BEOWULF
AND ITS ANALOGUES

BEOWULF
and its Analogues

Translated by
G. N. GARMONSWAY
and
JACQUELINE SIMPSON

including
Archaeology and Beowulf
by HILDA ELLIS DAVIDSON

With eight pages of
half-tone plates

LONDON: J. M. DENT & SONS LTD
NEW YORK: E. P. DUTTON & CO. INC.

Contents

CONTENTS

vi

Illustrations

Introduction

THE purpose of the present work is not only to offer a new translation of *Beowulf*, but also to gather between the covers of a single book translations of the numerous and scattered texts—of very varied types and periods—which may be held to have a bearing on our understanding of the characters and episodes in the poem.

Many of these analogues have been comparatively inaccessible to non-specialist readers, yet their considerable extent has forced editors and commentators on *Beowulf* to present only summaries or drastic selections from them; not infrequently, quotations have been given in the original languages without translation, and sometimes in so abbreviated and allusive a way that students have difficulty in grasping the significance of the proposed parallels or in assessing arguments based upon them. To present these texts in translation, and in generous quantities, may help those who are struggling to master the ramifications of scholarly controversy, or to judge how much light—or how little—a particular document can cast upon *Beowulf*. It may also serve to show how widely the various analogues differ in purpose, tone and literary merit, and to demonstrate the curious transformations which an incident or personage may undergo at the hands of writers of different periods and cultures. For these reasons, and because these stories are often of considerable interest for their own sakes, every effort has been made to present them as fully and coherently as possible, in chronological order within each sub-section.

The problems of translating *Beowulf* itself are well known: the rich diction with its traditional poetic terms, its wealth of near-synonyms, and its archaisms whose full connotations may or may not have been present to the poet's mind; the compressed imagery of compound words and kennings; the recurrence of words and phrases in varying contexts. In the matter of diction, the present translators, while conscious of the perils of archaism and Wardour Street English, felt that an aggressive modernity of idiom would be a betrayal of the spirit of the original, and so, when steering their course towards the noble but elusive ideal of 'good modern English', were more ready to respond to the claims of dignity and tradition than to those of contemporary colloquialism.

In dealing with poetic compounds and kennings, an attempt has been made to bring out fully the meaning of every element, even at the cost of using long phrases to render single words. True, this entails slowing the pace and, in the words of Professor Tolkien, risks 'dissipating the briefly flashed picture'; yet at least the reader has been forced to notice the existence and implications of the picture, and will return with enhanced appreciation to the rich concision of the original.

There has also been an attempt to be consistent in rendering words in the same way each time they recur, in so far as the claims of grammar and euphony permit, and to differentiate between Anglo-Saxon synonyms by allotting a separate word to each, if the resources of modern English allow. Naturally the initial decision to keep, say, 'combat' for *heaðo-*, 'war' or 'warlike' for *here-*, and 'battle' for *hilde-*, can only be arbitrary, and will sometimes give way to other considerations; nevertheless the procedure may perhaps bring out the technique of the original better than an unsystematic use of synonyms.

Consistency is particularly important in rendering the recurrent phrases on which the epic style so largely relies— *fyrene ond fǣhðe, mǣre þēoden, duguð ond geogoð, goldwine gumena* and many others. The existence of standard traditional formulas has been shown to be a basic factor in the technique of composing and transmitting heroic verse in many oral cultures, and their use in Anglo-Saxon written poetry is a stylistic feature which should on no account be obscured in translation. The pursuit of consistency will of course sometimes entail rejecting the word which springs to mind as the *mot juste* for a particular context, but this is not the disadvantage which it might at first appear. For the poet of *Beowulf* extracts a certain grim humour and irony out of applying heroic phrases to inappropriate situations, notably in describing the ravages of Grendel. One would lose a great deal by rendering *hūðe hrēmig* (l. 124) as 'gloating over his prey' rather than 'exulting over his booty' merely because the former suits a monster carrying off thirty murdered men; *hūðe hrēmig* is part of the heroic vocabulary, comparable to *since hrēmig*, applied to Beowulf himself at l. 1882, or to *frætwum hrēmig*, applied to Freawaru's proud young attendant who wears a slain man's sword (l. 2054); thus the poet's use of this noble phrase in gruesome circumstances comes as a well calculated shock.

Similar is the famous irony whereby Grendel is called a 'hall-thane' at Heorot, and the chain of related images which show Grendel and his kin as outcasts, exiles, wanderers who wage an endless feud against mankind. For twelve years Grendel enjoys sole possession of Hrothgar's lordly hall, night after night, yet he can never attain the privileges of thane-hood, symbolized by 'the precious throne, source of gifts', from which he is eternally debarred. Yet Grendel has a place of his own; 'the moors are his realms and the marshes his impregnable retreats' (*mōras hēold, fen ond fæsten*), just as the air is the realm of the dragon, and the home in which it takes its delight (*lyftwynne hēold*, l. 3043, echoes both the use of *healdan* as 'rule', and *ēþelwynn* 'delight in one's native land'). In such cases it is by the unexpected or ironic application of the heroic vocabulary that the poet makes his point; in other cases he may exploit an ambiguity in some word, as when he plays on the senses 'guest', 'newcomer' and 'hostile stranger' in the word *gist*, producing complexities that are lost in translation. Hengest is both guest and enemy at the court of Finn, and therein lies the paradox of his position; Beowulf is a stranger to the realm of Grendel's mother, but in an ironic sense he may be called her guest, so that it is a grotesque reversal of the laws of hospitality when she 'seats herself upon the guest in her hall' and draws a knife to kill him. The verbal subtleties of *Beowulf* repay close attention, even if this lingering upon details means that the story unfolds itself in translation at a pace even more leisurely than that of the original; the poet's own account of a minstrel composing a lay may perhaps justify a hope that he would have approved of this approach (ll. 872–4):

> *Secg eft ongan*
> *sīð Bēowulfes   snyttrum styrian,*
> *ond on spēd wrecan   spel gerāde,*
> *wordum wrixlan.*

The text used as a basis for translation is, in the main, that of Klaeber's edition; however, readings from those of Wyatt and Chambers and of Wrenn have sometimes been adopted, and the interpretations and comments of these and many other scholars have been taken into account. It would be beyond the scope of a work such as this to note all the various emendations and interpretations that have been proposed, but a few brief notes have been added to give the chief alternative renderings of some notorious cruxes. Very occasionally clarifications have been incorporated into the translation itself, particularly by substituting a proper name for an ambiguous 'he', or by expanding a compressed allusion such as the *āþum-swerian* of l. 84.

Our collaboration upon this work was tragically interrupted by the death of Professor Garmonsway in February 1967, and I was left to complete the task without the benefit of his scholarship and experience. At the time of his death he was polishing the final draft of the translation of *Beowulf* itself, and had worked over ll. 1–777 and 2200–2528; the remaining portions of the poem naturally reflect his views upon many points as known to me through correspondence and discussion, but the responsibility for any errors in these sections is mine. He had also chosen the texts to be included as analogues and had drawn up a scheme for their arrange-ment, but the actual translations are mine—except in the passages from Saxo Grammaticus, where I am grateful to the Folk-Lore Society for permission to quote extracts from the translation by Oliver Elton. Finally, I wish to express my gratitude to Dr. H. R. Ellis Davidson for contributing the section on archaeological evidence relating to *Beowulf*, and to the Controller of Her Majesty's Stationery Office for per-mission to reproduce the plan of the Yeavering excavations from *The History of the King's Works*.

JACQUELINE SIMPSON.

SELECT BIBLIOGRAPHY

TEXTS

The best edition is that of F. Klaeber, *Beowulf and the Fight at Finnsburg*, 3rd edition 1941; with supplements and full bibliography, 1951. Others are by A. J. Wyatt and R. W. Chambers, 2nd edition 1920; W. J. Sedgefield, revised edition 1935; M. Heyne, L. L. Schücking and E. von Schaubert, revised edition, 3 vols., 1946–1949; C. L. Wrenn, revised edition 1958.

TRANSLATIONS

J. R. Clark Hall and C. L. Wrenn, *Beowulf and the Finnsburg Fragment; A Translation into Modern English Prose*, with Prefatory Remarks by J. R. R. Tolkien 1940; revised edition 1950; G. Bone, *Beowulf in Modern Verse*, 1945; M. E. Waterhouse, *Beowulf in Modern English*, 1949; E. Morgan, *Beowulf: A Verse Translation*, 1952; D. Wright, *Beowulf* (Penguin Books), 1957.

CRITICAL STUDIES

R. Girvan, *Beowulf and the Seventh Century*, 1935; J. R. R. Tolkien, 'Beowulf: The Monsters and the Critics' in *Proceedings of the British Academy*, 22, 1936; S. O. Andrew, *Postscript on Beowulf*, 1948; A. Bonjour, *The Digressions in Beowulf*, 1950; D. Whitelock, *The Audience of Beowulf*, 1951; T. M. Gang, 'Approaches to Beowulf' in *Review of English Studies*, New Series, III, 1952; R. W. Chambers, *Beowulf: An Introduction*, 3rd edition with Supplements, 1959; A. G. Brodeur, *The Art of Beowulf*, 1959; W. W. Lawrence, *Beowulf and Epic Tradition*, 1961 (reprint of 1920 edition); K. Sisam, *The Structure of 'Beowulf'*, 1965; J. A. Leake, *The Geats of Beowulf*, 1967.

For fuller bibliographies, reference should be made to the most recent editions of Klaeber's *Beowulf* and Chambers's *Beowulf: An Introduction*, mentioned above; current publications will be found listed in the annual *Work in English Studies*.

BEOWULF

Beowulf

[* refers to the Notes on the Translation.]

WE HAVE indeed heard tell of the splendour of
warrior Danes in days gone by, of the kings of
that nation, and of how those high-born men achieved
deeds of valour.

4   Many a time did Scyld Scefing with troops of war-
riors deprive his foes among many races of their very
mead-benches, and strike terror into the Heruli, after
that time when he first was found destitute. He lived
to know consolation for that; beneath the skies he
throve and prospered in every honour, so that all
neighbouring nations across the whale-ridden seas
were forced to obey him and pay him tribute. A fine
king was he!

12   Later, there was born to him in his household a
young son, whom God sent to be a comfort to the
nation. He had perceived what cruel misery they once
had suffered, when for a long time they had been
without a sovereign; therefore the Lord of Life, the
Ruler of Glory, granted him honour throughout the
whole world. This Beowulf, offspring of Scyld, was
of high renown, and his fame spread far and wide
through the Danish realm. So it is that a young man,
while he is still under his father's care, should do noble
deeds, giving such brave gifts that later, when he is of
age, companions of his choice will stand beside him
when war comes, and give support to their chieftain.
Among all races, it is by praiseworthy generosity that
a man shall prosper.

26   Then at his destined hour Scyld departed, still full
of vigour, to pass into the keeping of the Lord; they
who were his cherished companions bore him away
to the driving surf, as he himself had ordered while
he still could master his speech—he, the friend of the
Scyldings, the beloved lord of that land which had
long been his.

3

32   There in the harbour lay the prince's vessel, a ship with curling prow, ice-covered, eager to put out to sea. Then they laid their beloved prince and ring-bestower within the ship, laying the renowned man beside the mast. Many treasures and rich adornments from distant lands were brought there. Never have I heard of any craft more handsomely furnished with weapons of war and raiments of battle, with swords and corselets; in its hold there lay a great number of treasures which were to go with him, far out into the sea's domain. They furnished him with offerings from the nation's wealth—and by no means so poorly as those others had done who, in the beginning, had sent him forth alone over the waves when he was but a child. Furthermore, they fixed aloft a golden standard high above his head; they trusted him to the deep to bear away, gave him to the rushing ocean; sad were their spirits, sorrowful their hearts. No man, none of those warriors beneath the heavens who are masters in their own halls, can say for certain into whose possession that cargo came.

I

53   Then in that stronghold the beloved king of the people, Beowulf of the Scyldings, was for a long time famous among the nations (his father, the sovereign, having passed away from his land), until to him in his turn there was born Healfdene the Tall, who ruled the gracious Scyldings as long as he lived, and even as an aged man was fierce in the fray.

59   To Healfdene, leader of armies, four children in succession were born into this world: Heorogar, Hrothgar, and Halga the Good, and a daughter, who, as I have heard, became Onela's queen, the cherished consort of the warlike Scylfing.

64   Next, it was to Hrothgar that success was granted in war, and such glory in battle that his friends and kinsmen gladly obeyed him, until his band of young warriors grew to a mighty retinue. It came into his mind that he would bid men fashion a palace, a mighty mead-hall greater than any children of men had ever

4

heard tell of, and that within it he would share out among young and old everything which God had bestowed on him, save for his royal lands and the lives of his men.

74   I have heard tell how orders for this work were then laid upon many races far and wide throughout the world, to adorn this place for the nation. Thus it came about in due time, with the utmost speed, that this greatest of halls came to be fully ready; he whose word was law far and wide chose for it the name Heorot. Nor did he fail to be true to his vow; he shared out rings and riches at the feasting. There stood that lofty towering hall with its broad horns; yet it was for swirling flames of war and for destroying fire that it waited. Not yet, however, was that time at hand when the sword's edge would prove what hatred had arisen between the king and his son-in-law, the result of murderous slaughter.

86   Then the savage being that lurked in dark places found it hard to bear this time of torment, when day after day he heard loud rejoicing in the hall; the sound of the harp was there, the clear song of the bard. He who knew how to unfold the tale of the first creation of man in far-off times spoke now, and told how Almighty God had formed the earth, a plain fair to see, which the waters encircle; how, glorying in His triumph, He had established the sun and moon as radiant light for earth-dwellers; how He had bedecked every corner of the world with branches and leaves; and how He had also created life for every race of beings that live and move.

99   Thus the men of that court lived in blessedness and joy, until one creature, a fiend from hell, began to work evil. Grendel was the name of that grim newcomer; he was renowned as a prowler in the borderlands, one whose realm was the moors, and the marshes his impregnable retreats. For a long time this outcast wretch had made his home in the regions where monsters dwell, ever since the Creator had sentenced him to exile. Upon Cain's whole kindred the Eternal Lord had taken vengeance for the blow by which he slew Abel; he won no joy by that deed of blood, for

on account of that crime Providence drove him into banishment, far from mankind. From him sprang all unholy broods, ogres and elves and the walking dead, and those giants, too, who for long ages waged war upon God—He paid them their due reward for that!

II

115   So when night had come Grendel went forth to seek out that lofty hall and see what guard the mail-clad Danes had set upon it after their beer-drinking. He found within it a company of high-born men sleeping after the feasting; they had no thought of grief, or the sorrow fated for men. This creature cut off from grace, grim and greedy, fierce and fell, at once set to work and seized thirty thanes from their couches. Back he turned, exulting over his booty, journeying homewards to seek his own place, carrying with him his fill of carnage.

126   Then in the half-light at the first coming of day, Grendel's strength in the fray was no longer hidden from men. Voices were raised in wailing, for the good days of feasting were over; a great cry went up throughout the morning. The renowned prince, a man of high birth and proven merit, sat joyless; he suffered, though mighty in power; he grieved for the loss of his thanes, when men examined the tracks of that hateful and accursed being. Too fierce was that strife, too relentless and long-lasting.

134   Nor was the time of respite long; on the very next night he again wrought more murderous havoc, more violent and bloody deeds, and felt no remorse; he was too deeply rooted in such ways. It was not hard now to find a man seeking elsewhere for some resting place farther afield or some bed among the outbuildings, when once it had been clearly shown, and proved by so plain a token, what hatred filled this thane in their hall. From that time onwards, whoever escaped the foe kept himself at a safe distance for the future. Thus did Grendel make himself master and wage a wrongful war against them all, single-handed, until that finest of halls stood empty.

146   This went on a long time; for twelve years' space

the kindly lord of the Scyldings bore this affliction, woes of every kind, and deep sorrows. It therefore became generally known to the children of men, through many a sad lay, that Grendel had long waged war on Hrothgar, pursuing through many seasons his spiteful hatred with violent and bloody deeds, a conflict which had no end. No peace did he wish with any man of the Danish host, nor was he willing to cease this deadly havoc, nor to offer blood-money in settlement; nor need any counsellors there expect compensation in bright gold from the slayer's hand. This monster, this dark shadow of death, would for ever hunt down both tried warriors and youths; he lurked near by and ensnared them; all night long he haunted the misty moors. Men cannot tell whither those who share the secrets of Hell may stalk abroad in their roamings.

164   Thus time and time again this foe of mankind, this fearsome being that walked alone, would inflict many violent deeds and harsh humiliations. He took Heorot, the hall gleaming with riches, to be his abode in the black nights; yet, under Providence, he had never been permitted to come near the precious throne, the source of gifts, nor did he feel any regard for it.*

170   This was great anguish and heartbreak for the friend of the Scyldings. Many a great man often sat in council discussing what to advise, what action would be best for stout-hearted warriors to take against these sudden fearful onslaughts. At times they vowed holy sacrifices to honour the shrines of idols, and prayed aloud that the Destroyer of Souls might render them aid against the calamities of their nation. Such was their custom, such was the hope of the heathen. It was towards Hell that they turned their minds; they knew nothing of Providence, Judge of men's deeds, nor did they know of the Lord God, nor did they at all know how to worship the Protector of the Heavens, the Ruler of Glory. Evil will be his fate who through dire wrongdoing must thrust his soul into the fire's embrace, without hope of comfort or of any respite! Well will it be for him who at the day of his death can go to the Lord and crave refuge in the bosom of the Father!

III

189   Thus the son of Healfdene brooded unceasingly on the sorrows of his time, nor could the far-sighted hero set aside those griefs. Too cruel was that strife which had befallen his people, too relentless and long-lasting —an inescapable torment sprung from savage malice, the worst of all baleful evils that come by night.

194   Away in his homeland among the Geats, Beowulf, a house-thane of Hygelac, heard of Grendel's deeds. In his strength he was the mightiest of all mankind in that day and age; he was of high birth, and of more than human stature. He gave orders for a good sea-going ship to be fitted out for him; he said that he wished to seek out the warrior-king, the renowned prince, over the swan-ridden seas, since he had need of men. Far-sighted men did not reproach him at all for that venture, dear though he was to them; they encouraged his bold spirit, and scanned the omens. The hero had with him picked champions of the Geatish people, the bravest he could find; with fourteen men he went down to the water-borne timbers. One of the warriors, a man skilled in sea-lore, guided them along the coast.

210   So time went by; the ship rode the waves, afloat under the lee of the cliff. Warriors, fully equipped, stepped aboard by the prow; the currents eddied, the sea lapped the shore. Into the vessel's hold the men bore their shining trappings, their armour so splendidly wrought for the fray. The warriors setting out on their chosen venture thrust their well-braced timbers out to sea.

217   Then away went the ship over the rolling deeps; sped by the wind, so like a bird, it drove onwards with foam-ringed neck, until, about the due time on the following day, its curving prow had gone so far that the voyagers could get sight of land, see the sea-cliffs gleaming, the tall crags and broad headlands. Thus the sea had been crossed, the voyage was at an end. The men of the Wederas swiftly set foot on level ground and moored their sea-borne timbers; their mail-coats, the garb of war, rang out; they gave God

8

thanks that the crossing of the waters had been easy
for them.

229   Then from a rampart the watchman of the Scyldings,
whose duty it was to stand guard on the sea-cliffs, saw
them bearing down the gangway, their bright bucklers
and armour ready for use. Curiosity pricked his mind
to find out who these men might be.

234   Down to the beach went Hrothgar's thane, riding
on horseback; powerfully he shook the mighty spear-
shaft in his hand, and challenged them in formal words:
'What kind of armed men are you who thus have
come clad in corselets, steering hither your tall craft
over the deeps and the highways of the sea? Long
indeed have I been guardian of this outpost and have
kept watch by the sea, so that none of our foes might
harry the land of the Danes with a ship-borne host.
Never have warriors bearing shields made their
approach more openly, and yet you had no knowledge
of the warriors' password agreed on by our kinsfolk.
Nor have I ever anywhere seen a mightier champion
than that outstanding man in your midst, that hero in
armour; he is no mere serving-man with weapons to
lend him dignity—unless his looks and his matchless
appearance belie him.

251   'I now must know your origin, in case you go
farther on your way as false spies, deeper into the land
of the Danes. So now, you foreigners who have trav-
elled the seas, I would have you know my plain
thought—it is best to be swift in revealing whence
you have come, and why.'

IV

258   The chief of them, the leader of the company,
answered him, revealing his noble eloquence: 'As for
race, we are liegemen of the Geatish people, and
belong to the fellowship that sits at Hygelac's own
hearth. My father was famous among many nations,
a high-born war-leader whose name was Ecgtheow.
He lived to see many winters, until in old age he
passed away from his courts; every wise man in all
parts of the world remembers him well.

267   'It is with friendly hearts that we have come to visit your lord, the son of Healfdene, the protector of your people; show goodwill to us by your advice! We have weighty business with the renowned lord of the Danes, and I intend that none of it should remain hidden once we are there.

272   'You know—if what we have heard tell as the truth is so—that in the land of the Scyldings there is some sort of scourge, some mysterious foe whose deeds give proof of hatred, and who in the darkness of night, by the terror he brings, reveals unbelievable spite through humiliations and carnage. In this matter I can give Hrothgar good counsel from a generous heart, teaching him how he, so noble and ripe in wisdom, may overpower his foe, so that his restless cares may be quieted—if indeed his tormenting troubles are ever fated to change, and if relief is to be found. If not, he will for evermore endure a time of hardship and inescapable distress, so long as that finest of halls still stands as his royal seat.'

286   The watchman, that fearless officer, spoke, sitting there on his horse: 'Any keen fighter who can think rightly must know the difference between words and deeds. I have heard how this company of men is loyal towards the lord of the Scyldings. So go on your way, bearing your weapons and war-gear, and I will guide you. Also I will order my young squires to stand guard over your vessel against every foe, and place a guard of honour over the freshly tarred craft on our shore, until those same timbers with their curving neck will once again bear their dear master over the sea's currents to the coast of the Wederas. It will surely be granted to one engaged in such a brave undertaking that he will survive the shock of battle unharmed!'

301   So they set forth on their way. Their floating vessel, a broad-bottomed craft, rode quietly upon its hawser, held fast by the anchor. Above their cheek-guards shone the figures of boars, adorned with gold; a gleaming pig, tempered in the flame, in its fierce spirit stood guard over stern men.* The warriors made haste, going onwards together till they were able to catch sight of a timbered hall, splendid and gleaming with

10

gold. Of all buildings beneath the skies, this palace in which a mighty ruler dwelt was the most renowned among all men in the world. Light blazed from it over many lands.

312 The brave warrior pointed out to them that splendid court of high-hearted men, so that they might make straight for it; the fine fighting-man turned his horse, and thereupon spoke these words: 'It is time for me to return. May the All-Ruling Father mercifully keep you safe in your venture! I will go back to the sea, to keep watch against any band of enemies.'

V

320 The highway gleamed with bright stones; the path guided the warriors as they marched together. Each corselet of war was shining, hard, and with hand-forged links; each glittering ring in their harness rang out, as they came striding into the hall for the first time in their fearsome war-gear. Weary from their sea voyage, they laid against the wall of the building their broad shields with bosses surpassingly strong. Then they seated themselves on the bench; these men's corselets and warlike armour rang out. The spears that were the seamen's weapons stood stacked together, shafts of ash-wood tipped with the grey sheen of the blade; the steel-clad troop was made more glorious by its weapons.

331 Then a proud warrior there questioned those champions about their birth: 'Where do you come from, with gold-plated shields, mail-shirts of grey sheen, and vizored helms, and that pile of war-spears? I am Hrothgar's herald and officer. Never have I seen a company of so many strangers bear themselves more gallantly. I am confident that it was through proud courage and boldness of heart that you sought Hrothgar out, and not through the misfortune of exile.'

340 The proud chieftain of the Wederas, famed for his valour and hardy beneath his helm, spoke these words in reply: 'We are companions who feast at Hygelac's table; Beowulf is my name. I wish to tell my errand

to the son of Healfdene, that renowned prince who is your sovereign, if he who is so noble will grant us leave to approach his presence.'

348   Wulfgar spoke—he was a chieftain of the Vendels, and his spirit and wisdom and prowess in the fray were known to many—'As for this, I will ask the friend of the Danes and lord of the Scyldings, the ring-bestower, the renowned prince, concerning your journey, as you have requested; and I will swiftly acquaint you with whatever answer the noble king is pleased to give me.'

356   Then he quickly turned away to where Hrothgar, old and quite grey, was sitting among his retinue of earls; this warrior famed for valour went forward till he stood face to face with the lord of the Danes, for he knew the right ways of a courtly retainer.

360   Wulfgar spoke thus to his kindly lord: 'Men of the Geats have voyaged here, coming from afar over the broad sweep of the ocean. These champions name their leader Beowulf. It is their request, my lord, that they might have speech with you; do not refuse to grant them a reply, O gracious Hrothgar! From their fighting-gear, they seem worthy of the respect of earls, and the chieftain who has led these battle-warriors here is indeed a man of prowess!'

VI

371   Thus spoke Hrothgar, helm of the Scyldings: 'I knew him when he was a boy. His father was named Ecgtheow, and it was to him that Hrethel of the Geats gave his only daughter in marriage; now his son has come here, a hardy man, to visit a kindly friend. Moreover, the seafarers who have carried rich gifts for the Geats to that land, as a sign of our regard, have said that he is famed for his combats, and has the strength of thirty men in his hand-grip. Holy God, in His mercy, has sent him to us, the Danes, to face the dread power of Grendel—or such is my hope. I shall offer treasures to the hero for his gallant daring. Go in haste, bid this company of kinsmen enter together to see me;

tell them also in your speech that they are welcome guests to the Danish people.'

389   Then Wulfgar went to the door of the hall, and standing within he gave his message: 'My victorious lord, the sovereign of the Danes, bids me tell you that he knows your high birth, and that you are welcome guests to him, you stout-hearted sailors from over the billows of the sea. Now you may enter Hrothgar's presence, in your armour, and wearing your vizored helms; but leave here your battle-shields and spears, those deadly shafts, to await the outcome of your meeting.'

399   The mighty man then arose, with many a warrior round him, a splendid band of thanes; others remained behind to guard their battle array, as their hardy leader had bidden. The rest, with the man guiding them, turned to go under the roof of Heorot. The warrior, hardy beneath his helm, stepped forward till he stood by the hearth.

405   Thus spoke Beowulf—upon him there shone a corselet, a web cunningly linked by the smith's skilful craft—'Hail to you, Hrothgar! I am a kinsman and a young thane of Hygelac; even in youth, I have undertaken many glorious deeds. Grendel's doings became well known to me on my native soil; seafarers say that this hall, this most noble building, stands empty and useless to every warrior, as soon as the setting sun is hidden in the afterglow of the sky. Then, O prince Hrothgar, my own countrymen (the noblest and most far-sighted among them) advised me that I ought to visit you, for they knew the strength of my might. They had themselves been watching once when, stained with the blood of foes, I returned from a struggle in which I had laid low a brood of ogres, bound five of them, and struck down sea-monsters in the waves by night. I had suffered dire straits, yet I avenged the wrongs done to the Wederas, and utterly crushed those raging creatures—they had courted trouble for themselves. And now I alone shall settle the account with Grendel, that monster and troll.

426   'Now therefore, chieftain of the glorious Danes and bulwark of the Scyldings, I beg of you one boon.

13

Now that I have come thus far, do not refuse me this,
O shield of warriors and noble friend of your people—
that I alone may cleanse Heorot, with my retinue of
followers, this band of hardy men. Also, I have dis-
covered that in his rashness this monster holds weapons
in contempt; so, since I truly desire that my liege-
lord Hygelac should be kindly disposed towards me,
I scorn to bear a sword or broad shield or yellow
buckler into the fray; with my own bare hands I will
grapple with this fiend and fight him to the death,
foe against foe. He whom death carries off must resign
himself to the judgment of the Lord.

442 'I expect that if he can get the upper hand, he will
without fear devour the Geatish people in this hall,
the scene of the fray, as he has often before done to the
chivalry of the Danes. You will have no need to cover
my head in burial, for if death carries me off, Grendel
will have me for himself, all stained with dripping
gore; he will carry away my bloody corpse in order
to savour it. The lone prowler will devour me remorse-
lessly, staining the hollows of the moor. You will
have no need to trouble further about the disposal
of my corpse. But if battle carries me off, send to
Hygelac this peerless battle-raiment, this most excel-
lent of corselets that protects my breast. It is a heir-
loom from Hrethel, and the handiwork of Weland.
Fate goes as it must go!'

VII

456 Thus spoke Hrothgar, helm of the Scyldings:
'Beowulf, my friend, you have come to visit us out of
kindness, and because of deeds done in the past, when
your father at one blow brought about the most
bloody of feuds, when with his own hand he slew
Heatholaf of the Wylfings. His own kindred, the
Wederas, could not keep him among them for fear
of the horrors of war, so from there he sought out the
Danish people, the honoured Scyldings, over the rolling
waves. At that time I had just begun my rule over the
Danish folk, and, despite my youth, I governed a

14

broad kingdom and this rich stronghold of warriors. My elder brother Hereogar, Healfdene's son, was by then dead and lifeless—he was a finer man than I! Thereupon I offered blood-money in settlement of that feud, sending ancient treasures to the Wylfings over the crest of the waves; your father swore oaths to me.

473   'It grieves my heart to speak to any man of the humiliations that Grendel has inflicted on me in Heorot by his sudden fierce onslaughts, filled with thoughts of hatred. My great host of fighting-men in this hall has been lessened; fate has swept them away into Grendel's dire clutches. Yet God can easily hinder this foolhardy ravager from such deeds!

480   'Very often, champions roused by their beer have vowed over the ale-flagon that with their dreaded swordblades they would wait in the banquet-hall for Grendel's attack. Then by morning, when the light of day came, this mead-hall, this lordly chamber, would be stained with dripping gore; all the bench-boards would be drenched with blood, and the hall covered in such gore as drips from swords. I had all the fewer loyal men, fewer picked warriors dear to me, because of those whom death had carried off.

489   'Now sit at the feast, and reveal to the heroes your thoughts and your triumphant victories, as your own heart moves you.' *

491   Then one bench of the banquet hall was cleared for all the men of the Geats together; the stout-hearted men went to sit there, proud in their strength. An attendant fulfilled his allotted task, bearing in his hand a richly adorned flagon of ale, and pouring out the flashing liquor. From time to time a bard sang in Heorot, with a clear voice. There was rejoicing among the heroes; this was no petty company, but the pick of the hosts of Danes and Geats.

VIII

499   Unferth, son of Ecglaf, who sat at the feet of the lord of the Scyldings, spoke thus, unloosing secret

words to stir up strife. The venture of Beowulf, the gallant seafarer, caused him great displeasure, for he would not willingly grant that any other man on earth had ever performed more glorious deeds beneath the heavens than he himself:

506 'Are you the Beowulf who pitted himself against Breca, and competed in swimming the broad seas, when you two in your pride tested the force of the tides, and for the sake of a foolhardy boast risked your lives in the deep waters? Nor could any man, friend or foe, dissuade you both from that hazardous venture, as you struck out to sea. There you cut through the water's currents with arms outstretched, ranging the highways of the sea and weaving your way with your hands as you glided over the rushing ocean; the depths were surging with waves and the billows of winter.

516 'For seven days both of you toiled in the grip of the waters, but he outstripped you in swimming, for he had the greater strength. Then one morning the high sea washed him ashore in the land of the Heatho-Ræmas; from there he, who was dear to his people, reached his cherished homeland, the land of the Brondings, and the fair peaceful stronghold where he ruled over his people, and his citadel with its wealth. Beanstan's son had faithfully carried out all he had sworn to do in his contest with you.

525 'I therefore expect that the outcome will be the worse for you, however well you may have proved yourself everywhere in the shocks of combat and in grim warfare, if you dare to wait all night long for Grendel, at close quarters.'

529 Thus spoke Beowulf, son of Ecgtheow: 'Yes indeed, my friend Unferth, roused by your beer, you have spoken much about Breca and talked of his venture! But I claim that the truth is that I showed more strength in swimming and bore greater hardships in the waves than any other man. When we were boys we two agreed, and made a vow on it—for we still were both youngsters then—that we would risk our lives out in the rushing ocean; and this we accordingly did. We each had a strong naked sword in our hand as we struck out to sea, meaning to defend ourselves against

16

whales. He was utterly unable to gain on me in swimming through the waves of the flood, or to pass more swiftly than I over the high seas; nor did I mean to get ahead of him. Thus we stayed together in the sea for the space of five days, till the flood and the rolling tides drove us apart, and most bitter foul weather and lowering night, and a fierce cutting wind from the north veered against us.

548 'The waves were savage, and the anger of the ocean fish was aroused; but my mail-shirt, stout with its hand-forged links, afforded me help there against those foes; the robe woven for battle, bedecked with gold, lay across my breast. One fell and murderous foe dragged me down to the bottom of the sea, and the grim creature held me fast in its grip. Yet my fortune granted that I might plunge the point of my battle-sword into the monster; the shock of combat carried off that mighty sea-beast by my hand.

IX

559 'These loathsome attackers often pressed hard upon me in this way, but with my good sword I gave them such service as it was fitting that I should. These wicked evil-doers did not have the joy of eating their fill, taking me for their food, or of sitting round their feast at the bottom of the sea; rather, on the morrow they were lying high and dry on a shore left bare by ebbing waves, wounded by blades and sent by the sword to their last sleep, so that never again would they hinder sea-travellers from their voyage across the high seas.

569 'Light, God's bright token, sprang up from the east; the swell died down, so that I could see headlands, those windswept walls. Fate will often spare a man, so that he is not marked for death, if his courage holds good. Indeed, such had been my fortune that I had struck down nine sea-monsters with the sword. Never have I heard of a harder fight by night under the vault of heaven, nor of a man in more wretched plight in the water's currents; yet I escaped with my life from my foes, though wearied by my adventure. Then the

17

sea with its rolling tides swept me away on a flood of driving waters to the land of the Lapps.

581 'I have never heard tell anything of such skilled combats of yours, Unferth, or of such horror wrought by your broadsword. Nor am I boasting too much if I say that never yet in the sport of combat has Breca, or you either, achieved so bold a deed with your gleaming swords—although indeed you were the slayer of your brothers, your closest kin. For that you shall suffer damnation in Hell, clever as you are!

590 'Truly I tell you, son of Ecglaf, the fearsome monster Grendel would never have committed so many dreadful deeds against your sovereign or brought such humiliation on Heorot, if your heart and spirit had been as grim in combat as you yourself make out. But he has found that he need not much dread a feud, or a fearsome storm of blades from the victorious Scyldings, your people. He levies his toll upon them, showing no mercy to any of the Danish people; he take his pleasure, he lays men low and sends them to death, expecting no strife from the spear-wielding Danes. But very soon now I shall show him in the fray the strength and valour of Geats. Then tomorrow morning, as soon as light dawns over mankind, and the sun, clad in heavenly brilliance, shines from the south, anyone who so wishes will be able to walk once again with a bold heart to the mead-drinking!'

607 The bestower of riches, white-haired with age, and famous in the fray was full of happiness then; the prince of the fair Danes, the shepherd of his people, placed his trust in this aid, having heard the steadfast purpose in Beowulf's words.

611 There was glad laughter among the warriors; merry voices rang out, and their words were cheerful. Wealhtheow, Hrothgar's queen, stepped forth, mindful of the duties of hospitality. The gracious lady, bedecked with gold, welcomed the men in the hall, and then gave the goblet first to the guardian of the of the Danish homeland, bidding him who was dear to his people drink beer with a light heart. The king, famed for his victories, gladly took part in the feast, accepting the goblet that passed round the hall. Then

18

the lady of the Helmings went to and fro everywhere among both tried warriors and youths, offering the rich vessel, till the moment came when the ring-decked queen of excellent nature brought a goblet of mead to Beowulf. She welcomed the chieftain of the Geats, and in words of wisdom gave thanks to God that her desire had come to pass, since there was a hero whom she could trust to bring relief from violent deeds.

628   The fighter, so fierce in slaughter, received the goblet from Wealhtheow's hand, and then, filled with zeal for the fray, poured forth his eloquence. Thus spoke Beowulf, son of Ecgtheow: 'I was resolved, when I put out to sea and took my place in the ship with my retinue of followers, that I would carry out the wishes of your people once and for all, or else fall slain, held fast in the grip of the foe. I must achieve this deed of heroic valour, or meet my last day in this mead-hall!'

639   These words of the Geat's proud vaunting speech pleased the lady well; the gracious queen of the people, bedecked with gold, went to sit beside her lord.

642   Then once again, as of old, there were brave words spoken within that hall, and the sound of a victorious host rang out, for the company was full of happiness, till presently the son of Healfdene wished to go to his night's rest. He knew that the monster had been planning his attack against that lofty hall from the time that they were able to see the light of the sun, until lowering night came down upon everything, and forms shrouded in shadow came stalking, black beneath the clouds.

651   The whole company rose. The two heroes saluted each other; Hrothgar wished Beowulf success, and gave the banquet hall into his charge, speaking these words: 'Never before, since I could lift hand and buckler, have I entrusted the lordly dwelling of the Danes to any man, save now to you. Keep and guard this, the finest of houses; remember your glory, show forth your mighty valour, keep watch against the enemy! You shall lack nothing that you may desire, if you come back alive after that deed of valour.'

X

662   Then Hrothgar, bulwark of the Scyldings, went from the hall with his retinue of warriors; the war-leader wished to seek repose with Weahltheow, his consort. The King of Glory, so men had learnt, had appointed a guardian for the hall, to face Grendel; he would render special service to the Danish sovereign, for he mounted guard against an ogre. Truly, the chieftain of the Geats gladly trusted in his own gallant strength, and the favour of Providence, when he put off his steel corselet, took the helm from his head, and gave his richly wrought sword, the choicest of blades, to his attendant squire, bidding him take charge of this battle-gear.

675   Then did the hero, Beowulf of the Geats, make a proud vaunting speech before mounting his bed: 'I think no less well of myself for my vigour in war, proved by deeds done in the fray, than Grendel does of himself; and so it is not with the sword that I shall lay him low and deprive him of life, although I very well might. He knows nothing of the advantage of striking back at me or hacking at my buckler, however famous he may be for his spiteful deeds, so tonight we will both dispense with the sword, if he dare seek a fight without weapons—and then let Wise God, the Holy Lord, adjudge the glory to whichever side may seem fitting to Him!'

688   The brave fighter then laid himself down, and put his cheek to the pillow. Around him, many a bold seaman lay down on his couch in that hall. Not one of them thought he would ever again return from there to his beloved homeland, to his own folk, or to the noble stronghold where he had been brought up; they had learnt how deadly slaughter had already carried off all too many of the Danish people in that banquet hall. But to these men, the people of the Wederas, the Lord had granted that the web of their fate would be woven with victories, giving them His comfort and support, so that by one man's strength and mighty deeds they all overcame their foe. It is a

well-known truth that through long ages Almighty God has governed mankind.

702 Then, stalking through the black night, came he who prowled in the shadows. The marksmen whose duty it was to guard that horned building were asleep, all save one. It was well known to them that this spectral foe could not hurl them down into the shadows if Providence did not so will it; for Beowulf, watchful in his anger against the enemy, waited in rising fury for the outcome of the struggle.

XI

710 Then from the moor came Grendel, making his way along the foot of the misty slopes; he bore with him the wrath of God. The wicked ravager meant to ensnare one of the human race in that lofty hall. He strode onwards beneath the clouds, till he came where he could very clearly make out that banquet chamber, the warriors' hall of gold, gleaming with gold plating. Nor was this the first time that he had sought Hrothgar's home, but never in all the days of his life, before nor since, did he meet with more cruel fortune in finding such thanes in a hall!

720 On he came, making his way to the building, an attacker bereft of all joys. The door gave way at once, though held by fire-forged bars, when he touched it with open palm; then, with his mind set on havoc, he thrust back the doors of the building, for fury was rising in him. Next, the fiend swiftly set his foot upon the bright-hued floor, and advanced with wrathful heart; from his eyes there flashed an ugly gleam, much like a flame. Inside the building he saw many a warrior, a friendly company of young warlike kinsmen sleeping together. At this his heart laughed within him, for the fearsome monster meant, before day came, to tear the life out of the body of every single one of them, now that the chance of a lavish feast had come his way.

734 But never again would fate decree that he could take any more of the human race for his food after that night. The kinsman of Hygelac, mighty in his strength, was watching to see how the wicked ravager

would set about making his sudden onslaught. Nor did the monster mean to delay, but for a start he quickly clutched a sleeping warrior, and, tearing him apart without resistance, he bit into the muscles that held the bones, drank the blood from his veins, and swallowed him down, chunk after chunk, so that soon he had devoured the lifeless man, feet, hands and all.

745   He came a step nearer; then with one hand the fiend laid hold of a stout-hearted warrior lying on his couch, reaching out towards him with his open palm. But the other quickly received him with a cunning trick, and fastened upon his arm.* All at once that master of violent deeds discovered that nowhere on earth, in no corner of the world, had he met with a mightier hand-grip in any other man. He grew frightened in heart and soul, yet he was unable to get away any faster. He longed to be gone; he wanted to flee into the darkness and make for the rout of devils, for what he was now feeling was something he had never met with before in all the days of his life.

758   Then Hygelac's noble kinsman, calling to mind what he had spoken that evening, stood erect and took a firm grip on him. Fingers were cracking. The ogre moved towards the door; the warrior took a step forward. The renowned Grendel meant to make a dash for the open as soon as he could, and flee away from there to the marshy hollows; he knew that the strength of his fingers was mastered by his fierce enemy's grip. Bitter was the journey that baleful ravager had undertaken to Heorot!

767   The lordly hall echoed; on all the Danes, on all who dwelt in the fortress, on every brave man and on every earl there came the taste of deadly fear. Fierce and furious grew the two who strove for mastery of that hall; the building resounded. It was a miracle that the banquet hall stood firm despite those fierce fighters, and that the fair dwelling did not crash to the ground; it was too firmly held, inside and out, by clamps of iron skilfully forged. Many a mead-bench enriched with gold was wrenched away from the floor, or so I heard tell, where the furious opponents struggled. The counsellors of the Scyldings had not thought that a

man could ever shatter it by any normal means, superb as it was, and decked out with antlers, or by his cunning lay it in ruins—not unless the all-embracing flame should swallow it up in its blaze.

782　　A sound rose up, a new sound, and often repeated. A terrible fear sprang up in every one of the Danes who from the outer wall heard that wailing, heard God's enemy keening his chant of dread, a song that told of no victory—Hell's slave howling over his wound. He who held him fast was the mightiest man in his strength in that day and age.

XII

791　　Beowulf, shield of heroes, would on no account let that deadly visitant go alive, for he held that his life would bring no good to any man.

794　　Many of Beowulf's followers brandished some weapon, some ancient heirloom, wishing to defend the life of their noble lord and renowned prince wherever they could. One thing they did not know, as these comrades in battle, filled with stern purpose, joined in the struggle, thinking they would hack him from every side and threaten his life—this wicked ravager was one whom no sword on earth, not the choicest of steel blades, could touch; he had cast a spell to blunt the edges of all victorious weapons. Yet his death was to be a wretched one in that day and age, and the being from the otherworld was to pass far away into the power of fiends.

809　　Then he who for so long had wrought many violent deeds against mankind out of a murderous heart, he who was at feud with God, found that his own body would not obey him, for Hygelac's valiant kinsman kept a hold on his hand. Each would be foe to the other as long as he lived. The fearsome monster felt agony in his own body; on his shoulder a vast gash appeared, plain to see; the sinews were tearing apart, the muscles that bound the bones were splitting. To Beowulf was granted triumph in the fray; Grendel, stricken to death, must flee away to the shelter of fenland slopes, to seek out his cheerless abode; all too well he knew that the end of his life had come, and his allotted days were over. The wish of all the Danes was fulfilled through this mortal struggle.

825   The far-sighted, stout-hearted man who had come from afar had cleansed Hrothgar's hall and saved it from spite. He rejoiced in that night's work, in his deed of glorious valour. This lord of the men of the Geats had fulfilled the vaunt he had made to the Danes, and also brought a cure for all the distress and the grievous malice which they had endured, being forced by dire need to bear it—no small affliction! The token was plain to see, once the brave warrior had placed the hand, arm and shoulder high up under the broad roof—there was Grendel's whole grasp, complete.

XIII

837   Then on the morrow, so I heard tell, there was many a warrior round that gift-hall; leaders of the people travelled from far and near along distant roads to look on that marvel, the tracks of the hateful creature. Those who examined the footprints of the dishonoured foe did not think it sad that he should lose his life; they saw how with weary heart, overcome in combat, put to flight and marked out for death, he had left a trail of life-blood all the way from there to the mere of the water-monsters. There the water was seething with blood; the fearsome whirlpool of waves, all mingled with hot gore, seethed with drops such as drip from swords. Death-doomed, there he had died when, losing all joys, he laid down his life and his heathen soul in that fenland refuge; there Hell had received him.

853   The aged retainers turned back again, and also many a gallant youth returned from that gay hunting, riding back from the mere on their glossy steeds. Beowulf's glory was proclaimed; many a man declared that nowhere in the wide world, north or south, from sea to sea, was there another shield-bearer nobler than he beneath the broad sweep of the brilliant sky, nor any more worthy of kingship. Yet indeed they did not

find any fault in their kindly lord, the gracious Hroth-
gar, for he was a good king.

864   Sometimes these famous fighters would set their
tawny steeds to gallop in rivalry, wherever the paths
seemed fair and were known to be good. Sometimes
one of the king's thanes, a man with a rich store of
high-sounding words and a memory filled with
lays, one who remembered a whole host of tales from
olden times, would devise some new poem linked in
true metre. Or again, this man would set out to relate
Beowulf's exploit according to his art, reciting the
well-wrought tale to good effect, and varying his words.

874   He spoke too of all he had heard tell about Sigemund
and his valiant deeds, and much that was not known,
about the warfare of the son of Wæls, his wide journey-
ings, and his violent and bloody deeds. No son of man
knew the full story of these, save only Fitela, to whom
Sigemund would say something of such matters, as
uncle to nephew, since in every combat they were
always companions in peril; very many of the ogres'
race had they laid low with their swords.

884   No little renown sprang up for Sigemund after the
day of his death, for, hardy in fighting, he had slain a
serpent, guardian of a treasure-hoard. He, son of a
high-born man, had ventured alone on that perilous
deed under the grey rock; Fitela was not with him.
Yet such was his fortune that his sword pierced the
wondrous snake so well that the lordly steel stuck fast
in the rock; the dragon perished by this murderous
blow. By his valour the dread warrior had won the
right to enjoy the hoard of rings at his own choice;
Wæls' offspring loaded a sea-going boat, carrying
bright adornments into the ship's hold. The serpent,
all fiery, melted away. Of all exiles, Sigemund, shield
of fighting men, was most renowned among many
nations for his valiant deeds, for by these he had
prospered—after the prowess, the strength and the
valour of Heremod dwindled away.

902   Heremod was lured into the power of his foes
among the Jutes, and speedily sent to his death.
Restless cares had tormented him too long; he caused
his people and all his nobles to fear for their lives. In

25

earlier times too many a far-sighted man had grieved over this stern warrior's way of life—the same who once had believed he would relieve their misfortunes, thinking that this son of a prince would prosper, inherit his father's noble rank, and so would guard his people, his hoarded wealth, his safe stronghold, and that kingdom of warriors, the homeland of the Scyldings. But whereas one man, Hygelac's kinsman, grew to be an ever greater source of joy to his friends and to all mankind, violence took a hold on that other man.

916 Sometimes they would range the tawny highways on their steeds, pitting them against one another. By then the morning sun was launched and speeding on its way. Many a retainer had gone with resolute heart to the lofty hall to gaze at the strange object so curiously made. The king himself, the guardian of ring-hoards, famous for his virtues, also came pacing from his wife's quarters with a great train of followers; and with him his queen made her way along the path to the mead-hall with a troop of maidens.

XIV

925 Thus spoke Hrothgar—he went to the hall and stood on the flight of steps, gazing up at the high roof gleaming with gold, and at Grendel's hand—'Let thanks for this sight be given forthwith to the Ruler of All! Many hateful wrongs and miseries have I suffered at Grendel's hands, but God, the Shepherd of Glory, can always work marvel on marvel. Not long ago I never hoped to see any relief for my woes in all my life, while this finest of houses stood stained with blood and wet with such drops as drip from swords. This was a deep-rooted sorrow to all my counsellors, who for long ages could not hope that they would ever protect the fortress of our people from these foes, these demons and spectres. Truly, whoever was the woman who gave birth to such a son among men, she may well say, if she is yet living, that Eternal Providence showed favour to her in her child-bearing!

946 'Now, Beowulf, best of warriors, as my son will I

cherish you in my heart; henceforth be true to this new kinship. You shall lack nothing in this world which you may desire, if it lies in my power. Often enough I have granted rewards for less than this, bestowing the honour of rich gifts on a lesser man, weaker in the fray. By your deeds you have achieved this—that your renown shall live to the end of time. May the Ruler of All reward you with success, as He did even now!'

957   Thus spoke Beowulf, son of Ecgtheow: 'With great goodwill we undertook this fight, this deed of valour, and braved the terrible might of an unknown being. I dearly wish that you could have seen the foe himself in all his splendid array, fainting with weariness! I had meant to coil my arms quickly round him in a hard lock, so that he would lie on his death-bed struggling for life in the grip of my hand, but his body slipped away from me. I could not prevent him from going, for Providence did not so will it; I could not cling closely enough to my deadly opponent, for the foe proved all too strong as he pulled back.

970   'He left his hand, arm and shoulder behind him as the price of his life, though even so the hapless creature did not gain any comfort. The loathsome attacker will not live any the longer, weighed down by his sins, for agony has taken firm hold on him in its relentless grip and cruel bonds; stained with his crimes, he must thus await the Great Judgment, and whatever sentence Providence in Its bright glory may choose to pass on him.'

980   Unferth, son of Ecglaf, was readier then to keep silent from vaunting speech about warlike deeds, when, thanks to this hero's might, the high-born warriors examined the hand on the high roof overhead, and the fingers of the foe. The bed of each nail was just like steel from in front; each claw on the hand of that heathen warrior was a hideous spike. They each declared that no hardy warriors' steel, even of proven worth, could have bitten into him to shear off the monster's bloody and warlike hand.

XV

991   Then orders were swiftly given that Heorot should again be bedecked inside, by men's hands; there were many, both men and women, who made ready the banquet-chamber, the hall for the guests. On the walls shone woven hangings, gleaming with gold, and much that was wonderful to see for all men who gaze on such things. The bright dwelling was much shattered and its hinges split apart, though it was held together by the iron clamps within; only the roof had remained quite unharmed when the monster, guilty of violent deeds, turned to flight, despairing of life. Never is it easy to flee death, though he who so wishes may try! He will have to seek out the place made ready for all living souls, all children of men, all who dwell on this earth—a place forced on him by necessity, where his body, held fast in the grave where it lies, will sleep when the feasting is ended.

1008   The time was then fitting for Healfdene's son to come into the hall; the king himself wished to take part in the feasting. Never, so I have heard tell, did a greater company of that people gather round their king, the giver of riches, or bear themselves more nobly. The men of high renown seated themselves on the benches and rejoiced as they took their fill; Hrothgar and Hrothulf, those kinsmen of resolute hearts, with due courtesy accepted many a goblet of mead in that lofty hall. Heorot was filled with friends; at that time the Scylding race pursued no treacherous arts.

1020   Then, in reward for victory, the son of Healfdene bestowed on Beowulf a gilded and adorned standard to be his emblem in battle, a helm and a corselet; also there was a renowned sword of great worth, which many saw carried before the hero. Beowulf accepted the goblet in that hall; he had no cause to be ashamed before men for so costly a gift. I have not heard of many men showing more friendship in giving to another on the ale-bench four such treasures trimmed with gold. A crest round the crown of the helm, bound with

28

metal threads, guarded the head from outside, so that
the sword (that legacy left by the files, hardened by the
showers that quenched it) could do it no savage harm
when the daring shield-bearer had to go forth to face
furious foes.*

1035   Then Hrothgar, shield of earls, ordered that eight
steeds, with cheek-straps all plated with gold, should
be led through the courtyards and on to the floor of the
hall. On one of them lay a saddle gleaming with skilful
craftsmanship, its splendour enhanced by rich adorn-
ments; in battle this was the high-king's seat, whenever
Healfdene's son wanted to share in the sword-play—
never had the prowess of this most famous king faltered
in the front rank when the slain were falling. Then he
who was the rampart of the Ingwine bestowed pos-
session both of horses and weapons on Beowulf, and
wished him joy in the use of them. Thus, as a man
should, did the renowned prince, the guardian of
heroes' hoards, give such steeds and treasures in
reward for the combat that no one who means to speak
truthfully and justly could ever find fault with them.

XVI

1050   Moreover, on the mead-bench the lord of earls gave
some treasure, some heirloom, to each of those who
had made the sea-crossing with Beowulf; also, he
promised to pay in gold the blood-money for the man
whom Grendel in his wickedness had killed—as he
would have killed more among them, if the Wise God
and the courage of one man had not averted that fate.
Providence governed the whole human race, as it does
still; it is therefore best to be always aware of this when
one's mind looks into the future. Much good and evil
must a man endure, if he has long experience of this
world in these days of strife.

1063   In the presence of the warrior who once had led
Healfdene's host to battle, there now was singing and
music too; the merry harp was plucked and many a
lay recited, when Hrothgar's bard, passing along the
mead-bench, spoke thus, to bring joy to the hall:

1068 'It was at the hands of the sons of Finn that Hnæf of the Scyldings, champion of the Half-Danes, had to fall on a Frisian field of slaughter, when the sudden onslaught came on them. Little cause indeed did Hildeburh have to praise the good faith of Jutes! Though guiltless herself, in that shield-play she was bereft of those she loved, her children and brothers; they sank down as was foredoomed, wounded by the spears. A sad woman was she! Truly, the daughter of Hoc had reason to mourn over the decrees of destiny, for when the morrow had come she could see beneath the brilliant skies how her kinsmen had been murderously slaughtered in the very place where she had once known the greatest bliss on earth.

1080 'But this strife had also carried off all Finn's thanes, save only a few, so that there where they had foregathered he could not fight to the bitter end in his struggle with Hengest, the thane of Prince Hnæf, nor could he dislodge the sad survivors by force. Therefore they offered them terms: that they would clear all one side of the room for them, to be their hall and high-seat, so that they would have possession of half, sharing it with the men of the Jutes; and that in giving out riches, Finn son of Folcwalda would every time show the Danes honour, favouring Hengest's company with rings and rich wealth in plated gold just as freely as he encouraged men of Frisian race in his banquet hall.

1095 'Then on both sides they pledged their faith in a strong treaty of peace. Eagerly and without argument Finn declared to Hengest, on oath, that in accordance with the judgement of his counsellors he would treat those sad survivors with honour; that no man there would break the treaty by word or deeds, or would ever in cunning malice mention the fact that now, having lost their prince, they were giving allegiance to the slayer of their own ring-giver, since this had been forced on them by necessity; and that if by some rash speech any Frisian were to rouse memories of that deadly feud, it would then be the sword's edge that would settle the quarrel.

1107 'A funeral pile was made ready, and gold in its

30

splendour was brought from the hoard. The finest
warrior among the warlike Scyldings was made ready
for the pyre. Upon the pile one could plainly see the
blood-stained mail-shirt, the image of swine or boar
all gilded and hard as iron, and many a man of high
birth dead of his wounds; great men had fallen in that
slaughter. Then Hildeburh gave orders that the bodies
of her children, her own sons, should be committed
to the blaze on Hnæf's pile, and be placed shoulder to
shoulder with their uncle upon the pyre. The woman
mourned, wailing the funeral chants. The warrior was
raised aloft. The huge fire for the slain went twisting
up towards the clouds, and roared in front of the burial
mound. Heads melted away; yawning wounds and
deadly gashes on the corpse burst open as blood gushed
out. Fire, that most ravenous creature, swallowed up
all the men of both peoples whom the battle there had
carried off; their breath of life had fled.

XVII

1125 'Then Finn's fighting men, bereft of their friends,
departed to make their way to their own abodes and
see the land of the Frisians, their homes and their
lofty stronghold. But Hengest still dwelt with Finn
throughout that slaughter-stained winter—most un-
happy was his lot. He remembered his homeland,
although he could not put out to sea in his ship with the
curling prow, for the waters were heaving in storm
and contending with the wind. Winter locked the
waves in fetters of ice, until the next year came to the
courts of men, even as it still does now, with days of
glorious fair weather, that always observe their due
seasons.

1136 'Then winter had slipped away, and the bosom of
earth was fair. The exile, the stranger, longed to be
gone from those courts; yet he thought even more of
avenging his wrongs than of crossing the sea, and
whether he might contrive some vengeful meeting,
since in his heart he remembered the men of the Jutes.
Thus he did not reject what the whole world would

31

counsel, when Hunlafing placed a flashing battle-
blade, finest of broadswords, upon his lap; its edges
were well known among Jutes.*

1146　　'A cruel death by the sword likewise came on the
bold-hearted Finn in his own home, when Gudlaf and
Oslaf spoke again of the grim onset and the sorrow at
the end of their sea voyage, laying on him the blame
for their many woes; a spirit shaken with fury could
not be pent up in the heart. Then the hall was reddened
with the life-blood of foes; Finn too was slain, a king
in the midst of his bodyguard, and the queen was seized.
The Scylding marksmen carried to their ships all the
goods of that king's household, with whatever jewels
and skilfully worked gems they could find in the home
of Finn; as they crossed the sea, they carried the noble
lady back to the Danes, and so brought her back to
her own people.'

1159　　The song, the minstrel's lay, was sung to the end.
Once again, merriment rose high; the sound from the
benches rang out more clearly; cup-bearers proffered
wine in wondrous vessels. Then Wealhtheow came
forth, wearing a golden circlet, and went over to
where those two fine men, uncle and nephew, were
sitting—as yet, there was peace between them, and
each was true to the other. There too sat Unferth the
spokesman, at the feet of the Scyldings' lord; all of
them relied on his bold spirit, believing that he had
great courage, although in the play of sword blades he
had shown no mercy to his kinsmen.

1168　　Then said the lady of the Scyldings: 'Accept this
goblet, my noble lord, bestower of riches! Let your
heart be full of happiness, O ring-giving friend of men,
and speak kindly words to the Geats, for so should a
man do. Be gracious to the Geats, not forgetting what
gifts from far and near you now possess. I have been
told that you wish to take this warrior to be as a son
to you. Heorot, the bright hall of the ring-giving, is
cleansed; rejoice while you may in giving many
rewards, and then leave this people and this kingdom
to your kinsmen, when you shall have to go forth to
meet destiny's decree.

1180　　'I know my gracious Hrothulf, and know that he

32

will hold these youths in honour if you, O friend of the
Scyldings, should leave this world sooner than he. I
can count that he will repay your offspring and mine
with his favour, if he remembers all the honours that
we both bestowed on him when he was still a child,
to be his delight and his glory.'

1188   Then she turned and went along the bench to where
her children Hrethric and Hrothmund sat with the
sons of warriors, a company of youths together; there
too sat Beowulf of the Geats, that noble man, between
the two brothers.

XVIII

1192   A goblet was carried to him, and words of friendly
cheer spoken, and twisted gold was bestowed with
much goodwill—two ornamental arm-bands, a robe,
rings, and the greatest neck-ring which I ever heard
tell of on earth. No finer treasure beneath the brilliant
sky have I ever heard tell of among heroes' hoards,
since Hama carried off the necklace of the Brosings,
both the jewel and its rich casket, to a fair strong-
hold; he fled from Eormenric's crafty spite, and chose
everlasting gain.

1202   Hygelac of the Geats, grandson of Swerting, had
this neck-ring with him on his last expedition, when
at the foot of his standard he defended his riches and
guarded the spoils of slaughter. Fate carried him off,
after he had courted misfortune by his proud courage,
seeking a feud with the Frisians. The powerful prince
had borne that rich ornament with its precious gems
across the brimming waves; beneath his buckler he
fell slain. The king's body then fell into the hands of
the Franks, and so too did the mail that clothed his
breast, and this circlet as well; fighters less worthy
than he plundered the slain after the carnage of battle;
men of the Geats remained on the field of corpses.

1214   The hall re-echoed with sound. Thus said Wealh-
theow, speaking before all that host: 'Have joy of this
circlet, beloved Beowulf, and may good fortune go
with it, O young warrior! Make use of this robe, one

of the treasures of our people, and may you prosper well! Prove what you are by your might, and show kindness to these boys by your counsel; I will remember to reward you for that. But already you have done so much that men far and near will praise you through long ages, even as far as the sea, home of the winds, encircles the cliffs. May you be blessed as long as you live, O high-born hero! I wish that rich treasures may be yours in abundance. And you who have joy yourself, be a friend to my sons by your deeds! Here every earl is true to the other, gentle of heart, and loyal to his liege lord; the thanes are all of one mind, the people are eager in their duty, and the men of this court, having drunk of our wine, will do as I bid.'

1232　Then she went to her seat. There was the finest feasting there, and men drank wine. They knew nothing of the fate, the grim destiny laid down of old, which was to come upon many an earl.

1235　After this, evening came on, and Hrothgar went to his chamber; the powerful lord went to his couch. A countless host of warriors remained in the great building, as earlier they often had done; they stripped the benches bare, and the whole place was spread with bedding and pillows. Among those who had shared in that feast, there was one who was marked out for death, hastening to his doom as he laid himself down on his couch in the hall. By their heads they placed their warlike bucklers, shields of bright wood; one might clearly see there on the bench, above each noble, a towering battle-helm, a ringed corselet, a magnificent stout spear-shaft. It was their custom both at home and in the field that they should always be ready for warfare in either case, at whatever hour it might be that need came upon their liege lord; a fine nation were they!

XIX

1251　Then they sank into sleep. One paid bitterly for his night's rest, just as had so often befallen them since Grendel took up his abode in the hall of gold and

34

followed his wrongful ways, until the end came and he died for his sins. It became clear and known to men far and wide that there still was an avenger who survived their foe, a long while after that bitter fight.

1258   The mother of Grendel, a mighty woman among monsters, had not forgotten her misery. She it was who had had to dwell in waters of terror and ill-omened streams, ever since Cain slew his only brother, his father's son, with the sword's edge. He then went forth, stained with guilt, with the mark of murder upon him, to flee the joys of mankind, and made his abode in the wilderness. From him there sprang many beings whose coming was destined from of old; one of these was Grendel, the hateful and cruel outcast who at Heorot had found one man wakeful, waiting for the fight. The monster had tried to get to grips with him there; but the other bore in mind the strength of his might, that ample gift God had given him, and put his trust in the One Ruler for help, for comfort and support, and by these means overcame the fiend, and laid low the creature from Hell. Then the foe of mankind had gone forth, humbled, bereft of joy, to seek the place of his death. And still his mother, ravenous and savage in her grief, wished to set forth on a journey that would bring sorrow, to avenge her son's death.

1279   She came then to Heorot, where mail-clad Danes were sleeping all about the hall. All at once the luck of these warriors changed, once the mother of Grendel had found her way in. Yet her onslaught was less dreadful than his, in the same degree as a woman's strength and the dread she inspires in the fray can compare with an armed man, when the bound blade of a hammer-forged sword, stained with gore, doughty of edge, shears off opposing boar-images over the helms.

1288   Then in that hall many a hard-edged sword was seized from above the benches, and many a broad buckler was held in a firm grip, but no man spared a thought for helm or broad corselet when that thing of horror set eyes on him. She herself was in haste, wanting to get out from there and save her life, now that she was discovered. Swiftly she wrapped her arms tightly round one high-born man, as she turned back towards the fens. He whom she had thus struck down on his couch was the dearest to Hrothgar of all warriors from sea to sea with the rank of companion, a powerful shield-bearing fighter, a hero of great renown. Beowulf was not there, for a separate lodging had been assigned to the renowned Geat after the giving of treasure. There was uproar in Heorot. She carried off that hand she knew well, all covered in gore; the burden of care was renewed, returning once more to that dwelling. No good barter was this, where those on both sides must pay with the lives of friends!

1306   Then the wise, grey-haired warrior-king was troubled to the heart when he knew that his princely thane, the dearest of all, was lifeless and dead. Beowulf, the hero blessed with the luck of victory, was swiftly fetched to the king's chamber; at the first light of day the high-born champion, the peerless hero himself with his companions, went where the wise man waited to see whether the Ruler of All would ever bring some change to pass after such tidings of woe.

1316   The man who excelled in warfare strode across the floor with his small band of picked men—the hall timbers echoed—till he could address his words to the wise lord of the Ingwine, and ask whether his night had been quiet, since there was so urgent a summons.

XX

1321   Thus spoke Hrothgar, helm of the Scyldings: 'Do not ask for happy tidings! The sorrow of the Danish people has been renewed. Æschere is dead—the elder brother of Yrmenlaf, a wise man who knew my secrets and was my counsellor, a comrade who fought by my side as we defended our lives in the strife, when marching hosts clashed together and rained blows upon boar-helms. Every earl, every man of high birth and proven merit, should be such as Æschere was!

1330   'A being, shaken with fury for slaughter, has slain him in Heorot with her bare hands; I do not know

whither that fearsome creature, glorying over such a
corpse and made famous by such a slaying, has turned
in her homeward journey. She has taken vengeance
for that bloody deed when last night you killed Grendel
by main force in your hard arm-lock, because all too
long he had injured my people and lessened their
numbers. He fell in that fight, his life being forfeit;
but now a second mighty and wicked ravager has come,
wishing to avenge her son. Indeed, she has gone far in
pursuing vengeance in her feud—or so it may well
seem to many a thane whose heart weeps for his lord,
the giver of riches, with cruel grief in his breast. Now
dead lies the hand which had proved willing to give
you all your desires!

1345 'I have heard my people who dwell in this land and
the counsellors in my hall saying that they have seen
two such huge prowlers of the borderlands, whose
realm is the moors, creatures from the otherworld.
One of these, as far as they could best tell, had the
likeness of a woman; the other miscreated wretch trod
his outcast way in the form of a man, save that he was
more huge than any human being. From days of old,
those who dwell in this country have called him
Grendel; they know of no father of his, nor whether
any such mysterious beings had been born before him.

1357 'They have made their abode in a secret land of
wolf-haunted slopes, windswept crags and perilous
fen-paths, where a mountain torrent plunges down-
wards, hidden by the mists of the crags, and the flood
plunges under the earth. It is not many miles from here
that that mere lies; over it hang groves thick with
hoarfrost, and trees, held firm by their roots, stretch
a dark canopy over the water. There every night one
may see a deadly miracle—fire burning on the water.
No one alive among all the children of men has such
ripe wisdom that he knows where its bottom lies.

1368 'Though the strong-antlered stag that roams over
the heath may seek the trees of this forest, if hard
pressed by the hounds and pursued from far off, yet
he will rather give up life and breath on the bank
before he will leap in to hide his head. No pleasing
place is this! Swirling waves rise up from it, black, to

37

the clouds, when the wind stirs dire storms, till the air grows dim and the skies weep.

1376   'Now it is only through you that help may be found once again. You do not yet know that region, the perilous spot in which you may find the creature guilty of so many crimes—seek it if you dare! I will reward you for taking this feud on yourself, as I did before, with riches and ancient wealth and twisted gold, if you make your way back.'

XXI

1383   Thus spoke Beowulf, son of Ecgtheow: 'Do not grieve, O far-sighted man! It is better for every man that he should avenge his friend, rather than mourn much. We each must come to the end of life in this world; let him who can do so win renown before death, for that is the finest thing left to a lifeless man.

1390   'Rise up, guardian of the kingdom! Let us swiftly go to examine the trail of this woman of Grendel's kin. This I promise you: she shall not escape to any refuge, neither to the bosom of the earth, nor to the mountain forests, nor to the bottom of the sea, let her go where she will! For today, take patience under every woe, as I well believe that you will.'

1397   The aged man leapt to his feet and thanked God, the Lord Almighty, for what this man had spoken. Then a horse was bridled for Hrothgar, a steed with braided mane. The wise ruler rode forth in all his gorgeous array; a foot-troop of shield-bearers marched alongside. Footprints could be seen far and wide along the woodland tracks, the trail left on the earth as she went straight on over the murky moor, carrying a lifeless thane, the noblest of those who had held counsel with Hrothgar in his own hall.

1408   The son of high-born men went onwards over high rocky slopes, by a narrow track, by small paths where only one man could walk, by an unknown road, past beetling crags and many a haunt of water-monsters. With a few other wise men, he went ahead to examine the ground, until suddenly he came upon mountain trees leaning out above a grey rock—a cheerless wood. Below them lay the water, gory and troubled.

1417 There was anguish now for all Danes and friends of the Scyldings to suffer in their hearts, and distress for many a thane and for all the earls, when they came upon Æschere's head on that cliff by the deeps. The flood was seething with blood and hot gore; the people gazed upon it.

1423 At times a horn would sing out its eager battle-call. The marching host all seated themselves; upon that water they saw then many of the serpent brood and strange sea-dragons exploring those depths, and also water-monsters lying on the slopes of the crags, like those serpents and wild beasts which will often sally out at mid morning on the sea where ships ride, on a journey that brings sorrow. Away they plunged, savage and in swelling fury; they had noticed that clear sound, the war-horn ringing. With an arrow from his bow, the chieftain of the Geats stripped one of them of life and the power to master the waves, for the hard war-dart stuck in his vitals, so that he was the slower in swimming the deep, and death carried him off. Soon he was hard pressed among the waves by boar-spears with sword-like barbs, and was fiercely assailed and dragged up on to the crag—a wondrous creature that once cleft the waves. Men gazed on the dreadful stranger.

1441 Beowulf dressed himself in hero's garb; he felt no fear for his life. His hand-woven war-corselet, broad and gleaming with subtle work, would have to explore the depths; it was so well able to protect his bone-framed chest that no hostile grasp or malicious clutch of any wrathful foe might harm the life in his breast. The silvery helm that guarded his head would have to go down into eddying waters and churn up the bed of the mere; its splendour was enhanced by rich ornament, and it was clasped round with lordly bands, just as the weapon-smith had wrought it in days of old, shaping it most wonderfully and setting it with images of boars, so that henceforth no blade or battle-sword could bite upon it.

1455   Not least among his powerful aids was that which Unferth, Hrothgar's spokesman, lent him in his time of need—a hilted sword, the name of which was Hrunting. It was peerless among ancient treasures; the edge was of steel, gleaming with twigs of venom, hardened by blood shed in combats; never in battle had it failed any man who grasped it in his hand as he dared set out on dread adventures or go to where armies gathered. This was not the first time that it must accomplish a deed of valour. Truly, the son of Ecglaf, skilled in strength, no longer bore in mind what he had said earlier when roused by his drink, now that he was lending his weapon to a finer swordsman. He himself did not dare risk his life beneath the tumult of the waves; there he forfeited glory and fame for valiant deeds. It was not so with the other man, once he had made himself ready for the fray.

XXII

1473   Thus spoke Beowulf, son of Ecgtheow: 'Now, O renowned son of Healfdene, O far-sighted ruler, now that I am eager to set out on this adventure, think of what we spoke of before, O gold-giving friend of men—that if I should lose my life for the sake of your need, you would take my father's place for me when I was gone. Be a protector to my young followers and close comrades, if battle carries me off; also, O beloved Hrothgar, send the treasures you gave me to Hygelac. Then when he gazes on that wealth, the lord of the Geats, Hrethel's son, may see and understand by this gold that I had found a bestower of rings who was noble in bounty, and had joy of it while I could. And let Unferth, a man known far and wide, have this ancient heirloom, my wondrously fashioned sword with wave-patterned blade, hard of edge; it is with Hrunting that I will win renown for myself, or else death will carry me off!'

1492   With these words the chieftain of the Weder-Geats hastened boldly on his way, and would not stay for a reply; the billows swallowed up the warrior.

1495 A great part of the day passed before he could catch
sight of the level floor of the mere. Then all at once
she who for a hundred seasons had kept watch on the
broad sweep of the floods in her cruel hunger, grim
and greedy, realized that some human being from up
above was exploring the lair of alien creatures. She
grasped him, she clutched the warrior in a terrible
lock; yet for all that she did no harm to his unwounded
body, for there was ring-mail wrapped around it to
protect it, so that she could not thrust her hateful
fingers through the warlike coat, the interlinked mail-
shirt on his limbs.

1506 Then, when she had come to the bottom, this she-
wolf of the waters carried the mail-clad prince into
her dwelling, in such a way that he could not wield
his weapons, no matter how gallant he might be.
Many wondrous creatures pressed hard upon him in
those depths, and many a sea-beast sought to break
through his warlike mail-shirt; monsters harassed him.
The hero then observed that he was inside some enemy
hall, where no water could harm him, nor could the
sudden tug of the flood reach him, because of this
roofed chamber; he saw the light of a fire, a glowing
flame shining brightly.

1512 The noble warrior could then see that outcast
creature of the depths, the mighty water-hag; he gave
so powerful a sweep of the warlike broadsword, his
hand never checking its stroke, that the blade with
coiling patterns chanted its greedy war-song on her
head. But the newcomer then found that the flashing
battle-blade would not bite, nor harm her life, for the
edge failed the prince in his need. It had endured many
hand-to-hand encounters, and often it had sheared
through some helmet or some doomed man's battle-
garb; it was the first time for this precious treasure
that its honour failed.

1529 Hygelac's kinsman, never slow to valour, grew
resolute once more, and set his mind on glory. The
wrathful champion cast aside the sword with curving
patterns, all bound round with fine work, so that it
lay upon the ground, tough and steely edged; he put
his trust in his strength and the force of his hand-grip.

Thus should a man act when he means to win long-lasting renown in the fray, and should never be concerned for his life.

1537   Then the chieftain of the warlike Geats gripped Grendel's mother by the shoulder—he felt no remorse for the hostile deed—and flung down his deadly opponent so that she fell to the floor, for he was hardy in combat, and fury was rising within him. She quickly paid him back by her fierce grasp as she clutched at him. Then this strongest of fighting men, this champion among marching hosts, stumbled with weariness, so that he got a fall.

1545   She then seated herself on the guest in her hall, and drew her broad knife with its burnished edge; she meant to avenge her son, her only offspring. But across his shoulder lay the interwoven mesh that guarded his breast; this protected his life, preventing all entrance by point or edge. Ecgtheow's offspring, champion of the Geats, would have perished then down under the broad earth, had not the hard war-mesh of his corselet afforded him help, and had not Holy God held victory in His power. It was easy for the Wise Lord, Ruler of the Heavens, to decide this matter according to justice, when Beowulf had risen again to his feet.

XXIII

1557   Then he saw, among other weapons, a broadsword blessed with the luck of victory, an ancient sword of the ogres' making, doughty of edge, a thing of glory to fighting men. It was the choicest of weapons, save that it was too huge for any other man to carry it in the sport of battle—a fine sword, splendidly wrought, the work of giants. The daring champion of the Scyldings, savage and cruelly grim, grasped the hilt and its fastenings and drew the blade with coiling patterns. Recking nothing for his own life, he struck so wrathfully that the sword took her hard on the neck and broke the rings of bone; the broadsword passed straight through her death-doomed flesh. She fell to

the floor. The sword was gory; the warrior rejoiced
at his work.

1570 A flash blazed out; light sprang up in that place,
just as when the sun, the sky candle, shines in its
radiance from heaven. He looked all round that
dwelling, then turned to follow the wall. Wrathful
and resolute, Hygelac's thane held his weapon high,
gripping it hard by the hilt. The warrior still had use
for the blade, for he meant soon to give Grendel final
payment for those many onslaughts he had made
against the West Danes; on far more occasions than
one he had slain in their sleep the companions around
Hrothgar's hearth, devouring fifteen men of Danish
race as they slept, and carrying as many again from
the house as his loathsome booty. The fell champion
had paid him the reward due for this, to so good effect
that he now saw Grendel lying on his couch wearied
out from the fray, lifeless, so gravely had he been
injured in battle at Heorot. The corpse burst wide
open when, after death, he suffered the stroke of a
hard sword-blow, as Beowulf cut off his head.

1591 All at once the far-sighted men who were gazing
with Hrothgar at the deep waters saw that the swirling
waves were all mingled with gore, and the surface
stained with blood. The aged grey-haired men spoke
of the hero together, saying they did not expect ever
again to see the high-born man come, glorying in his
triumph, to seek their renowned prince; to many it
seemed certain then that the she-wolf of the waters
had struck him down. The ninth hour of the day had
come; the keen Scyldings abandoned the crags, and
Hrothgar, the kindly gold-giver, turned homewards.
But the strangers sat, sick at heart, and stared at the
mere, wishing, but not expecting, that they might see
their kindly lord himself.

1605 Then, because of the blood shed in that combat, the
sword, that fighting blade, began to dwindle away into
deadly icicles; it was a marvel of marvels how it all
melted away, just as ice does when the Father who has
power over times and seasons loosens the bonds of
frost and unbinds the fetters of the pool—such is true
Providence! The chieftain of the Weder-Geats took

43

no more treasures from that dwelling, although he saw many there, save only Grendel's head, and also that hilt gleaming with riches; the blade with its interwoven patterns had already burnt up and melted away, so hot was that blood, and so venomous the being of the otherworld who had perished there.

1618   So, having lived to see his enemies fall in the fight, he straightway set himself to swimming, and dived upwards through the water. The swirling waves, homes of creatures more than human, had all been cleansed, now that that being of the otherworld had given up his days of life and this fleeting order of creation.

1623   Then the protector of the seafarers came swimming with bold heart to land, rejoicing in the spoils won from the lake, the mighty burden which he brought with him. They went to meet him, and gave thanks to God; this glorious company of thanes rejoined over their prince, and at seeing him safe and sound. Helm and corselet were quickly unstrapped from the valorous hero. Beneath the clouds the lake waters sank into stillness, stained with the blood of slaughter.

1632   They set forth from that place, retracing their steps with joyful hearts, and made their way along the paths and well-known highways. Men brave as kings carried that head away from the cliff by the deep water, though this was too hard a task for any single one among these men of great courage; four of them, with much toil, had to convey Grendel's head on a spear-shaft to the hall of gold. So presently there came the fourteen bold Geats, keen in war, striding towards the hall; with them their lord trod the meadows by the mead-hall, proud in the midst of this throng. Then the chieftain of those thanes, a man of bold deeds and honoured with high renown, a warrior brave in battle, came striding in to greet Hrothgar. The head of Grendel was carried by the hair across the floor of the hall where men were drinking—a thing of terror to the earls and to the queen among them, a wondrous sight which men gazed upon.

44

XXIV

1651   Thus spoke Beowulf, son of Ecgtheow: 'See, son of Healfdene, chieftain of the Scyldings, gladly we brought you these spoils from the lake, in token of glorious victory—these which you look upon here. Not lightly did I escape with my life from this fight under the water, and it was among hardships that I dared this deed. In the very first moments my strength in the fray would have been stripped from me, had not God shielded me. Nor in this battle could I achieve anything with Hrunting, fine though that weapon may be; but the Ruler of Men granted that I might see hanging, fair on the wall, an ancient sword of more than human size (how often has He guided the friendless!), and that I might draw that weapon. Then in the struggle, when my opportunity came, I struck down the guardians of that dwelling. Then the warlike broadsword with its blade of interwoven patterns burnt itself up as the blood burst out, the hottest gore ever shed in combat. I brought the hilt back from there, in spite of the foes; I had wreaked vengeance, as was fitting, for their violent deeds and the deadly slaughter of the Danes.

1671   'This I promise you, that you can sleep in Heorot free from care, with your retinue of men and every thane among your people, with tried warriors and youths; and that you need not fear, as you did before, that deadly evil will come from that quarter upon your earls, O prince of the Scyldings!'

1677   Then the golden hilt, the work of giants of yore, was given into the hand of the aged warrior, the grey-haired leader in battle. Thus after the fiends had fallen, this work made by wondrous craftsmen passed into the possession of the Danish lord. When the savage-hearted creature guilty of murder, the opponent of God, and his mother too, had forsaken this world, it passed into the power of the noblest of all earthly kings from sea to sea, and of all who have shared out their wealth in the realm of Denmark.

1687   Then Hrothgar spoke, as he examined the hilt, this

ancient heirloom. There was engraved upon it the origin of that ancient strife after which the flood and the gushing ocean had struck down the giant race—they had brought that peril upon themselves. Theirs was a nation estranged from the Eternal Lord, and therefore the Ruler gave them their final reward by surging water. Also, by means of runic letters on foils of shining gold, it was rightly marked down, set forth and recorded, for whom that sword had first been wrought, the choicest of steely blades, with its hilt of twisting patterns and its gleaming serpent forms.

1698   Then the wise son of Healfdene spoke, and all were silent: 'Lo, one who has upheld truth and justice among his people, who remembers all that is past, who has grown old as the guardian of his homeland—such a man may well say that this hero was born for greatness! Thy renown, O Beowulf my friend, will be exalted among every nation and along distant roads. In patience and wisdom you control all your strength. I will carry out my pledges of friendship with you, of which we have already spoken together; and you shall live to be a long-enduring comfort to your nation, and a help to warriors.

1709   'Heremod, offspring of Ecgwela, was not such for the honoured Scyldings; he did not grow up to be a joy to them, but to bring slaughter and deadly destruction on the Danish people. In his rising fury he would cut down the companions who feasted at his table and the comrades who fought by his side, until this renowned prince turned aside, alone, from the joys of mankind, even though Almighty God had exalted him in the bliss of strength and power and had upheld him above all other men. Yet within his heart his secret thoughts grew bloodthirsty; never did he give treasures to the Danes for honour's sake. Joyless, he suffered torment and long-lasting affliction on account of this strife. Learn from this, and understand the virtue of bounty! I who am ripe with the wisdom of years have related this tale for your sake.

1724   'It is a wonder to tell how Almighty God shares out wisdom and land and lordly rank among men, according to His deep purpose; He has power over

46

all. Sometimes He will allow the soul of some man of a
renowned kindred to follow his heart's desire; He will
grant him earthly bliss in his own homeland, which
is his to rule, and is a safe stronghold to men; He will
make whole regions of the world a broad kingdom
subject to him, so that the man himself in his folly
cannot imagine any end to it. He lives on, in plenty
and joy; no sickness or age hampers him at all, no
grievous malice overshadows his spirit, no enmity
anywhere reveals its murderous hate, for the whole
world goes according to his will.

XXV

1739   'He knows nothing of a worse evil, until all too much
pride grows and flourishes in him, while the guardian
and watchman of the soul is slumbering—too sound
a sleep is this, ensnared in the cares of this world, and
all too close is the slayer who in wickedness shoots a
a dart from his bow. Then this helmed man, knowing
no way to protect himself, is smitten to the heart by a
biting arrow, by the crooked, mysterious promptings
of the accursed spirit.

1748   'All he has held so long now seems too little for him.
He is covetous, his thoughts are savage, and it is
never his proud vaunt that he gives away gold-
plated circlets; he forgets and ignores what is ordained
for the future, because of the great share of honour
which God, the Ruler of Glory, had bestowed upon
him. And yet at the latter end it shall come to pass that
this fleeting body must crumble away and fall, marked
out for death. Another man takes the inheritance—
one who ungrudgingly shares out the treasures and
ancient wealth of this earl, heeding no terror.

1758   'Be on guard against such baleful evil, O beloved
Beowulf, noblest of men, and choose for yourself the
better part, the everlasting gains. Do not set your mind
upon pride, O renowned champion! Now, for a little
while, your might is at its full glory; yet soon it will
come to pass that sickness or the sword's edge will
strip you of your strength; or it will be the embrace

of fire, or the surge of the flood, or the bite of a blade, or the flight of a spear, or fearsome old age; or else the clear light of your eyes will fade and grow dim; presently it will come about that death shall overpower you, O warrior!

1769   'In the same way, for a hundred seasons I ruled the mail-clad Danes under these skies, and in war I protected them with spear and with sword-edge against so many races throughout this earth that I did not reckon there was any opponent against me beneath the broad sweep of the sky. Yet see how in my very homeland there came a reversal of fortune, misery following mirth, when Grendel, that ancient enemy, made his way into my dwelling! Because of this persecution, I ceaselessly bore great anxiety of mind. Thanks be to Providence, the Eternal Lord, that I have lived long enough to gaze with my own eyes on this head, wet with such drops as drip from swords, at the close of this ancient struggle!

1782   'Go now to your seat and rejoice in the joys of the feast, your glory enhanced by this fight; when the morrow comes, we shall share between us a whole host of treasures.'

1785   The Geat was glad at heart, and straightway went to take his seat, as the far-sighted man had bidden. Then once again, as before, a feast was courteously made ready for the men, famed for their valour, who sat in that hall.

1789   The dark cowl of night grew black above the men of that court. The tried warriors all arose, for the aged grey-haired Scylding wished to go to his bed. The Geat, that famous shield-warrior, was exceedingly well pleased to rest; straightway, a chamberlain who, as was proper, saw to all a thane's needs and all that war-like travellers ought to have in those days, led him forth, for he was wearied by his exploit and had come from afar.

1799   Then the great-hearted hero took his rest. There stood the towering building, wide-gabled and gleaming with gold; within it the guest slept, till the black raven with blithe heart heralded the sun, the sky's joy. Then came the bright sunshine, streaming up over the

48

shadows. The fierce warriors made haste, for these men of high birth were eager to journey back to their own people; he who had come with a bold heart wished to seek out his craft, which lay far from there.

1807 The hardy warrior then ordered that Hrunting should be borne to the son of Ecglaf, bidding him take his sword, that well-loved steel. He gave him thanks for that loan, saying he reckoned it a good friend in the fray and powerful in battle, and he spoke no word of blame against the edge of that blade—a gallant warrior was he! By then the fighters, eager for their journey, were ready in their armour. The high-born man whom the Danes greatly honoured went to the high-seat where Hrothgar was, and one warrior brave in battle greeted the other.

XXVI

1817 Thus spoke Beowulf, son of Ecgtheow: 'We sea-farers who came from afar now wish to say that we long to visit Hygelac. All was well with us here; we were entertained as nobly as heart could desire; you have shown great bounty to us. If ever on this earth, O lord of men, I can by warlike deeds earn any more of your heart's love than I have yet done, I shall be ready at once. If I hear from across the broad sweep of the floods that surrounding nations threaten terrible things against you, as those who hate you have some-times done, then I will bring a thousand thanes and heroes to your aid. As for Hygelac, lord of the Geats and shepherd of our people, I know that though he is young he would be willing to support me by words and deeds, so that I could prove how dearly I value you, and could bring my shafted spear and the support of my strength to your aid when you might have need of men.

1836 'Furthermore, if Hrethric, that son of a prince, should decide to come to the Geatish court, he would find many friends there; it is most right that one who is himself a fine man should visit far-distant lands.'

1840   Thus spoke Hrothgar in answer: 'The wise Lord sent into your mind those words you have just uttered! I have never heard a man so young in years discourse with such far-sightedness. You are mighty in strength and ripe in mind, O you who speak such wise words! If it should ever come about that the spear, or some cruelly fierce battle, or sickness, or steel should carry off Hrethel's offspring, your sovereign and shepherd of your folk, then I think it likely that if you were still living the Sea-Geats would have no finer man to choose as king and guardian of the warriors' hoard, if you were willing to hold your kinsmen's kingdom. The longer I know you, beloved Beowulf, the better your mind and spirit please me.

1855   'You have achieved so much that there shall be mutual peace between our peoples, Geats and Spear-Danes; that the conflicts and hostile inroads in which they once indulged shall now cease; that so long as I rule this broad kingdom there shall be mutual giving of treasures, so that many a man shall greet another with goodly gifts across the waters where gannets bathe, for some ship with curling prow will bring offerings over the sea in token of love. I know that it it is the nature of your race to be steadfast towards both friend and foe, living lives above all reproach, according to the ways of old.'

1866   Then Healfdene's son, shield of heroes, gave him twelve more treasures within the hall, bidding him journey safely back to his cherished people with these gifts, and speedily return again. Then the king who was lord of the Scyldings, noble and of high birth, kissed that finest of thanes and clasped him round the neck; tears fell from the grey-haired man. Being old and full of the wisdom of years, there were two things that he might expect, though the second was the more likely—that never would they see one another again in such a meeting of gallant men. This man was so dear to him that he could not hold down the surging grief in his breast; a hidden longing in his heart for this dearly loved man burnt in his blood, and was held fast by his heart-strings.

1880   Beowulf departed, a warrior proudly decked with

gold, and trod the grassy earth, exulting in rich treasure. The sea-going craft that rode at anchor was waiting for its lord and master. As they went on their way, Hrothgar's gift was many times praised; he was a peerless king, utterly without flaw, until old age took from him the joy of his strength—old age, that has often brought ruin to many.

XXVII

1888   So this band of most gallant young men came down to the sea flood, wearing their mail-shirts, the interlocked mesh of rings. The guard at the coast noticed the return of the warriors, as he had done before; he did not greet the newcomers with insult from the crest of the hill, but rode down to meet them, and said that these fighters in shining mail who were going down to the ship would prove welcome to the people of the Wederas. Then on that shore the broad sea-going vessel with its curling prow was laden with warlike raiment, with horses and with treasure; the mast towered high over wealth from Hrothgar's hoard. Beowulf gave a gold-bound sword to the man who had guarded their boat, so that henceforth he was held in greater honour on the mead-bench because of that treasure and heirloom.

1903   Then the vessel put off to ruffle the deep water, and forsook the land of the Danes. At the mast was a fine sail, a robe for the seas, made fast by a rope; the waterborne timbers creaked. No wind from over the waves held the floating vessel back from its journey. Away went the sea-going ship, floating onwards over the waves with foam-ringed neck, its iron-bound prow passing over the currents, until they could catch sight of the cliffs of the Geats and the well-known headlands; sped by the breeze, the craft drove ahead until it beached on the shore.

1914   The harbour-guard was quickly ready there at the water's edge; for a long while he had gazed far out over the driving waters, yearning for these well-loved men. He moored the broad-bottomed ship fast to the shore with hawsers, lest the force of the waves should drive those fair timbers out to sea. He gave orders that the high-born heroes' wealth, their rich adornments and plated gold, should be carried ashore; they would not have far to go to find Hygelac, son of Hrethel, the bestower of riches, where he himself dwelt with his companions in his home near the edge of the sea.

1925 Glorious was that building; the high king in that hall was of princely fame; Hygd too, the daughter of Hareth, was very young, wise, and highly accomplished, though she had lived only a few years within that enclosed fortress, and yet she was not mean-spirited, nor too niggardly in giving treasured wealth to the Geatish people.

1931 One noble queen of a nation showed arrogance and cruel violence.* There was no brave man among the cherished companions, save for the great lord himself, who dared, even by day, to turn his eyes towards her. Whoever did, could be certain that deadly bonds, hand-twisted, would be meted out for him, and that after they had laid hands on him the sword would be his portion, so that a blade with branching patterns would settle the matter and proclaim the cruel slaughter. Such a custom is not queenly, nor fitting for a woman to follow, matchless though she may be—that she who fashions peace should exact the life of some well-loved man because of a fancied wrong.

1944 Yet Offa, Hemming's kinsman, put an end to all this. Men at their ale-drinking then told a different tale, saying that she brought fewer afflictions and spiteful wrongs on the people as soon as she had been wedded, gold-bedecked, to that young champion, well loved and high born, and had set forth at her father's bidding for Offa's hall over the grey-green sea. Henceforth as long as she lived she had joy in her destined life on the throne, and was renowned for her goodness; she kept her deep love for that prince of heroes who was, as I have heard tell, the noblest of all mankind, of all the vast race of men from sea to sea. So Offa, the brave spearman, was honoured far and wide for his gifts and his wars, and ruled his homeland with wisdom. To him was born Eomer, to be a help to heroes—a kinsman of Hemming, a grandson of Garmund, and skilful in combats.

XXVIII

1963   The hardy Beowulf himself walked on along the shore with his handful of picked men, treading the wide beaches and the meadows by the sea. Hastening from the south, the sun shone forth, a candle to the world. They went on their way, going eagerly on towards the place where, so they had heard, the fine young warrior-king, the shield of earls, the slayer of Ongentheow, was sharing out rings in his stronghold. The news of Beowulf's voyage was quickly brought to Hygelac—news that this shield of fighting-men, his own comrade-in-arms, had come within the bounds of the homestead, alive and unharmed in the sport of combat, and was going up to the court. Inside, one floor of the hall was swiftly cleared for the guests who were coming on foot, as the powerful ruler bade.

1977   Then he who had survived the strife took the seat facing the king himself, kinsman facing kinsman, after he had greeted his gracious liege lord in the solemn words of courtly speech. Hareth's daughter passed to and fro in the hall with tankards of mead, showing her love for the people, and gave flagons of drink into the hands of the Hæthnas.

1983   Hygelac began courteously to question his companion in that lofty hall; curiosity pricked him to know what the adventures of the Sea-Geats had been: 'What befell you in your voyage, beloved Beowulf, after you had suddenly resolved to seek strife and battle far off over the salt waters, at Heorot? Did you bring any cure for the widely known sorrow of Hrothgar, the renowned prince? I have brooded over this with anxious mind and restless care, not trusting what might come of my dear liegeman's adventure; I had long begged you not to make any attack on that slaughtering spirit, but to let the Danes themselves settle their feud with Grendel. I thank God that I was allowed to see you safe and sound!'

1999   Thus spoke Beowulf, son of Ecgtheow: 'My lord Hygelac, many men now know of that famous encounter, and what long-drawn struggle there was between Grendel and me in the very place where for long ages he had brought misery and a whole host of sorrows upon the victorious Scyldings. I took vengeance for it all, so that none of Grendel's kinsfolk on earth need boast of the din that rose in the half-light before dawn—not even he who lives longest of all that loathsome race, entrammelled in treachery.

2009   'First I came into the hall of the ring-giving, to greet Hrothgar there; straightway, Healfdene's renowned kinsman assigned me a seat beside his own sons, as soon as he knew my mind. The company were filled with delight; never in the whole of my life had I seen greater joy over the mead among those sitting in any hall under heaven's vault. Sometimes the renowned queen, pledge of peace between nations, would pass to and fro through the whole hall, kindling the courage of youthful warriors; often she would give a twisted circlet to some man, before she went to her own seat. Or sometimes, before the flower of the host, the daughter of Hrothgar would bear a flagon of ale to all the earls in turn—I heard those sitting in the hall name her Freawaru, as she gave heroes the richly studded vessel.

2024   'She, so young and bedecked with gold, is betrothed to Ingeld, the gracious son of Froda. This has been settled by the friend of the Scyldings, the shepherd of the kingdom, and he thinks it a wise plan to bring a settlement to so many slaughterous feuds and conflicts, by means of this woman. Yet how often the slaying spear will scarcely lie idle after a prince's fall, even for a little while, noble though the bride may be!

2032   'It may displease the prince of the Heathobeards and all the thanes of those peoples, when he treads the hall floor with that lady, and when young men from the Danish court are entertained among the flower of their host. On these Danes there glitter heirlooms from the men of old, hard ring-patterned blades which had been the treasures of the Heathobeards for as long as they could wield those weapons, until amid the shield-play they brought destruction on their cherished companions and on their own lives.

XXIX

2041 'So then at the feast some old spear-fighter who sees the ring of a sword-hilt speaks out, remembering all the slaying of men by the spear. Grim is his spirit! Sad at heart, he begins to test some young champion's mettle by uttering the thoughts in his heart, waking the havoc of war, and speaks these words: "My friend, can you recognize that blade, that precious steel which your father in his vizored helm bore into battle on his last expedition? There the Danes, the keen Scyldings, slew him and remained masters on the field of slaughter, when Withergyld lay dead after the fall of heroes. Now the son of some man among those slayers, exulting in rich adornments, treads the hall floor, boasts of that murder, and bears the treasure which you by rights should possess."

2057   'Time after time he prompts him thus and rouses his memory with bitter words, till the moment comes when a retainer of that lady must sleep stained with blood from a sword's slash, his life forfeit for his father's deeds; the other escapes from there alive, for he knows the land well. Then the sworn oaths of earls will be broken by both sides; after that, mortal hatred will well up in Ingeld, and because of the restless cares within him, his love for his wife will grow cooler. Therefore I do not think that the goodwill of the Heathobeards or this lordly alliance is sincerely meant towards the Danes, or that this friendship will hold firm.

2069   'Now, O bestower of riches, I shall speak once again of Grendel, so that you may clearly know the outcome of the hand-to-hand struggle of champions. After heaven's jewel had glided over the earth, there came a wrathful being, fearsome and savage in the dusk, to seek us out where we, as yet unharmed, were

guarding the hall. This attack proved fated for Hond-
scio, bringing deadly destruction to a doomed man;
he, the girded champion, was the first to lie dead.
Grendel slew the renowned young thane with his
jaws, swallowing the whole body of the dearly loved
man.

2081   'Even then the bloody-toothed slayer, with his
mind set on havoc, did not mean to leave the hall of
gold empty-handed, but, being famous for his might,
he put me to the test, grasping at me with eager hand.
A pouch hung there, broad and strange and held fast
by cunning clasps; it had all been fashioned from
dragons' hides, by artifice and the devil's crafts. Though
I was guiltless, this bold doer of mighty deeds wanted
to thrust me inside it, one among many others; but
this he could not do, when once I stood upright in
wrath.

[XXX]

2093   'It would be too long to unfold the tale of how I
paid back that scourge of the people for all his evils;
by my deeds there I brought honour on your people,
O my prince! He escaped away, and for a little while
longer enjoyed the delights of life; however, his right
hand remained in Heorot to mark the trail, and he went
from there humbled and sad at heart, and sank to the
bottom of the mere.

2101   'For this mortal struggle the friend of the Scyldings
amply rewarded me with plated gold and with many
treasures, when the morrow came and we sat down at
the feast together. There was singing of lays there, and
gay minstrelsy; the aged Scylding himself, who had
heard tell of so many things, unfolded tales of far-off
times. Sometimes he, so brave in battle, would pluck
the merry harp for his delight; sometimes he would
utter some lay of true and bitter grief; sometimes this
great-hearted king would rightly unfold some strange
tale; or sometimes again the old warrior, bowed with
age, would bewail his youth and his strength in battle.
His heart was overflowing within him as, wise with
the ripeness of years, he remembered so much.

2115 'Thus all day long we took our pleasure there, until
another night came down upon men. By then Grendel's
mother was swiftly ready to avenge her wrongs, and
set out on a journey fraught with sorrow; death, and
the warlike enmity of the Wederas, had carried off her
son. This hideous woman avenged her child, and
valiantly killed a warrior; it was there that life departed
from Æschere, an aged counsellor of ripe wisdom.
Nor when the morrow came could the Danish people
burn him in the blaze now he was dead, nor lay the
well-loved man on a pyre; she had carried the body
off in her fiendish embrace, down under the mountain
torrent. For Hrothgar this was the most grievous of
the afflictions which had so long befallen the leader
of the people.

2131 'Then the prince, in troubled mood, besought me
for your sake to accomplish some heroic deed amid
the tumult of deep waters, risking my life and achiev-
ing a deed of glory; he promised me recompense.
Then, as is known far and wide, I found a grim and
dreadful creature guarding the bottom of the surging
flood. There for a while we fought hand to hand; the
deep waters were seething with blood, and in that
hall where battle raged I cut off the head of Grendel's
mother with a blade of more than human size. Not
lightly did I get away from there alive, but I was not
yet marked for death.

XXXI

2142 'The shield of earls, Healfdene's kinsman, once
again gave me great numbers of treasures. Thus did
the king of that nation live, following noble customs;
truly, I did not lose my reward, the recompense due
to my strength, for Healfdene's son gave me treasures
of my own choice. These I wish to bring to you, O
warrior-king, and bestow them with all goodwill.
Always I look to you for every favour; I have few
kinsmen near in blood save for you, O Hygelac!'

2152 Then he bade them bring in the mighty standard
with a boar image, the towering battle-helm, the grey

57

corselet, the gorgeous war-sword; after that, he thus continued his tale: 'Hrothgar, the far-sighted ruler, gave me this garb of battle, and in one speech he bade me first tell you whose legacy this is. He said that King Heorogar, prince of the Scyldings, had owned it a long while; yet even so, Hrothgar did not wish to give this mail which had clothed his breast to his son, the bold Heoroweard, although he was loyal to him. Have joy in the use of it all!'

2163   I have heard that besides these adornments there also remained four swift steeds, all alike, tawny as apples; the steeds and the treasures too he bestowed upon Hygelac. Thus should a kinsman act; never should he weave webs of malice against the other in hidden cunning, nor devise the death of his close companion. Hygelac's nephew, so hardy in combat, was very loyal to him, and each of them bore in mind what would benefit the other.

2172   I have heard that he gave to Hygd the neck-ring, that marvel, that wondrous treasure which Wealhtheow, a prince's daughter, had given to him, together with three horses, graceful and with gay saddles; after receiving that neck-ring, her breast was more nobly adorned.

2177   Thus Ecgtheow's son, a man well known for his combats and noble deeds, gave proof of his boldness and acted as honour bade. Never, when roused by drink, did he slay the comrades by his hearth; his heart was not savage, but, being bold in battle, he made good use of the ample gift God had given him, the greatest strength that man could have. He had long been lowly, for the sons of the Geats had not thought him a fine man, nor had the lord of the Wederas been willing to do him much honour on the mead-bench; they had firmly believed he was slothful—a man of high birth, but not keen in warfare. But there came a change from all afflictions for this man, blessed with glory.

2190   Then Hygelac, the shield of earls, the king famous in combat, bade them fetch in the gold-trimmed heirloom of Hrethel; among the Geats there was no finer treasure in the shape of a sword. This he laid in

Beowulf's lap, and gave him seven thousand hides of land, a hall, and a princely throne. Thus both of them by hereditary right owned land in that country, a domain to leave to their heirs; but the larger region, the broad kingdom itself, was for him whose rank was higher.

2200   In later days, amid the din of battle, it came to pass —after Hygelac lay dead, after battle-blades had been the death of Heardred beneath the shelter of his shield, when the warlike Scylfings sought out this hardy and daring fighter among his victorious people, assailing the nephew of Hereric with their enmity—after these things, it came to pass that the broad kingdom passed into Beowulf's hands.

2208   For fifty winters he guarded it well, until, when he was a king ripe in wisdom and grown old as guardian of his homeland, one creature began to make himself master in the dark nights—a dragon, which on the high heathland kept watch over a hoard and a tall rocky barrow, under which ran a passage unknown to men.* Into this, a certain man had gone; he had found a way in close to that heathen hoard, and his hand gripped a large flagon gleaming with rich ornament. Afterwards the dragon did not hide his loss, though he had been tricked while asleep by a thief's cunning; the nation of warriors dwelling near by soon found out what fury filled him.

XXXII

2221   The man who had so bitterly wronged the dragon did not break into the serpent's hoard by set purpose or by his own choice, but through dire necessity; being a slave of some warrior or other and troubled by guilt, he fled from a hateful flogging and, needing some shelter, found his way into that place. As soon as he looked inside, horror and dread fell upon the new-comer; yet the unhappy wretch . . . when the sudden onslaught came on him. A rich vessel. . . .

2231   There were many such ancient riches in that earthen house, just as some unknown man, after much thought, had hidden them there in days gone by—precious treasures, the vast legacy of a noble race. Death had carried them all away in former times, and the one man left from the flower of that race, the last remaining alive as guardian of the treasure, grieved for his friends and expected the same fate as theirs, knowing that he would enjoy for only a brief space the wealth gathered over the years.

2241   A barrow stood ready on open ground by the water's waves; it had been newly built by the headland, and secured by arts that made it hard to enter. Into this the keeper of the rings bore great heaps of princely treasures and plated gold, worthy of being hoarded, and spoke but few words:

2247   'O earth, guard now what earls have owned, now that heroes cannot! Indeed, it was from you that noble men once won it. Death in the fray, that fierce destroyer of life, has carried off every single man of my race, and they have forsaken this life and seen the last of the joys of the hall. I have none to bear the sword, none to burnish the gold-plated flagon or the precious drinking-vessel; the flower of the host has passed swiftly away. The hard helm must be bereft of its plates and golden ornament; the burnishers whose task it was to polish the vizored helm are now sleeping in death. So too the warlike mail-coat which, amid the crashing of shields, endured the slash of steel blades in battle, will crumble away along with the warrior; nor can the ringed corse-let travel far and wide with the war-leader, or be at the hero's side. There comes no delight from the harp, no mirth from the wood that brought good cheer; nor does the good hawk swoop through the hall, nor the swift steed stamp in the courtyard. Deadly slaughter has carried away many of the race of the living!'

2267   Thus, sad at heart, the sole survivor mourned in his grief for them all, joylessly wandering by day and by night until death's surging tide reached his heart.

2270   The ancient scourge that haunts the half-light of dawn found the hoard standing open to be his delight. This smooth-skinned, spiteful dragon seeks out bar-rows of the dead, and flies by night, burning and encircled in fire; those who dwell in that land dread him greatly. He is wont to seek out what is hoarded in the earth, and there takes up his abode beside the heathen gold, growing wise in ripeness of years, and yet for all that he is no better off.

2278   Thus for three hundred years this scourge of the nation guarded that immense house of treasure through his more than human might, until this one man roused fury in his heart. He took the gold-plated flagon to his lord, begging his prince for terms of peace. Thus was the hoard ransacked and the hoarded wealth carried off, and the wretched man was granted his boon. For the first time his lord looked on the handiwork of men of the days of old.

2287   When the serpent awoke, a new source of trouble arose. He slithered along the rock, and with ruthless rage found the footprints of his foe, for in his stealthy cunning he had stepped too far forward and close to the dragon's head. Thus a man who is not marked for death, and whom the favour of God the Ruler protects, may easily survive sorrow or the misery of exile. Eagerly the guardian of the hoard searched along the ground, meaning to find the man who had acted so cruelly towards him as he slept. Burning with savage rage, he went circling again and again round the whole outer wall of the barrow, but there was no one to be found in that waste land. Yet he rejoiced at the thought of a fight and deeds of battle, while from time to time he turned back into the barrow to search for the rich cup; he soon discovered that some man or other had tampered with the gold and the lordly wealth.

2302   The guardian of the hoard waited with difficulty until nightfall, for the keeper of the barrow was swollen with fury, and that hateful foe wished to pay men back with flame for the loss of the precious drinking-vessel. At last day slipped away, as the serpent desired; no longer would he wait within the walled barrow, but sped forth, armed with flame and fire. This was the beginning, bringing terror to the men of that land; so too the swift ending was to be bitter for their king, the giver of riches.

XXXIII

2312 Then this newcomer began to spew forth coals of fire and burn the bright dwellings. The glow of the burning rose up, bringing horror to men; the hateful creature that flew through the air meant to spare no living thing. From far and near could be seen the spiteful onslaught of the serpent, their cruel foe, showing how the warlike ravager hated the Geatish people and was humbling them. Before daybreak, he darted back to the hoard and to his hidden lordly hall. He had encircled the men of that land with blazing, burning flame; he put his faith in the wall and the barrow and in his own fighting ability, but this faith deceived him.

2324 A true account of this horror was speedily brought to Beowulf, telling how his own home, that finest of buildings, together with his throne, source of gifts to the Geats, had melted away in surges of burning fire. This brought suffering to the heart of that noble man, and great trouble to his mind; the wise man imagined that he had bitterly offended the Eternal Lord and Ruler by sinning against some ancient law; his heart within him was overflowing with dark forebodings, as was not usual with him.

2333 With his live coals the fiery dragon had utterly destroyed all the coastline and the nation's impregnable fortress, the stronghold of that region; the warlike king, the prince of the Wederas, planned to take revenge on him for this. The protector of fighting-men, the lord of earls, gave orders that a wondrous shield made entirely of iron should be fashioned for him; he was well aware that no forest timber, no shield of linden wood, could help him against fire. This prince of proven merit was now to see the end of his fleeting days and the finish of life in this world; so too was the dragon, even though he had long guarded the hoarded wealth. The ring-giving ruler was too proud to go with a host and a great force to seek out the creature that flew far and wide. He did not dread what this strife might bring, nor did he think much of the serpent's fighting prowess, his strength or his valour, because he had proved his mettle in many dangerous straits

62

and had survived many combats and the clashes of
battle, ever since the time when he had cleansed
Hrothgar's hall, being a man blessed with the luck of
victory, and had crushed to death a loathsome race,
the kindred of Grendel.

2354   Not the least of those hand-to-hand encounters
was that in which Hygelac was slain, when in the shock
of the fray the offspring of Hrethel and king of the
Geats, a kindly lord to his people, died in Friesland by
the thirsty sword that drank his blood, and was beaten
down by its blade. Beowulf came safely away from
there by his own strength, and by using his skill in
swimming; alone, he carried thirty mail-coats in his
arms when he leapt into the sea. No need had the
Hetware to be exultant about their fight on foot, when
they carried their linden shields forward against him;
very few escaped with their lives from that daring
warrior, to seek their own homes.

2367   Then, solitary and wretched, the son of Ecgtheow
swam back to his own people across the expanse of
waters. There Hygd offered him both the kingdom
and its hoarded wealth, riches and the royal throne;
now that Hygelac was dead, she did not trust that her
son would be able to hold his ancestral throne against
foreign peoples. Yet for all that, these unhappy men
could in no way prevail upon the high-born hero to be
lord over Heardred or to agree to accept the kingdom.
However, he upheld him among his people by friendly
counsels, goodwill and respect, until he grew up and
ruled over the Weder-Geats.

2379   It was Heardred whom the exiled brothers Eanmund
and Eadgils, sons of Ohthere, sought out from across
the sea; they had rebelled against Onela, the helm of
the Scylfings, a renowned prince and the noblest of
the sea-kings who distributed riches in the kingdom
of Sweden. It was this that set a term to Heardred's
life, for it was the lot of Hygelac's son to receive a
deadly wound by strokes of the sword in return for
this hospitality. And when Heardred lay dead, Onela,
the son of Ongentheow, turned back to seek his home
again, and let Beowulf hold the princely throne and
rule the Geats—a fine king was he!

XXXIV

2391   In later days he did not forget the vengeance he owed for his prince's fall; he befriended the hapless Eadgils, the son of Ohthere, and supported his cause with a host of armed men across the broad lake. After this, Eadgils took his own vengeance, bringing trouble by his expeditions through the bitter cold; he deprived King Onela of his life.

2397   Thus the son of Ecgtheow had survived every combat, and all perilous onslaughts and deeds of valour, until that final day when he had to do battle against the serpent. Then the lord of the Geats, filled with fury, went with eleven others to look upon the dragon. He had learnt by then how this feud had arisen to become a baleful affliction to men; the vessel, that renowned precious treasure, had come into his possession from the finder's hand. He who had been responsible for the start of the strife was the thirteenth man in that company; this lowly captive, downcast in spirit, had to lead the way from there. Against his will he went onwards to where he knew the earthen hall stood solitary, a mound covered over with soil, near the surging water and the tumult of the waves. Inside, it was full of finely worked objects and filigree. A hideous guardian, a ready fighter bold in the fray, had grown old there beneath the earth, keeping watch over treasures of gold; they were no easy prize for any man to win.

2417   Then the king so hardy in combats seated himself on the headland, and from there the gold-giving friend of the Geats bade farewell to his hearth-companions. His spirit was sad, yet shaken with fury and ready for slaughter; very near now was the fate which was to come upon the aged man, threaten the treasure of his soul, and part asunder his life from his body; not much longer would the high-born hero's spirit be clothed in flesh.

2425   Thus spoke Beowulf, son of Ecgtheow: 'Many were the clashes of battle in times of war which I survived in my youth; I remember it all. I was seven years old when the princely giver of riches and kindly lord of the people took me in fosterage from my father; King Hrethel cherished me and kept me by him, gave me riches and feasted me, and was ever mindful of our kinship. As a young warrior in his strongholds, I was never in any degree less dear to him during his lifetime than any one of his own sons, Herebeald, Hæthcyn, or my own Hygelac.

2435   'For the eldest a bed of slaughter was prepared—and not as might befit him, but through his own kinsman's deed, when Hæthcyn struck him with an arrow from his horn-inlaid bow, striking down his kindly lord; he missed his mark and shot his kinsman dead, brother slaying brother with a bloody shaft. That was a slaying for which there could be no blood-money, an act of guilty violence, a weary burden to heart and mind; yet for all that, the noble prince had to lose his life unavenged.

2444   'In like manner, it is tragic for an aged man to bear it if his son, so young, must swing on the gallows. Then indeed let him utter a song of bitter grief as his lay, while his son hangs there to the raven's delight, and he himself, though old and full of the wisdom of years, can bring no help to him! Morning after morning, he is always reminded of his child's passing; he has no wish to wait for any second son to be born in his stronghold, now that the first one has found his deeds ending in inescapable death. In sorrow and care he gazes at his son's dwelling, and his banquet hall laid waste and bereft of joy, a home now for the winds. The horsemen are sleeping, the warriors lie hidden in their graves; there is no sound of the harp, no such mirth in these courts as there had been long ago. Then he goes to his couch; alone, he keens his sorrowful dirge for his only son; all his fields and dwelling-places now seem to him too spacious.

XXXV

2462   'In like manner did the helm of the Wederas feel sorrow for Herebeald welling up in his heart; he could never make the slayer pay the price for his bloody deed, nor could he show his hatred for that warrior by any hostile acts, although he was far from dear to him. So then, in this sorrow which had fallen all too bitterly upon him, he forsook the joys of men and chose the light of God; when he departed from life he left his sons lands and the stronghold of their people, as a wealthy man does.

2472 'Then, after Hrethel had died, there was enmity and strife between Swedes and Geats, with mutual grievances and harsh warlike conflict across the wide water. The sons of Ongentheow were keen and bold in warfare; they would not keep friendship across the lakes, but would often, in their malice, inflict fearful carnage round Hreosnabeorh. As is well known, my dear kinsmen took vengeance for that violent and bloody deed, although one of them paid for it with his life— a hard bargain! This attack proved fatal for Hæthcyn, lord of the Geats. I have heard how on the morrow, when Ongentheow sought out Eofor, as kinsman he revenged himself on his kinsman's slayer with the edge of the sword; the war-helm split and the aged Scylfing sank down, pale from the sword. The hand of Eofor, remembering the great toll of bloody deeds, did not check its deadly stroke.

2490 'In that fray fortune granted that I might repay Hygelac with my bright sword for the treasures he had given me; he had bestowed land on me, a domain to enjoy and leave to my heirs. There was never any need for him to seek for some champion, of less worth than I, among the Gifthas or the Spear-Danes or in the Swedish kingdom, and hire him at a price. I would always go before him in the marching host, alone in the van, and thus, while life lasts, I shall do battle, as long as this sword endures. It has often done me good service, early and late, ever since I slew Dæghrefn, the champion of the Franks, with my own hand before the flower of the host. Never was he able to bring to the Frisian king the rich jewel which had adorned Hygelac's breast, for the standard-bearer fell slain in the contest, a high-born man in all his valour. Nor did the sword's edge slay him, but my hostile grasp crushed the beating of his heart and the framework of his bones.

Now the edge of this blade, this hand and this hard sword, must fight for the hoard.'

2510   Thus spoke Beowulf, uttering for the last time the words of a vow: 'I ventured into many a fray in my youth; now that I am old and wise and the guardian of my people, I will once more undertake a feud and achieve a deed of glory, if that evil ravager will come out from his earthen hall to meet me.'

2516   Then for the last time he greeted each of his bold men in their helms, his cherished companions, saying: 'I would not bear a sword as weapon against the serpent, if I knew how else I could come to grips with the monster to fulfil my vaunt, as I did against Grendel long ago; but I expect this combat will be fought with hot fire and a breath of venom, and therefore I have a shield and a corselet upon me. I shall not retreat by so much as one foot from the guardian of the barrow, but whatever fate and the Providence guarding all men may hold in store for us both shall come upon us there, by the wall. My heart is keen for the fray, so I forgo further vaunts against the flying foe.

2529   'Wait near the barrow, you men in armour, protected by corselets, to see which of us two can better bear his wounds in the murderous onslaught. This is no adventure for you, nor is it in any man's power save mine alone to pit his strength against the monster and achieve this heroic deed. I will win the gold by my valour, or else warfare, the perilous destroyer of life, shall carry off your lord!'

2538   Then the famous champion rose, leaning on his buckler, hardy beneath his helm, and went in his shirt of mail to the foot of the rocky cliff, placing his trust in a single man's strength—that is not the way of a coward! He who was noble in bounty and had survived so many wars and the din of battles where marching hosts clashed, saw arches of rock piercing that wall, and a stream gushing out through them from the barrow. The surging waters of that brook were hot fierce fire; because of the dragon's flame he would not be able to survive long unburnt in the deep places near the hoard.

2550   Then the prince of the Weder-Geats let a cry burst

67

forth from his breast, for he was filled with fury, and he shouted aloud in ruthless rage; his voice, a ringing challenge to combat, went roaring in under the grey rock. The guardian of the hoard recognized human speech, and his hate was aroused; there was no more time left to sue for peace.

2556 First the monster's breath came from among the rocks, a hot reek of battle; the ground echoed. The warrior at the foot of the barrow, the lord of the Geats, swung his round buckler up to face the dread newcomer. This creature of twisting coils felt his heart eager to seek out strife. The noble warrior-king had already drawn his sword, an ancient heirloom whose edges were very keen; each of them, intent upon havoc, felt horror at the other. With firm heart, the ruler of loyal men stood by his towering shield, while the serpent swiftly coiled himself together; in his armour he waited.

2569 Then he came gliding out, burning and coiling, and hastened towards his doom. The shield protected the renowned prince well in life and limb, but for a briefer while than his purpose required; there at that moment, for the first time, he had to stand his ground without fate assigning to him the triumph in the battle. The lord of the Geats swung his arm up, and with his sword, a mighty heirloom, he dealt a stroke at that dread creature gleaming with many hues, but its burnished edge gave way on meeting the bone, and it bit less strongly than the king required of it in his hour of need, when hard pressed by his troubles.

2580 After this fierce stroke, the guardian of the barrow grew savage in mood, and breathed out slaughtering fire; the flashing light of battle sprang up far and wide. The gold-giving friends of the Geats could not boast of triumphant victory, since the naked war-blade had failed in the combat as it should not have done, being steel of proven worth. This was no easy adventure, for the renowned son of Ecgtheow was to forsake the level plains of this earth, and against his own will would have to find a dwelling in some other place; even so must every man leave this fleeting life. Nor was it long before these dread opponents met once more. The guardian of the hoard took fresh heart; once again his breast heaved with his breathing, so that he who had ruled the people suffered cruel straits, lapped about with fire.

2596   His close companions, sons of high-born men, did not take their stand in a group around him, as honour demands in battle, but turned back into the wood and saved their own lives. But in one of them was a heart overflowing with sorrow; nothing can ever set aside the bonds of kinship, for a man who thinks rightly.

XXXVI

2602   His name was Wiglaf, the son of Weohstan, a well-loved shield-warrior, a chieftain among the Scylfings and a kinsman of Aelfhere; he saw his liege lord in his vizored helm suffering this heat. Then he remembered the honourable gifts which he had bestowed on him, the wealthy dwellings of the Wægmundings, and the rightful share of the common land which his father had had. He could not now hold back; his hand grasped his buckler of yellow linden wood, and he drew an ancient sword.

2611   That sword was known to men as the heirloom of Eanmund the son of Ohthere, whom Weohstan had slain in battle with the edge of his blade, when he was a friendless exile, carrying home to his own kinsfolk the gleaming burnished helm, the corselet of rings, the ancient sword made by ogres. All this armour ready for use Onela gave to him, though it had been the war-garb of a man of his own blood; nor did Onela take up the blood-feud, though it had been his brother's son that Weohstan slew. For many seasons Weohstan kept these rich adornments, sword and corselet, until his son was able to accomplish heroic deeds as his father before him had done; then, among the Geats, he gave him that garb of war whose worth was beyond all counting, before he himself, ripe in wisdom, passed away from this life. And now it was the first time for this young champion that he must fight beside his noble lord in the shock of the fray. His mind and spirit did not waver, nor did his father's heirloom give way in the fray, as the dragon found out as soon as they met.

2631 Thus spoke Wiglaf, uttering many just reproaches to his comrades; sad was his spirit: 'I remember the time when in the banquet hall where we took our mead we promised our lord who gave us these treasures that we would repay him for the war-gear, the helms and hard swords, if any need such as this were to come upon him. By his own will he chose us from his hosts for this expedition, thinking of us when there was glory to be won; these treasures also he gave me, because he judged us to be good warriors and keen men in our helms—even though the lord and shepherd of our people meant, for our sakes, to achieve this deed of valour alone, since he, above all other men, had achieved deeds both glorious and rash.

2646 'Now the day has come when our liege lord has need of the strength of good warriors in the fray. Let us go forward to help our leader in battle, for as long as this heat lasts, and this grim terror with coals of fire! God knows that for my part I had far rather that those live coals should engulf my body beside my lord who gave me gold. I do not think it fitting that we should carry our bucklers home again, unless we can first fell this foe and defend the life of the prince of the Wederas. I know well that for the sake of his past deeds he does not deserve to suffer torment and sink in the strife, alone among the flower of the Geatish host; he and I together will share sword and helm, corselet and mail-coat.'

2661 Then he strode through the deadly smoke to the help of his lord, wearing his war-helm; few words did he speak: 'O beloved Beowulf, perform your whole task well, just as you declared long ago, in the days of your youth, that you would never let your honour dwindle while you were alive. Now, O resolute prince, famous for your deeds, you must defend your life with all your strength; I will aid you.'

2669 After these words, that fearsome serpent, full of malice and glowing with surging fire, advanced in wrath for the second time to seek out his foes, the men he hated. In these waves of flame Wiglaf's shield

was burnt up to the boss, nor could the corselet afford
aid to the young spearman; but the youthful warrior
valiantly took his place behind his kinsman's shield
when his own had been utterly destroyed by coals of
fire.*

2677 Then once again the warrior king set his mind upon
glory, and in his mighty strength he dealt such a
stroke with his warlike sword that it stuck fast in the
head, driven deep by his violence. Nægling broke in
two; Beowulf's ancient sword with its grey glinting
blade had failed him in combat. It had not been
granted him that steely edges might help him in
battle; his was too strong a hand—so I heard tell—
which would overtax every blade by its stroke, when-
ever he carried into combat some wondrously hard
weapon, so that for all that he was no better off.

2688 Then for the third time, when his opportunity came,
the perilous fire-dragon, the scourge of the nation,
with his mind set on some bloody deed, rushed hot
and fiercely grim against the bold hero and gripped his
whole neck between cutting teeth. Beowulf was
stained with his own dripping life-blood; gore gushed
out in floods.

XXXVII

2694 I have heard how in the king's hour of need the
hero at his side showed the valour, strength and bold-
ness which were his birthright. He took no heed of the
head, though the hand of this brave man in his armour
was burnt as he helped his kinsman by striking rather
lower down at the spiteful creature, so that his gleam-
ing gold-plated sword plunged in so well that from
that time the fire began to die down. By then the king
himself was master of his senses once more, and he
drew a deadly knife, sharp and biting in battle, which
he wore with his corselet; the helm of the Wederas
ripped the serpent open in the middle. They had felled
the foe, their valour taking his life by force; both these
high-born kinsmen had struck him down together.
That is what a warrior should be, a true thane in the
hour of need!

71

2709   For the prince, this was the last time that he would win victory by his own deeds, the last of his great acts in this world. The wound which the earth-dragon had dealt him began then to burn and swell; all at once he found that the venom, in its deadly evil, was welling up in his heart. Then the high-born hero went as far as a ledge by the wall, and there sat, pondering deeply; he gazed on that work of giants, seeing how the age-old earthen dwelling held the rocky arches within it firm upon their columns. Meanwhile that most excellent thane with his own hands bathed his kindly lord, the renowned prince, weary now from the battle, and stained with such drops as drip from swords.

2724   Beowulf spoke; he spoke despite his hurt, his deadly and pitiful wound. He knew well enough that he had seen the last of his days of earthly bliss; all the number of his days had slipped away, and death was exceedingly near:

2729   'I would now wish to give my war-garb to my son, if it had been granted me that any heir of my body would remain after me. I have ruled this nation for fifty winters; there was no king among all neighbouring peoples who dared attack me with trusty swords, or threaten terror against me. In my own land I awaited the fate allotted for me. I guarded well what was mine, I did not pursue crafty spites, I did not swear any oaths unjustly. I can rejoice in all this, though I am stricken with deadly hurt, for when my life slips from my body the Ruler of men will have no cause to accuse me of the murderous slaughter of any kinsmen.

2743   'Now, beloved Wiglaf, go swiftly to look upon the hoard under the grey rock, now that the serpent lies there, sleeping his last sleep through a bitter wound, and bereft of his riches. Make haste now, that I may gaze on the ancient wealth, a heritage of gold, and look eagerly at brilliant gems skilfully worked. Because of this wealth of treasure I shall the more gently depart from life, and from my chieftainship which I have held for so long.'

XXXVIII

2752 I have heard how, after these words were spoken,
the son of Wihstan speedily obeyed his wounded lord,
stricken in combat, and went in under the roof of the
barrow, wearing his mail-shirt, a mesh of rings inter-
woven for battle. As he passed along by the ledge, this
brave young thane, glorying in his triumph, saw many
a precious jewel, gold glinting as it lay on the ground,
and marvels hanging from the walls. He saw too the
lair of the serpent, the ancient being that flew in the
half-light of dawn, and bowls that had been the vessels
of men of old, lying with none to burnish them, and
stripped of their rich trappings. There was many a
helm, now old and rusty, many an arm-ring twisted
with skilful craft. How easily the riches and gold in
the ground may overwhelm any man, though he who
so chooses may hide them! Also he saw a standard all
worked with gold swinging high above the hoard, the
finest and most wondrous thing that hands had ever
woven. A flash of light sprang from it, so that he could
have sight of the level floor, and gaze at all these objects
so finely worked. There was no sign of the serpent
there, for the sword's edge had carried him off.

2773 I have heard how one man then plundered the hoard
in the mound, the ancient work of giants, and loaded
his arms with goblets and dishes at his own choice;
he also took the standard, that most shining of
emblems. The aged lord's sword, the edge of which
was of steel, had injured the creature who had so
long been the protector of these treasures, and who for
the sake of this hoard had brought terror of hot fire
fiercely welling out at dead of night, until he died a
violent death.

2783 The messenger made haste, being eager to return,
and spurred on by the rich adornments; he was pricked
by anxiety as to whether he would find the bold-
hearted prince of the Wederas still alive, though
stricken, in the place where he had left him. Coming
then with those treasures, he found his lord, the
renowned prince, covered with dripping blood and

almost at the point of death; he began to sprinkle him again with water, until fresh words burst forth to reveal his hidden thoughts.

2792   The warrior king spoke, an aged man in his grief, and looked upon the gold: 'To the Lord of All, the King of Glory, the Eternal Lord, will I utter my thanks aloud for these rich adornments on which I gaze here, thanking Him that I was able to acquire such things for my people before the day of my death. Now that I have paid for this treasure hoard with my full span of life, you must yourself still supply the needs of my people; no longer can I remain here. Bid men renowned for combats build a fair burial-mound on the headland by the sea, after the funeral pyre; it is to tower high upon Hronesnæs as a reminder to my people, so that seafarers who sail their tall ships from afar through the mists upon the floods may henceforth call this Beowulf's Barrow.'

2809   The staunch-hearted prince took a torque from his neck and gave it to the young spearman, his thane, together with his helm that gleamed with gold, his arm-ring, and his corselet, and wished him joy in the use of them: 'You are the last remaining man of our kin, the Wægmundings; fate has swept away all my kinsmen, the valiant earls, as destiny decreed; I must follow them.'

2817   These words were the last to reveal the thoughts in the aged man's breast, before he chose the funeral pyre and the hot destroying flames; his soul passed away from his breast, to seek the glory of the righteous.

XXXIX

2821   It was hard for the untried youth to bear what had befallen, when he saw this most loved of men lying in pitiful plight upon the ground, at his life's end.

2824   His slayer too, the terrible earth-dragon, lay bereft of life, beaten down in ruin. No longer could the serpent with his twining coils guard the hoard of rings, for the edges of a steely blade, hard and notched in the combat, a legacy of the hammer, had destroyed him; he who had flown far and wide had sunk to the

ground near his treasure-filled dwelling, and lay still
with his wounds. Never would he circle through the
air for his sport at dead of night, nor let himself be
seen abroad, glorying in the treasures he owned; he
had sunk down upon the earth, through the deed of
the war-leader's hand. Yet not one of the mighty men
in that land, daring though he might be in every deed,
had ever succeeded—or so I heard tell—in facing the
breath of that venomous destroyer or laying hands on
the rings in that hall, if he found the guardian that
lurked in the barrow awake. Beowulf had paid with
death for his share in these lordly treasures; thus they
had each come to the end of this fleeting life.

2845   It was not long before ten men came out together
from the wood—men slow to do battle, weaklings,
troth-breakers, who had not dared bring their javelins
into play in the hour of their liege lord's great need.
Filled with shame they came, bearing shields and in the
garb of war, to where the aged man lay; they gazed at
Wiglaf. The champion was sitting, wearied out,
beside his lord's shoulders, and seeking to rouse hm
with water; he did not succeed. He could not retain
the chieftain's life in this world, dearly though he
wished to do so, nor could he turn aside what came
from God the Ruler, for the decree of God ruled
every man's actions, as it does even now.

2860   This youth had a grim answer ready then for every
man who had lost his valour. Thus spoke Wiglaf the
son of Weohstan, as with a bitter heart he looked at
these men for whom he had no love: 'Any man who
wishes to speak the truth can surely say of the liege
lord who gave you those treasures, the war-gear in
which you stand there—as so often this prince would
give some helm or corselet to the thanes sitting on the
mead-benches in his hall, the most splendid he could
find anywhere, far or near—that when the time came
for fighting, he had utterly and grievously wasted
those trappings of war! The king of our people had
no cause to boast of his comrades in arms; yet God,
the Ruler of Victories, granted him that when he stood
alone and had most need of valour, he would with his
sword avenge his own death himself.

2877 'I could do little to protect his life in the fray, yet
I strove all the same to help my kinsman, to the utter-
most limit of my strength. When I smote the deadly
adversary with my sword, he was henceforth the
weaker for it, and the fire welled out less strongly
from his head. There were too few defenders thronging
round our prince when the time of peril came upon him.

2884 'Now the accepting of riches, the bestowing of
swords, and all your delight in your own land and
your beloved homes—all this must come to an end
for your race. Every man within the circle of your
kindred will have to become a wanderer, stripped of all
right to hold land, once high-born men far away have
heard of your flight—a deed that brings no renown!
For any man, death is better than a life disgraced!'

XL

2892 Then he ordered that the news of the warlike deed
should be brought to the encampment high on the
cliff edge, where a band of shield-bearing warriors
had sat all morning long, expecting one of two things
—either the death or the return of the man they loved.

2897 The man who rode to the headland left nothing of
the new tidings untold, but spoke the truth in front
of them all: 'He who granted all desires of the Wederas,
he who was lord of the Geats, now lies still on his
deathbed and rests on a couch of slaughter, through
the serpent's deed. At his side lies the foe who took
his life, stricken down by knife-wounds; with his sword
he could inflict no wound at all on that monster.
Wiglaf, the son of Wihstan, sits by Beowulf, warrior
by lifeless warrior; with heavy heart he keeps the
death-watch over friend and foe.

2910 'Our people must now expect a time of strife, once
the king's fall becomes openly known far and wide
among Franks and Frisians. Our cruel grievance
against the Franks took shape when Hygelac went
journeying with his ship-borne host into Frisian
lands, where the Hetware assailed him in battle, and
by their valour and their greater strength forced the
mail-clad warrior to bow down in death, and fall in

the midst of his troops. No rich adornments did our
sovereign give to the flower of his host. From that
time, the favour of the Merovingian king has never
been granted to us.

2922   'Nor do I expect the least friendship or good faith
from the Swedish nation, since, as was widely known,
Ongentheow took the life of Hæthcyn, Hrethel's son,
at Hrefnawudu, when the Geatish people in their
arrogance had first attacked the warlike Scylfings.
Ongentheow, the wise old father of Ohthere, terrible
in his old age, at once struck his counter-blow at
Hæthcyn. He cut down this leader of seamen and
rescued his own wife, the mother of Onela and Ohthere,
an aged woman bereft of her gold; then he pursued
his deadly adversaries until they retreated into Hrefnes-
holt, with much difficulty, and having lost their lord.

2936   'With his great army he then besieged those whom
swords had left alive, though wearied by wounds; all
night long he vowed again and again to bring disaster
on that unhappy band, saying that on the morrow he
would spill the blood of some of them with the blade's
edge, and hang others on the gallows tree as sport for
the birds. But with the first light of day came fresh
comfort for their grieving minds, when they caught
the chanting of Hygelac's horn and trumpet, as that
hero came with the flower of his host, following on
their tracks.

XLI

2946   'Far and wide one could see a trail of blood shed by
Swedes and Geats, a token of how the two peoples had
stirred their feud to the pitch of deadly onslaught.
Then the lord Ongentheow turned aside to higher
ground; the wise hero, bitterly disappointed, went with
the men of his race to seek some impregnable retreat.
He had learnt to know proud Hygelac's skill in battle
and war; he did not trust that he could hold back the
seafarers by resistance, or make a stand to guard his
hoarded wealth and the women and children against
those who came in war. The old man drew back behind
an earthen rampart.

2957   'The Swedish people were then pursued, and the banners of Hygelac overran their place of refuge, once Hrethel's Geats had broken into their encampment. There the white-haired Ongentheow was brought to bay by swords' edges, and thus the king of that nation had to submit to the power of Eofor alone. Wulf, son of Wonred, lunged so wrathfully at Ongentheow with his weapon that at this stroke blood sprang from the veins under his hair. Yet for all that the aged Scylfing was not afraid, for, as soon as the king swung round again, he quickly paid Wulf back for the murderous blow, dealing him a worse one in return. Nor could Wonred's brave son deal the old man any counter-stroke, for he had sheared through the helm on his head, so that he was forced to bow down, stained with blood, and he fell to the earth. He was not yet marked for death, but recovered, though the wound had bitten deep. Then, while his brother lay there, Eofor, Hygelac's hardy thane, swung his broad blade, an ancient sword made by ogres, so that it broke Ongentheow's giant-wrought helm above his covering shield; the king, the shepherd of his people, bowed down, smitten to death.

2982   'There were many there to bind the wounds of Eofor's kinsman and raise him at once, when the way was cleared before them so that they were masters on the field of slaughter. Meanwhile, one warrior stripped the other; Eofor took from Ongentheow his steely corselet, his hard hilted sword, and his helm as well. He brought the grey-haired man's costly trappings to Hygelac, who accepted the rich adornments and courteously promised to reward him among his own people, and fulfilled this promise. When he had returned home, the lord of the Geats, offspring of Hrethel, repaid Eofor and Wulf for that combat by exceedingly great riches; to each of them he gave land and interlinked rings to the value of a hundred thousand sceattas, because they had won glory there by their strokes—no man on earth need reproach him for these rewards! To Eofor he then also gave his only daughter, to bring honour on his home, and to be a pledge of his favour.

78

2999   'This, then, is the feud and enmity and murderous hate between men, because of which I expect that the Swedish people will come to attack us when they hear that our lord has lost his life—our lord, who guarded his hoarded wealth and his kingdom against those who hated him, and after the fall of heroes guarded the bold shield-warriors, achieving much good for his people, and accomplishing yet further heroic deeds.

3007   'Now it is best to make haste, that we may look on the king of our nation there, and escort him who gave us treasures on his way to the pyre. There shall be more than one single portion of wealth to melt away with that gallant man; there is a hoard of treasures and gold uncounted, purchased at a grim price, for now at the last he has bought these rings with his own life. These the fire shall devour and the blaze swallow up; no man shall wear these treasures in memory of him, no bright maiden shall have these rings as adornment about her neck. Rather, she shall tread some alien land, sad at heard and bereft of gold, and this not once but many times, now that the leader of armies has laid aside all laughter and mirth and glad joy. Because of this, many a spear, cold in the morning air, shall be grasped and raised in the hand; no sound of harp shall awaken the fighters, but the black raven, eager for doomed men, shall have much to speak of as he tells the eagle how he fared in his feeding, when with the wolf he plundered the slain.'

3028   Thus did the bold man tell hateful tidings; he did not falsely conceal any words or deeds.

3030   The whole company rose; joyless, they went to the foot of Earnanæs, to look through welling tears upon that wondrous sight. There they found him lying lifeless on the sand, not stirring from his bed of rest—he who had given them rings in times gone by. The last day had come for that noble man; the warlike king, prince of the Wederas, had perished thus by a wondrous death.

3038   But first they had seen there a stranger creature, the loathsome serpent lying on the level ground before them; the grim-looking fire-dragon, dreadful in gleaming hues, was scorched with live coals; he measured fifty feet long as he lay. The air had once been his delight and his realm in the hours of night, till he swooped down again to seek his lair; now he was held fast by death, and had used earth's caverns for the last time.

3047   Beside him stood goblets and bowls; dishes lay there, and costly swords, rusty and eaten away, as if they had rested there in earth's bosom for a thousand years. That heritage of gold from the men of yore was of more than human power, being encircled with such a spell that no man could ever have reached that ring-filled hall, had not God Himself, the true King of Victories, who is the protector of men, granted to the man whom He chose the power to uncover the hoard— and this He might have granted to whatever man He thought fitting.

XLII

3058   It was then plain to see that this adventure had brought no gain to the creature who had wrongfully kept those fine things hidden inside there, beneath the wall. Yet the guardian had first slain a man who had few with him, and then grievous vengeance was taken for that deed of blood. It is a mystery where a hero famed for valour may meet the end of his destined life, when a man can no longer dwell in his mead-hall, among his kinsmen. So it was with Beowulf, when he went to meet the guardian of the barrow and his crafty hate—he himself did not know through what means his death would be brought about. For the renowned princes who had placed that treasure there had spoken solemn words over it, to last till the Day of Doom, saying that whatever man might rifle that place would be guilty of sin, kept captive in the shrines of false gods, held fast in hell's bonds, tormented with plagues. Beowulf had not first examined well enough the owner's legacy of abundant gold.*

3076   Thus spoke Wiglaf, son of Wihstan: 'Many an earl must often endure anguish through the will of one man, as has now come to pass for us. We could not give our beloved prince, the shepherd of the kingdom, the good advice not to attack the guardian of the gold, but to let him lie where he had been so long, and remain in his own abode till the world's end; he followed his high destiny.

3084 'The hoard so grimly won has been examined— too cruel was fortune, that spurred the king towards it! I myself have been in and gazed round at all the riches in this dwelling, once a way had been cleared for me, though not by peaceful means, and once entry was allowed under the walls of earth. I hastily caught up in my arms a great and mighty burden of hoarded riches, and carried it out here to my king. He was still alive then, conscious and sound in mind. Many things did the aged man say in his grief; he bade me greet you, and asked that in memory of your kindly lord's deeds you should build a barrow on the place of the pyre—a high one, to be great and renowned, even as he was the most honoured fighter among all men upon the wide earth, while he still could rejoice in the wealth of his stronghold.

3101 'Now let us hasten to seek out and see for the second time the pile of gems so cunningly wrought, the wonders beneath this wall. I will guide you, so that from near by you will gaze upon arm-rings in plenty, and upon massive gold. Let a bier be quickly prepared, and be ready when we come out; and then let us carry this lord of ours, this much loved man, to where he must long abide in the keeping of God the Ruler.'

3110 Then Wihstan's son, a hero brave in battle, bade them give orders to many warriors and owners of homesteads, so that these leaders among the people might bring wood from far off for this noble man's pyre: 'Now, as the dark flame grows, live coals shall devour this chieftain of fighting men, who has often endured the steely shower, when a storm of arrows sped by bowstrings came darting in over the shield-wall, and when the eager feather-clad shaft did its duty, aiding the arrow-head on its way.'

3120 Indeed, Wihstan's far-sighted son chose seven men together from the thanes of the king's bodyguard, the noblest among them, and he himself went in under that treacherous roof as the eighth of those battle-

81

warriors; one man, he who walked at the head of them, bore a blazing torch in his hand. There was no drawing lots as to who should rifle the hoard, as soon as the men saw that some part of it remained unguarded in the chamber, lying there to perish; little did anyone grieve that they should hastily carry those precious treasures outside. Also they thrust the dragon over the cliff, letting the waves take the serpent, and the floods engulf the keeper of rich adornments. Then twisted gold beyond all counting was loaded on to a wagon, and the grey-haired warrior prince was borne to Hronesnæs.

XLIII

3137 Then the Geatish people made ready a funeral pile for him on that spot—no petty one, but one hung round with helms and battle-shields and bright corselets, as had been his request. Then in the midst of it the lamenting warriors laid the renowned prince, their beloved lord. The fighters then began to kindle the greatest of funeral fires upon that crag; woodsmoke rose up, black above the blaze, and the roaring of flames was mingled with wailing, while the swirling winds fell still, until fire had split his bony frame and lay hot about his heart. With cheerless spirits they mourned the killing of their lord, a heavy grief to them. Also a Geatish woman, with her hair bound up, in her sorrow and care sang again and again a funeral chant, saying she sorely dreaded that she would know days of mourning, and a time of great slaughter and terror among the host, with humiliation and captivity. Heaven swallowed up the smoke.*

3156 Then the people of the Wederas built a shelter on the headland; it was high and broad, and could be seen far and wide by those who travel the waves.* In ten days they had built up this memorial to a man bold in combat; they raised a wall round what the fire had left, the worthiest that men of deep knowledge could devise. In this barrow they placed armrings and jewels, and all the rich trappings which men intent upon strife had taken from the hoard; they left this wealth of earls for the earth to guard, laying the gold in the ground, where it still exists, and now, as before, is set apart from the use of men.

3169   Then round the burial mound rode men brave in battle, sons of high-born men, twelve in all; they wished to lament their sorrow and mourn for their king, to utter a lay and to speak of this man. They praised his heroism, and proclaimed the excellence of his deeds of valour, for it is fitting that a man should thus honour his liege lord by his words, and show him heartfelt love when his spirit has been taken from his body. Thus did men of the Geats, his own hearth-companions, bewail the fall of their lord; they said that among all the kings in this world he had been the gentlest of men and the most gracious, the most kindly to his people, and the most eager to win renown.

NOTES ON THE TRANSLATION

169 The last clause of this sentence could also mean: 'nor did he feel any regard for Him [i.e. God].'

305–6 In rendering this passage, *ferh* has been taken to mean 'pig', with *fāh ond fȳrheard* and *gūðmōd* in apposition to it, and *grimmon* has been taken as a dative plural, 'stern men'. Several other arrangements of syntax and punctuation are possible: in particular, *ferh* may be part of a compound *ferhweard*, 'the guarding of life'. In that case, the rendering would be: 'Above their cheek-guards shone the figures of boars, adorned with gold, gleaming, tempered in flame; with fierce spirit, it stood guard over the lives of stern men.' A further possibility is that the reading *gūðmōd grummon* should be kept, and interpreted as the first clause of the next sentence: 'Above their cheek-guards shone the figures of boars, adorned with gold; gleaming and tempered in flame, it stood guard over their lives. Their stern hearts were filled with wrath; the warriors made haste. . . .'

489–90 In rendering this passage, *onsæl* has been taken as a verb, 'reveal', and *meoto* as a noun, 'thought'. Alternatively, *meoto* may be a verb, 'listen' or 'consider', and *on sæl* a phrase meaning either 'in this hall' or 'at this time', according to whether the vowel is short or long. With these readings, and emending *secgum* to *secga*, the lines could be rendered: 'Now sit at the feast, and in this hall (or: at this time) think upon the triumphant victories of men, as your own heart moves you.'

748–9 The translation assumes that the point of these lines is to record a vital stage in the fight, the moment when Beowulf first gets his grip upon Grendel's arm. Therefore *gesæt* has been taken to mean 'got possession of', and *inwitþancum* is interpreted as referring to Beowulf's stratagem which tricked Grendel into unwarily stretching his arm out. The alternative rendering is: 'He [Beowulf] perceived his [Grendel's] malicious intention, and sat up, propping himself up on one arm.'

84

1033 *Scūrheard* has been taken as an allusion to the quenching of blades to harden them, since it follows a reference to files, which obviously alludes to the processes of smithying. However, the image might also be that of a sword 'hardened by showers of blows' (either hammer-blows, or strokes in battle), or 'hard in the storm [of battle]'.

1142 The translation follows the reading *worold rādenne*, not the emendation *weorod-rādende*, 'ruler of the host'. If the latter is accepted, it could apply either to Finn or to Hunlafing, and the lines would mean either that Hnæf did not now refuse to fight Finn, or that he did not reject Hunlafing's appeal.

1931–2 This rendering takes *mōdþrȳðo* as a compound abstract noun, 'arrogance of mind', rather than as a proper name, which would give the meaning: 'Modthryth, noble queen of the nation, showed cruel violence.' The emendation *mōd þrȳðe ne wæg* requires the rendering: 'This noble queen of the nation (i.e. Hygd) did not show the pride and cruel violence of Thryth.' It is also possible to read *mōd þrȳtho wæg*, and render: 'Thryth, the noble queen of the nation, showed pride and cruel violence.'

2212–31 The translation follows the conjectural readings adopted in Klæber's edition.

2672–3 A different division of words and lines gives the reading: *Līg ȳðum fōr./Born bord wið rond*. The rendering then would be: 'He [i.e. the dragon] advanced in waves of flame. The shield [of Wiglaf] burnt up to the boss.'

3074–5 This rendering is based on the unamended text, taking *gold-hwæte* in agreement with *ēst*, 'gift' or 'legacy'. The point of the passage seems to be that if Beowulf had known of the curse laid on all who touched the gold, he might have avoided death; it has indeed been suggested that *gold-hwæte* might mean 'accursed' rather than 'abundant' gold. Among other possible renderings are: 'He had by no means looked too eagerly upon the owner's legacy of abundant gold' (i.e. Beowulf was not avaricious, so the curse could not touch him); or, taking *ēst* as 'grace' and *āgend* as a kenning for God, 'Never before had he beheld more fully the gold-abounding grace of God' (i.e the gold was God's last and best gift to Beowulf). It is also possible, by emending *næs* to *næfne*, to take the lines as a continuation of the previous sentence: '. . . whatever man might rifle that hoard would be . . . tormented with plagues, unless God's grace had already looked favourably upon him who was eager for gold (*gold-hwæte*).'

3150–5   The rendering adopts the readings *Gēatisc* in l. 3150, *swīðe* in l. 3152, and *heofung-dagas* in l. 3153.

3157   The rendering adopts the reading *hlēo on hōe*.

86

GENEALOGIES

1. THE ROYAL HOUSE OF THE GEATS

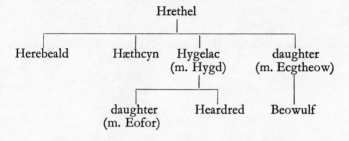

2. THE ROYAL HOUSE OF THE DANES (SCYLDINGS)

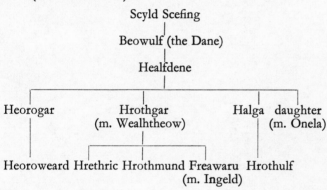

3. THE ROYAL HOUSE OF THE SWEDES (SCYLFINGS)

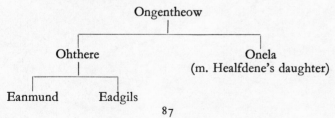

4. THE ROYAL HOUSE OF THE GEATS

[Bēahs]

Herebeald	Hæthcyn	Hygelac	daughter	daughter
		(m. Hygd)	(m. Eofor?)	
		daughter	Heardred	Beowulf
		(m. Eofor?)		

5. THE ROYAL HOUSE OF THE DANES (SCYLDINGS)

Scyld Scefing

Beowulf (the Dane)

Healfdene

Heorogar	Hrothgar	Halga	daughter
	(m. Wealhtheow)		(m. Onela)

Heoroweard   Hrethric   Hrothmund   Freawaru   Hrothulf
(m. Ingeld)

6. THE ROYAL HOUSE OF THE SWEDES (SCYLFINGS)

Ongentheow

Ohthere	Onela
	(m. Healfdene's daughter)

Eanmund   Eadgils

ANALOGUES

AND

RELATED DOCUMENTS

I. The Geats—O. N. Gautar.

A. BĒOWULF—O.N. Bǫðvarr Bjarki/Bierghi— Lat. Bodvarus Biarki/Biarci.

1. *Old English Charter of King Æðelstan* (A.D. 931).

> [The charter is defining the boundaries of a grant of land.]

> ... from there north over the hill . . . to the fence of Beowa's Patch [*Beowan hamm*], and then eastwards to Blackberry Copse . . . then to the long meadow, and from there to Grendel's Mere. . . .

2. *Liber Vitae Ecclesiae Dunelmensis.*

> A seventh-century entry in this list of benefactors of Durham Cathedral mentions a monk named *Biuulf.*

3. *Bjarkamál* (*c.* 905?)

> [This lay, extant only in fragments and paraphrase, is the earliest text to mention Bǫðvarr Bjarki. See below, II G 3 and 8.]

4. *Skjǫldunga saga* (*c.* 1200) in an abstract by Arngrímur Jónsson (1596), ch. 12.

> Rolfo [Hrólfr Kraki, King of Denmark] had a most celebrated champion named Bodvarus, a Norwegian, who for his courage won praise above all others; on him he bestowed his daughter Scura.

> [For this saga's account of the part played by Rolfo's champions in the conflict between Adilsus of Sweden and Alo of the Upplands, see below, III E 4.]

5. Saxo Grammaticus, *Danish History* (*c.* 1200), II § 56.

At that time, a certain Agnarus, son of Ingellus, being about to wed Ruta, the sister of Rolfo [i.e. Hrólfr Kraki, King of Denmark; see below, II G], celebrated his bridal with a great banquet. The champions were rioting at this banquet with every sort of wantonness, and flinging from all over the room knobbed bones at a certain Hialto. But it chanced that his messmate, named Biarco, received a violent blow on the head through the ill aim of the thrower; at whom, stung both by the pain and the jeering, he sent the bone back, so that he twisted the front of his head to the back, and wrung the back of it to where the front had been; punishing the wryness of the man's temper by turning his face sidelong. This deed moderated their wanton and injurious jests, and drove the champions to quit the palace.

The bridegroom, nettled at this affront to the banquet, resolved to fight Biarco, in order to seek vengeance by means of a duel for the interruption to their mirth. At the outset of the duel there was a long dispute, which of them ought to have the chance of striking first. For of old, in the ordering of combats, men did not try to exchange their blows thick and fast; but there was a pause, and at the same time a definite succession in striking; the contest being carried on with few blows, but those terrible, so that honour was paid more to the mightiness than to the number of the blows. Agnarus, being of higher rank, was put first; and the blow which he dealt is said to have been so furious, that he cut through the front of the helmet, wounded the skin of the scalp, and had to let go of his sword, which became locked in the vizor-holes. Then Biarco, who was to deal the return stroke, set his foot against a stock, in order to give the freer poise to his steel, and passed his fine-edged blade through the midst of Agnarus' body. Some declare that Agnarus, in supreme suppression of his pain, gave up the ghost with his lips relaxed into a smile. The champions passionately sought to avenge him, but were visited by Biarco with like destruction, for he used a sword of wonderful sharpness and unusual length which he called Lövi.

When he was triumphing in these deeds of prowess, a beast of the forest furnished him fresh laurels. For he met a huge bear in the thicket, and slew it with a javelin; and then bade his companion Hialto put his lips to the beast and drink the blood that came out, that he might be the stronger afterwards. For it was believed that a draught of this sort caused an increase in bodily strength. By these valorous achievements he became intimate with the most illustrious nobles, and even became a favourite of the king, took to wife his sister Ruta, and had the bride of the conquered as the prize of the conquest.

[For Saxo's paraphrase of the *Bjarkamál* and his account of Biarco's part in Rolfo's last battle, see below, II G 8.]

6. Snorri Sturluson, *Edda*, *Skáldskaparmál*, chs. 53-4.

[For this mention of Bǫðvarr Bjarki among Hrólfr's champions, see below, II G 10.]

7. *Series Runica Regum Daniae Altera* (fourteenth century).

Then Rolf Krake, Helhe's son, was king; in his time lived Hialti and Bierghi . . .

8. *Hrólfs saga kraka* (*c.* 1400), chs. 24-7, 30-6.

Now the tale there is to be told is how, away in the north of Norway, a king named Hringr ruled over Uppdalir. He had a son who was called Bjǫrn [i.e. 'Bear']. Now it is said that the queen died, and this was felt as a heavy loss for the king and for many others too. The men of that land and the king's counsellors asked him to marry again, and so it came about that he sent men south through the realm to woo a wife for him. But they were met by strong contrary winds and heavy storms, so that they were forced to turn their ship's prow and run before the wind, and the end of the matter was that they were driven north to Lappland and spent the winter there.

One day they went up inland and came to a house, in which sat two women, lovely to look at; the women greeted them pleasantly and asked where they had come

93

from. They told them all about their journey, and
what its purpose was; then they asked the women where
they were from, and for what reason they had come there
all on their own, and so far from other people, being
such lovely and beautiful women.

The older woman said: 'There is reason for every-
thing, my friends. We are here because a powerful king
asked for my daughter's hand, but she would not have
him; in reply he threatened her with harsh treatment,
and so I am keeping her here secretly as long as her
father is away from home—for he is away on raiding
expeditions.'

They asked who her father was.

The mother said: 'She is the daughter of the King of
Lappland.'

They asked these women what their names were.

The older one said: 'My name is Ingibjǫrg, and my
daughter's name is Hvít; I am the mistress of the King
of Lappland.'

There was only one maid there to wait on them. The
king's men thought highly of these women, and they
agreed it would be a good plan to ask whether Hvít
would be willing to go with them and become King
Hringr's wife. The one who was the leader among the
king's messengers made this proposal to her; she did
not, however, give her answer hastily, but referred the
matter to her mother's authority.

'It's an ill wind that blows nobody any good, as they
say,' said her mother; 'yet I think it wrong that this
should be done without her father's leave. All the same,
we must take this risk, if she is ever to do well for
herself.'

Thereupon she made ready for the journey with
them, and so they went their way and returned to King
Hringr. The messengers at once asked the king whether
he wished to take this woman, or whether she should
be sent back by the way she came. The king thought
well of the girl, and at once arranged his wedding with
her. He would pay no heed to the fact that she was not
wealthy. But the king was somewhat advanced in years
—as one was very soon able to tell by looking at the
queen.

94

There was a peasant whose home was not far from the king's; he had a wife and one child, a daughter called Bera [i.e. 'She-Bear'], who was young and lovely to look at. Bjǫrn the king's son and Bera the peasant's daughter had played together as children, and got on very well together. This peasant was rich and wealthy; in youth he had been long away on raids, and he was a very valiant man. Bjǫrn and Bera loved one another dearly, and would often meet.

Some time now went by without anything happening worth speaking of. Bjǫrn the king's son grew up fast and became tall and strong; he gave proof of great manliness in all kinds of feats of strength. King Hringr used to spend long periods out of the country on raiding voyages, but Hvít stayed at home and governed the country. She was not well-liked among the common people, but to Bjǫrn she behaved with great friendliness, though he hardly welcomed it.

On one occasion when the king was about to set out from home, the queen told him that his son Bjǫrn ought to stay at home with her to help govern the country. The king too felt that this would be advisable; the queen by then was growing imperious and haughty. So the king told his son Bjǫrn that he was to stay at home and keep guard over the land, together with the queen. Bjǫrn said that he did not much like this, and that he felt a deep dislike for the queen; but the king said that he had to stay behind. So now the king left the country, with a great troop of men.

Bjǫrn now went home after his talk with his father, each feeling convinced that his own view had been the right one. He went off to his sleeping-quarters, in a rather gloomy mood, and as red as blood. The queen went to talk to him, wishing to cheer him, and spoke of her friendliness towards him. He told her to go away, and so she did for the time being.

However, she often came again to talk to him, and she said it would be most suitable that they should share the same bed while the king was away, and that it would be far more fitting that they should live together than that she should be married to so old a man as King Hringr. Bjǫrn received this suggestion angrily and struck her a heavy blow on the chin, and told her to take herself off, and tried to drive her away.

She said she was not used to being driven out or struck: 'You prefer holding that peasant's daughter in your arms, Bjǫrn, rather than me. It's a most fitting match for you, or so one might think, even though there's greater disgrace in that than in enjoying my love and favours! And the time may not be far off when something comes to thwart your desires and your folly.'

Thereupon she struck him with a wolf-skin glove, and said he was to turn into a fierce and savage bear— 'and, furthermore, you are to eat no other food than your father's cattle. You shall slaughter them for your meat, in greater numbers than has ever been known up to now. You shall never be freed from this curse, and this vengeance will seem to you worse than none'.

After that Bjǫrn disappeared, and no one knew what had become of him; and when men noticed that Bjǫrn was missing they went searching for him, but he was nowhere to be found—as was only too likely. It must also be said that the king's cattle were now being slaughtered in heaps, and that a grey bear was preying on them, a huge and fierce one.

One evening it so happened that the peasant's daughter saw this fierce bear. The bear went up to her and showed her great friendliness, and she thought that in the eyes of this bear she recognized the eyes of the king's son Bjǫrn, and she did not try to avoid him. The beast then walked ahead of her, and she followed all the way till he came to a certain cave. And as she came up to the cave, there was a man in front of it who greeted the peasant's daughter Bera. She recognized that this was Bjǫrn, Hringr's son, and theirs was a most joyful meeting. They stayed there in the cave for some while, for she did not want to part from him as long as she had the choice; he told her, however, that it would not be fitting for her to stay there with him, for he was a beast by day, but a man by night.

King Hringr now came home from his raiding, and he was told of all that had happened while he was away: the disappearance of his son Bjǫrn, and also the other matter of the huge beast that had come into the country and was preying most on the king's own cattle. The queen urged him to have the beast killed, but still it was put off for a while. The king did not seem to like the sound of all this, and he thought that very strange things were happening.

One night when Bera and the king's son were in bed together, Bjǫrn began to speak, and said: 'I have a foreboding that tomorrow is to be the day of my death, for they will succeed in hunting me down. Indeed, I have no joy in life on account of this evil spell that hangs over me; and though I do have this one delight that you and I are together, this too is now going to be changed. I will give you this ring which is under my left arm. Tomorrow you will see the troop of men attack me, and when I am dead you are to go up to the king and ask him to give you whatever is under the beast's shoulder on the left side, and he will grant you this. The queen will suspect who you are as you are about to leave, and she will give you some of the beast's flesh to eat; but this you must not eat, for you are a pregnant woman, as you know, and you are going to bear three sons that are yours and mine, and it is on them that the mark of it will be seen if you eat the beast's flesh—for that queen is the worst of trolls. Then go home to your father's house, and there you will give birth to the boys. One of them, however, will seem the finest to you. And if you cannot rear them at home because of the evil spell on them and their own reckless ways, then bring them with you to this cave here. Here you will see a chest with three compartments; the runes on the side will tell you what each of them is to have. There are three weapons set in the rock, and each of them is to have the one destined for him. The first of our sons is to be called Elg-Fróði, the second Þórir, the third Bǫðvarr; and I think it likely that they will be no petty men, and that their names will be long remembered.'

He spoke to her about many things, and then the bear-skin wrapped itself round him; and so the bear went out, and she went out after him. She looked round about, and then she saw a great troop of men advancing along the shoulder of the mountain, and many big hounds going ahead of the troop. The bear now ran away from the cave, and off along the mountain; the hounds and the king's men went to meet him, and he was strongly attacked by them. He maimed many men among them before he was overcome, and all the hounds he killed. At last they encircled him, and he turned round and round inside the circle, and saw that things had come to such a pass that he would not manage to escape. Then he turned to where the king stood and seized hold of the man standing next to him and tore him apart alive. By then the bear was so weary that he threw himself flat on the ground, and they swiftly ran forward and killed him.

The peasant's daughter saw this. She went up to the king and said: 'Sire, will you give me whatever is under the beast's left shoulder?'

The king agreed, saying it could only be something which it would be quite fitting for him to give her. By this time the king's men had flayed much of the bear's body, so Bera then went up and took away the ring and kept it; but the men did not see what she took, nor were any questions asked about it. The king did ask her who she was, as he did not recognize her; she gave herself whatever name she thought best, and it was not the true one.

The king now went home, and Bera was one of the king's company. The queen was very cheerful, and gave her a gracious welcome and asked who she was; she answered as before, not with the truth. The queen now prepared a great feast, and ordered that the bear's flesh should be cooked as a treat for the men. The peasant's daughter was in the queen's bower and could not get away, for the queen suspected who she must be. And along came the queen, sooner than might have been expected, with a dish with bear's flesh on it, and she bade Bera enjoy it. Bera refused to eat.

'It's an outrageous thing,' said the queen, 'that you should turn up your nose at a treat which the queen herself does you the honour to offer you. Take it quickly, or it will be the worse for you.'

She carved a piece for her, and in the end it happened that she swallowed that mouthful. Then the queen cut off another piece and put it in Bera's mouth, and one small crumb of that mouthful went down her throat; but then she spat the rest out of her mouth and said she would eat no more, not even if the queen tortured or killed her.

The queen said: 'Maybe there's been enough already to have some effect.' And she laughed.

Then Bera went home to her father. The unborn children were a painful burden to her. She told her father the whole story of her marriage, and of what kind it had been. And shortly after, her pains came on her and she bore a boy, though of a rather strange sort—the upper part of him was human, but he was an elk from the navel down, and he was given the name Elg-Fróði. Another boy now came forth, and he was named Þórir; below the instep his feet were dog's paws, and so he was given the name Þórir Houndsfoot. He was a most handsome-looking man apart from that. The third boy came forth, and he was the handsomest of them all; he was called Bǫðvarr, and there was no blemish on him at all. It was Bǫðvarr that she loved the best. . . .

[The two elder boys grow up, take their shares of the wealth and weapons in Bjǫrn's cave, and set out to win fame in distant lands.]

Bǫðvarr stayed at home with his mother, who loved him dearly; he was the most accomplished of men, and the most handsome to look at; he was not very ready to talk with other people.

One day he asked his mother who his father had been. She told him how he had died, and all that had happened, and how an evil spell had been laid on him by his stepmother.

Bǫðvarr said: 'We still owe this ogress some payment for this evil.'

Then she told him how she had been forced by the queen to eat some of the bear's flesh—'and the mark of it can be still seen on your brothers Elg-Fróði and Þórir.'

Bǫðvarr said: 'I would have thought it no less

99

pressing a duty for Elg-Fróði to avenge our father's
death on this bitch of an ogress than to kill guiltless
men to win himself wealth, or to do other such evil
deeds. In the same way, I think it strange that Þórir
should have gone away without giving this witch some
reason to remember him. I think it would be best if I
gave her some reason to remember us, on behalf of us
all.'

Bera said: 'Make quite sure that she cannot use any
wizardry which might do you harm.'

Bǫðvarr said he would see to that.

After this Bǫðvarr and Bera went to see the king;
and, on Bǫðvarr's advice, she now told the king all that
had happened, and showed him the ring which she had
taken from beneath the beast's left shoulder, which had
belonged to his son Bjǫrn.

The king said he certainly knew the ring—'and I have
sometimes almost suspected that all these terrible things
which have happened were caused by the queen's
plotting, but for the sake of my love for her I let the
matter rest'.

Bǫðvarr said: 'Send her away now, or we will take
vengeance on her.'

The king said he would give him as much money as
he wanted as compensation, if he would still let matters
rest, and would give him lands to rule over, and the
title of earl straight away, and the kingdom itself after
his death, provided no harm was done her.

Bǫðvarr said he did not want to be king himself, and
would rather remain with the king and serve him—
'but you are so enslaved by this evil creature that you
are hardly master of your own wits, or of your law-
ful kingdom. From now on she must never flourish
here'.

Bǫðvarr was by then so fearsome to deal with that
the king dared not oppose him. Bǫðvarr went to the
queen's bower, and he had a kind of bag in his hand.
The king followed him, and so did his mother. And
when Bǫðvarr came into the bower he went up to Queen
Hvít and put this bag of wrinkled skin over her head
and pulled it down right to the neck. Then he struck
her in the face and battered her to death after torturing

her in various ways, and so dragged her through all the streets. Many of the people there in the hall, most of them indeed, thought it had been no case for half-measures; but the king took it very badly, though he could do nothing about it. Thus Queen Hvít lost her wretched life.

Bǫðvarr was eighteen years old when this took place. Shortly afterwards, King Hringr fell sick and died, and thereupon Bǫðvarr took the kingdom and remained there contentedly for a little time. After a while he summoned an Assembly of the people of that country, and there at the Assembly he said that he wanted to leave. . . .

[Bǫðvarr goes to visit his two brothers; Elg-Fróði is living as a bandit, but Þórir is King of Gautland. On Elg-Fróði's advice he decides to seek a place at the court of Hrólfr Kraki, and so travels from Gautland to Denmark, arriving in the neighbourhood of Leire.]

One day there was a heavy rainstorm and Bǫðvarr got very wet; his horse was growing completely exhausted and was about to founder under him, as he had ridden it so hard, and the ground was extremely mushy and made the going heavy. As night fell the darkness grew thick and there came a downpour, and before he was aware of anything the horse had stumbled over some jutting slab of rock. Bǫðvarr got down and looked about him and noticed that there was a sort of house there, and he found the doorway and knocked on the door. Then a man came out. Bǫðvarr asked for a night's hospitality. The master of the house said he would not turn him away at dead of night, as he was a stranger; this householder thought he looked an impressive figure, by what he could see of him. Bǫðvarr stayed the night there, and the hospitality was good. He asked many questions about the great deeds of King Hrólfr and his champions, and whether it was far to get there.

'No,' said the old peasant, 'it is very close now. Do you mean to go there?'

'Yes,' said Bǫðvarr, 'that is my plan.'

The peasant said that place would suit him very well —'as I see that you're a big man and a strong one, but they think they are such warlike fellows'.

And at this, as they were speaking of King Hrólfr and his champions at Hleiðargarðr [Leire], the peasant's old wife wept aloud.

'What are you weeping about, you poor helpless old woman?' said Bǫðvarr.

The old woman said: 'My man and I had only one son, the one called Hǫttr, and one day he went over to the stronghold to enjoy himself, and the king's men mocked him, and he took it badly. So then they took him prisoner and stuck him on the rubbish-heap of bones; and now it is their meal-time habit that as soon as they have gnawed each bone clean, they throw it at him. Sometimes if it hits him he gets a great wound, and I don't know if he's alive or dead. And the return I would like to have from you for my hospitality is this—that you should just throw smaller bones at him rather than bigger ones, if he's not quite dead of it yet.'

Bǫðvarr said: 'I will do as you ask. And I don't think it very warlike to throw bones at people, or to persecute children or low-born men.'

'Then you will be acting nobly,' said the old woman, 'for your hand looks strong to me, and I know for sure that he could never stand up to your blows if you did not choose to hold yourself in check.'

After this Bǫðvarr went on his way to Hleiðargarðr, and he came to the king's dwelling. He led his horse into a stall next to the king's best horses, and asked nobody's permission. Then he went into the hall, and there were few men there; he sat down at the far end of the bench, and when he had been there for a while he heard a sort of scuffling coming from a certain spot, away out in a corner. Bǫðvarr looked over there, and saw a man's hand reaching up out of the middle of a great pile of bones that stood there; this hand was very black. Bǫðvarr went over and asked who it was in the pile of bones.

The answer came, rather timidly: 'My name is Hǫttr, good master.'

'Why are you there?' said Bǫðvarr. 'And what are you doing?'

'I'm making myself a shield-wall, good master.'

Bǫðvarr said: 'You're a miserable wretch, you and your shield-wall!' And Bǫðvarr grabbed at him and jerked him out of the pile of bones.

At this Hǫttr shrieked aloud, and said: 'So now you want to be the death of me! Don't do this, just when I'd got everything all nice and ready! And now you've broken my shield-wall to bits—I had built it up all round me, so high that it sheltered me from all your blows, so that no blow has reached me this long while. And even so, it wasn't as well built as I'd planned it would be.'

Bǫðvarr said: 'You'll not manage to make shield-walls any longer.'

Hǫttr wept, and said: 'Are you going to be the death of me now, master?'

Bǫðvarr told him not to make such a noise; then he picked him up and carried him out of the hall, and down to a lake which lay near by—few people took any notice of this—and washed him from head to foot. After this, Bǫðvarr went back to the seat he had taken before, and led Hǫttr behind him and sat down him beside him there; but Hǫttr was so frightened that he trembled in every limb, even though he was beginning to understand that this man wanted to help him.

After this, evening drew on, and men came crowding into the hall; and Hrólfr's champions saw that Hǫttr had been given a seat up on a bench, and they thought that the man who had taken it on himself to do this had shown himself to be pretty bold. Hǫttr pulled a long face when he saw these acquaintances of his, for he had known nothing but ill-treatment from them; he would dearly have liked to stay alive and get back into his pile of bones, but Bǫðvarr was holding on to him so that he could not get away—for Hǫttr was thinking that if only he could get back there he would not be so exposed to their blows as he was now.

Now the retainers followed their usual habit, throwing bones—small ones at first—across the room at Bǫðvarr and Hǫttr. Bǫðvarr acted as if he hadn't seen. Hǫttr was so frightened that he could not swallow food or drink, thinking at every other moment that he was about to be hit.

And now Hǫttr said to Bǫðvarr: 'Good master, there's a big knuckle-bone coming straight at you now! It must be meant to do us an injury.'

Bǫðvarr told him to hold his tongue. He put his cupped hand up to meet the knuckle-bone, and so caught it—and it had the leg-bone still attached to it. Then Bǫðvarr sent the bone back, hurling it at the man who had thrown it, and it caught him such a hard blow full in the face that this was the death of him. Then a great fear came over the retainers.

Now the news came to King Hrólfr and his champions up in the castle, that an impressive-looking man had come into the hall and killed one of his retainers, and that they wanted to have him killed. King Hrólfr inquired whether the retainer had been killed for no reason. 'Practically none,' they said. And then the whole truth of the affair came out in the king's hearing.

King Hrólfr said it was quite out of the question to have the man killed—'You have taken up a wicked custom, flinging bones at guiltless men; it is a dishonour to me and a great disgrace to yourselves to do such a thing. I have often spoken to you about it before, but you have paid no heed. I think the man you have attacked this time will prove to be no petty weakling; call him to me, so that I may know who he is.'

Bǫðvarr came into the king's presence and greeted him courteously. The king asked him his name.

Bǫðvarr said: '"Hǫttr's safe-conduct" is what your men call me, but my name is Bǫðvarr.'

'What compensation will you offer me for my retainer?' said the king.

'He was asking for what he got,' said Bǫðvarr.

'Are you willing to become my man, and take his place?' said the king.

Bǫðvarr said: 'I am not refusing to become your man, but as things are at present the two of us, Hǫttr and I, are not to be parted, but should both of us remain near you—nearer than that man used to sit—or else both of us will be gone from here.'

The king said: 'I can't see that he will be an honour to us, but I won't grudge him food.'

So now Bǫðvarr walked over to the seat which pleased him best, and would not occupy the one which the other man had had. He lifted three men bodily off a certain bench, and then he and Hǫttr sat themselves down on it, farther up the hall than the place assigned to them. The men thought it would be rather a difficult matter it tackle Bǫðvarr, and they felt great anger against him.

Now as it drew on towards Yule the men grew gloomy. Bǫðvarr asked Hǫttr what this meant, and he said that a beast, a huge and terrible one, had come there two winters running—'and it has wings on its back, and it is always flying. For two autumns now it has come visiting us here, and done a great deal of damage. No weapons bite on it, and the king's champions, even the best among them, do not come back again'.

Bǫðvarr said: 'The king's hall is not as well manned as I thought, if a single wild beast lays waste this realm and destroys the king's cattle.'

'This is no wild beast,' said Hǫttr. 'On the contrary, it's the worst of trolls.'

Now came the eve of Yule. The king said: 'It is my will that men should keep quiet and silent tonight, and I forbid all my men to put themselves in danger from this beast; the cattle can fare as fate will have it, but my men I do not wish to lose.'

They all promised faithfully to do as the king asked.

During the night Bǫðvarr slipped out secretly; he made Hǫttr go with him, which he did much against his will, declaring that he was being led out to his death. Bǫðvarr said things would turn out better than that. They set out from the hall, and Bǫðvarr had to carry him, he was so frightened. They now caught sight of the beast, and at once Hǫttr shrieked as loud as he could, saying the beast would swallow him up. Bǫðvarr told this whelp of his to hold his tongue, and threw him down on some moss, and there he lay, not exactly free from fear—but on the other hand, he dared not go home either.

Now Bǫðvarr advanced towards the beast, and it so happened that his sword stuck fast in the sheath; he now managed to shift the sheath so that the sword came from the scabbard, and he at once plunged it in under the beast's shoulder so firmly that it pierced the heart, and at this the beast crashed down dead to the ground.

After this, Bǫðvarr went over to where Hǫttr lay, picked him up and carried him over to where the beast lay dead; Hǫttr was trembling violently.

'Now you must drink the beast's blood,' said Bǫðvarr. For a long time he was loath to do it, but still he certainly did not dare do otherwise. Bǫðvarr made him drink two great gulps, and also made him eat part of the beast's heart. After this, Bǫðvarr took hold of him, and they wrestled for a long time.

'Now you have become extremely strong,' said Bǫðvarr, 'and I don't expect that you'll be afraid of King Hrólfr's retainers now.'

'From now on,' said Hǫttr, 'I shall not be afraid of them, or of you either.'

'So things have turned out well, comrade Hǫttr. Now let us go and pick the beast up, and arrange it in such a way that the others will think it's alive.'

So this they now did; after that they went home and kept quiet about their doings, and nobody knew what they had achieved.

In the morning the king asked whether they knew anything about the beast, and whether it had come visiting there that night. He was told that all the livestock was in the folds, safe and sound. The king told his men to inquire whether anyone had seen any trace of its having come near their home. The watchmen did so, and quickly came back and told the king that the beast was on its way there, rushing straight towards the stronghold. The king bade his retainers be valiant, and each act bravely as his heart prompted, and so do away with this monster; and so they made themselves ready, as the king bade.

The king turned towards the beast, and thereupon he said: 'I see no sign that the beast is advancing. Now, who wants to make a good bargain and go out to meet it?'

Bǫðvarr said: 'That would be a cure for even the boldest man's curiosity! Now, comrade Hǫttr, clear yourself of that slanderous charge which some have

made against you, saying there is no spirit or valour in
you. You go out now, and kill that beast! You can see
that none of the others is very eager to.'

'Yes,' said Hǫttr, 'I will undertake this.'

The king said: 'I don't know where you got such
valour from, Hǫttr; there has been a great change in
you in a very short while.'

Hǫttr said: 'Give me the sword Gullinhjalti [Golden-
hilt] which you are holding, and then I will either fell
the beast or meet my death.'

King Hrólfr said: 'This sword is not to be borne
except by a man who is a good fighter, and valiant too.'

'You will have to believe that my nature is such,' said
Hǫttr.

'What is one to think,' said the king, 'except that
there has been a greater change in your character than
meets the eye? Very few men would think they recog-
nized you as the same man. Now take this sword and
use it, noblest of men—for so you are, if this deed is
well done.'

Then Hǫttr walked boldly up to the beast and struck
at it as soon as he got within striking distance, and the
beast fell down dead.

'See what he has accomplished, sire!' said Bǫðvarr.

'Certainly he has changed greatly,' said the king. 'But
Hǫttr has not slain the beast alone—rather, it is you who
did it.'

'That may be so,' said Bǫðvarr.

The king said: 'I knew, as soon as you came here,
that there would be few who would be your match;
even so, this seems to me your most glorious deed, that
you should have made a second champion out of Hǫttr,
who hardly seemed likely to turn out very lucky. And
now it is my will that he should no longer be called
Hǫttr, and from now on he is to be called Hjalti—you
shall take your name from the sword Gullinhjalti.'

And that is the end of the tale about Bǫðvarr and his
brothers.

[For this saga's account of Bǫðvarr Bjarki's part
in Hrólfr's encounter with Aðils at Uppsala, and in
Hrólfr's last stand at Leire, see below, II G 11.]

9. *Bjarkarímur* (*c.* 1400).

(*a*) I stanzas 20–53; II 4–40; III 30–40. (Summary.)

[There was an earl named Bjór who had three
sons, Bǫðvarr, Fróði and Þórir; this earl was a
widower, and on the advice of his counsellors he
decided to remarry. The messengers he sends out
to fetch him a bride are lured aside by an elf-like
woman, Hvít, and bring her to Bjór, who weds
her. Hvít clothes the earl's sons in magic kirtles,
thus changing Bǫðvarr to a bear, Fróði to an elk,
Þórir to a hound; the latter two kill one another,
but Bǫðvarr escapes to the woods, and lives by
preying on his father's herds. He makes love to
Hildr, a peasant's daughter, who bears him three
sons, and these too are named Bǫðvarr, Fróði and
Þórir; they are quite normal. Soon after, the elder
Bǫðvarr is killed, still in bear-form, by his father's
huntsmen. Hvít sends some of his flesh to Hildr, and
in her absence the children suck a little of it; Fróði
gets elk's legs to the knee, Þórir a hound's foot,
and Bǫðvarr a bear's claw on his toe. The two elder
boys take heirlooms left them by their father, and set
out on adventures; later Bǫðvarr does so too,
having first killed the enchantress Hvít. Eventually
Bǫðvarr decides to seek Hrólfr Kraki's court.]

(*b*) IV stanzas 28–66.

Bjarki parted from his brother . . . and went as the
road led, making his way out to Denmark. So now he
went to a place where the road grew bad, and I know
what was the first place where he spent a night; I have
heard that the champion turned his steps to where an
old peasant and his wife lived.

The hero asked about Hrólfr's ways and the man
answered: 'They drive mad with terror all those with
whom they play their sports. In the court of Leire there
stands a stone which twelve men could hardly lift; he
who would join Hrólfr's band must lift it, and then he
is reckoned a strong man. There are two dogs at the
gates, and both are very grim; not a withered stick can

get in there, for they tear everything to pieces. I had a
son named Hjalti—a fairer lad have I never seen—he
risked himself at Leire Court, and all the spirit has been
beaten out of him. Now they call Hjalti Hǫttr; they call
him sow and clumsy lubber and wretched milksop—
he would be better off dead.'

Next morning Bǫðvarr made ready to leave; the man
bowed before him and the woman was in tears. Bǫðvarr
asked why she was weeping.

'I fear that the bone-throwing comes hard and fast
at Hjalti, and that if you throw bones at him with your
whole strength, it will go badly with him.'

'More likely I will strike him lightly; I would be
giving a poor repayment for your good hospitality if I
did him any harm. Rather, if he is willing, we will both
help one another; it may well be that if there are two of
us, the men will strike him no longer.'

The old woman handed him two loaves which Bǫðvarr
was to take with him—'the hounds may snatch at them,
if you get to the gates of the castle'.

Bǫðvarr bade them farewell and went to the hall; he
turned towards the rampart on which the watchdogs
lay. Both the hounds made for him; he threw the loaves
down, then he turned the back of his axe against them
and slew those two evil gallows-tikes.

A man came into the prince's hall, saying a troll was
going about the castle—'he has not acted as he should,
but has beaten the king's hounds to Hell'.

Hrólfr bade him raise the war-whoop and chase this
ruffian away, but said he had a foreboding that the hero
would not be much terrified. The courtiers made a loud
outcry; he never flinched at this, but himself whooped
with them, for he had now come into the street. The
people said, 'Let us crowd on him and drive him from the
castle'—then many a man was frightened indeed, if he
laid hands on them. He came in amongst a great crowd of
men; he crushed the life out of two champions, and so
at last made his way in to them.

The hero said as he came in: 'Where shall I sit, my
lord Hrólfr?'

'Away out by the door, at the side of Hǫttr!'—and
he did not obtain pledge of peace.

Bǫðvarr sat himself down on a bench; facing it was a pile of bones, and there was a man between it and the dais, and many made mock of him. Bǫðvar picked the man up by the neck, though it was not easy to talk with him—'Is this fellow still asleep? You never sit upright like other men.'

Hjalti spoke, hiding himself: 'Don't treat me badly! You have taken my pile of bones from me, yet warriors here throw things for their sport.'

'Sit up here and see how things go. Whoever hurls bones will get the worst of it, and they will send you smaller ones if you are sitting up beside me.'

Hjalti obeyed, and scrambled up on to the dais; the knuckle-bone of an ox came hurtling at him, but Bǫðvarr caught it, and sent the ox-bone back, so that he who had first started the bone-throwing got his death-blow, for it took him hard on the ear. Another bone came flying in the middle of the meal, for warriors got harsh treatment there; it came hurtling outwards from the man in the highseat facing the king's, but Bǫðvarr knocked it aside with the back of his hand. He sent the ox-leg back again; the man in the highseat shook his beard and fell dead to the floor—any faint-heart must have felt fear.

Hrólfr bade them bear him word speedily: 'Let my words be told to Bjarki—he is to sit now in the seat in which that man used to drink.'

Bjarki did as the chieftain bade; he set Hjalti down on the bench, but he himself sat on the shoulders of those who were sitting on either side.

Many there used to jeer at Hǫttr because he was not bold in speech. One day they both left the hall without all the courtiers knowing.

Hjalti, struck with terror, said: 'Don't let us go near the forest; there is a she-wolf there that eats men up, and she will kill us both together.'

The she-wolf sprang from a thicket, fearsome, with gaping mouth; Hjalti was most wretched, and every limb and joint of him trembled. Bjarki went fearlessly up to her; he did not delay longer, but drove his axe in up to the hammer; vast quantities of blood gushed from her.

'One of two choices you must choose, Hjalti'—so

spoke the champion Bǫðvarr. 'Drink the blood, or
I'll kill you here. You seem to me to have no spirit in
you.'

Hjalti replied sorrowfully: 'I hardly dare drink
blood, yet most things can be done when one is driven
to do them, and there is no better choice for me now.'

Hjalti did as Bǫðvarr bade; I have heard that he lay
down in the blood, then drank three gulps, and that
was enough to make him able to wrestle against any
one man. His spirit grew bold and his might increased;
it was far from him to hesitate in front of any little
thing; he was wondrously strong and as powerful as a
troll, and all his clothes split on him. He had become so
hardy in spirit that he never feared hurtling weapons;
gone now was his coward's name; he was equal to
Bǫðvarr in valour.

(c) V stanzas 3–15.

. . . I will speak a while of Bone-Hjalti. He has
obtained a bold heart and hardy courage; all his spirit
and strength he got from the she-wolf's blood.

A certain grey bear used to visit the sheepfolds at the
court of Leire; this beast did harm to many a man and
to the sheep far and wide. Bjarki was blamed for it, as
he had killed the watchdogs, but it was not fitting for
him to squabble with men.

Hrólfr and all his courtiers made ready to hunt the
bear—'He who overcomes the beast shall be the greatest
man in my hall'.

The bear rushed roaring from its lair; it whirled its
cruel paws about, so that men shrank back. Hjalti
turned and watched when the struggle began; he had
nothing in his hands at the time, just his bare fists. Then
Hrólfr flung his own war-sword to Hjalti; the champion
stretched out his hand and grasped it. Then he rapidly
smote the bear on the right shoulder; the bear fell to
earth and bore himself more meekly.

That was the first deed he did to win glory, and many
more followed; he was by far the best warrior in the
play of weapons. Because of this Hjalti got the name
'Noble-Hearted'; Bjarki was no more than equal to
him when gold was being shared out.

(d) VIII stanzas 1–12.

[According to the *Bjarkarímur*, the feud in the
Danish royal family was as follows: Ingjaldr and
Hálfdan were brothers, and the former killed the
latter; then Hálfdan's sons Hróarr and Helgi killed
Ingjaldr, and later maimed Ingjaldr's son Hrærekr
in a quarrel over a ring. Then Ingjaldr's illegitimate
son Agnarr, a fearsome berserk, made war on
Hróarr's son Hrólfr Kraki, and Hrólfr and his
champions faced Agnarr in a lengthy battle.]

Agnarr roused fierce spear-play, and it was a wonder
how many men fell. This hero did not give mere wounds
and scratches; he hacked heads off as fast as possible,
five at a blow. At every single sweep of his sword, this
shield-bearer split three men asunder on each side of him.

The bold Hrólfr cried aloud: 'Where are you, valiant
Bjarki? Show us your great might, you who love battle!'

Fearlessly Bǫðvarr drew and flourished Laufi, and
then men fled from him like children. The fighters saw
a white bear running among them; Agnarr himself laid
his hard sword on this bear's head, but it broke at the
hilts, to his great grief. Then Laufi ripped his life out,
as Bjarki took part in the game; he drove the naked
blade in the chieftain's breast, and it reached its mark
on him. The bright blade pierced the heart of the mighty
heir of a prince; all men saw how Agnarr laughed—
such men are a great loss. This berserk died smiling,
breathing out hot breath; they all thought Agnarr had
been overcome by a cunning trick.

I B.   HYGELÁC—O.N. Hugleikr—

Lat. Huiglaucus/Higlacus/Hyglacus/Hugletus/
Chochilaicus/Chlochilaichus

1. Gregory of Tours (*d.* 594), *History of the Franks*, III ch. 3.

After all this had happened, the Danes, together with
their king, whose name was Chlochilaichus, attacked

the Frankish lands by sea in a ship-borne raid. Having gone up on shore, they laid waste one district of the kingdom of Theuderic [King of the Franks], and carried off captives; then, having loaded their ships with these captives as well as with the rest of their booty, they set out to return to their own land. But their king remained on shore while the ships were taking to the deep sea, for he was to follow in due course. Now when the news had been brought to Theudericus that a region belonging to him had actually been laid waste by foreigners, he sent his son Theudebertus to those parts with a strong army and a great store of arms. And he, having first killed the king, fell upon the enemy in a naval battle, overwhelmed them, and restored all the plunder to his own land.

2. *The Book of Monsters* (*Liber Monstrorum*) (eighth century?). Part I ch. 2.

Concerning King Huiglaucus of the Getae, and his amazing hugeness.

Now there are also these monsters of amazing hugeness, namely, King Huiglaucus, who ruled the Getae and was slain by the Franks. Even when he was twelve years old, no horse could carry him. His bones are preserved on an island in the Rhine, where it flows into the sea, and are shown as a prodigy to people who come from afar.

3. *The Book of the History of the Franks* (*Gesta Francorum*) (*c.* 727), ch. 19.

In those days the Danes, together with their king, whose name was Chochilaicus, attacked the Frankish lands over the deep sea with a ship-borne host. They laid waste a district belonging to Theuderic, that of the Atuarii or others, and carried off captives; then they went aboard their ships, which were full of captives, setting out for the deep sea, with their king remaining on the sea shore. When this news had been brought to Theudericus, he sent his son Theudobert to those parts with a large army. And he, pursuing them, fought against them and routed them with great slaughter, killed their king, seized the booty, and restored it to his own land.

4. Saxo Grammaticus, *Danish History* (*c.* 1200), IV § 117.

After this Hugletus was king [of Denmark], who is said to have defeated in battle at sea Hömothus and Högrimus, the despots of Sweden.

5. Saxo Grammaticus, *Danish History*, VI §§ 185–6.

Therefore [Starkatherus] took his fleet into Ireland with Haco [King of Denmark], in order that even the farthest kingdoms of the world might not be untouched by the Danish arms. The king of the island at this time was Hugletus, who, though he had a well-filled treasury, was yet so prone to avarice that once, when he gave a pair of shoes which had been adorned by the hand of a careful craftsman, he took off the ties, and thus by removing the latchets turned his present into a slight. This unhandsome act blemished his gift so much that he seemed to reap hatred for it instead of thanks. Thus he used never to be generous to any respectable man, but to spend all his bounty upon mimes and jugglers. For so base a fellow was bound to keep company with the base, and such a slough of vices to wheedle his partners in sin with pandering endearments. Still he had Gegathus and Suipdagerus, nobles of tried valour, who by the singular lustre of their warlike deeds shone out among their unmanly companions like jewels embedded in ordure; these alone were found to defend the riches of the king. When a battle began between Hugletus and Haco, the hordes of mimes, whose light-mindedness unsteadied their bodies, broke their ranks and scurried off in a panic; and this shameful flight was their sole requital for all their king's benefits. Then Gegathus and Suipdagerus faced all those thousands of the enemy single-handed, and fought with such incredible courage that they seemed to do the part not merely of two warriors, but of a whole army. Gegathus, moreover, dealt Haco, who pressed him hard, such a wound in the breast that he exposed the upper part of his liver. It was here that Starcatherus, while he was attacking Gegathus with his sword, received a very sore wound on the head; wherefore he afterwards related in a certain song that a ghastlier wound had never befallen him at

114

any time; for, though the divisions of his gashed head were bound up by the surrounding outer skin, yet the livid unseen wound concealed a foul gangrene below. Starcatherus conquered, killing Hugletus and also routing the Irish; and he had any of the actors beaten whom chance made prisoner, thinking it better to order a pack of buffoons to be ludicrously punished by the loss of their skins than to command a more deadly punishment and take their lives.

6. Snorri Sturluson, *Heimskringla* (c. 1223–35), *Ynglinga saga* ch. 22.

Hugleikr was the name of Álfr's son, who took the kingship over the Swedes after those brothers, since Yngvi's sons were children at the time. King Hugleikr was no warrior, but sat at home quietly in his own lands; he was a rich man, but was miserly over his wealth. He used to have all sorts of entertainers at his court, harpers and fiddlers; he also kept wizards about him, and all kinds of folk learned in magic lore.

There were two brothers named Haki and Hagbarðr, very excellent men; they were sea-kings and had a great following, and sometimes they sallied out together, and sometimes each on his own. There were many champions with them. King Haki went to Sweden with his host to attack King Hugleikr, and King Hugleikr gathered a host to meet him. Two brothers named Svipdagr and Geigaðr joined his host, most excellent men and great champions. King Haki had twelve champions with him, and Starkaðr the Old was also with him; King Haki was also a very great champion himself. They met at Fyrisvellir, and there was a very great battle, and Hugleikr's host soon fell. The two champions Svipdagr and Geigaðr made an attack, but six of King Haki's champions opposed them, and they were captured. Then King Haki broke through the shield-wall and reached King Hugleikr, and killed him and his two sons there; after this the Swedes fled, and King Haki subdued the country and made himself king of the Swedes.

II. The Danes

A. HEREMŌD—O.N. Hermóðr.

1. *Hákonarmál* (*c.* 965) ll. 38–9.

> [Óðinn sends dead heroes in Valhǫll to welcome a
> newcomer.]
>
> 'Hermóðr and Bragi!' cried the Lord of gods,
> 'Go forth to greet the prince!'
>
> [Cf. VII 1.]

2. *Hyndluljóð* (date uncertain; included in *Flateyjarbók c.* 1375)
strophe 2.

> [Freyja praises Óðinn's generosity.]
>
> To Hermóðr he gave a helm and corselet,
> And to Sigmundr a sword of his own.

3. For references to Heremōd in Anglo-Saxon and Norse
genealogies, see II B 1, 2, 4, 6, 10.

4. Snorri Sturluson, *Edda* (*c.* 1220), *Gylfaginning* ch. 49.

> [It is not clear whether the Hermóðr, son of
> Óðinn, who figures in this tale is the same as the
> human hero Hermóðr in the extracts given above.
> This tale tells how after the death of Baldr the gods
> sent an envoy to Hel, goddess of the Underworld,
> to plead for his release.]

He who was to go on this journey was named Her-
móðr the Bold, a son of Óðinn. Then Óðinn's horse

Sleipnir was taken and led forth, and Hermóðr mounted him and galloped away . . .

Now of Hermóðr there is this to tell, that he rode for nine nights through dales dark and deep, so that he could see nothing, till he came to the River Gjǫll and rode on to Gjǫll Bridge. It is roofed over with gleaming gold, and Móðguðr is the name of the maiden who guards this bridge.

She asked him his name and lineage, and said that the day before five troops of dead men had ridden across the bridge—'yet the bridge echoes no less to the tread of you alone, nor have you the look of a dead man. Why do you ride here on the road to Hel?'

He answered: 'I must ride to Hel to seek Baldr. Have you seen Baldr at all on the road to Hel?'

But she said that Baldr had indeed ridden there across Gjǫll Bridge—'and downwards and northwards runs the road to Hel'.

Then Hermóðr rode on till he came to the gates of Hel. He dismounted from his steed and tightened the girths, then remounted and set spurs to him, and the steed gave so great a leap clear over the gates that he came nowhere near touching them. Then Hermóðr rode right up to the hall, dismounted, walked into the hall, and saw his brother Baldr sitting on the highseat there; and Hermóðr stayed there that night.

In the morning Hermóðr asked Hel to grant that Baldr should ride home with him, and said how great was the weeping for him among the gods. But Hel said that one must put it to the proof whether Baldr was so dearly loved as they said—'and if everything in the world, alive or dead, weeps for him, then he shall return to the gods; but he shall stay with Hel if any creature refuses and will not weep'.

Then Hermóðr rose up, and Baldr went to the door of the hall with him, and took off the ring Draupnir and sent it to Óðinn as a keepsake; and Nanna sent her linen headdress and other gifts to Frigg, and a gold finger-ring to Fulla. Then Hermóðr rode off on his way, and came to Ásgarðr, and told all the tidings which he had seen and heard.

II B. SCYLD SCEFING (Scyldwa, Sceldwea, Scealdwa)—O.N. Skjǫldr—Lat. Sceldius/Scioldus

SCĒAF (Scef, Scēafa)—O.N. Seskef.

1. *The Anglo-Saxon Chronicle* (MSS. B & C), for the year 855.

> [A genealogy of King Æthelwulf of Wessex, traced back through twelve generations to Cerdic, then through nine generations from Cerdic to Woden, then continuing:]

> ... Woden, [Ā adds: the son of Frithuwald], the son of Freawine, the son of Frealaf, [Ā adds: the son of Frithuwulf], the son of Finn, the son of Godwulf, the son of Geata [Ā, D: Geat; C: Geatt], the son of Tætwa, the son of Beaw, the son of Scyldwa [Ā: Sceldwea; C: Scealdwa], the son of Heremod, the son of Itermon, the son of Hathra, the son of Hwala, the son of Bedwig [D: Beowi], the son of Sceaf, who is the son of Noah and was born in Noah's Ark. . . .

> [The genealogy then continues from Noah to Adam.]

2. Asser, *Life of King Alfred* (893), ch. 1.

> [The same genealogy of Æthelwulf as far as Woden, then:]

> ... Woden, who was the son of Frithowald, who was the son of Frealaf, who was the son of Frithuwulf, who was the son of Finn, who was the son of Godwulf, who was the son of Geata, and this Geata the heathens long ago worshipped as a god. This Geata was the son of Tætwa, who was the son of Beaw, who was the son of Sceldwea, who was the son of Heremod, who was the son of Hathra, who was the son of Hwala, who was the son of Bedwig, who was the son of Seth [i.e. Scef?], who was the son of Noah. . . Adam.

3. Æthelweard (*d. c.* 1000), *Chronicle* III 3.

[The same genealogy as Asser gives, as far as God-wulf, then:]

. . . Godwulf, the son of Geat, the son of Tetwa, the son of Beo, the son of Scyld, the son of Scef. This Scef was driven ashore in a warship on an island in the ocean which is called Scani, and was surrounded by weapons; he was indeed a very young child, and unknown to the inhabitants of that country. However, he was adopted by them, and they willingly looked after him as one of their own household, and later chose him as their king; and from his stock King Athulf [i.e. Æthelwulf] traces his descent.

4. William of Malmesbury (*d.* 1143), *De Gestis Regum Anglorum* II § 116.

[The same genealogy, ending:]

. . . Godulfus, the son of Getius, the son of Tetius, the son of Boewius, the son of Sceldius, the son of Sceaf. He, so they say, as a small child, was driven ashore in a boat without oars on a certain island of Germany called Scandza, of which Jordanes, the historian of the Goths, speaks. He was asleep, and at his head was laid a sheaf of corn; for this reason he was given the name Sceaf, and was received as a miracle by the men of that region, and carefully reared. As an adult he reigned in the town which was then called Sleswic, but is now in fact called Hedeby. That region is called 'Old Anglia'; from there the Angles came to Britain, and it lay between the Saxons and the Goths. Sceaf was the son of Heremodius. . . .

5. *Wīdsīð* (seventh century), l. 32.

Scēafa [ruled] the Longbeards.

6. *Langfeðgatal* (twelfth century).

(*a*) [A genealogy beginning with Japhet son of Noah, continuing through Greek gods and heroes, followed

119

by Norse gods, of whom the last named is Magi; it then proceeds like the Anglo-Saxon genealogies above:]

. . . his son Magi; his son Seskef or Sescef [i.e. *se Sceaf*]; Bedvig; Athra; Itermann; Heremotr; Scealdna; Beaf; Eat; Godulfi; Finn; Frealaf; Voden, whom we call Oden.

(*b*) [A genealogy of Danish Kings] Oden; Skioldr; Fridleifr; Fridefrode. . . .

7. Sven Aageson, *A Brief History of the Kings of Denmark* (*c.* 1187), ch. 1.

Skiold is said to have been the first to have ruled the Danes. And, as we have alluded to his name, the reason why he was known by such a name [Skjǫldr = 'Shield'] was because he admirably guarded all the boundaries of the kingdom by the protection which his defence afforded. It was from him that our kings took their title of 'Skioldungs', according to Icelandic fashion.

8. *Skjǫldunga saga* (*c.* 1200), in an abstract by Arngrímur Jónsson (1596), ch. 1.

[The Danes] do not spring from Dan, as Saxo Grammaticus says, but from a certain Scioldus, a son of Odinus (whom the vulgar tongue names Othin). The tradition says that this Odinus . . . assigned Denmark (which did not as yet have that name) to his son Scioldus and Sweden to his son Ingo. And that therefore from Scioldus those who today are Danes were in the olden days called 'Skiolldungs', and the Swedes 'Inglings' from Ingo. . . . Scioldus set up his abode in the stronghold of Hledra [Leire] in Sjælland (which was also the royal seat of many succeeding kings), after he had subdued Jutland, which, on account of its nearness, was the first land that he seized possession of.

9. Saxo Grammaticus, *Danish History* (*c.* 1200) I §§ 11–12, 18.

Scioldus, the son of Lotherus, inherited his natural bent, but not his behaviour; avoiding his inborn perversity by great discretion in his tender years, and thus escaping all traces of his father's taint. So he appropriated what was alike the more excellent and the earlier

share of the family character; for he wisely departed
from his father's sins and became a happy counterpart
of his grandsire's [Dan's] virtues. This man was famous
in his youth among the huntsmen of his father for his
conquest of a monstrous beast: a marvellous incident,
which augured his future prowess. For he chanced to
obtain leave from his guardians, who were rearing him
very carefully, to go and see the hunting. A bear of extra-
ordinary size met him; he had no spear, but with the
girdle that he commonly wore he contrived to bind it,
and gave it to his escort to kill. More than this, many
champions of tried prowess were at the same time of his
life vanquished by him singly; of these Attalus and
Scattus were renowned and famous. While but fifteen
years of age he was of unusual bodily size, and displayed
mortal strength in its perfection; and so mighty were
the proofs of his powers that the rest of the kings of the
Danes were called after him by a common title, the
Skioldungs. Those who were wont to live an abandoned
and flaccid life, and to sap their self-control by wanton-
ness, this man vigilantly spurred to the practice of
virtue in an active career. Thus the ripeness of Scioldus'
spirit outstripped the fulness of his strength, and he
fought battles at which one of his tender years could
scarce look on. And as he thus waxed in years and valour
he beheld the perfect beauty of Alvilda, daughter of the
King of the Saxons, sued for her hand; and for her sake,
in the sight of the armies of the Teutons and the Danes,
challenged and fought with Scattus, governor of Alle-
mania, and a suitor for the same maiden; whom he
slew, afterwards crushing the whole nation of the
Allemanians and forcing them to pay tribute, they being
subjugated by the death of their captain. Scioldus was
eminent for patriotism as well as arms. For he annulled
unrighteous laws and most heedfully executed whatever
made for the amendment of his country's condition.
Further, he regained by his virtue the realm which his
father's wickedness had lost. He was the first to proclaim
the law abolishing manumissions. A slave, to whom he
had chanced to grant his freedom, had attempted his
life by stealthy treachery, and he exacted a bitter penalty;
as if it were just that the guilt of one freedman should be

visited upon all. He paid off all men's debts from his
own treasury, and contended, so to say, with all other
monarchs in courage, bounty, and generous dealing.
The sick he used to foster, and charitably gave medicines
to those sore stricken, bearing witness that he had taken
on him the care of his country and not of himself. He
used to enrich his nobles not only with home taxes but
also with plunder taken in war, being wont to aver that
prize-money should flow to the soldiers, and the glory
to the general. Thus delivered of his bitterest rival in
wooing, he took as the prize of combat the maiden for
love of whom he had fought, and wedded her in
marriage. Soon after he had by her a son, Gram. . . .

Gram, for his marvellous prowess, was granted a
share in the sovereignty by his father, who was now in
extreme age. . . .

10. Snorri Sturluson, *Edda* (*c.* 1220), *Prologue* ch. 3.

[A genealogy similar to that in *Langfeðgatal*, no. 6
above, tracing descendants of the god Þórr by way
of various Norse mythological names to Magi, then
continuing like the Anglo-Saxon genealogies:]

. . . his son Magi; his son was Seskef [i.e. *se Sceaf*],
his son Beðvig, his son Aðra, whom we call Annan, his
son Ítermann, his son Heremoð, his son Skjaldun whom
we call Skjǫldr, his son Bjáf whom we call Bjár, his son
Ját, his son Guðólfr, his son Finn, his son Fríallaf whom
we call Friðleifr, and he had a son whose name was
Vóden and whom we call Óðinn.

11. Snorri Sturluson, *Edda*, *Skáldskaparmál* ch. 40.

Skjǫldr was the name of Óðinn's son, from whom the
Skjǫldungs are descended; he had his dwelling and
was ruler in those lands which now are called Denmark,
but were then called Gotland. Skjǫldr had a son named
Friðleifr who ruled the land after him. . . .

12. Snorri Sturluson, *Heimskringla* (*c.* 1223–35), *Ynglinga saga*
ch. 5.

Skjǫldr, the son of Óðinn, married her [Gefjun, a
goddess], and they lived at Leire.

13. *Annales Ryenses* (*c.* 1290).

> [This chronicle names 'Skiold' among the Danish kings, reckoning him the son of Lother and the father of Gram. It gives no details.]

14. *A Chronicle Roll* (of the reign of Henry VI of England, 1429–71).

> That Steldius [i.e. Sceldius] was the first man to inhabit Germany.

II C. BĒOWULF (BĒOWA, BĒOW, BĒAW), son of Scyld.

1. For references to Bēow, son of Scyld, in Anglo-Saxon and Norse genealogies, see above, II B 1, 2, 3, 4, 6, 10.

2. For the name Bēowa in an Anglo-Saxon place-name, see above, I A 1.

3. *Lokasenna* (date uncertain; included in the *Poetic Edda*, *c.* 1270), stanzas 43–6.

> [The poem concerns a feast of the gods, during which Loki exchanges insults with all the other gods in turn. Among these is one named Byggvir, unknown elsewhere, who in the prose introduction to the poem is called 'Freyr's serving-man'; since *bygg* means 'barley' in Norse, and so does *bēow* in Anglo-Saxon, Byggvir may be the same person as Bēow.]

Byggvir said:

> Were I as well born as is Ingunar-Freyr,
>   And sat in so goodly a seat,
> I'd grind you right down into marrow-pulp,
>   And crack all your joints, you crow!

Loki said:

What's that weeny thing wagging its tail,
    I see it go sniffing and snuffing?
You're always around at the ears of Freyr,
    And chattering under the quern.

Byggvir said:

Byggvir's my name, and I'm prompt to act,
    So all gods and all men do say;
It's a triumph for me that Óðinn's sons
    Drink ale together in here.

Loki said:

Byggvir, be quiet! You never know how
    To give out fair shares of food;
When fighting starts up, you're not to be found—
    You're down in the straw on the floor!

II D. HEALFDENE—O.N. Hálfdan(r)—
Lat. Haldanus.

1. *Hyndluljóð* (date uncertain; included in *Flateyjarbók* (*c.* 1375), strophes 18–19.

Hálfdan was of yore the highest of the Skjǫldungs;
Famous were the forays which those princes led,
Their deeds seemed to run to the ends of the earth.
He allied himself with Eymundr the Noble,
And Sigtryggr he slew with his icy blade;
He wedded with Almveig, noblest of ladies;
They bred, and gave birth to eighteen sons.

2. *Langfeðgatal* (twelfth century).

[A genealogy of Danish kings.]

. . . Frode the Bold; Ingialdr the foster-son of Star-kadar; Halfdan, his brother; his sons Helgi and Hroar;

124

Rolfr Kraki, the son of Helgi; Hrærekr Hnauggvanbaugi [Ring-Hoarder], the son of Ingialdr; Frode; Halfdan; Hrærekr Slaungvanbaugi [Ring-Hurler]. . . .

3. *Leire Chronicle* (*c.* 1170), chs. 3, 4.

[This text incorrectly makes Haldanus the son of Ro (Hróðgar)].

After the death [of Ro], his sons [Helgi and Haldanus] divided the kingdom in two shares; one was to have the land, the other the sea. Thus Haldanus was king over the land, and begot a son named Siwardus, nicknamed the White, who when his father Haldanus died laid him in a mound at Lethra [Leire].

4. Sven Aageson, *A Brief History of the Kings of Denmark* (*c.* 1187), ch. 1.

[Skiold] left behind him two heirs to the kingdom, namely Frothi and Haldanus. In the course of time these brothers quarrelled with each other through their ambition to rule, and Haldan, having slain his brother, obtained the kingship.

5. *Skjoldunga saga* (*c.* 1200), in the abstract by Arngrímur Jónsson (1596) ch. 10.

[In this saga Halfdanus and Ingialldus are half-brothers, sons of Frodo IV of Denmark by different mothers; Frodo is killed by Svertingus—see V A 2 and B 4.]

So when Frodo the Fourth had been slain . . . Halfdanus . . . betook himself to Scania; he avenged his father's fall by the slaughter of the twelve sons of Svertingus, who had throttled Frodo with their own hands. Then Ingialldus . . . bestowed one third of the kingdom on his half-brother Halfdanus, the avenger of their father's fall. . . . By his marriage with a certain Sigrida, Halfdanus had as children Signya, Roas and Helgo. The next thing was that Ingialldus, in his greed to reign alone, came upon his brother unawares with an army and slew him; he was therefore made King of Denmark, and married his brother's widow, by whom he had Rærecus and Frodo.

6. Saxo Grammaticus, *Danish History* (*c.* 1200) II § 51.

> [Frotho the First of Denmark] left three sons, Haldanus, Roe and Scatus, who were equal in valour and were seized with an equal desire for the throne. All thought of sway, none was constrained by brotherly regard; for love of others forsaketh him who is eaten up with love of self, nor can any man take thought at once for his own advancement and for his friendship with others. Haldanus, the eldest son, disgraced his birth with the sin of slaying his brethren, winning his kingdom by the murder of his kin; and, to complete his display of cruelty, arrested their adherents, first confining them in bonds and presently hanging them. The most notable thing in the fortunes of Haldanus was this, that though he devoted every instant of his life to cruel deeds, yet he died of old age, and not by the steel.

7. Snorri Sturluson, *Edda* (*c.* 1220), *Skáldskaparmál* ch. 80.

> There was a king named Hálfdan the Old, who was the most outstanding of all kings. He held a great sacrifice at mid winter, offering sacrifice that he might live in his kingdom for three hundred years. But he received the answer that he would not live longer than one long human life-span, but that for three hundred years there would be no woman among his descendants, and no man of common rank. He was a great warrior, and went far and wide among Baltic lands. There he slew in single combat a king called Sigtryggr. Then he married a woman named Alvig the Wise; they had eighteen sons, nine of whom were born at one birth.

8. *Annales Ryenses* (*c.* 1290).

> [A genealogy of descendants of Skiold.]
>
> . . . Haldanus; Ro; Haldean and Helgi. . . .

9. *Series Runica Regum Daniae Altera* (fourteenth century).

> Then Haldan, Frothe's son, was king; he slew his brother because he wanted to have the kingdom.

10. *Hrólfs saga kraka* (*c.* 1400) ch. 1.

There was a man named Hálfdan and another named Fróði, two brothers and sons of a king, and each of them ruled a kingdom of his own. King Hálfdan was cheerful, easy-going and good-natured, but King Fróði was an absolute brute. King Hálfdan had three children, two sons and a daughter named Signý; she was the eldest, and was married to Earl Sævill. All this happened while his sons were still young; one of them was called Hróarr and the other Helgi.

Reginn was the name of their foster-father, and he loved these boys dearly. A little way from the stronghold there lay an island, and on it there lived an old peasant named Vífill; he had been a lifelong friend of King Hálfdan. Old Vífill had two dogs, one called Hoppr and the other Hó; this old peasant had a well-stocked farm, and he knew much ancient lore if ever he were attacked.

Now to take up the tale—King Fróði dwelt in his own kingdom, and nourished a deep grudge against his brother King Hálfdan that he should rule over Denmark alone, whereas his own lot seemed to him less good. So therefore Fróði gathered together a mob and a mighty host and set out for Denmark, and arrived there at dead of night and set everything in fire and flames. King Hálfdan could make little defence; he was taken prisoner and slain, and those who could do so fled away. All common folk in the stronghold had to swear oaths of fealty to King Fróði, otherwise he had them tortured with various tortures.

II E. HRŌDGĀR—O.N. Hróarr—
Lat. Ro/Roe/Roas.

1. *Wīdsīð* (seventh century), ll. 45–9.

Very long did Hrōðwulf and Hrōðgār, nephew and uncle, keep peace as kinsmen together, after they had driven off the tribe of the Vikings and humbled Ingeld's battle-array, hewing down the host of the Heaðobards at Heorot.

2. For Hróarr in the *Langfeðgatal*, see above, II D 2.

3. *Leire Chronicle* (*Chronicon Lethrense*) (*c.* 1170), ch. 3.

> [This chronicle makes Ro the eldest of this group of kings, making him a son of Dan.]

> Thus Dan was King of Denmark for three years; by his wife Dannia he had a son whose name was Ro. He, on his father's death, inherited the kingdom; he raised a mound for his father at Lethra [Leire] in Zealand, where his father had established a royal seat, which he in his turn enriched with many treasures. At that time there was a large town in the middle of Zealand, where nowadays there is an uninhabited hill called Høkebjorg, from which Høkekøping takes its name. Now when Ro saw that it was very expensive for traders to transport their goods by road from their ships by driving wagons to this spot, he gave orders that the town should be transferred to a harbour that could be reached by the Isafjord, and that buildings should be laid out round a very beautiful fountain. There Ro built a most fair town, on which he bestowed a name in honour of himself and this fountain, a name taken partly from the word 'fountain' and partly from his own name, thus calling it 'Roskilde' in Danish; it was to be known by this name for ever. King Ro lived in such peace that no man drew a sword against him, nor did he himself lead any expedition abroad. His wife was fruitful and bore him two sons; the first was named Helgi and the second Haldan. When these boys began to grow and to come to their strength, their father died and was laid in a mound at Lethra.

4. *Skjoldunga saga* (*c.* 1200) in an abstract by Arngrímur Jónsson (1596), chs. 10, 12.

> [Ingialldus kills his brother Halfdanus and marries the widow, Sigrida—see above, II D 5.]

> Her daughter Signya was brought up by her, and later

Ingialldus married her off to Sevillus, Earl of Zealand. But the boys Roas and Helgo lived secretly in hiding on a certain island off Scania, and when they had grown up they paid their uncle Ingialldus back in his own coin, avenging the fall of their father Halfdanus by killing Ingialldus. Therefore Roas and his brother Helgo were hailed as the next kings of Denmark; Roas indeed lived quietly at home, while Helgo lived the life of a sea-raider. . . . Roas married the daughter of an English king.

[For the adventures of Helgo, see II F 7 below. After Helgo's death, Roas shared the throne with his young nephew Rolf Krake.]

Not long afterwards, Roas, the uncle of Rolfo, was slain by his own first cousins, Rærecus and Frodo, the sons of Ingialldus.

5. Saxo Grammaticus, *Danish History* (*c.* 1200) §§ 51, 52.

[Halfdanus's] sons were Roe and Helgo. Roe is recorded to have been the founder of Roskilde, which was later increased in population and enhanced in power by Sweyn, who was famous for the surname Forkbeard. Roe was short and spare, while Helgo was rather tall of stature. Dividing the realm with his brother, Helgo was allotted the domain of the sea . . . .

[For the adventures of Helgo, see II F 8 below. After some years there arose a warlike Swedish king called Hothbroddus.]

Not content with conquering the east, [Hothbroddus] assailed Denmark, challenged its king Roe in three battles, and slew him.

6. For Ro in the *Annales Ryenses*, see above, II D 8.

7. *Series Runica Regum Daniae Altera* (fourteenth century).

The next was Ro, Frothe's son; he was the first to build Roskilde.

8. *Hrólfs saga kraka* (*c.* 1400), chs. 1–5, 10–11.

[After the death of Hálfdan—see above, II D 10—his sons Helgi and Hróarr fled from Fróði.]

Reginn, the foster-father of Helgi and Hróarr, got them away and out to the island, to the peasant Vífill's home; they grieved bitterly over their wrongs. Reginn said that if Vífill could not manage to keep them safe from King Fróði, then indeed all shelters would be snowed up. Vífill said: 'This means playing tug-of-war with a strong man,' but said there was a strong obligation on him to help the boys. So he took them in and put them in an underground chamber, and they mostly stayed in there by night, but during the day they took the air in the thickets of the old peasant's woods, for half the island was overgrown with woods. And in this way they parted from Reginn.

Reginn had great possessions in Denmark, and wife and children, and he could see no other way open to him but to submit to King Fróði and swear oaths of fealty to him. King Fróði now subdued the whole kingdom with tribute and taxes. Most men submitted very unwillingly, for King Fróði was the most unpopular of men; and in the same way, he demanded tribute from Earl Sævill.

When all this had been achieved, King Fróði grew a little easier in his mind about not having found the boys Helgi and Hróarr. However, he now sent out spies after them in all directions, far and near, north, south, east and west; he promised great gifts to whoever could tell him anything about them, but threatened those who might hide them with various tortures if it were discovered—and still no one was able to tell the king anything about them. Then he had wise women and soothsayers brought from all over the country, and made them search up and down the country, and islands and outer skerries too, and still they were not found. And now he had wizards brought, who can pry into anything just as they choose, and these told him that they were not being brought up in the country itself, and yet that they were not far from the king.

King Fróði said: 'We have searched far and wide for

them, and I hardly think it likely that they should be near at hand; but there is an island near here where we have not searched thoroughly, for it is nearly uninhabited, save for one poor peasant who lives there.'

'Search there first,' said the wizards, 'for a great veil of fog lies over that island, and this makes it hard for us to see anything near this peasant's dwelling. We think he is a wise man, and that there is more in him than meets the eye.'

'Then one must search there once again,' said the king, 'but I think it very strange that a poor fisherman should be keeping these boys and should dare to keep people safe from me in this way.'

It happened one morning that the peasant Vífill woke and said: 'There's many a strange thing on the move, and the wraiths of great and mighty men have come hither to the island. Rise up, sons of Hálfdan, Hróarr and Helgi, and stay in my woodland thickets today.'

They ran off into the woods. Now it all happened as the peasant had guessed, that King Fróði's messengers came to the island and searched for them in every place which occurred to their minds, and found the boys nowhere. The peasant seemed to them most suspicious-looking, but all the same they went away leaving matters thus, and told the king that they could not find them.

'You must have searched badly,' said the king. 'This old peasant is a master of magic arts. Now go back there by the same road, so that he should be less well prepared to get them out of the way, if they are there.'

So now they had to do as the king said, and went back to the island a second time.

The peasant said to the boys: 'There's no sitting still for you! Make your way to the woods as fast as you can.'

The boys did so. After this the king's men came rushing up and demanded to ransack the place, and the peasant opened up everything for them; and they did not find them anywhere on the island, wherever they might search, and so they went home again leaving matters thus, and told the king.

King Fróði said: 'We mustn't use kid gloves any longer in dealing with this man. I shall go to the island myself as soon as morning comes.'

And so it was done, and the king went himself.

The old peasant awoke, feeling somewhat troubled, and saw once again that some plan must be quickly found. He said to the brothers: 'If I call loudly to my dogs Hoppr and Hó, you must realize that it means you. You must take this as a token that those coming to the island have not come in peace, and then you must run to your underground chamber and hide there; for your kinsman Fróði is now taking part in the search himself, and he is seeking your lives by hostile tricks and turns of every kind, and I cannot now foresee whether I shall be able to keep you safe.'

The peasant then went down to the shore, where the king's ship had arrived. He acted as if he had not seen it, and pretended to be looking hither and thither for his sheep so earnestly that he never once glanced at the king or his men. The king bade his men take the peasant prisoner, and so it was done, and he was led before the king.

'You are a very tricky old fellow, and a sly one,' said the king. 'Tell me where the king's sons are, for you do know that.'

The old peasant said: 'All hail to you, sire! Don't keep me captive, for the wolf will be tearing my sheep to pieces.' And then he called loudly: 'Hoppr, Hó! Help the sheep, since I can't save them now!'

'Who are you calling to?' said the king.

'Those are my dogs' names,' said the peasant. 'Now search wherever you like, sire, but I don't suppose that the king's sons will be found here. I am quite amazed that you should think I would keep men hidden against your will.'

The king said: 'You most certainly are a tricky old fellow, and from now on they will never again be able to find shelter here, even if they have done so up till now, and it would be only right if you were put to death.'

The peasant said: 'It is now in your power to do so. In that case you would have got some business done on the island, more so than if you go home leaving matters thus.'

'I cannot find it in me to have you killed,' said the king, 'even though I think this is a mistaken course.'

So now the king went home, leaving matters thus.

Now the old peasant went to find the boys and told them that they could not stay there any longer—'I will send you to Sævill, your brother-in-law, and you will both grow to be famous men, if you live long enough.'

At this time Hróarr was twelve years old and Helgi ten, and yet the latter was the bigger and bolder of them. They now went on their way, and wherever they came or met and talked with men, one of them gave his name as Hamr and the other as Hrani. The boys came to Earl Sævill and were there for a week before they spoke with the earl about whether they could stay.

'I don't think you are much of an acquisition,' said he, 'but I won't grudge you food for a while.'

They stayed there for some time, and proved rather troublesome; it was impossible to find out what kind of people they were or from what family they came, and the earl did not suspect who they were, for indeed they never made him any the wiser about their real standing. Some men said they must have grown up with the scurvy, and they made mock of them because they always had cowled cloaks on and would never push back the cowls, and therefore many people thought they must have the scurvy. They stayed there till the third winter.

On a certain occasion King Fróði invited Earl Sævill to a feast, and he had rather a suspicion that he must be keeping the boys hidden because of the family ties between them. So now the earl made ready for this journey, and took many men with him. The boys asked to go with him, but the earl said that they were not to go. Signý, the earl's wife, also went on this journey.

Hamr (who in fact was Helgi) got himself an unbroken colt to ride and galloped off after the earl's troop, but sitting with his face to the tail and acting just like a halfwit. His brother Hrani got himself another steed of the same sort, but he was facing the right way round. The earl now watched as they came after him, quite unable to master their steeds; the shaggy colts were bucking up and down under them, and the cowl of

Hrani's hood fell back. Their sister Signý caught sight of this, and she recognized him at once, and wept very bitterly. The earl asked why she was weeping. Then she spoke this verse:

> 'The race of the Skjǫldungs,
> Kin of Lund's king,
> To this have they come—
> Mere broken branches!
> I saw my brothers
> Bareback riding,
> But Sævill's warriors
> On saddled steeds.'

The earl said: 'Great tidings, but don't let them become known.'

Then he rode back to them and bade them take themselves off home again, saying they were an utter disgrace to a company of noble men. Both boys were on foot again by then. But the reason that he spoke in such a way was that he was on his guard lest anyone should guess from his words who the boys were. So now they ran to and fro on the outskirts of the company and were no more willing to turn back than before, and then they rode in the rear rank.

So now they came to the feast, and ran backwards and forwards in the hall, and at one moment they made their way to where their sister Signý was. She spoke to them, rather low: 'Do not stay in this hall, for you are not full-grown men.' They paid no heed to this.

King Fróði began to talk of how he wanted to have King Hálfdan's sons searched out, and said he would bestow great honours on anyone who could tell him anything about them. A wise woman who was named Heiðr had come there. King Fróði bade her use her arts and find out what she could tell him about the boys. He then prepared a splendid feast to welcome her, and made her sit on a high scaffolding used in sorcery.

Then the king asked what tidings she could see— 'for I know', said he, 'that many things will now appear before you, and I can see the marks of great good luck in you. Answer me as quickly as you can, O sorceress!'

Then she set her jaws wide open and yawned deeply,
and then a chant rose to her lips:

'There are two in here,
And neither I trust;
Glorious their birth,
By the fire they sit.'

The king said: 'Is that the boys, or those who have
sheltered them?'

She answered:

'Those who were long
On Vífill's island,
And there were known
By the names of hounds,
Hoppr and Hó.'

At this moment Signý threw a gold ring to her; she was
pleased with the present, and wanted to break off now.
'How has this come about?' said she. 'All I said was
a lie, and my second sight has gone quite astray.'

The king said: 'You shall be tortured into speaking if
you won't agree to what is best for you. Among so great
a crowd of men I understand what you are saying no
better than I did before, nor do I know why Signý is
not in her seat—and it may well be that there is wolf
plotting here with wolf.'

The king was told that Signý had fallen ill because of the
smoke coming from the stove. Earl Sævill bade her sit up
and bear herself boldly—'for there's many a thing that can
save the boys' lives, if that is what must happen. So don't
you show the least sign of what you are thinking, for there
is nothing we can do to help them as matters stand now'.

King Fróði now pressed the sorceress hard, bidding
her speak the truth if she did not wish to be tortured.

Then she yawned deeply, and the spell was hard to
work, and she now spoke this verse:

'I see where they're sitting,
Both safe and sound,
Hróarr and Helgi
Hálfdan's sons;
They will rob Fróði
Of life itself—

135

unless they themselves are swiftly destroyed, and that shall never be,' said she.

After this she leapt down from the sorcerer's scaffolding, and said:

'Fierce are the eyes
Of Hamr and Hrani;
Noble princes are they,
And wondrously brave.'

After that, the two boys ran away out into the woods in great fear. Their foster-father Reginn recognized them, and took this much to heart. And the wise woman, as she ran out from the hall, gave them the good advice that they should save their lives.

And now the king bade his men leap to their feet and go in search of them. Reginn put out every light in the hall, and now each man grappled with the next, for some were willing that they should get away, and so because of all this they got to the woods.

The king said: 'They came close this time, and there must be many here who were in this plot and scheme with them, and there will be grim revenge taken for this, as soon as there is time enough for it. But now we will be able to drink the whole evening, for they must have been glad enough to have got away, and the first thing they will try to is save their lives.'

Reginn set about pouring drink for the men, and he, and many others who were friends of his, served them with ale so zealously that they all fell down there, one on top of the other, fast asleep.

Now the brothers stayed quiet in the woods, as has been said before, and when they had been there some while they happened to see a man come riding towards them from the hall. They recognized quite clearly that it was their foster-father Reginn coming there; they were glad of the sight of him, and greeted him warmly. He gave no answer to their greetings, but turned his horse round, away from them and facing the hall. They were amazed at this, and discussed between them what it might mean. Reginn now turned his horse towards them once again, and looked as frowning as if he would attack them then and there.

'I think I understand what he wants,' said Helgi.

He now set off back towards the hall, and they went after him.

'My foster-father behaves like that', said Helgi, 'because he does not want to break his oaths to King Fróði, and so he does not want to speak to us, though he is very willing to help us.'

There was a grove which the king owned standing near the hall, and when they reached it Reginn spoke to himself: 'If I had great grievances against King Fróði, I would burn this grove down.' He said no more than that.

'What does it mean?' said Hróarr.

'What he wants,' said Helgi, 'is that we should go back to the hall and set fire to it everywhere except at one exit.'

'How shall we be able to do that, two youths like us, against such heavy odds as are facing us?'

'So it must be, even so,' said Helgi. 'We will have to take a risk some time or other, if we are to take vengeance for our wrongs.'

And so they did.

The next thing was that Earl Sævill came out, and all his men. He said then: 'Let's pile up the fires and help these boys! I have no duty towards King Fróði.'

Now King Fróði had two smiths who were past-masters of their craft, and both of them were named Varr [i.e. 'Wary']. Reginn shepherded all his host, both friends and kinsmen, out through the door of the hall.

Now King Fróði awoke in the hall, heaved a deep sigh, and said: 'I have dreamed a dream, lads, and it boded no good. I dreamed that I thought that a voice was calling out to us, and it was speaking thus: "You are coming home now, O King, you and your men." It seemed to me that I answered, rather resentfully: "Home where?" Then the call came again, so near me that I felt the breath of whoever was calling. "Home to Hel, home to Hel!" said whoever was calling. And at this I awoke.'

At this moment they heard something from outside

137

the hall door, Reginn the foster-father speaking this
verse:

'It is Reginn outside,
And Hálfdan's warriors,
Resolute foemen—
Tell this to Fróði.
Wary forged nail-spikes,
Wary set heads on,
Wary for Wary
Wary-nails forging.'

The king's men who were indoors said that that was
no great news, even if it was raining [reginn = rain]
outside, or if the king's smiths were at their smithying,
whether they were forging nails or any other piece of
work.

'You think this no news?' said the king. 'It will not
prove so for me. Reginn has surely told me of some
threat, and has given me a sign that I ought to be wary;
he has been sly and cunning with me.'

Then the king went to the door of the hall and saw
enemies facing him outside. By then the whole hall had
begun to blaze. King Fróði asked who was leader at
this fire-raising. They said that the leader was Helgi,
and his brother Hróarr.

The king asked them to come to terms with him, and
offered them the right to fix whatever terms they liked
—'for it is a monstrous way to behave between us, who
are kinsmen, that any one of us should wish to be the
other's slayer'.

'No one can trust you,' said Helgi. 'Will you be less
ready to betray us than to betray my father Hálfdan?
You shall pay for that now.'

Then King Fróði turned away from the door of the
hall towards the mouth of his underground chamber,
meaning to make his way through it to the woods, and
so save himself. But as he reached the underground
chamber, Reginn was there to meet him, and he did not
look very peaceable. Then the king turned back, and
burned to death indoors, and many of his host with him.
Sigríðr, the mother of the brothers Helgi and Hróarr,
also burned indoors, because she would not go out. The

brothers thanked their brother-in-law Earl Sævill for
his good help, and their foster-father Reginn, and all
their followers; and they gave many men fine gifts, and
in this way they won themselves the kingdom and all
the wealth which King Fróði had owned, both in land
and treasure.

These brothers were by nature different in character.
Hróarr was a cheerful and easy-going man, but Helgi a
very warlike man, and he was far more highly thought
of; and so things went on for some while. And this now
is the end of the tale of Fróði, and the beginning of the
tale of Hróarr and Helgi, Hálfdan's sons.

[For Helgi, see below, II F 12. Hroarr married
the daughter of the King of Northumberland and
settled in England.]

King Helgi had a ring which brought great fame with
it, and both he and his brother wished to own it, and so
did their sister Signý. One day King Hróarr came into
the realm of his brother King Helgi, and King Helgi
made a magnificent feast to welcome him.

King Hróarr said: 'You are certainly the better man
of us two, and because of the fact that I have settled
myself in Northumberland, I am very willing to grant
you this kingdom which we both held in common, if
you are willing to share some precious possession with
me. I want to take that ring, which is the finest treasure
among your possessions, and we would both own it in
common.'

'The only right and proper thing, brother,' said Helgi,
'is that the ring should be truly yours.'

This conversation pleased them both. King Helgi
brought the ring to his brother King Hróarr, and now
King Hróarr went away home to his own kingdom and
lived there quietly.

It so happened that their brother-in-law Sævill died,
and his son Hrókr took his earldom after him; he was a
grim man, and most covetous. His mother told him a
great deal about the ring which her brothers owned—
'and I would have thought it rather fitting', said she,
'if my brothers had shown by the gift of some kingdom
that they remembered us, for we stood by them in the

vengeance for our father; yet they have not shown your father or me that they remembered this'.

'What you say is as true as day,' said Hrókr, 'and such a thing is quite abominable. Now I will take up the case with them, to see what honours they are willing to give us in return for this.'

After this, he went to find King Helgi and demanded one-third of the kingdom of Denmark, or else that fine ring—for he did not then know that Hróarr had it.

The king said: 'You state your claim very harshly and with hasty pride. We won the kingdom through our valour, for we staked our lives to get it, with the support of your father, and of my foster-father Reginn, and of other noble men who were willing to help us. Now we are certainly willing to make you some return, if you will accept it, on account of our kinship; but this kingdom has cost me so much that I will not lose it on any account. And King Hróarr has taken the ring now, and I should think that he won't part with it to you.'

With that, Hrókr went away, very ill-pleased, and now sought a meeting with King Hróarr, who gave him a warm and honourable welcome; and he stayed with him for some while.

And one day when they were out at sea, lying in a certain fjord, Hrókr said: 'I think it would do you great honour, uncle, if you were to give me that fine ring, and so show that you remembered our kinship.'

The king said: 'I have given up so much to get this ring that I will not let it go on any account.'

'Then you will surely let me see the ring,' said Hrókr. 'I have the greatest curiosity to know about it, whether it is such a treasure as they say.'

'That is a small gift for you,' said Hróarr, 'and it shall certainly be granted.'

Hrókr now considered the ring for a while, and declared it impossible to speak too highly of it—'and I have never seen any treasure like it, and there is the strongest excuse for you to think the ring extremely fine. The best plan now would be that neither of us should enjoy it, nor anyone else either'—and he flung the ring from his hand, out to sea, as far as he could.

'You are a most wicked man,' said King Hróarr.

After this he had Hrókr's feet cut off, and had him sent back to his domain in this state. He was soon whole again, as his stumps healed over.

Then he gathered a host and wanted to take vengeance for his disgrace; he found himself a great host and came to Northumberland unawares, at a place where King Hróarr was at a feast, with few men with him. Hrókr attacked at once, and then there began a hard battle, and the difference in the odds was very great. There King Hróarr died, and Hrókr conquered that country.

[For the connection between Hrókr and Hreðric, see below, II J].

9. For Hróarr in the *Bjarkarímur*, see below, II J 6.

II F. HĀLGA—O.N. Helgi—Lat. Helgo.

1. *Helgakviða Hundingsbana* II (tenth century? Included in the *Poetic Edda, c.* 1270).

[The poem is very fragmentary, and its hero is said to be a Vǫlsung, not a Dane; however, his two chief exploits, the slaying of Hundingr and of Hǫðbroddr, are ascribed by Saxo to Helgi the Dane —see below, II F 8. The opening stanzas allude obscurely to an episode in which Helgi visits the court of Hundingr, disguised as a slave-woman; stanza 12 states that Helgi later killed Hundingr.]

You tell of warfare; at Helgi's feet
Hundingr the king must needs sink low;
In combat you met, you avenged your kin,
Blood spurted out on the edge of the blade.

[A valkyrie named Sigrún appeals to Helgi to save her from an unwelcome wooer, Hǫðbroddr; they meet in battle, and Helgi kills Hǫðbroddr. The

141

poem is chiefly concerned with the love of Helgi
and Sigrún and his return from the dead for a last
meeting with her.]

2. *Helgakviða Hundingsbana* I (eleventh century; included in
the *Poetic Edda, c.* 1270).

[The poem tells how at Helgi's birth norns and
ravens foretold his prowess; stanzas 10–14 tell of
his feud with Hundingr and his sons.]

Not long did this lord for warfare wait;
When he was fifteen winters old,
Hundingr he slew, a hardy man
Who long had ruled over lands and men.

Then Hundingr's sons all claimed their due
In wealth and rings, from Sigmundr's heir,
For they had wergeld to get from him
For plunder taken and father slain.

The chieftain would not grant their pleas,
Nor could these kinsmen wergeld get;
He said that a mighty storm was near,
A storm of grey spears and Óðinn's wrath.

The warriors went to their chosen field,
A field they laid out at Logafjǫll;
Peace was shattered between the foes;
Greedy for prey, wolves roamed the isle.

The prince took his seat beneath Eagle Rock,
When he had slain Alfr, and Eyjolfr too,
And Hjǫrvarðr and Hávarðr, Hundingr's sons;
He had slain the whole of the spear-lord's race.

[The valkyrie Sigrún then appears and bids Helgi
make war on Hǫðbroddr for her sake; the rest of the
poem describes preparations for battle, an exchange
of taunts between supporters of each side, and
Sigrún's praise of Helgi when Hǫðbroddr has fallen.]

3. For *Grottasǫngr* stanza 22 see below, II G 2. Its allusion to
the incestuous origin of Hrólfr Kraki implies knowledge
of the story of Helgi the Dane and Yrsa.

4. For Helgi's place in the *Langfeðgatal* genealogy, see above, II D 2.

5. *Leire Chronicle (Chronicon Lethrense)* (*c.* 1170), ch. 4.

But Helgi was a sea-king, and gathered many ruffians about him, for he was well suited to sea warfare; he would seek out various regions, sometimes in peace, but sometimes in sea-borne raids. So it happened on one occasion that Helgi, needing a harbour and wearied by rowing, came to a certain harbour near Laland; there, in his brother's realm, he remained quietly with his host for three nights, his tents pitched peacefully on shore. Then, filled with physical yearnings, he sent out his men to seek some girl fit for a king. They brought to the king the daughter of a certain earl called Rolf the Old, though they were pursued by her father; her name was Thora. She was made pregnant by him, and later bore a daughter, whom she named Ursula. King Helgi went on his way, and laid many regions waste. But many years later it happened once again that this same Helgi was driven ashore in the harbour we have already spoken of; he had forgotten his former deed there, and gave orders that some girl should be shown to him—and thus he raped his own daughter Ursula, whom he received from the hands of Thora Rolfsdaughter. She was made fruitful by her own father's seed, and bore a son whom she named Rolf after her grandfather. Meanwhile Thora, who was both wife and mother-in-law to Helgi, died, and was buried on an island which is named Thorey; and later on her father, Rolf the Old, was also buried there. Also the sea-king Helgi, his son- and grandson-in-law, was buried there too.

6. Sven Aageson, *A Brief History of the Kings of Denmark* (*c.* 1187), ch. 1.

[Halfdan had been slain by his brother Frothi—see above, II D 4.]

He had begotten a son as heir to his kingdom, namely Helghi, who, because of his exceptional courage and

143

energy, always led the life of a sea-raider. Since he de-populated the coastal territories of every one of the surrounding kingdoms with his raiding fleet, and made them subject to his rule, he was given the title 'Sea-King'.

7. *Skjǫldunga saga* (*c.* 1200), in an abstract by Arngrímur Jónsson (1596), ch. 11.

[Helgo and Roas avenged their father—see II E 4 above.]

Therefore Helgo and his brother Roas were hailed as the next kings of Denmark; Roas indeed lived quietly at home, while Helgo lived the life of a sea-raider. One day he happened to land in Saxland (which was then ruled by Earl Geirtiofus, who was away at the time), and betook himself with his army to a town where he knew there lived a queen or countess whose name was Olava the Rich. He was given a friendly welcome, as she was unable at once to resist his unexpected arrival. A sumptuous feast was arranged, minds grew heated with wine, and Helgo asked Olava to grant him her favours for the night. Although she was unwilling, she pre-tended not to repulse him, for truly her abilities lay not in strength but in cunning. With his wits clouded by wine, he was led to her chamber; the rest lay here and there, sunk in wine and slumber. Olava, who planned to come to bed only after much loitering, contrived great delays in taking off her feminine adornments and tidily putting away what she had taken off; meanwhile Helgo, overcome by slumber, fell asleep.

Then she arranged for him to be laid in a cart, still sleeping, and carried down to the ships, after his com-panions had been given a message that their leader had gone back to the ships. Now when they got there they saw approaching a great crowd of local people, whom Olava had summoned by secret messengers, and so they thought the only safe thing for them to do was to go on board. In fact, Olava had had Helgo's head shaved and befouled with tar and feathers, and so, having made a mockery of him, sent him away. So Helgo went home to Denmark, bearing the bitterness of this treatment.

But the following year Helgo returned to Saxland and

took revenge for his former injury. He appeared un-
expectedly and kidnapped Olava when she left home
with a group of female attendants, carried her off into
the trackless depths of thick forests, and kept her with
him for three days in this lair, forcing her to serve his
lust. From this intercourse was born a daughter, Yrsa,
who was brought up with her mother in Saxland, and
later, so they say, became Queen of Sweden. After this,
Helgo gave up his raiding for a while, and exchanged
positions with Roas; Roas had married the daughter
of an English king.

Later, King Helgo of Denmark reverted to plundering
and sea-raiding, made war on Sweden, and was vic-
torious. He kidnapped the queen Yrsa, carried her
back with him to Denmark, and thus through ignorance
the father wedded his own daughter—though against
the wishes and advice of his brother Roas, who said he
could recognize her as a kinswoman by her features. A
son was born to them, Rolfo, who was later nicknamed
Krag. When news of this affair reached Countess Olava
in Saxland, she set out secretly for Denmark as soon as
three years had passed since the marriage; she summoned
her daughter Yrsa, revealed the truth, and ordered her
to go back to Sweden, and abandon so wicked a marriage.
Yrsa told her father-husband everything, asked leave to
depart, and obtained her request. Five years later, Helgo
died in battle.

8. Saxo Grammaticus, *Danish History* (*c.* 1200) §§ 51–3.

Dividing the realm with his brother, Helgo was
allotted the domain of the sea; and attacking Scalcus,
the King of Sclavia, with his naval force, he slew him.
Having reduced Sclavia into a province, he scoured the
various arms of the sea in a wandering voyage. Savage
of temper as Helgo was, his cruelty was not greater than
his lust; for he was so immoderately prone to love, that
it is doubtful whether the heat of his tyranny or of his
concupiscence was the greater. On Thorey he ravished
the maiden Thora, who bore a daughter, to whom she
afterwards gave the name of Ursa.

Then he conquered in battle, before the town of Stad,
the son of Syrik, King of Saxony, Hundingus, whom he

challenged, attacked, and slew in a duel. For this he was called Hunding's Bane, and by that name gained the glory of his victory. He took Jutland out of the power of the Saxons, and entrusted its management to his generals, Heske, Eyr and Ler. In Saxony he enacted that the slaughter of a freedman and a noble should be visited with the same punishment; as if he wished it to be clearly known that all the households of the Teutons were held in slavery, and that the freedom of all was tainted and savoured equally of dishonour.

Then he went back freebooting to Thorey. But Thora had not ceased to bewail her lost virginity, and planned a shameful device in abominable vengeance for her rape. For she deliberately sent down to the beach her daughter, who was of marriageable age, and prompted her father to deflower her. And though she yielded her body to the treacherous lures of delight, yet she must not be thought to have abjured her integrity of soul, inasmuch as her fault had a ready excuse by virtue of her ignorance. Insensate mother, who allowed the forfeiture of her child's chastity to avenge her own! . . . A great crime, but with one atonement; namely, that the guilt of this intercourse was wiped away by a fortunate progeny, its fruit being as delightful as its repute was evil. For Rolfo, the son of Ursa, retrieved the shame of his birth by signal deeds of valour; and their exceeding lustre is honoured with bright laudation by the memory of all succeeding time. For lamentation sometimes ends in laughter, and foul beginnings pass to fair issues. So that the father's fault, though criminal, was fortunate, being afterwards atoned for by a son of such marvellous splendour.

Meantime Regnerus died in Sweden; and Suanhuita his wife passed away soon after. . . . Their son Hothbroddus succeeded them. Fain to extend his empire, he warred upon the East. . . . Not content with conquering the East, he assailed Denmark, challenged its king, Roe, in three battles, and slew him. Helgo, when he heard this, shut up his son Rolfo in Leire, wishing, however he might have managed his own fortunes, to see to the safety of his heir. When Hothbroddus sent in governors, wanting to free his country from alien rule, he posted his people about the city and prevailed and slew them. Also he annihilated Hothbroddus himself and all his forces in a naval battle, so avenging fully the wrongs of his country as well as of his brother. Hence he who before had won a nickname for slaying Hunding, now bore a surname for the slaughter of Hothbroddus. Besides, as if the Swedes had not been enough stricken in battles, he punished them by stipulating for most humiliating terms; providing by law that no wrong done to any of them should receive amends according to the form of legal covenants. After these deeds, ashamed of his former infamy, he hated his country and his home, went back to the East, and there died. Some think he was affected by the disgrace that was cast in his teeth, and did himself to death by falling on his drawn sword.

9. Snorri Sturluson, *Heimskringla* (*c.* 1223–35), *Ynglinga saga* chs. 28–9.

[In this version Aðils of Sweden kidnaps Yrsa, daughter of Queen Álof of Saxland, and makes her his queen. Not long after, King Helgi raids Sweden, captures and carries off Queen Yrsa; they marry, and their son is Hrólfr Kraki. When Hrólfr is three, Álof appears at Leire and reveals the truth. Yrsa returns to Sweden, to Aðils. Helgi falls on a raiding expedition when Hrólfr is eight years old. For the full text, see below, III E 7.]

10. *Annales Ryenses* (*c.* 1290).

Helgi . . . a zealous warrior, slew Hothbrodus, the King of Sweden.

11. *Series Runica Regum Daniae Altera* (fourteenth century).

King Helhe, [Ro's] brother, slew King Hotbrod of Sweden, and exacted tribute from Thythistaland for the third time.

12. *Hrólfs saga kraka* (*c.* 1400), chs. 7–9, 13–14, 16.

[For this saga's account of Helgi's youthful adventures, see above, II E 8.]

At that time there was a queen reigning in Saxland,

whose name was Ólof. She lived like warrior kings; she would wear a sword and mailcoat and helmet, girt with a sword, and with a helm on her head; and her nature was that though she was fair of face she was cruel of heart and proud. It was generally said that she was the best match in the Northern Lands at that time, as far as men had heard tell, but she did not wish to have a husband. Now King Helgi heard tell of this proud queen, and he thought it would greatly add to his glory if he could possess this woman, whether she were willing or no.

So one day he came there with a great host; he landed in the region where this powerful queen ruled, and came there unexpectedly. He sent his men up to her hall, and bade them tell Queen Ólof that he and his host wished to banquet there. The messengers told the queen this, and it took her unawares, so that she did not have a chance to gather a host. So then she took the best course open, and invited King Helgi and all his host to a feast. Now King Helgi came to the feast, and he was assigned a place on the highseat beside the queen, and they drank from the same horn all evening; there was no lack of anything, and no sign of displeasure to be seen in Queen Ólof.

King Helgi said to the queen: 'This is how it is,' said he. 'I wish that we should drink our bridal ale tonight. There are men in plenty here to witness it, and then we can both sleep in the one bed tonight.'

She said: 'I think we are going about this too quickly, sire; but if I must needs agree to take a husband, then I think there is no man more courteous than you, and so I can expect that you will do me no dishonour in this.'

The king said that it would be quite fitting for her, considering her haughtiness and pride, 'that we should live together for as long as it pleases me'.

'We must choose several of our friends here,' said she, 'for there is nothing I can do about it, and you are bound to have your way; you will surely behave honourably towards me.'

The drinking was heavy that evening and far into the night, and the queen was very merry, and for all that anyone could see she seemed very well pleased at this match.

Some while later he was led up to bed, and she was there waiting for him. The king had drunk so heavily that he at once fell down on the bed asleep, and the queen took advantage of this to prick him with a sleep-thorn. And when all the men had left, the queen got up again. She shaved all his hair off and smeared him with tar; then she took a sleeping-bag and put some clothes in it, and after that she took hold of the king and stuffed him into this sleeping-bag; then she found some men, and had them carry him down to his ships.

Then she woke his men, and said that their king had gone to his ships and was wanting to sail, as a fair wind had just sprung up. They leapt to their feet each as fast as he could; they were fuddled with ale, and did not clearly know what they were doing. And so they returned to the ships, and nowhere could they see their king, but they did see that a sleeping-bag had been brought there, a huge one. They were curious to find out what was in it while they were waiting for the king—for they thought he would be coming later. And when they opened it, they found their king in it, made mock of and put to shame; the sleep-thorn fell out, and the king awoke from a dream which was no pleasant one—and he was in very ill humour with the queen.

Now on the other hand it must be said that Queen Ólǫf had gathered her hosts during the night, and there was no lack of men to be had, and so King Helgi saw that he had no chance of getting at her now; they could hear the sound of trumpets and battle-calls up on shore. The king saw that it would be best to get away as fast as possible; the wind was favourable at the time. King Helgi now sailed home to his kingdom, having suffered this humiliation and disgrace, and he was extremely ill-pleased, and often thought of how he could take vengeance on the queen.

Now Queen Ólǫf stayed in her kingdom for a while, and her overbearing ways and tyranny had never been greater than now. She kept a strong guard always about her after this feast she had given King Helgi; the news of it spread far and wide through the land, and everyone thought it quite unheard-of that she should have made a mockery of such a king. Not long afterwards King

Helgi put out to sea in his ship, and in the course of this voyage he came ashore in Saxland, where Queen Ólǫf had her seat. She had a great host of men on guard. He ran his ship into a hidden creek, and told his men that they were to wait for him till sunrise of the third day, and then go on their way if he had not returned by then. He had two chests with him, full of gold and silver; he had got himself wretched rags for his outer clothing.

Then he went on his way to a wood, and there he hid the money, and then went off to the neighbourhood of the queen's hall. He found one of her thralls on his way, and asked news of the land. The thrall said things were all peaceful, and asked who he was. He said he was a wandering beggar—'Yet a great find of treasure has fallen into my hands out in the wilds, and I think it would be a good plan for me to show you where the money is.'

So now they went back into the woods, and he showed him the money, and the thrall thought it was a most remarkable thing that he should have had such luck.

'How eager is the queen for wealth?' said the beggar. The thrall said there was no woman who was more eager.

'Then this will please her,' said the beggar, 'and she will consider that she owns the wealth I have found here, since this land must be hers. But it would be wrong to turn good luck into bad, so I shall not conceal this money, and the queen can assign me whatever share of it she pleases, and that will be good enough for me. Would she be willing to make the effort of coming here to fetch the money?'

'I think so,' said the thrall, 'if it is done in secret.'

'Here's a necklace and a ring which I'll give you', said the beggar, 'if you bring her here into the wood alone; and if she is displeased with you, I'll find a plan for you.'

So they agreed on this, and struck their bargain.

Now he went home and told the queen that he had found great wealth in the wood, enough to bring happiness to many men, and he asked her to come quickly with him to see the wealth.

'If what you say is true', said she, 'you will get good

luck from the telling, but if not, your head will be off. But since in the past I have found you to be a truthful man, I will believe what you say.'

So now she gave proof that she was eager for wealth; she went off with him secretly in the dead of night, without anyone knowing but the two of them. And when they came to the wood, there was Helgi waiting for them, and he gripped her in his arms, and said that this meeting was just right for him to avenge his disgrace.

The queen said she had treated him badly—'but now I will make full amends to you for everything, and you can wed me as is fitting'.

'No,' said he, 'that choice is no longer open to you. You must come down to my ships with me, and stay there for as long as I like; for the sake of my honour I cannot forbear to take vengeance on you when I was so cruelly and shamefully treated.'

'You must have your own way this time,' said she.

The king slept beside the queen during many nights. And after that the queen went home, and he had taken his revenge on her as was said just now, and she was very ill-pleased with her lot.

After that, King Helgi went off raiding, and was a famous man. And when some time had passed, Ólǫf gave birth to a child, and it was a girl; she was utterly indifferent to this child. She had a dog which was named Yrsa, and she called the girl after it, so that her name was to be Yrsa. She was lovely to look at. And when she was twelve years old she had to tend sheep, and she never knew anything about herself except that she was the daughter of a peasant and his wife—for the queen had managed things so secretly that few people knew that she had been pregnant and borne a child. And so things went on, till the girl was thirteen years old.

It so happened at that time that King Helgi landed on that coast and was curious to have news of the country. He was wearing beggar's clothes. Near a forest he saw a large flock, and tending it was a young woman who was so lovely that he thought he had never seen a lovelier woman. He asked what her name was, and of what family she came.

'I am a peasant's daughter,' she said, 'and my name is Yrsa.'

'Your eyes are not those of a thrall,' said he—and he fell in love with her at once, and said that it would be quite fitting that a beggarman should have her, since she was a peasant's daughter. She begged him not to do this, but in spite of that he seized her and went off to his ships, and then sailed home to his kingdom.

Queen Ólǫf, when she heard of this, showed herself to be deceitful and false-hearted; she behaved as if she knew nothing of how matters stood, and the idea came into her head that this would bring grief and disgrace on King Helgi, not fame, nor happiness either. King Helgi now held his wedding with Yrsa, and he loved her dearly. . . .

King Helgi and Yrsa loved one another dearly, and they had a son who was named Hrólfr, who later became a man of great renown.

Queen Ólǫf heard of how dearly Helgi and Yrsa loved one another and were happy in their marriage. This did not please her, and she set out to visit them; and when she arrived in their land she sent a message to Queen Yrsa. And when the two women met, Yrsa invited her to her hall, but she said she would not agree to that, and said she had received no honour for which to repay King Helgi.

Yrsa said: 'You treated me very scornfully when I was with you. Do you know nothing which you could tell me about my family and what it may be, for I suspect that it is not what I have been told, that is, that I was the daughter of a peasant and his wife?'

'It is not beyond possibility', said Ólǫf, 'that I might know something to tell you about that. Indeed, that was my chief errand in coming here, that I wanted to reveal it to you. Are you happy in your marriage?'

'Yes,' said she, 'and well I might be happy, for I am married to the most noble of kings, and the most famous.'

'You haven't got such good reason to be happy as you think,' said Ólǫf, 'for he is your father, and you are my daughter.'

Yrsa said: 'Of all mothers I think mine is the worst

and most cruel, for this is such a monstrous thing that it can never be forgotten.'

'It is on Helgi's account, and on account of my anger, that you have had to pay in this way,' said Ólǫf. 'But now I am willing to invite you to come home with me in honour and esteem, and I will do the best I can for you in every way.'

Yrsa said: 'I do not know how that will turn out, but I cannot stay here now that I know of this monstrous thing which weighs upon us.'

After this she went to find King Helgi and told him what a hard fate had come upon them.

The king said: 'Cruel indeed is the mother you had! But I would wish that things should stay as they are.'

She said that things could never be the same, nor could they live together from then on. So now Yrsa went home with Queen Ólǫf and stayed in Germany for a while. This was such a blow to King Helgi that he took to his bed and was utterly downcast. Everyone thought there was no better match than Yrsa to be found, and yet kings were slow to ask for her hand; the chief reason for this was that it always seemed very possible that Helgi might come to take her back, and would show his displeasure if she were married off to anyone else.

There was a king called Aðils, a powerful and greedy man, who ruled over Sweden and lived in his chief stronghold at Uppsala. He heard of this woman Yrsa, and thereupon he made his ship ready and set out to meet Ólǫf and Yrsa. Ólǫf held a feast to welcome King Aðils, and received him with all her skill and courtesy. He asked for Queen Yrsa as his wife.

Ólǫf answered: 'You must have heard tell of how matters stand in her affairs, but we will not raise any objection if her consent can be got.'

The question was then laid before Yrsa. She answered by saying that it would not turn out well—'for you are a king who is not much liked'. But the plan was carried out all the same, whatever she might or might not say about it, and Aðils went away with her; King Helgi was not asked his opinion about this, because Aðils reckoned himself to be a greater king than he. King Helgi did not

153

find out about it before they had gone home to Sweden, when King Aðils held a splendid wedding feast for her; and now King Helgi heard tell of it, and felt twice as badly about it as before. He slept in an outer building, with no one else there. And now Queen Ólǫf is out of the story; and so things went on for a while. . . .

[Helgi then has an affair with an elf-woman, on whom he begets a daughter, Skuld, who grows up into a fierce sorceress. For Skuld's part in the death of Hrólfr Kraki, see below, II G 5, 8, 11.]

Meanwhile King Aðils was living at Uppsala. He had twelve berserks, and they were always with him to guard the land and prevent all wars and perils. King Helgi now made ready for an expedition to Uppsala to fetch Yrsa away. He came to land there, and when King Aðils heard tell that King Helgi had come to land, he asked Queen Yrsa in what way she wished King Helgi to be welcomed.

'It is for you to decide that,' said she, 'but you already know that there is no man to whom I am more deeply bound than him.'

So King Aðils thought it best to invite him to a feast, but he did not mean this feast to be wholly free from trickery. King Helgi accepted and went to the feast with a hundred men, but the greater number stayed down by the ship. King Aðils welcomed him with open arms. Queen Yrsa was planning to reconcile the two kings, and she treated King Helgi with the greatest honour. King Helgi was so filled with joy at seeing the queen that he let everything else pass him by unnoticed, and he wanted to talk with her at every hour that he could take advantage of, and in this manner they sat down to the feast.

The next thing that happened was that King Aðils' berserks came home; and as soon as they had landed, King Aðils went to meet them without the others learning of it. He told them to go off into a wood that lay between his stronghold and King Helgi's ship, and to rush out from it at King Helgi as he was going back to his ship—'I will also send out a troop to help you, and this will come on them from behind so that they will be caught in a cleft stick. I want to make quite sure that King Helgi does not get away, for I realize that he loves the queen so much that I will not risk what he might do.'

Meanwhile King Helgi was sitting at the feast, and this treacherous plot was carefully hidden from him, and from the queen too. Now Queen Yrsa told King Aðils that she wished him to give King Helgi very noble gifts of gold and precious things; he agreed to do so, but in fact he meant to have them all for himself. After this King Helgi set off, and King Aðils and the queen saw him on his way, and the queen and the two kings parted on good terms. But very soon after King Aðils had turned back, King Helgi and his men became aware of enemies, and battle broke out at once. King Helgi pressed onwards and fought valiantly, but because of the overwhelming odds against him he fell there, having won much glory and received many great wounds, for some of King Aðils' forces got round behind them, so that they were caught between the hammer and the anvil. Queen Yrsa knew nothing of all this until King Helgi had fallen and the battle was over. And there ends the story of King Helgi.

II G. HRŌDULF—O.N. Hrólfr Kraki— Lat. Rolfo Krake/Krag.

1. *Wīdsīð*, ll. 45–9—see II E 1.

2. *Grottasǫngr* stanza 22 (*c.* 950? Quoted by Snorri Sturluson, *Edda, Skáldskaparmál* ch. 52, *c.* 1220).

[Two giantesses, working at a handmill, prophesy doom on King Fróði and his descendants.]

Let us grind still faster! Yrsa's son
Shall take vengeance on Fróði for Hálfdan's death;
He shall be called her son and her brother—
We two know of that!

3. *Bjarkamál* (*c.* 950?).

[This lay, describing the last stand of King
Hrólfr and his warriors when attacked at Leire, now
survives only fragmentarily in three sources:
(1) A paraphrase by Saxo Grammaticus, see below,
II G 8; (2) Three stanzas of doubtful authenticity
about Hrólfr's generosity to his followers, which
are quoted by Snorri Sturluson, *Edda*, *Skáldskapar-
mál* ch. 56, because of the many kennings for gold
they contain; (3) The two opening stanzas, quoted
by Snorri in *Heimskringla*, *Óláfs saga helga* ch. 220,
because the lay was recited by Óláf's poet at dawn
before the battle of Stiklastaðir, 1030. These two
stanzas are as follows:]

> Day has risen,
> The cocks' wings are rustling,
> 'Tis time now for toilers
> To set to their tasks.
> Awake now, awake,
> O friends well-loved!
> Awake, all ye keenest
> Companions of Aðils!
>
> Hárr the Hard-gripper,
> Hrólfr the Marksman,
> Noble-born warriors
> Who never will flee!
> Not for wine do I wake you
> Nor for women's lore,
> Nay, I wake you for warfare,
> The hard battle-play.

4. For Rolfr in the *Langfeðgatal*, see above, II D 2.

5. *Leire Chronicle* (*Chronicon Lethrense*) (*c.* 1170), chs. 4, 7.

The son of Helgi and Ursula, the young Rolf, grew
up to be vigorous and valiant. His mother Ursula, now
a widow, was married to Athislus, King of Sweden;

she bore him a daughter named Sculd, who was thus
sister to Rolf by the same mother.

[At this point the *Leire Chronicle* inserts accounts
of two non-Skjǫldung kings allegedly imposed on
Denmark by Athislus of Sweden.]

Meanwhile, while Rachi and Snyo were reigning,
Helgi's son Rolf (nicknamed Kraki) was growing mighty;
after the death of Snyo the Danes chose him to be their
king. Like his forefathers, he very often dwelt at Lethra
in Zealand. He had his sister Sculd living with him—
the daughter of his mother Ursula and King Athislus,
of whom we have spoken above. He gave her a province
of Zealand called Hornshereth to support her waiting-
maids, in which he built a village named after Sculd,
from whom it took the name Sculdelef.

At that time there was a certain Earl of Scania named
Hiarward, of German race, owing tribute to Rolf; he
sent wooers to him, asking that he should give his sister
Sculd to Hiarward as wife. As Rolf was unwilling, he
secretly carried off the girl according to her own wish,
and made her his spouse. Because of this, Hiarward and
Sculd laid a plot, debating between themselves how Rolf
could be killed, so that Hiarward as survivor might be
made heir to the kingdom. So, not very long after,
Hiarward, taking courage from his wife's exhortations,
led a fleet to Zealand; he pretended to be bringing tribute
to his brother-in-law Rolf. As day was dawning, he sent
word to Rolf, bidding him come to see the tribute. When
Rolf saw no tribute but an armed host, he was over-
whelmed by warriors and killed by Hiarward. The men
of Zealand and Scania who were with Hiarward took him
as their king; only for a short time, from morning till the
hour of prime, did he hold the name of king. For then
there came Aki, brother of Haghbard and son of Hamund;
he slew Hiarward, and was made king of the Danes.

6. Sven Aageson, *A Brief History of the Kings of Denmark,*
(*c.* 1187) ch. 1.

[After Helgi] his son Rolf Kraki succeeded to the
kingdom. He was outstanding for ancestral courage; he

was slain at Lethra, which at that time existed as a very famous royal residence, but is now hardly inhabited, being one of the humblest villages in the neighbourhood of the city of Roskilde.

7. *Skjǫldunga saga* (*c.* 1200), in an abstract by Arngrímur Jónsson (1596), chs. 12, 13.

Rolfo, nicknamed Krake, or, in Danish, Krag (the name by which we know the sea-crow), was born of such intercourse that Helgo was at the same time his father and his grandfather; he succeeded to the throne at eight years old. Not long after, Roas, Rolfo's uncle, was slain by his own first cousins, Rærecus and Frodo, the sons of Ingialldus.

Rolfo Krake, most famous among the kings of this line, was outstanding for many qualities: wisdom, power, wealth, courage, moderation, amazing generosity, and his tall and thin stature. There is a tale about him, that one day he was visited by a certain Woggerus, who had long burned with curiosity to see this king. As Woggerus was staring fixedly at him, Rolfo asked whether he wanted anything of him. The other asked whether this was Rolfo, the very famous King of Denmark; to which the king said that he was indeed generally so called.

'O how fickle is rumour, and how little like the truth!' cried Woggerus. 'I used to imagine that this king excelled all others in physical as in mental gifts, but I could more truly call him a crow than a king!'

The king said: 'What little gift will you bestow on me with this nickname?' (For such was the custom for those giving nicknames.)

'I have no fit gift to bring you, O king,' said Woggerus.

In answer the king said: 'Then it is for whichever of us is better placed to do so to give a gift to the other'— and at the same time he gave Woggerus, as a gift, a ring which he had at hand.

Gratefully accepting the gift, Woggerus exclaimed: 'I vow to the gods that one day I will avenge your death, if it is your fate to fall by the sword!'

The king said, laughing: 'It takes little to make Woggerus happy!' (This remark passed into a proverb, if

someone makes as much display over some small gift
as if he were about to give a big one.)

Rolfo Krake had a daughter Driva, and another whose
name was Scura. The former he gave in marriage to a
man of great reputation, the Swede Witserchus, who
by his deeds had won no less glory than the famous
Starcardus; for Witserchus, all alone, had slain six
giants when fighting twelve of them all at once, whereas
Starcardus had never slain so many all at one time. Rolfo
also had another most celebrated champion named
Bodvarus, a Norwegian, who for his courage won praise
above all others; on him he bestowed his daughter
Scura. Besides these, he had ten outstanding wrestlers
constantly in attendance at his court, for which reason
he began to strike awe all his neighbours.

It was through the services of Bodvarus that Rolfo
secured the death of his father's first cousin, a son of
Ingialldus, the incomparable sea-raider and warrior
Agnarus, when nobody else dared to face him [cf. I A
5 and 9(d)].

He also made war upon King Hervardus of Eyland,
who without consulting Rolfo had married Scullda, the
daughter of King Adilsus of Sweden and Queen Yrsa,
and therefore sister to Rolfo on the mother's side; he
subdued him and made him pay tribute.

After this, hostility arose between this King Adilsus
of Sweden and Alo, king of the Upplands in Norway,
and both sides appointed to meet in battle; the place
fixed upon for the battle was Lake Wæner, which was
frozen over. Realizing that he would be inferior in forces
at this meeting, he begged his stepson Rolfo for help,
promising in repayment that Rolfo could carry away as
his reward whichever three most precious things he
might prefer in the whole kingdom of Sweden; more-
over each of his twelve champions would be granted
three pounds of pure gold, and each of the other warriors
three marks of silver. Rolfo, though remaining at home
himself, sent his twelve champions as reinforcements for
Adilsus, and through their deeds he who would other-
wise have been defeated obtained the victory. They
demanded the reward that had been proposed for them
and for their king, but Adilsus denied that he owed any

reward to Rolfo, since he was absent. The Danish warriors therefore spurned what was offered to them as soon as they understood that their king was being cheated in this way, and when they had returned home again they explained what had happened.

Rolfo therefore betook himself to Sweden with an army, and, leaving all the rest of his forces down by the ships, himself went on horseback to Uppsala with those twelve most valiant warriors of his—wonderful boldness, to dare trust himself thus among foes! The Danes bade the Swedes care so well for their horses that they would not carelessly incur the least taint of dirt. The Danish king also had an outstanding hawk, and they gave strict instructions that it should be properly cared for by the men of that town. But on the orders of the Swedish king the horses' tails were cut off, and the hawk was thrown in among thirty hawks that the Swedish king owned, in order that it might be torn to pieces.

They then entered a hall which was splendid but had hidden traps in it; for the Swedish king had seen to it that an underground pit should be dug in the middle of the floor, into which those who entered carelessly would fall. However, they thought the darkness suspicious, detected the pit by using their swords as staffs, and leapt across it. After this the windows were opened, and fire was brought in for the feasting, and smoking torches for the drinking. They saw a great fire being kindled in the middle of the hall, which was in fact being done because Rolfo was in the habit of boasting that he never fled, whether from fire or steel; when it had increased to such a degree that the Danes' garments were beginning to burn (they had come without corselets), Rolfo flung his shield on the flames, crying: 'Look, we will stoke up the fires with you!'—and at the same time he leapt across the flames on which he had flung his shield, and his twelve companions followed his example. Then the servants of the Swedish king said: 'This man is surely Rolfo, who will not flee fire or steel!' Then Rolfo said: 'He does not flee the fire who leaps across it,' and so saying he hurled all the Swedes who were present into the flames and so burned them to death.

Soon afterwards Queen Yrsa came in, and brought

her brother-son Rolfo a huge horn filled with gold, which would have been the reward of the twelve champions for their former deeds of valour; at the same time she brought a most valuable spear, a corselet of the same quality, and a very fine horse, all of which had been taken by Adilsus as spoils from Alo of the Upplands, as has been said before. At the same time she lovingly bade them mount the finest horses which she had had saddled for them, and leave their own behind because of their mutilated tails, and so escape from the approaching armies of Adilsus. Rolfo obeyed the warning of his mother-sister; and when he went to fetch his hawk he found that the thirty hawks that were Swedish had been killed by this one.

As they left Uppsala the Danes were pursued at once by a very numerous army, and they would have been overtaken if the Danish king had not deceived them by a very pretty trick. This was how it was: when Rolfo saw that the Swedes were drawing near, he scattered the gold coins he had received from his sister Yrsa along the road, and the others were far keener to gather them than to pursue. When Adilsus at length noticed the trick, he strongly urged his men on, but in vain; then, setting spurs to his horse, he forced it to gallop ahead of the rest of his army. As the Danish king saw that Adilsus could not be tempted with gold coins, he produced a ring of pure silver which his forebears had once carried off as booty from a defeated Swedish king, and threw it down in the path of Adilsus. Now Adilsus, who had a yearning for wealth, did not feel he could despise so precious an object; so turning his horse back, he bent right down and made haste to pick up the ring with his spear. The name of this ring was Svíagrís, that is, 'Piglet of the Swedes'. Seeing Adilsus bending down to pick up the ring, Rolfo cried out: 'Now I have made the mightiest of the Swedes stoop like a pig!' Adilsus, seeing he was striving in vain to achieve what he wanted, turned back to Uppsala.

The Danish king now spent the night in the house of a certain countryman, but next day he refused to accept a corselet and cloak which this man was offering him; and when they had gone only a little way farther, the peasant's hut vanished. By this, Rolfo knew for certain that it had been Odinus, the god of warriors, and that because he had scorned the offered weapons, in future victory would be denied to him, and his fated end was drawing near. However, for many years he lived free from tumults and disturbance.

Thus did his fate come upon him: his own brother-in-law Hiorvardus, who had once been defeated by him in battle, secretly cherished hatred for Rolfo, which he was at length able to satisfy by a trick. His wife Scullda (Rolfo's sister, as has been said) agreed with his plan, and indeed urged him on in it; she sent men to ask Rolfo in his name for a remission of two years' tribute, which Rolfo granted to his brother-in-law without making difficulties. By the use of this money Hiorvardus won over the neighbouring princes as allies, and by every means, whether by entreaties or bribes, he enticed them to take up arms with him against the Danish king; he was sure that Odinus, angry with the Danes, had destined the victory to him. (They worshipped Odinus as a second Mars, for which reason those who fell in battle were said to be dedicated to Odinus.)

So in the third year (for, as we have said, the tribute had been excused for two years) Hiorvardus set sail for Zealand with several ships, pretending that he meant to pay the tribute. He halted towards nightfall not far from the gates of Lethre [Leire], which was the royal seat; a large number of wagons which were to carry the goods unloaded from the ships had been sent out by road, and these too stopped for the night near the gates, because darkness was falling. But during the night Hiorvardus captured the wagoners, put them in chains, and filled all the wagons with soldiers hidden under rugs; meanwhile, in the silence of night and by the grey light of dawn, the rest of Hiorvardus' fleet, which certainly had not been far away, without delay gathered one after another in the harbour. Besides the warriors shut inside the wagons, a number of men on foot followed Hiorvardus as an escort, as if for the sake of pomp; they advanced, and appeared before the town gates, which were opened for them without delay or inspection, as if they were bringing tribute and tax, not armed might.

But as soon as this host held the gates, the men who had been left by the ships came running up in great number. They attacked the hapless Rolfo, who all this while had been sunk in deep slumber, and also the men of the town, who, caught unawares, had taken no steps to protect their town beyond setting guards and watchmen. With heroic courage Rolfo seized his weapons, dedicated the foe to the gods, and drove them from the gates; but then, overpowered by some mysterious lethargy, he allowed them back in again. Battle raged till evening; Odinus himself was seen in human form, fighting in the front rank of the foe; dead bodies too were seen to spring to life again (Satan having evidently entered into them), and raise a hideous tempest against the Danes. What more need I say? Rolfo fell, with almost all his men, and night had come before the signal for retreat was sounded.

On the very next day Hiorvardus was hailed by everyone as King of Denmark, and oaths of allegiance were offered. The custom was that one should swear by laying one hand on a sword which the king, seated on his throne, held resting in his lap. Woggerus, who has been already mentioned (it was he who gave Rolfo his nickname), came forward among the rest, declaring that he wished to offer his oath of allegiance with the others; he was the only one of the king's men to have survived the final battle. When, following the solemn ritual, he set his hand on the sword, he gripped the hilt and drove the outstretched blade into the breast of King Hiorvardus. Thus Hiorvardus was the only man who has ruled the Danish kingdom for barely six hours.

8. Saxo Grammaticus, *Danish History* (*c.* 1200), §§ 53–68.

Helgo was succeeded by his son Rolfo, who was comely with every gift of mind and body, and graced his mighty stature with as high a courage. In his time Sweden was subject to the sway of the Danes; wherefore Athislus, the son of Hothbroddus, in pursuit of a crafty design to set his country free, contrived to marry Rolfo's mother Ursa, thinking that his kinship by marriage would plead for him and enable him to prompt his stepson more effectually to relax the tribute; and fortune prospered his wishes. But Athislus had been from his boyhood imbued with a hatred of liberality, and was so grasping of money that he accounted it a disgrace to be called open-handed. Ursa, seeing him so steeped in filthy covetousness, desired to be rid of him; but, thinking she must act by cunning, veiled the shape of her guile with marvellous skill. Feigning to be unmotherly, she spurred on her husband to grasp his freedom, and urged and tempted him to insurrection; causing her son to be summoned to Sweden with a promise of vast gifts. For she thought that she would best gain her desire if, as soon as her son had got his stepfather's gold, she could snatch up the royal treasures and flee, robbing her husband of bed and money to boot. . . .

Accordingly, Rolfo, tempted by the greatness of the gifts, chanced to enter the house of Athislus. He was not recognized by his mother owing to his long absence and the cessation of their common life; so in jest he first asked for some victuals to appease his hunger. She advised him to ask the king for a luncheon. Then he thrust out a torn piece of his coat, and begged of her the service of sewing it up. Finding his mother's ears shut to him, he observed, 'That it was hard to discover a friendship that was firm and true, when a mother refused her son a meal, and a sister refused her brother the help of her needle.' Thus he punished his mother's error, and made her blush deep for her refusal of kindness.

Athislus, when he saw him reclining close to his mother at the banquet, taunted them both with wantonness, declaring that it was an impure intercourse of brother and sister. Rolfo repelled the charge against his mother by an appeal to the closest of natural bonds, and answered that it was honourable for a son to embrace a beloved mother. Also, when the feasters asked him what kind of courage he set above all others, he named Endurance. When they also asked Athislus what virtues above all he desired most devotedly, he declared, Generosity. Proofs were therefore demanded of bravery on the one hand and munificence on the other, and Rolfo was asked to give evidence of courage first. He was placed to the fire, and defending with his target the side that was most hotly assailed, had only the firmness of his endurance to fortify the other, which had no defence. How dexterous, to borrow from his shield protection to assuage the heat, and to guard his body, which was exposed to the flames, with that which sometime sheltered it amid the hurtling spears! But the glow was hotter than the fire of spears; and though it could not storm the side that was entrenched by the shield, yet it assaulted the flank that lacked its protection. But a waiting-maid who happened to be standing near the hearth saw that he was being roasted by the unbearable heat upon his ribs; so, taking the stopper out of a cask, she spilt the liquid and quenched the flame, and by the timely kindness of the shower checked in its career the torturing blaze. Rolfo was lauded for supreme endurance, and then came the request for Athislus' gifts. And they say that he showered treasures on his stepson, and at last, to crown the gift, bestowed on him an enormously heavy necklace.

Now Ursa, who had watched her chance for the deed of guile, on the third day of the banquet, without her husband ever dreaming of such a thing, put all the king's wealth into carriages, and going out stealthily, stole away from her own dwelling and fled in the glimmering twilight, departing with her son. Thrilled with fear of her husband's pursuit, and utterly despairing of escape beyond, she begged and bade her companions to cast away the money, declaring that they must lose either life or riches. . . . She added that it was not paying a great price to lay down the Swedes' own goods for them to regain; if only they could themselves gain a start in flight, by the very device which would check the others in their pursuit, and if they seemed not so much to abandon their own possessions as to restore those of other men. Not a moment was lost; in order to make the flight swifter, they did the bidding of the queen. The gold is cleared from their purses; the riches are left for the enemy to seize. Some declare that Ursa kept back the money, and strewed the tracks of her flight with copper that was gilt over. . . . So Athislus, when he saw the necklace that he had given to Rolfo left among the

165

other golden ornaments, gazed fixedly upon the dearest treasure of his avarice, and, in order to pick up the plunder, glued his knees to the earth and deigned to stoop his royalty unto greed. Rolfo, seeing him lie abjectly on his face in order to gather up the money, smiled at the sight of a man prostrated by his own gifts, just as if he were seeking covetously to regain what he had craftily yielded up. Two Swedes were content with their booty, and Rolfo quickly retired to his ships, and managed to escape by rowing violently.

Now they relate that Rolfo used with ready generosity to grant at the first entreaty whatsoever he was begged to bestow, and never put off the request to the second time of asking. For he preferred to forestall repeated supplication by speedy liberality, rather than mar his kindness by delay. This habit brought him a great concourse of champions; valour having commonly either rewards for its food or glory for its spur. . . .

[There follows the episode of Biarke and Agnar— see above, I A 5.]

When Rolfo was harried by Athislus he avenged himself on him in battle and overthrew Athislus in war. Then Rolfo gave his sister Sculda in marriage to a youth of keen wit, called Hiarthwarus, and made him governor of Sweden, ordaining a yearly tax; wishing to soften the loss of freedom to him by the favour of an alliance with himself.

Here let me put into my work a thing that is mirthful to record. A youth named Viggo, scanning with attentive eye the bodily size of Rolfo, and greatly smitten with wonder thereat, proceeded to inquire in jest who was that 'Krage' whom nature in her bounty had endowed with such towering stature?—meaning humorously to banter his uncommon tallness. For 'Krage' in the Danish tongue means a tree-trunk whose branches are pollarded, and whose summit is climbed in such wise that the foot uses the lopped timbers as supports, as if leaning on a ladder, and, gradually advancing to the higher parts, finds the shortest way to the top. Rolfo accepted this random word as if it were a name of honour for him, and rewarded the wit of the saying with a heavy bracelet. Then Viggo, thrusting out his right arm decked with the bracelet, put his left behind his back in affected shame, and walked with a ludicrous gait, declaring that he, whose lot had so long been poverty-stricken, was glad of a scanty gift. When he was asked why he was behaving so, he said that the arm which lacked ornament and had no splendour to boast of was mantling with the modest blush of poverty to behold the other. The ingenuity of this saying won him a present to match the first. For Rolfo made him bring out to view, like the other, the hand he was hiding. Nor was Viggo heedless to repay the kindness; for he promised, uttering a strict vow, that if it befell Rolfo to perish by the sword, he would himself take vengeance on the slayers. Nor should it be omitted that in old time nobles who were entering the court used to devote to their rulers the first-fruits of their service by vowing some mighty exploit; thus bravely inaugurating their first campaign.

Meantime Sculda was stung with humiliation at the paying of the tribute, and bent her mind to devise deeds of horror. Taunting her husband with his ignominious estate, she urged and egged him to break off his servitude, induced him to weave plots against Rolfo. . . . Accordingly she ordered huge piles of arms to be muffled up under diverse coverings and carried by Hiarthwarus into Denmark, as if they were tribute; these would furnish a store wherewith to slay the king by night. So the vessels were loaded with the mass of pretended tribute, and they proceeded to Leire, a town which Rolfo had built and adorned with the richest treasure of his realm, and which, being a royal foundation and a royal seat, surpassed in importance all the cities of the neighbouring districts. The king welcomed the coming of Hiarthwarus with a splendid banquet, and drank very deep, while his guests, contrary to their custom, shunned immoderate tippling. So while all the others were sleeping soundly, the Swedes, who had been kept from their ordinary rest by their eagerness for their guilty purpose, began furtively to slip down from their sleeping-rooms. Straightway uncovering the hidden heap of weapons, each girded on his arms silently and then went to the palace. Bursting into its recesses, they drew their swords upon the sleeping figures. Many awoke; but, invaded as much by the sudden and dreadful carnage as by the drowsiness of sleep, they faltered in their resistance; for the night misled them and made it doubtful whether those they met were friends or foes.

Hialto, who was foremost in tried bravery among the nobles of the king, chanced to have gone out in the dead of that same night into the country and given himself to the embraces of a harlot. But when his torpid hearing caught from afar the rising din of battle, preferring valour to wantonness, he chose rather to seek the deadly perils of the War-God than to yield to the soft allurements of Love. . . . As he went away, his mistress asked him how aged a man she ought to marry if she were to lose him? Then Hialto bade her come closer, as though he would speak with her more privately; and, resenting that she needed a successor to his love, he cut off her nose and made her unsightly, punishing the utterance of that question with a shameful wound, and thinking that the lecherousness of her soul ought to be cooled by the outrage to her face. When he had done this, he said he left her choice free in the matter she had asked about. Then he went quickly back into the town and plunged into the densest of the fray, mowing down the opposing ranks as he gave blow for blow. Passing the sleeping-room of Biarco, who was still slumbering, he bade him wake up, addressing him as follows:

'Let him awake speedily, whoso showeth himself by service or avoweth himself in mere loyalty, a friend of the king! Let the princes shake off slumber, let shameless lethargy be gone; let their spirits awake and warm to the work; each man's right hand shall either give him glory, or steep him in sluggard shame; and this night shall be either end or vengeance of our woes.

'I do not now bid ye learn the sports of maidens, nor stroke soft cheeks, nor give sweet kisses to the bride and chafe the soft thigh and cast eyes upon snowy arms. I call you out to the sterner fray of War. We need battle, not light love; nerveless languor has no business here, our need calls for battles. Whoso cherishes friendship for the king, let him take up arms. Prowess in war is the

readiest appraiser of men's spirits. Therefore let warriors
have no fearfulness and the brave no fickleness; let
pleasure quit their soul and yield place to arms. Glory
is now appointed for wages; each can be arbiter of his
own renown, and shine by his own right hand. Let
nought here be tricked out with wantonness; let all be full
of sternness, and learn how to rid them of this calamity.
He who covets the honours or prizes of glory must not
be faint with craven fear, but go forth to meet the brave,
nor whiten at the cold steel.'

At this utterance Biarco, awakened, roused up his
chamber-page Scalcus speedily, and addressed him as
follows:

'Up, lad, and fan the fire with constant blowing;
sweep the hearth clear of wood, and scatter the fine
ashes. Strike out sparks from the fire, rouse the fallen
embers, draw out the smothered blaze. Force the slack-
ening hearth to yield light by kindling the coals to a
red glow with a burning log. It will do me good to
stretch out my fingers when the fire is brought nigh.
Surely he that takes heed for his friend should have warm
hands, and utterly drive away blue and hurtful chill.'

Hialto said again: 'Sweet is it to repay the gifts re-
ceived from our lord, to grip swords, and devote the
steel to glory. Behold, each man's courage tells him
loyally to follow a king of such deserts, and to guard
our captain with fitting earnestness. Let the Teuton
swords, the helmets, the shining armlets, the mail-coats
that reach the heel, which Rolfo of old bestowed on his
men, let these sharpen our mindful hearts to the fray.
The time requires, and it is just, that in time of war we
should earn whatever we have gotten in the deep idle-
ness of peace, that we should not think more of joyous
courses than of sorrowful fortunes, nor always prefer
prosperity to hardship. Being noble, let us with even
soul accept either lot, nor let fortune sway our behaviour;
let us pass the years of sorrow with the same countenance
wherewith we took the years of joy.

'Let us do with brave hearts all the things that in our
cups we boasted of with sodden lips; let us keep the
vows which we swore by highest Jove and the mighty
gods. My master is the greatest of the Danes; let each

man, as he is valorous, stand by him; far, far hence be
all cowards! We need a brave and steadfast man, not
one who turns his back on a dangerous pass, or dreads
the grim preparation for battle. Often a general's greatest
valour depends on his soldiery, for the chief enters the
fray all the more at ease that a better array of nobles
throngs him round. Let the thane catch up his arms with
fighting fingers, setting his right hand on the hilt and
holding fast the shield; let him charge upon the foes,
nor pale at any strokes. Let none offer himself to be
smitten by the enemy behind, let none receive the swords
in his back; let the battling beast ever front the blow.
"Eagles fight brow foremost," and with swift gaping
beaks speed onwards in the front; be ye like that bird
in mien, shrinking from no stroke, but with body facing
the foe.

'See how the enemy, furious and confident overduly,
his limbs defended by the steel, and his face by a gilded
helmet, charges the thick of the battle-wedges, as though
sure of victory, fearless of rout and invincible by any
endeavour! Ah, misery! Swedish assurance spurns the
Danes. Behold, the Goths with savage eyes and grim
aspect advance with crested helms and clanging spears;
wreaking heavy slaughter in our blood, they wield their
swords and their battle-axes hone-sharpened.

'Why name thee, Hiarthwarus, whom Sculda hath
filled with guilty purpose, and hath suffered thus to
harden into sin? Why sing of thee, villain, who hast
caused our peril, betrayer of a noble king? Furious lust
of sway hath driven thee to attempt an abomination,
and, stung with frenzy, to screen thyself behind thy
wife's everlasting guilt. What error hath made thee to
hurt the Danes and thy lord, and hurled thee into such
foul crime as this? Whence entered thy heart the treason
framed with such careful guile?

'Why do I linger? Now we have swallowed our last
morsel. Our king perishes, and utter doom overtakes
our hapless city. Our last dawn has risen—unless per-
chance there be one here so soft that he fears to offer
himself to the blows, or so unwarlike that he dares not
avenge his lord, and disowns all honours worthy of his
valour.

'Thou, Rute, rise and put forth thy snow-white head, come forth from thy hiding into the battle. The carnage that is being done without calls thee. By now the council-chamber is shaken with warfare, and the gates creak with dreadful fray. Steel rends the mail-coats, the woven mesh is torn apart, and the midriff gives under the rain of spears. By now the huge axes have hacked small the shield of the king; by now the long swords clash, and the battle-axe clatters its blows upon the shoulders of men, and cleaves their breasts. Why are your hearts afraid? Why is your sword faint and blunted? The gate is cleared of our people and is filled with the press of the strangers.'

And when Hialto had wrought very great carnage and stained the battle with blood, he stumbled for the third time on Biarco's berth, and thinking he desired to keep quiet because he was afraid, made trial of him with such taunts at his cowardice as these:

'Biarco, why art thou absent? Doth deep sleep hold thee? I prithee, what makes thee tarry? Come out, or the fire will overcome thee. Ho! Choose the better way, charge with me! Bears may be kept off with fire; let us spread fire in the recesses, and let the blaze attack the door-posts first. Let the firebrand fall upon the bed-chamber, let the falling roof offer fuel for the flames and serve to feed the fire. It is right to scatter conflagration on the doomed gates.

'But let us who honour our king with better loyalty form the firm battle-wedges, and having measured the phalanx in close-knit rows, go forth in the way the king taught us—our king, who laid low Roricus, the son of Bokus the covetous [i.e. Hrærekr Ring-Hoarder] and wrapped the coward in death. . . .

[There follows the account of how Rolfo defeated Roricus—see below, II J 4.]

'Nothing was so fair to [Rolfo] that he would not lavish it, or so dear that he would not give it to his friends, for he used treasure like ashes, and measured his years by glory, not by gain. Whence it is plain that the king who hath died nobly had lived also most nobly,

that the hour of his doom is beautiful, and that he graced
the years of his life with manliness. For while he lived his
glowing valour prevailed over all things, and he was
allotted might worthy of his lofty stature. He was as swift
to war as a torrent raging down to the sea, and as speedy
to begin battle as a stag is to fly with cleft foot upon his
fleet way.

'See now, among the pools dripping with human
blood, the teeth struck out of the slain are carried on by
the full torrent of gore, and are polished on the rough
sands. Dashed on the slime they glitter, and the torrent
of blood bears along splinters of bone and flows above
lopped limbs. The blood of the Danes is wet, and the
gory flood stagnates far around, and the stream pressed
out of steaming veins rolls back the scattered bodies.

'Tirelessly against the Danes advances Hiartwarus,
lover of battle, and challenges the fighters with out-
stretched spear. Yet here, amid the dooms and dangers
of war, I see Frotho's grandson smiling joyously, who
once sowed the fields of Fyriswald with gold. Let us too
be exalted with an honourable show of joy, following
in death the doom of our noble father. Be we therefore
cheery in voice and bold in daring; for it is right to
spurn all fear with words of courage, and meet our
deaths in deeds of glory. Let fear quit heart and face;
in both let us avow our dauntless endeavours, that no
sign anywhere may show us to betray faltering fear. Let
our drawn sword measure the weight of our service.
Fame follows us in death, and glory shall outlive our
crumbling ashes! And that which perfect valour hath
achieved during its span shall not fade for ever and ever.
What want we with closed doors? Why doth the locked
bolt close the folding-gates? For it is now the third
cry, Biarco, that calls thee and bids thee come forth
from the barred room.'

Biarco rejoined: 'Warlike Hialto, why dost thou call
me so loud? I am the son-in-law of Rolfo. He who
boasts loud and with big words challenges other men to
battle, is bound to be venturous and live up to his words,
that his deed may avouch his vaunt. But stay till I am
armed and have girded on the dire attire of war.

'And now I tie my sword to my side, now I first get

my body guarded with mail-coat and headpiece, the helm keeping my brow and the stout iron shrouding my breast. None shrinks more than I from being burnt a prisoner inside, and made a pyre together with my own house; though an island brought me forth and though the land of my birth be bounded, I shall hold it a debt to repay to the king the twelve hundreds which he added to my honours.

'Hearken, warriors! Let none robe in mail his body that shall perish, let him last of all draw tight the woven steel; let the shields go behind the back; let us fight with bared breasts, and load all your arms with gold. Let your right hands receive the bracelets, that they may swing the blows more heavily and plant the grievous wound. Let none fall back! Let each zealously strive to meet the swords of the enemy and the threatening spears, that we may avenge our beloved master. Happy beyond all things is he who can mete out revenge for such a crime, and with righteous steel punish the guilt of treacheries.

'Lo, methinks I surely pierced a wild stag with the Teutonic sword which is called Snyrtir; from which I won the name of Warrior when I felled Agnarus, son of Ingellus [see above, I A 5] and brought the trophy home. He shattered and broke with the bite the sword Hoding which smote upon my head, and would have dealt out worse wounds if the edge of his blade had held out better. In return I clove asunder his left arm and part of his left side and his right foot, and the piercing steel ran down his limbs and smote deep into his ribs. By Hercules, no man ever seemed to me stronger than he! For he sank down half-conscious, and, leaning on his elbow, welcomed death with a smile and spurned destruction with a laugh, and passed rejoicing into the world of Elysium. Mighty was the man's courage, which knew how with one laugh to cover his death hour, and with a joyous face to suppress utter anguish of mind and body!

'Now also with the same blade I searched the heart of one sprung from an illustrious line, and plunged the steel deep in his breast. He was a king's son, of illustrious ancestry, of noble nature, and shone with the brightness of youth. The mailed metal could not avail him, nor his sword, nor the smooth target-boss; so keen was the force of my steel, it knew not how to be stayed by obstacles.

'Where then are the captains of the Goths, and the soldiery of Hiartwarus? Let them come, and pay for their might with their life blood. Who can cast, who can whirl the lance save scions of kings? War springs from the nobly born; famous pedigrees are the makers of war. For the perilous deeds which chiefs attempt are not to be done by the ventures of common men. Lo, greatest Rolfo, thy great ones have fallen, thy holy line is vanishing! No dim and lowly race, no low-born dead, no base souls are Pluto's prey, but he weaves the dooms of the mighty, and fills Phlegethon with noble shapes.

'I do not remember any combat wherein swords were crossed in turn and blow dealt for blow more speedily. I take three for each I give; thus do the Goths requite the wounds I deal them, and thus does the stronger hand of the enemy avenge with heaped interest the punishment that they receive. Yet singly in battle have I given over the bodies of so many men to the pyre of destruction, that a mound like a hill could grow up and be raised out of their lopped limbs, and the piles of carcases would look like a burial barrow. And now what doth he who but now bade me come forth, vaunting himself with mighty praise, and chafing others with his arrogant words, and scattering harsh taunts, as though in his one body he enclosed twelve lives?'

Hialto answered: 'Though I have but scant help, I am not far off. Even here, where we stand, there is need of aid, and nowhere is a force or a chosen band of warriors ready for battle more wanted. Already the hard edges and the spear-points have cleft my shield in splinters, and the ravening steel has rent and devoured its portions bit by bit in the battle. The first of these things testifies to and avows itself. Seeing is better than telling, eyesight faithfuller than hearing. For of the broken shield only the fastenings remain, and the boss, pierced and broken in its circle, is all that is left me. And now, Biarco, thou art strong, though thou hast come forth more tardily than was right, and thou retrievest by bravery the loss caused by thy loitering.'

But Biarco said: 'Art thou not yet weary of girding at me and goading me with taunts? Many things often cause delay. The reason why I tarried was the sword in my path, which the Swedish foe whirled against my breast with mighty effort. Nor did the guider of the hilt drive home the sword with little might; for though the body was armed he smote it as far as one might when it is bare and defenceless; he pierced the armour of hard steel like yielding waters, nor could the rough, heavy breastplate give me any help.

'But where now is he that is commonly called Odin, the mighty in battle, ever content with a single eye? If thou see him anywhere, Rute, tell me.'

Rute replied: 'Bring thine eye closer and look under my arm akimbo; thou must first hallow thine eyes with the victorious sign if thou wilt safely know the War-God face to face.'

Then said Biarco: 'If I may look on the awful husband of Frigg, howsoever he be covered with his white shield, and guide his tall steed, he shall in no wise go safe out of Leire; it is lawful to lay low in war the war-waging god.

'Let a noble death come to those that fall before the eyes of their king. While life lasts, let us strive for the power to die honourably and to reap a noble end by our deeds. I will die overpowered near the head of my slain captain, and at his feet thou also shalt slip on thy face in death, so that whoso scans the piled corpses may see in what wise we rate the gold our lord gave us. We shall be the prey of ravens and a morsel for hungry eagles, and the ravening bird shall feast on the banquet of our body. Thus should fall princes dauntless in war, clasping their famous king in a common death.'

I have composed this particular series of harangues in metrical shape, because the gist of the same thoughts is found arranged in short form in a certain ancient Danish song, which is repeated by heart by many conversant with antiquity.

Now, it came to pass that the Goths gained the victory and all the array of Rolfo fell, no man save Viggo remaining out of all those warriors. For the soldiers of the king paid this homage to his noble virtues in that battle, that his slaying inspired in all the longing to meet their end, and union with him in death was accounted sweeter than life.

Hiartwarus rejoiced, and had the tables spread for feasting, bidding the banquet come after the battle, and fain to honour his triumph with a carouse. And when he was well filled therewith, he said it was a matter of great marvel to him that out of all the army of Rolfo no man had been found to take thought for his life by flight or fraud. Hence, he said, it had been manifest with what jealous loyalty they had kept their love for the king, because they had not endured to survive him. He also blamed his ill fortune, because it had not suffered the homage of a single one of them to be left for himself; protesting that he would very willingly accept the service of such men. Then Viggo came forth, and Hiartwarus, as though he were congratulating him on the gift, asked him if he were willing to fight for him. Viggo assenting, he drew and proffered him a sword. But Viggo refused the point and asked for the hilt, saying first that this had been Rolfo's custom when he handed forth a sword to his soldiers. For in old time those who were about to put themselves in dependence on the king used to promise fealty by touching the hilt of the sword. And in this wise Viggo clasped the hilt, and then drove the point through Hiartwarus; thus gaining the vengeance which he had promised Rolfo to accomplish for him. When he had done this, the soldiers of Hiartwarus rushed at him, and he exposed his body to them eagerly and exultantly, shouting that he felt more joy in the slaughter of the tyrant than bitterness at his own. Thus the feast was turned to a funeral, and the wailing of burial followed the joy of victory. . . . Thus the royalty of Hiartwarus was begun and ended on the same day.

9. *Annales Ryenses* (c. 1290).

. . . Rolf Kraki, the son of Helgi. After many very famous victories, he was treacherously slain in his bed at Leire, the royal seat in Zealand, by Earl Hiartwarus of Scania, who had had his sister as wife; with him too were slain those most famous champions Biarki and Hialti, together with the king's whole household. Hyarwarus succeeded him. Hyarwarus reigned only a short while, indeed only from morning till the hour of prime. Haki son of Hamund killed him, and was made King of Denmark.

10. Snorri Sturluson, *Edda* (*c.* 1220), *Skáldskaparmál* chs. 53–4.

Why is gold called 'Kraki's Seed'?

There was a king in Denmark named Hrólfr Kraki; he was the most glorious among ancient kings, the first among them for generosity, valour and simplicity. There is one proof of his simplicity which is much mentioned in the stories, about a little lad, a poor one who was named Vǫggr. This lad came into King Hrólfr's hall; the king was young at the time, and thinly built. Vǫggr stood before him and looked up at him.

Then the king said: 'What do you want to say, lad, that you stand there looking at me?'

Vǫggr said: 'When I was at home I heard people say that King Hrólfr at Leira was the greatest man in the Northlands, and now here's a little pole sitting here in the highseat, and you all call him king!'

Then the king answered: 'You've given me a name, lad, so now I will be called Hrólfr Kraki [i.e. 'pole']. But it is the custom to give a gift to go with the name-giving. Now I can see that you have no gift ready to give me with this name—none, at least, that I could accept. It's for those who have to give to those who have not,'—and he took a gold ring from his hand, and gave it to him.

'Good luck to you above all kings for this gift!' said Vǫggr. 'And this oath I swear, that I will be the slayer of the man who slays you.'

Then the king said, laughing; 'It takes little to make Vǫggr happy.'

Another proof concerning Hrólfr Kraki's valour is what is told about the king ruling at Uppsala, whose name was Aðils and who had married Yrsa, the mother of Hrólfr Kraki. He was at war with a king who ruled over Norway, whose name was Áli. They arranged to meet and do battle on the ice of the lake which is called Vænir. King Aðils sent a message to his stepson Hrólfr Kraki that he should come with his forces to aid him, and promised rewards for all his host while they were

177

on this campaign, and that King Hrólfr could have for
himself any three treasures in Sweden which he chose.
King Hrólfr could not go, because of a war he was
waging against the Germans, but he sent his twelve
berserks to Aðils; one was Bǫðvarr Bjarki, then Hjalti
the Noble-Hearted, Hvítserkr the Bold, Vǫttr, Veseti,
the brothers Svipdagr and Beiguðr. In this battle fell
King Áli and a great part of his men. King Aðils took
from him, when he was dead, the helmet Hildisvín and
his horse Hrafn. Then Hrólfr's berserks asked to take
their reward, three pounds of gold for each of them,
and furthermore they asked that they might take away
for King Hrólfr the treasures they would choose on his
behalf; these were the helmet Hildigǫltr and the corselet
Finnsleif, on which no steel would bite, and the gold
ring which was called Svíagríss, which Aðils' fore-
fathers had owned. But the king refused all these treas-
ures, nor would he pay the rewards. So the berserks
went away and were ill-pleased with their lot, and told
Hrólfr Kraki how things had turned out.

Very soon he set out upon his journey to Uppsala,
and when he had brought his ships into the Fýri River
he rode towards Uppsala, and with him were his twelve
berserks, none of whom had been granted safe-conduct.
His mother Yrsa welcomed him and found him quarters,
not in the king's hall. Then fires were kindled before
them, and they were given ale to drink. Then King
Aðils' men came in and piled wood on the fires and
built them up so huge that the clothes of Hrólfr and
his men were burning, and Aðils' men said: 'Is it true
that Hrólfr Kraki and his berserks never flee either
from fire or from steel?'

Then Hrólfr Kraki and all the rest leapt up, and he
said:

'Let us stoke up the fires
In the stronghold of Aðils!'

and took up his shield and threw it on to the fire and
leapt across the fire while the shield was burning, and
spoke once again:

'He does not flee the fire,
He who leaps across it.'

178

His men all did the same, one after the other, and they also seized those who had stoked up the fire and threw them into the fire.

Then Yrsa came, and she handed Hrólfr Kraki a cow's horn full of gold, and the ring Svíagríss with it, and bade them ride back to their host. They ran to their horses and rode down to the plains of Fýrisvellir, and then they saw that King Aðils was riding after them with his host fully armed, wishing to slay them. Then with his right hand Hrólfr Kraki took gold from the horn and sowed it all along the path. But when the Swedes saw that, they leapt from their saddles and each man took what he could get, though King Aðils bade them ride on, and himself rode ahead at full speed. His steed was called Sløngvir, the swiftest of all steeds. Hrólfr Kraki saw that King Aðils was riding nearer to him, so then he took the ring Svíagríss and threw it at him, bidding him take it as a gift. King Aðils rode up to the ring and took it up on the point of his spear, and it slipped up on to the socket. Then Hrólfr Kraki turned back and saw how he was stooping low, and so he said: 'Now I have made the mightiest of the Swedes stoop like a pig!' And so they parted.

For this reason gold is called 'Kraki's Seed', or 'the Seed of Fýrisvellir'.

11. *Hrólfs saga kraka* (*c.* 1400) chs. 22–3, 38–52.

King Hrólfr now sent men to Sweden to see his mother Queen Yrsa, and he asked her to send him the wealth which his father King Helgi had owned and which King Aðils had taken for himself when King Helgi was slain. Yrsa said it would be very fitting for her to further this plan, if only it were possible for her to do so—'and if you should come to fetch this wealth yourself I will give you good counsel, my son. But King Aðils is so greedy for money that he does not care what he does to get it.' And she bade them tell this to King Hrólfr, and at the same time she sent him noble gifts.

King Hrólfr now set out upon raiding voyages, and because of this he delayed before going to seek a meeting with King Aðils. Meanwhile he gathered great power into his hands, and he forced all the kings whom he encountered to pay him tribute; and what did most to bring this about was that all the greatest champions wished to be with him and serve no other man, because he was far more generous with his wealth than any other king. King Hrólfr set up his chief seat at the place called Hleiðargarðr [Leire]; it is in Denmark, and is a large stronghold and a strong one, and there was more splendour and courtly pomp there than anywhere else, and more of all which contributes to magnificence than anyone can have heard tell of.

There was a powerful king named Hjǫrvarðr, and he married Skuld, the daughter of King Helgi and half-sister of King Hrólfr; this was done with the consent of King Aðils and Queen Yrsa and her half-brother Hrólfr. And on one occasion King Hrólfr invited his brother-in-law Hjǫrvarðr to a feast. One day while he was there for this feast it so happened that the two kings were standing out of doors, and that King Hrólfr unbuckled his belt and handed his sword to King Hjǫrvarðr while he did so. And when King Hrólfr had buckled the belt round him once more, he took the sword back, and said to King Hjǫrvarðr: 'We both know', said he, 'that it has long been a saying that whoever holds another man's sword while he is unbuckling his belt shall be this man's underling ever afterwards. So now you shall be a tributary king under me, and bear it willingly, like the rest.'

Hjǫrvarðr was extremely angry over this, yet he had to let it remain at that. He went home leaving matters thus, and was dissatisfied with his lot; nevertheless he did send tribute to King Hrólfr in the same way as his other tributary kings who owed obedience to him. . . .

Now it is told how one day King Hrólfr sat in his kingly hall with all his champions and mighty warriors with him, and held a costly feast. Now King Hrólfr looked to left and right of him, and said: 'A mighty and overwhelming force is gathered together here within one hall!' Then King Hrólfr asked Bǫðvarr whether he knew of any king equal to himself, or ruling over champions equal to these.

Bǫðvarr said he knew of none such—'but there is one thing which I think sets limits to your kingly glory'. King Hrólfr asked what this was.

Bǫðvarr said: 'What is lacking, sire, is that you have not laid claim to the heritage your father left for you in Uppsala, which your stepfather King Aðils wrongfully keeps for himself.'

King Hrólfr said it would be a hard task to seek for that—'for Aðils is no simple man, but rather one who is wise in magic lore, crafty, cunning, cruel-hearted, and the worst of men to have dealings with'.

'Yet, sire,' said Bǫðvarr, 'it would be fitting for you to seek your own property, and to go to see King Aðils some time and find out what answer he makes to this claim.'

King Hrólfr said: 'This matter you have stirred up is very weighty, for it is also our duty to seek vengeance for my father's death. King Aðils is very covetous and full of crafty tricks, but we must take the risk.'

Bǫðvarr said: 'I won't object to it if one day we find out what one must face in facing King Aðils.'

King Hrólfr now made ready for his journey with a hundred men, and also his twelve champions and his twelve berserks. There is nothing to tell about their journey until they came to the house of a certain farmer. He was standing outside as they came up, and he invited them all to stay there.

'You're a brave fellow,' said the king, 'but have you means enough to do this? We are not such a small company as all that, and it's not for a petty farmer to take us all into his house.'

The man laughed and said: 'Yes, sire,' said he, 'I've sometimes seen men coming where I might be, no fewer than these. You shall not lack drink or anything else all night long, whatever you may need.'

'Then we will take the risk,' said the king.

The farmer was pleased at this, and now their horses were taken in, and they were offered hospitality.

'What is your name, farmer?' said the king.

'Some men call me Hrani,' said he.

The hospitality there was so good that they could hardly believe that they had ever come to a more hospitable place, and the farmer was very cheerful, and there was nothing they could ask him which he could not explain, and they thought him a man of great wisdom. They now settled down to sleep. And when they awoke they were so frozen that their teeth were chattering in their heads, and they all huddled up together and piled clothes and everything they could find on top of them— all except King Hrólfr's champions, who contented themselves with the clothes they had on already. They were all frozen all night long.

Then the farmer asked: 'How did you sleep?'

Böðvarr answered: 'Very well,' said he.

Then the farmer said to the king: 'I know that some of your retainers think it was a little cool in this hall last night, and so it was; as they found this so hard to bear, they certainly can't expect to be able to stand the hardships with which King Aðils at Uppsala will test you. Send home half your troop, sire, if you wish to keep your life, for it is not by a great host of men that you will win victory over King Aðils.'

'You are a fine man, farmer,' said the king, 'and I shall take the advice you give me.'

They now went on their way as soon as they were ready, bidding the farmer farewell, and the king sent home one half of his troop. So now they rode on their way, and all at once there appeared another farm in front of them, a small one. They thought they recognized the same farmer here as they had lodged with before, and it seemed to them that things had taken a very strange turn. Once again the farmer welcomed them warmly, and asked why they came so often.

The king said: 'We scarcely know what tricks are being played on us, and you can be called a really tricky fellow.'

'This time too', said the farmer, 'I shan't give you a poor welcome.'

They stayed a second night there amid fine hospitality, and settled down to sleep, and awoke because so great a thirst had come on them that they thought it nearly unbearable, so great that they could hardly move their tongues in their heads. They got up, and went over to where a great cask of wine was standing, and drank from it.

In the morning farmer Hrani said: 'Once again, sire, it happens that you must pay heed to me, for I think that the men who were forced to drink during the night have little power of endurance in them. You will have greater tests than that to endure when you come to King Aðils.'

Then a great storm broke, and they sat indoors there all day, and the third night came. Towards evening a fire was lit in front of them, and those who were sitting near the fire thought it very hot to the hand; most of them ran from the seats which Hrani had assigned to them, and they all rushed away from the fire—all except King Hrólfr and his champions.

'Sire,' said the farmer, 'you can again take your pick from your troop, and it is my advice that none should go any farther except yourself and your twelve champions; in that case there is some hope that you may come back, but otherwise none.'

'I think so well of you, farmer Hrani,' said the king, 'that we will take your advice.'

They stayed three nights there. Then the king rode from there with twelve men, but sent home all the rest of his troop.

King Aðils got news of this, and declared it a good thing that King Hrólfr should wish to visit him—'for he shall certainly find business to do here, such business that it will seem well worth talking of, before we part'.

After this King Hrólfr and his champions rode up to King Aðils' hall, and all the folk of the fortress ran up into its highest tower to see the pomp of King Hrólfr and his champions, for they were sumptuously decked out, and many people thought very highly of such courtly-looking knights. At first they rode slowly and in stately fashion, but when they were only a little way from the hall they set spurs to their steeds and galloped them right into the hall, so that everybody in their path fled from them. King Aðils had them welcomed with great good cheer, and bade them let their horses be taken from them.

'Take good care, lads,' said Bǫðvarr, 'that not one hair of the forelock or tail of these horses is out of

place, and look after them well, and keep careful watch
that they don't foul themselves.'

King Aðils was told at once what detailed orders they
had given about the care of their horses, and he said:
'Their pride and arrogance is quite extraordinary! Now
listen to my plan and do as I tell you—chop off their
tail-stumps right up against the rump, and cut off their
forelocks so that the hide of the forehead comes away
too, and ill-treat them in every way as shamefully as you
can, and leave them so that they are only just alive.'

Meanwhile Hrólfr and his champions were led to the
doors of the hall, but King Aðils kept out of sight.

Then Svipdagr said: 'I have known this place before
now, and I'll be the first to go in, for I am most suspici-
ous of how we may be welcomed and what preparations
have been made for us. Let's not say a word as to which
of us is King Hrólfr, so that King Aðils should not
recognize him among our band.'

So then Svipdagr walked ahead of them all, and after
him came his brothers Hvítserkr and Beigaðr, and then
King Hrólfr and Bǫðvarr, and the rest one after the
other. There were no servants to be reckoned with, for
those who had shown them into the hall had disappeared.
They had their hawks on their shoulders, for in those
days that was thought high pomp; King Hrólfr had a
hawk which was called Hábrók [High-Breeks]. Now
Svipdagr walked forward, keeping a careful watch in all
directions; he saw great changes everywhere. They
passed over so many traps laid in their path that it
would be no easy task to describe them, and the farther
they went into the hall the more difficult it was for
them.

And now they came so far along the hall that they
reached a spot from which they saw where King Aðils
sat in his highseat, all puffed up with pride, and both
thought it no small thing that they should set eyes on
one another. All the same, they saw that it would still
be no easy matter to stand right in front of King Aðils,
though they had now come near enough to one another
to be able to hear one another's words.

It was King Aðils who then spoke first: 'So you've
got here by now, friend Svipdagr? And what errand can

bring such a champion here? And is he really like he
looks to me—

> A split in the nape of his neck,
> One eye gone from his head,
> An arrow-head stuck in his brow,
> Two gashes cut on his hands.

And his brother Beigaðr is just the same, all twisted
up!'

Svipdagr spoke so loudly that all could hear: 'I want
to have a promise of peace from you now, King Aðils,
according to what you and I settled once—peace for
these twelve men who have come here with me.'

King Aðils answered: 'I am willing to grant that. So
walk right into the hall, quickly and boldly and with
fearless hearts.'

They thought they could see that pitfalls had been
dug in the hall-floor ahead of them, and that it would
not be safe to make trial of these things that had been
prepared for them; and there was so deep a gloom
hanging over King Aðils that they could not clearly see
his face. They also saw that the hangings, which were all
round the inside of the hall to add to its pomp, were
torn away from the wall, and that there must be armed
men under them. And it was only too true, for men in
armour came rushing from every corner as soon as they
had got across the pits, and King Hrólfr and his men
fought very fiercely and clove these men's skulls down
to the teeth. This went on for some while, and still
King Hrólfr did not reveal which one of them was he, and
the enemy host were falling in swathes.

King Aðils in his highseat was swelling with fury as
he saw how Hrólfr's champions were slaughtering his
men like the dogs they were, and he could see that this
game would not do, so he stood up and said: 'What's the
meaning of all this great turmoil? These men of mine
are miserable scoundrels—why do you start playing
tricks and pretending to attack such notable men as
these who have come to visit us? Stop it at once and sit
down! Let us all enjoy our good cheer together, stepson
Hrólfr.'

Svipdagr said: 'You have hardly kept your promise

of peace, King Aðils, and you have acted dishonourably over this.'

After this they sat down, with Svipdagr in the best place, then Hjalti the Noble-Hearted, and then Bǫðvarr and the king together, for they did not wish him to be known.

King Aðils said: 'I see that you do not travel as befits your rank when in a foreign land. Why has my stepson Hrólfr no larger band than this?'

'And I see', said Svipdagr, 'that you spare no pains to lay treacherous plots against King Hrólfr and his men; and there is no great cause for wonderment, whether he rides here with few men or many.'

And this was the end of their talk. After this King Aðils had the hall cleaned up; the dead were carried away, for many of King Aðils' men had been slain, and great numbers wounded.

King Aðils said: 'Let us now light fires down the length of the hall for these friends of ours, and show our sincere love for such men as these, so that we should all enjoy ourselves.'

Now some men were fetched to light the fire in front of them. Hrólfr's champions always sat with their weapons about them, and would never let them out of their hands. The fire caught quickly, as they were not sparing with pitch or dry sticks. King Aðils chose seats on one side of the fire for himself and his retainers, and on the other side for King Hrólfr and his champions, and each band sat on its own long-bench and talked together in most friendly fashion.

King Aðils said: 'There's no exaggeration in what is said of the valour and hardihood of you champions of Hrólfr; you do indeed think yourselves above everyone else, and the tales told about your strength are no lie. Now build the fires up,' said King Aðils, 'for I cannot see clearly which is the king. You will not flee from the fire, though you may get a little too hot.'

So this was now done as he ordered. He wanted in this way to find out for sure where King Hrólfr was, for he felt sure that he would not be able to stand the heat so well as his champions, and he thought that it would then be easier for him to catch him when he knew which

he was, for he truly did wish to bring Hrólfr to his doom.
Bǫðvarr realized this, and so did most of the others, and
they sheltered him from the heat as best they could, yet
not in such a way that he would be the more easily
recognized. And while the fire blazed most fiercely at
them, King Hrólfr set his mind on remembering within
himself what he once had sworn, never to flee either
from fire or from steel; and thereupon he saw that King
Aðils wanted to put this to the test, so that they would
either burn there or else fail to keep his oath. They also
saw that King Aðils' throne had moved right back
through the wall of the hall, and so had the seats of his
men. The fuel was now burning fast, and they saw that
they would be on fire themselves unless something was
done about it. By now much of their clothing was on
fire, and they had thrown their shields on to the blaze.

Then Bǫðvarr and Svipdagr cried:

> 'Let us stoke up the fires
> In the stronghold of Aðils!'

Then each of them caught hold of a man among those
who had kept the fires going, and flung them on to the
fires, and said: 'Now you can enjoy the warmth of the
fire in return for your toil and trouble, since we are now
perfectly baked. You can bake yourselves now, as you
both worked so hard to keep the fire going for us for a
while!'

Hjalti caught hold of another and flung him on to the
fire at his end of it, and it went the same way with each
of these who were stoking the fires. They burned to
ashes there, and there was no rescue for them, because
nobody dared come close enough.

After that had been done, King Hrólfr began to speak:

> 'He does not flee the fire,
> He who leaps across it.'

And after this they all vaulted over the fire, meaning
to set upon King Aðils and take him prisoner. And when
King Aðils saw this, he fled for his life and ran to a
wooden post which stood in the hall and was hollow
inside, and so he got out of the hall by means of his
magic crafts and spells.

Thus he got into Queen Yrsa's chamber and tried to talk to her, but she greeted him with contempt and spoke many harsh words to him: 'First you had my husband King Helgi killed', said she, 'and behaved vilely towards him, and withheld wealth from him who owned it. And now, over and above that, you want to kill my son, and you are a more wicked and cruel man than all the rest. Now I will do all I can to see that King Hrólfr gets this wealth, and you will have only dishonour for your share, as is right and fitting.'

'The way things are going here,' said King Aðils, 'neither he nor I shall ever trust the other again. From now on I'll never let them set eyes on me.'

After that they ended their talk. Queen Yrsa then went to find Hrólfr and gave him a most glad welcome, and he returned her greeting warmly. She sent a man to serve them and give them good hospitality, and when this man came before King Hrólfr, he said: 'This man is thin-faced, with a face like a pole. Is this your king?'

King Hrólfr said: 'You have given me a name which will stick to me [Kraki, 'pole'], and what gift will you give me to go with it?'

'I have nothing at all to give,' said Vǫggr, 'for I am penniless.'

'It's for those who have to give to those who have not,' said the king, and he drew a gold ring from his hand and gave it to this man.

'All good luck to you for this gift!' said Vǫggr. 'It is the finest of treasures!'

And when the king saw that he thought so much of it, he said: 'It takes little to make Vǫggr happy.'

Vǫggr spoke, as he set one foot on the block: 'This oath I swear, that if I live longer than you, and if you are defeated by men, then I shall avenge you.'

The king answered and said: 'You do rightly, even though there may be others no less likely than you to do that.'

They realized that this man would be loyal and true in doing the little he could, but they thought he would only be able to achieve little, because the man was a worthless fellow. They hid nothing from him now. After this they decided to sleep, feeling sure that they could lie without fear in the quarters the queen had found for them.

Bǫðvarr said: 'All is prepared well for us here, and the queen wishes us well, but King Aðils wishes us all the evil he can. I shall think it strange if we are forced to put up with things as they are.'

Vǫggr told them that King Aðils was an ardent worshipper of heathen gods, 'so much so that there's nothing like it to be found. He makes blood-offerings to a boar. I don't believe there is any other foe to match him, so be on your guard, for he has set his whole mind on destroying you in one way or another'.

'It's even more likely, so I think,' said Bǫðvarr, 'that he will bear a grudge against us for the way he fled from the hall before us this evening.'

'You must also reckon on this,' said Vǫggr, 'that he will prove sly and cruel.'

After that they slept, and awoke because there was so great an uproar to be heard outside that everything echoed, and the building they were lying in seemed to shake as if it were swaying to and fro.

Vǫggr was the first to speak: 'Now the boar must be out and about, and it must have been sent by King Aðils to wreak vengeance on you, and it is so great a troll that no one can stand up against it.'

King Hrólfr had a huge hound which was called Gramr, and he was with them; he was quite outstanding for strength and valour. The next thing was that in came the troll in the likeness of a boar, and horrible was the behaviour of so evil a troll. Bǫðvarr set the hound on the boar, and he did not let himself be dismayed but rushed against the boar, and a very hard struggle began. Bǫðvarr went to the help of the hound and struck at the boar, but the sword never bit on his back. The hound Gramr was so fierce that he tore off the boar's ears and all the flesh of the cheeks as well, and then two things happened at once, for the boar plunged down again to where he had come from, and then King Aðils came up to the building with a great host and at once set fire to it. And at this King Hrólfr and his men became aware that, once again, there would be no lack of fuel.

Bǫðvarr said: 'It would be a wretched death-day if

189

we had to burn to death in here, and a wretched end to King Hrólfr's life if that were to come to pass. I would rather choose to fall by weapons in an open field. I can see no better plan for us now than to batter the wooden wall so hard that it gives way, and so break our way out of the house, if that can be done'—and indeed it was no child's play, for the house was sturdily built—'and then when we get outside let each tackle the man in front of him, and then they will soon give way again.'

'That is an excellent plan,' said King Hrólfr, 'and it will serve very well for us.'

So now they followed this plan and flung themselves against the wooden wall so hard and so wildly that it all broke apart, and so they got outside. The street of the stronghold was packed tight with men in armour. Then there began a very hard battle against them, and King Hrólfr and his champions fought their way forward grimly. The host facing them soon proved very feeble; they never met a single man so proud or haughty that their mighty blows would not make him crawl on his knees.

And in the middle of this hard battle, King Hrólfr's hawk came flying out of the fortress and perched on the king's shoulder, acting as if he had some great victory to boast of.

'He acts as if he won himself fame,' said Bǫðvarr.

The man who was in charge of the hawks hurried to the loft in which they were kept, thinking it strange that King Hrólfr's hawk should have got away, and he found all King Aðils' hawks dead.

The battle ended in their killing great numbers of men, and no one could stand against them at all; but King Aðils had disappeared by then, and none of them could tell for sure what had become of him. Those of King Aðils' men who could still stand begged for quarter, which they granted them.

After that they went back to the hall, and boldly walked in. Bǫðvarr asked on which bench King Hrólfr wished to sit, and King Hrólfr answered: 'We will all seat ourselves on the king's own dais, and I myself will sit on the highseat.'

King Aðils did not come into the hall, and he thought

he had had bitter things to bear and had been greatly put to shame, in spite of all the tricks he had played. So now they sat there for a while in peace and quiet.

Then said Hjalti the Noble-Hearted: 'Wouldn't it be a good plan if someone went to see our horses and find out whether they are not short of anything they need?'

And so now this was done, but as soon as the man came back he said that the horses had been shamefully ill-treated and quite ruined, and he told them in what way they had been treated, as has been told already. King Hrólfr did not give away his feelings over this, except that he said that King Aðils was quite consistent in everything he did.

Now Queen Yrsa came into the hall and went up to King Hrólfr and greeted him in eloquent and stately words, and he answered her greetings warmly. She said: 'You have not been as well received here, kinsman, as I would have wished or as would be right; nor ought you to remain here any longer, my son, amid such evil welcome, for there is a great mustering of men throughout all Sweden, and King Aðils means to slay you all, as he has long wished to do if only he were able to—though at present your good luck has more strength in it than his trollish powers. Now here is a silver horn which I will give you, and in it are kept all King Aðils' finest rings, and among them the one called Svíagríss, which he thinks finer than all the rest.'

And together with these she also gave him much gold and silver in other forms; all this wealth together was so great one man that would scarcely be able to reckon up its value. Vǫggr was close at hand, and received much gold from King Hrólfr for his loyal service.

The queen had twelve horses led out, all reddish in hue except one which was as white as snow, which King Hrólfr was to ride. Of all King Aðils' horses, it was these that had proved the finest, and all were fully caparisoned. She got them shields and helms and coats of mail and other good clothes, the best to be had, because the fire had spoilt their clothes and weapons; and she got them everything which they needed, and all of the noblest and most costly.

191

King Hrólfr said: 'Have you given me as much wealth as is mine by right and as my father had?'

'This is greater by far', said she, 'than what you could rightly have claimed, and you and your men have won yourselves great fame here. Now equip yourselves as well as you can, so that no one can assail you, for you will once again be put to the test.'

After that they mounted their steeds. King Hrólfr spoke lovingly to his mother, and they parted on friendly terms. So now King Hrólfr and his champions rode on their way from Uppsala, and across the plain which is called Fýrisvellir, and there King Hrólfr saw a great gold ring gleaming in front of them on the path, and it rattled as they rode over it.

'The reason it cries so loud', said King Hrólfr, 'is that it does not like being alone,' and he let a gold ring slip from his own hand to join the other on the path, and said: 'It shall be told that I do not pick up gold though it lies in my path; and let no man of mine be so bold as to pick it up! It was thrown down there so that it might delay our journey.'

They promised this, and at that very moment they heard trumpet calls from every side, and they saw an innumerable host riding after them. This host was rushing onwards so wildly that every man in it was galloping as fast as his horse could go. King Hrólfr and the others rode straight on, just as before.

'These men are pursuing us hotly,' said Bǫðvarr, 'and I would certainly like them to have some return for their trouble, since they clearly want to find us.'

'Let us not take much notice of them,' said the king. 'They themselves will be delayed.'

He stretched out his hand for the horn in which the gold was, which Beigaðr was holding in his hand as he rode. Now he sowed the gold far and wide along the path as they rode right across Fýrisvellir, so that the path gleamed like gold. But when the host which was riding after them saw how there was gold gleaming far and wide along the path, most of them jumped down from their horses, and whoever was quickest to pick it up thought that he had the best of the game. There was much robbing and brawling there, and whoever was strongest got the most, and because of this they were slow to take up the pursuit.

And when King Aðils saw this he very nearly went out of his mind, and he abused them with bitter words, saying that they were picking up petty prizes but letting the greatest prize slip away, and that the tale of this foul shame would be told in every land—'that you should let a mere twelve men get away from us, when I have gathered such a countless host from every region in the Swedish realm!' So now King Aðils galloped off ahead of them all, for he was as angry as might be, and a crowd of men followed him.

Now when King Hrólfr saw King Aðils come dashing up close behind him, he took the ring Svíagríss and threw it down on the path. And when King Aðils saw the ring, he said: 'Whoever gave this precious treasure to King Hrólfr was more loyal to him than to me, but none the less it is I who will have joy of it now, and not King Hrólfr,'—and he stretched out his spear-shaft to where the ring lay, wanting to get hold of it by this means, and stooped down very low over his horse as he thrust his spear down into the circle of the ring.

Now King Hrólfr saw this, and turned his horse back, and said: 'Now I have made the mightiest of the Swedes stoop like a pig!'

And while King Aðils was trying to pull back his spear-shaft with the ring on it, King Hrólfr galloped up to him and cut off both his buttocks right down to the bone, using the sword Skǫfnungr, which was the finest of all swords that have ever been borne in the Northlands.

Then King Hrólfr spoke to King Aðils and bade him live with this shame for a while—'and now you can recognize King Hrólfr, and know which is the man whom you have long sought to find'.

Then great loss of blood overwhelmed King Aðils so that he grew faint, and he now had to turn back again leaving matters worse than ever, but King Hrólfr took back Svíagríss. Thus they parted for that time—and indeed it is not said that they ever met again. They also slew all the men who had ridden farthest ahead and taken the greatest risk, for these men did not need to wait long for King Hrólfr and his champions, nor did any of them think himself too good to become their servant if he got the chance, and none found fault with the other for doing so.

King Hrólfr and his men now went on their way and rode on almost all day, and as night drew on they came upon a farmstead and went up to the door. Farmer Hrani was there to meet them, and he offered them every hospitality, and said that things had not turned out very differently from what he had guessed concerning their journey. The king agreed that this was true, and said there was no smoke in Hrani's eyes.

'Here are some weapons which I want to give you,' said farmer Hrani.

'These weapons are hideous, old fellow,' said the king—it was a shield, sword and mailcoat—and King Hrólfr would not accept the weapons.

At this Hrani came near to anger, and thought himself much insulted. 'You are not acting as is worthy of you, King Hrólfr,' said he, 'though you may imagine that you are. And you are not always as wise as you think.'

The farmer took this very badly, and now nothing more was said of their being given hospitality for the night, so now they wanted to ride on their way, even though the night was dark. Hrani was scowling when one looked him in the face, for he thought they had treated him with little honour as they refused to accept gifts from him, and now he did not stop them from riding wherever they liked. So now they rode off leaving matters thus, and no farewells were spoken.

And before they had gone very far, Bǫðvarr Bjarki came to a halt and spoke these words: 'Fools think of things when it's too late, which is what is happening to me now. I suspect that we may not have acted very wisely in refusing what we should have accepted, and it may well be victory that we have refused.'

'I have the same suspicion,' said King Hrólfr, 'for that may have been Óðinn the Old, and indeed the man had but one eye.'

'Let us turn back as fast as we can,' said Svipdagr, 'and put it to the test.'

194

So now they went back again, but by then the farm-
stead and the old man had disappeared.

'There is nothing to be gained by searching for him,'
said King Hrólfr. 'He is an evil spirit.'

So now they went on their way, and there is nothing
more to be told of their journey till they got back to his
own realm of Denmark, and settled there in peace.
Bǫðvarr gave the king this advice, that from then on he
should take little part in warfare. They thought it more
than likely that they would be hardly ever attacked even
if they remained quiet, but Bǫðvarr said he doubted
whether the king would have the luck of victory in
future, if he still relied on that.

King Hrólfr said: 'Fate rules each man's life, not that
evil spirit.'

'Never would we wish to leave you,' said Bǫðvarr,
'as long as we have any say in the matter. But yet I have
a strong suspicion that it will not be long before there are
heavy tidings for us all.'

That was the end of their talk; and they became
immensely famous for this expedition.

Now things went on the same way for a long time,
and King Hrólfr and his champions sat peacefully in
Denmark, and no one attacked them. All his tributary
kings kept their allegiance to him and paid him their
tribute, and so did Hjǫrvarðr, his brother-in-law.

Now it happened one day that Queen Skuld spoke to
her husband King Hjǫrvarðr, with a heavy sigh: 'It
pleases me little that we should have to pay tribute to
King Hrólfr and be forced into submission to him, and
it must no longer be that you are his underling.'

'It will be best for us, like the others, to put up with
it and stay quiet,' said Hjǫrvarðr.

'You are not much of a man', said she, 'if you are
willing to bear every kind of shame that is put on you.'

'It is quite impossible to put oneself against King
Hrólfr,' said he, 'for no one dares lift shield against
him.'

'You are none of you real men,' said she, 'for you
have no spirit in you, and he who takes no risks never
wins the game. One cannot tell until one has tried it
whether King Hrólfr is proof against blows, or his

champions either. As things stand at present', said she, 'I believe he will prove to have lost all chance of victory, and I would feel quite ready to put the matter to the test, and if so I would not spare him, even though he is my kinsman. Indeed, the reason he is constantly at home is that he himself suspects that victory would escape him. Now I shall set a plan on foot, if only it may strike home, and now I shall not neglect to bring every one of my tricks into play, so that this may succeed.' (Now Queen Skuld was a most powerful witch and was born of the elves on her mother's side, and for this King Hrólfr and his champions paid the price.) 'First, I shall send men to King Hrólfr and ask him if he will allow me to pay no tribute for the next three years, and then I shall pay him the whole amount at once—in so far as he has any right to it. Now I think there is a good chance that this trick will work, and if it does succeed we must keep quiet about it.'

So now messengers were sent to and fro with the queen's request, and King Hrólfr agreed to the request about the tribute. During this time Skuld gathered together all the men who were the best fighters, and all the wicked rabble from every district near by. Yet all this treachery was so well hidden that King Hrólfr knew nothing about it, nor did his champions have any suspicion of it, for the whole thing was done with much witchcraft and spells. Skuld set strong sorcery at work to overcome her half-brother King Hrólfr, so that she had the help of elves and norns and innumerable other evil beings, so that no human power could stand against them. But King Hrólfr and his champions enjoyed good cheer and fine pastimes in Leire, and in every kind of sport of which men had any knowledge they acquitted themselves skilfully and with courtly grace. Each one of them had a mistress for his delight.

And now it is time to tell how the host of King Hjǫrvarðr and Queen Skuld was quite ready, so that they set out for Leire with this innumerable army and arrived there at Yule. King Hrólfr had had great preparations made for Yule, and his men drank hard on Yule-Eve. Hjǫrvarðr and Skuld pitched their tents outside the stronghold, and these were large and long and strangely fitted out; there were many wagons there, all filled with weapons and armour.

King Hrólfr paid no heed to this. His mind was now more set on his grandeur and splendour and pride, and on all the valour which filled his heart, and on holding his feast for all who had come there, and that his honour should be known far and wide—for indeed he had everything which could add lustre to the glory of an earthly king. But it has never been said that King Hrólfr and his champions ever at any time offered sacrifices to heathen gods; rather, they put their trust in their own strength and might, because at that time the Holy Faith had not been preached here in the Northlands, and those who lived in the northern half of the world had little knowledge of their Creator.

Now the next thing to be told is that Hjalti the Noble-Hearted went to the house in which his mistress was. He saw plainly that things were not peaceful in the tents of Hjǫrvarðr and Skuld, yet he let matters be and did not even raise an eyebrow at it, but lay down with his mistress. She was the loveliest of women.

And when he had been there for some time he jumped up and said to his mistress: 'Which would you like best, two men of twenty-two, or one man of eighty?'

'I would like two men of twenty-two better than old fellows of eighty,' said she.

'You'll pay for those words, you whore,' said Hjalti, and he went up to her and bit her nose off. 'You can blame that on me, if ever any men start a fight over you—but I should think that from now on most people will think that you're not much of a prize.'

'You have been cruel and unjust to me,' said she.

'One can't foresee everything,' said Hjalti.

He snatched up his weapons, for he saw that all round the stronghold was a tight circle of men in armour with standards set up. He now understood that they need no longer hide from themselves the fact that warfare was at hand. He made his way into the hall and up to where King Hrólfr sat with his champions.

Hjalti said: 'Awake, my lord and king, for the foe is at the gates, and there is greater need for fighting than for embracing women. I think the gold in your hall will not increase much through the tribute of your sister Skuld; she has the grimness of the Skjǫldungs, and this much I can tell you—this host is no small one, with hard swords and weapons of war, and they march round about the stronghold with drawn swords. King Hjǫrvarðr's errand to you can be no friendly one, and never again from now on does he intend to ask for his kingdom from your hands. Now is the time', said Hjalti, 'when we must lead forth the army of our king, who never grudged us anything. Let us now nobly fulfil our vows that we should defend this king, the most famous now living in all the Northern lands! Let us so act that the tale of it may be told in every land! Let us now repay him for weapons and war-gear and many other favours too, for we must not give him grudging service in return. Mighty portents also have appeared, though for a long time we have closed our eyes to them, and strongly do I suspect that such mighty happenings will now follow on them as shall be long remembered. Some men may say that I speak words of despair, but yet it may prove true that King Hrólfr now drinks for the last time among his champions and retainers. Up with you now, all you champions!' said Hjalti. 'And be swift in bidding your mistresses farewell, for another task is close at hand, to prepare yourselves for what shall follow. Up with you, all you champions, up now all at once and arm yourselves!'

Then up sprang Hrómundr the Hardy and Hrólfr the Swift-Handed, Svipdagr and Beigaðr and Hvítserkr the Bold, Haklangr the sixth man, Harðrefill the seventh, Haki the Valiant the eighth, Vǫttr the Strong the ninth, the tenth was called Starólfr, the eleventh was Hjalti the Noble-Hearted and Bǫðvarr Bjarki the twelfth. He was so called because he had driven all King Hrólfr's berserks out because of their pride and injustice, and killed some of them, so that not one of them came out of it well, for they were all like women compared to him when it came to the test, even though they had always thought themselves greater than he and had always laid treacherous plans against him.

Bǫðvarr Bjarki stood up straightway and put on his armour and said that King Hrólfr would now have need of proud warriors: 'And all who take their stand beside King Hrólfr must have heart and courage to serve their needs.'

Then King Hrólfr sprang to his feet, and fearlessly he spoke: 'Bring us drink, the best that there is, and before all else we shall drink and be merry, and so show what manner of men are these, the champions of Hrólfr. Let our one care be that our valour be always remembered, for now the greatest and most fearsome champions of all the neighbouring lands have come against us here. Tell this to Hjǫrvarðr and Skuld and their doughty fighters—that we will drink and be glad before we collect our tribute!'

It was done as the king said. Skuld answered: 'King Hrólfr, my brother, is unlike all others, and men such as he are the greatest loss; but, for all that, our quarrel must come to a head.'

There was so much that was admirable in King Hrólfr that he was praised by both friend and foe.

Now King Hrólfr sprang down from the highseat where he had been drinking for some time with his champions; they bade farewell to their good drink for a while, and the next thing was that they were all outside, except for Bǫðvarr Bjarki. Nowhere could they see him, and they wondered greatly at this, and thought it not impossible that he had been either taken prisoner or slain.

And as soon as they came outside, a terrible battle broke out. King Hrólfr himself went forward with the standards, and his champions were with him on either side, and there were all the other folk from the stronghold, who would be numerous enough to count, though they proved of little worth. There one might see mighty blows struck on helm and mail-coat, swords and spears might one see brandished aloft, and so many heaps of corpses that the ground was all covered with them.

Hjalti the Noble-Hearted spoke: 'Many a mail-coat is split now, and many a weapon broken; and many a helm is shattered, and many a valiant knight thrust down from his horse's back. Great is our king's spirit, for he is as glad now as when he drank ale most deeply, and ever he smites with both hands. He is most unlike to other kings in battle, for it seems to me that he has the strength of twelve kings, and many a valiant man has he slain; and now King Hjǫrvarðr may see that the sword Skǫfnungr bites deep, and it now clangs aloud on their skulls'—for the virtue of Skǫfnungr was such that it cried aloud when it felt the bone.

Now the fighting broke out again with great violence, so that nothing could withstand King Hrólfr and his champions. King Hrólfr smote so hard with Skǫfnungr that it seemed a marvel, and this did great work among King Hjǫrvarðr's host, which fell in swathes. Hjǫrvarðr and his men saw that a huge bear was advancing in the van of King Hrólfr's men, and always he was nearest to where the king was. He slew more men with his paw than any five of the king's champions; blows and missiles glanced aside from him, and he trampled underfoot both men and horses of King Hjǫrvarðr's host, and he crunched everything near him between his teeth, so that murmurs of dismay arose in King Hjǫrvarðr's host.

Now Hjalti looked around and could not see his comrade Bǫðvarr, and he said to King Hrólfr: 'What can this mean, that Bǫðvarr should shelter himself and not come near the king—such a champion as we thought him to be, and as he has often proved himself?'

King Hrólfr said: 'Wherever it is best for us that he should be, that is where he is, if he is his own master. Be true to your own glory and courage, and speak no ill of him, for not one of you is his equal—yet I do not reproach any of you, for you are all most valiant champions.'

Now Hjalti went off in haste back to the king's dwelling, and saw where Bǫðvarr was sitting there, never stirring.

'How long must we wait for our most famous champion?' said Hjalti. 'It is a thing unheard of that you should not stand up on your own feet and put those strong arms of yours to the test, arms which are as strong as a bear's. Up with you now, Bǫðvarr Bjarki, my chieftain, or I will burn this house and you in it! It is a shame above all shames, to such a champion as you are, that the king should put himself in peril for our sakes,

and that you should thus lose that high praise which you
have had till now.'

Then Bǫðvarr stood up, and heaved a sigh, and said:
'You need not try to frighten me, Hjalti, for I have
never yet been afraid, and now I am ready to go. When
I was young I never fled from fire or steel; fire I have
seldom met with, but the clash of steel I have borne
from time to time, and from neither of them have I run
till now. And you shall truly say that I will fight full
well; King Hrólfr has always called me champion in
front of his men. I have also much for which to repay him
—first the fact that I am his son-in-law, then twelve
homesteads which he gave me, and many precious
treasures with them. I slew Agnarr, who was a berserk
and a king as well, and that deed is still remembered.'—
Then in front of Hjalti he reckoned up the many mighty
deeds which he had done, and how he had been the
slayer of so many men, and he bade him understand that
he would go fearless into battle.—'But yet I think that
there are far stranger things to face here than anywhere
else where we have been before. But you have not done
such fine service for the king by this deed of yours as
you think, for otherwise it would have been almost
settled by now which side would have the victory. Yet it
is more because folly has come upon you, not that you
do not wish well to the king; no other of his champions
would have got away with calling me out except you,
or except the king himself, for I would have killed any
other man—and now everything must now go as it
needs must, and no plan shall be of any use. I tell you,
in good truth, that I can now give the king far less help
than before you called me away from here.'

'One thing is clear,' said Hjalti, 'that my deepest
bonds are those that bind me to you and to King Hrólfr;
but it is hard to know the best thing to do, when things
are as they are now.'

After Hjalti's egging on of him, Bǫðvarr stood up and
went out to the battle. The bear had vanished from the
host, and now the battle began to turn against them. So
long as the bear was with King Hrólfr's host, Queen
Skuld had not been able to work any of her tricks from
where she sat in her black tent on her sorceress's

scaffold, but now there came a change, as when dark
night comes on after bright day. King Hrólfr's men now
saw how there came from among King Hjǫrvarðr's
host a fearsome boar. To look at, he was no smaller
than a three-year-old ox, and wolf-grey in hue, and from
each of his bristles there flew an arrow, and in this
monstrous fashion he laid King Hrólfr's retainers low.

Bǫðvarr Bjarki now cleared an open space about him,
hacking with both hands, and with his mind set on
nothing save on doing what he could before he fell;
and now they fell before him, one on top of another,
and both his arms were bloodied to the shoulder, and
he piled the corpses round about him on every side. He
seemed as if he was mad. But however many men he and
Hrólfr's other champions slew among the host of Hjǫr-
varðr and Skuld, it was a most wondrous thing that their
host never grew any less; it was as if they had done noth-
ing at all, and they thought they had never come upon
such a marvel.

'Vast are the numbers of Skuld's host,' said Bǫðvarr,
'and now I suspect that the dead are on the move, and
that they rise up again and fight us; and it will prove
hard indeed to fight against the walking dead. However
many limbs are sheared off and shields split apart, or
helms and corselets hacked into little pieces, or many a
chieftain cut in two, such dead men as these are the
grimmest of all to deal with, and we have no power to
master them. And where now is that champion of King
Hrólfr who so much challenged my courage and called
on me so often to come out, before I would answer him?
I do not see him now, and yet it is not my wont to speak
ill of men.'

Then said Hjalti: 'What you say is true, you are not
the man to speak ill of others. Here stands he whose
name is Hjalti--and I have work enough on my hands
now, and there is no great distance between us. I have
need of good warriors, for all my armour is hacked away,
foster-brother, and though it seems to me that I fight
with all my strength, yet I get no vengeance for all the
strokes I receive. But there must be no hanging back
now, if we are to lodge in Valhǫll tonight. Truly, never
have we met with such marvels as face us now, and we

have long had forebodings of the happenings which have come upon us now.'

Then spoke Bǫðvarr Bjarki: 'Hear what I say! I have fought in twelve pitched battles, and always been called stout-hearted, and never fled before any berserk. It was I who roused King Hrólfr to go to seek King Aðils, and there we met with certain tricks, but those were of little account beside these evils. My heart is so heavy now that I have not such joy in fighting as before. Not long ago I met King Hjǫrvarðr in an earlier onslaught, so that our paths crossed and each of us hurled taunts at the other. We exchanged blows for some while. He made a thrust at me which made me think I was bound for death's doors, but then I hacked off his hand and foot, and another stroke took him on the shoulder so that I split him down one side and down the back, and it took such effect on him that he ceased breathing and lay for a while as if asleep, so that I thought him dead—but there can't be many like him to be found, for afterwards he fought again no less boldly than before, and I shall never be able to tell what it is that gives him strength. Many men have now gathered here against us, great and simple alike, who are pressing on us from all quarters so that none can lift shield against them, but as yet I have not recognized Óðinn here. Yet I much suspect that he must be working here against us, that foul and faithless son of Satan! If anyone should bring me word of him, I would crush him like any other evil and tiny mouseling, and that wicked and poisonous creature would be shamefully ill-treated if only I could lay hands on him! Who would feel more deadly hate in his heart if he saw his liege lord so ill-treated as we now see ours?'

'It is not easy to turn fate aside,' said Hjalti, 'nor to stand fast against magic powers.'

And so they ceased their talk.

King Hrólfr defended himself well and valiantly and with greater gallantry than anyone has ever heard of. They pressed hard upon him, and he was encircled by picked men from Hjǫrvarðr's and Skuld's host. Skuld had now come into the fight, and earnestly urged her rabble to attack King Hrólfr, for she saw that his champions were not very near to him. And it was that which bitterly grieved Bǫðvarr Bjarki, that he could not come to the aid of his lord, and so too with the rest of the champions, for they were now as eager to die beside their lord as they had been to live beside him while they were in the flower of their youth. By now the king's whole bodyguard had fallen so that not one of them was still standing, and most of the champions had got their death-wounds, and so things went as was only too likely. Master Galterus says that human strength cannot stand up against the strength of such fiends unless the power of God should come to oppose them—'and that was the one thing that stood in the way of your victory, King Hrólfr, that you had no knowledge of your Creator'.

There now came such a storm of sorcery that the champions began to fall, one across the other, and Hrólfr left the shield-wall, and he was like one dead from weariness. There is no need to spend more words on this, for there fell King Hrólfr and all his champions, winning great renown.

And no words will ever tell what great slaughter they had wrought there. King Hjǫrvarðr fell there, and all his host, except that a few shameful wretches remained alive, together with Skuld. She took King Hrólfr's realms for herself, and ruled them badly, and for a short while only. Elg-Fróði and King Þórir Houndsfoot avenged their brother Bǫðvarr Bjarki as they had promised him (as has been told in the Tale of Fróði), and they got great forces from Sweden from Queen Yrsa, and men say that Vǫggr was the leader of that host. They made their way to Denmark with all their host, without Queen Skuld suspecting it at all. They managed to lay hands on her in such a way that she could make no spells to prevent it, and they slew all her rabble, and killed her with various tortures; and so they won back the kingdom for King Hrólfr's daughters, and then each of them went back to his own home.

A burial mound was raised for King Hrólfr and the sword Skǫfnungr laid beside him; and each of the champions was given a mound, and some weapon beside him. And here ends the saga of King Hrólfr Kraki and his champions.

12. *Bjarkarímur* (*c.* 1400), I, stanzas 7–17.

. . . Mighty, say I, was Hrólfr the king, who ruled the courts of Leire. He was a chieftain well known for valour, held in awe by all his neighbours; as long as this world lasts, tales will be told of him in the Northlands.

One day there came before the king's table a certain merry fellow, a peasant's son with a witty tongue, who said his name was Vǫggr—'I thought, when I ran off from home, that Hrólfr must be outstanding, but the man I see here is smaller than would have seemed at all likely.'

He never made a bow, so I heard tell, but stood facing the king, and was silent.

'What do you think of me now?' asked Hrólfr.

'Most tales are very great lies,' said this worthy fellow. 'I would think there was a tall thin pole in the king's highseat.'

'What rich gift have you in readiness, O keeper of the snake's sweat [i.e. gold]? You must be meaning to give me something, if I am to be called by this name.'

'I know no way of doing so, nor anything I could offer in exchange.'

'Then he who has the more must share it; you will accept some little thing.'

Hrólfr gave him a gold ring, and it weighed half a mark; the court saw that most honourable deed, and every man's tongue praised him.

'I have vowed to avenge you, O mighty King Hrólfr; that is all I hope for, since there is no man like you to be found. You are not stingy with your wealth; noble is your way of life!'

It took very little to make Vǫggr happy; the prince sat and smiled.

13. *Landnámabók* (*Hauksbók*) (*c.* 1330), ch. 140.

[An adventure ascribed to the son of one of the settlers of Iceland.]

Skeggi of Miðfjǫrðr was a man of very strong character. He went plundering round the Baltic coasts, and then went ashore in Denmark, near Zealand. He was

incited to break into the burial mound of King Hrólfr
Kraki, and he took out from it Hrólfr's sword Skǫfnungr,
and Hjalti's axe, and many other precious objects. But
he did not get Laufi, for Bǫðvarr tried to attack him, but
King Hrólfr defended him. After this, he went back to
Iceland and lived at Reykjar in Miðfjǫrðr.

II H. HEOROWEARD—O.N. Hjǫrvarðr—
Lat. Hiartwarus/Hiarwardus/Hervardus.

1. *Leire Chronicle*, see above, II G 5.

2. *Skjǫldunga saga*, see above, II G 7.

3. Saxo Grammaticus, *Danish History*, see above, II G 8.

4. *Annales Ryenses*, see above, II G 9.

5. *Hrólfs saga kraka*, see above, II G 11.

II I. HEALFDENE'S DAUGHTER—
O.N. Signý—Lat. Signya.

1. *Skjǫldunga saga*, see above, II D 5, II E 4.

2. *Hrólfs saga kraka*, see above, II D 10, II E 8.

II J. HRÉDRÍC—O.N. Hrœrekr—
Lat. Roricus/Rokil.

1. For Hrærekr Hnauggvanbaugi and Hrærekr Slaungvan-
baugi in the *Langfeðgatal*, see above, II D 2.

2. Sven Aageson, *A Brief History of the Kings of Denmark* (*c.* 1187), ch. 1.

After him [i.e. Rolf Kraki], there ruled his son Rokil, known by the nickname Slaghenback.

3. *Skjǫldunga saga* (*c.* 1200) chs. 12 and 14.

(*a*) Roas, Rolfo's uncle, was slain by his own first cousins, Rærecus and Frodo, the sons of Ingialldus.
(*b*) After Hiorvardus had thus been slain at the very outset of his reign, there succeeded Rolfo's kinsman Rærecus, who was first cousin on the father's side to Helgo, Rolfo's father [i.e. Rærecus was son of Ingialldus, see above, II D 5]. A certain Wallderus, grandson of Waldemarus, waged war on him . . . and after some time of fighting they shared Denmark between them: Rærecus was to be King of Zealand and Wallderus of Scania.

4. Saxo Grammaticus, *Danish History* (*c.* 1200) II § 62; III §§ 82–5.

[Saxo describes two unconnected figures named Roricus; the first is mentioned in the course of his paraphrase of the *Bjarkamál* as a former victim of Rolfo's prowess.]

. . . our king [Rolfo], who laid low Roricus the son of Bokus the covetous [probably a misunderstanding of the nickname *hnøggvanbaugi*, 'Covetous of Rings', 'Ring-Hoarder'] and wrapped the coward in death.

He was rich in wealth, but in enjoyment poor, stronger in gain than in bravery; and thinking gold better than warfare, he set gold above all things, and ingloriously accumulated piles of treasures, scorning the service of noble friends. And when he was attacked by the navy of Rolfo, he bade his servants take the gold from the chests and spread it out in front of the city gates, making ready bribes rather than battle, because he knew not the soldier, and thought that the foe should be attempted with gifts and not with arms; as though he could fight with wealth alone, and prolong the war by using, not men, but wares! So he undid the heavy coffers and the

rich chests, he brought forth the polished bracelets and
the heavy caskets; they only fed his destruction. Rich
in treasure, poor in warriors, he left his foes to take
away the prizes which he forbore to give to the friends
of his own land. He who once shrank to give little rings
of his own will, now unwillingly squandered his masses
of wealth, rifling his hoarded heap. But our king in his
wisdom spurned him and the gifts he offered, and took
from him life and goods at once; nor was his foe profited
by the useless wealth which he had greedily heaped up
through long years. But Rolfo the righteous assailed
him, slew him, and captured his vast wealth, and shared
among worthy friends what the hand of avarice had
piled up in all those years; and, bursting into the camp
which was wealthy but not brave, gave his friends a
lordly booty without bloodshed. . . .

[After Hiartwarus had been killed by Viggo—see
above, II G 8—the next king of Denmark in Saxo's
account was Hotherus—a figure in fact drawn from
mythology. In due course he was succeeded by his
son Roricus, who went to war to quell a revolt of
tributary Slavs.]

Roricus, in order to check this wrong-doing, sum-
moned his country to arms, recounted the deeds of his
forefathers, and in a passionate harangue urged them unto
valorous deeds. But the barbarians . . . hid two companies
of men in a dark spot. But Roricus saw the trap; and
perceiving that his fleet was wedged in a certain narrow
creek among the shoal water, took it out from the sands
where it was lying and brought it forth to sea. . . . Also
he resolved that his men should go into hiding during
the day, where they could stay and suddenly fall on the
invaders of his ships. . . . And in fact the barbarians who
had been appointed to the ambuscade knew nothing
of the wariness of the Danes, and sallying against them
rashly, were all destroyed. . . .
Now among [the Slavs] there was a man of remarkable
stature, a wizard by calling. He, when he beheld the
squadrons of the Danes, said: 'Suffer a private combat to
forestall a public slaughter, so that the danger of the

many may be bought off at the cost of the few. And if
any of you shall take heart to fight it out with me, I shall
not flinch from these terms of conflict. . . .'

One of the Danes, whose spirit was stouter than his
strength, heard this, and proceeded to ask Roricus what
would be the reward for the man who met the challenger
in combat. Roricus chanced to have six bracelets, which
were so intertwined that they could not be parted from
one another, the chain of knots being inextricably laced;
and he promised them as a reward for the man who
would venture on the combat. But the youth, who
doubted his fortune, said: 'Roricus, if I prove successful,
let thy generosity award the prize of the conqueror,
do thou decide and allot the palm; but if my enterprise
go little to my liking, what prize canst thou owe to the
beaten, who will be wrapped either in cruel death or in
bitter shame? . . . It is folly to lay hands on the fruit
before it is ripe, and to be fain to pluck that which one
is not yet sure is one's due. This hand shall win me the
prize, or death.'

Having thus spoken, he smote the barbarian with his
sword; but his fortune was tardier than his spirit, for
the other struck him back, and he fell dead under the
force of the first blow. Thus he was a sorry sight unto
the Danes, but the Slavs greeted their triumphant com-
rade with a great procession, and received him with
splendid dances. On the morrow the same man, whether
he was elated with the good fortune of his late victory,
or was fired with the wish to win another, came close
to the enemy, and set to girding at them in the words of
his former challenge. . . .

So Roricus was vexed that . . . in all his host not one
man should be found so quick of spirit or so vigorous
of arm that he longed to sacrifice his life for his country.
It was the high-hearted Ubbo who first wiped off this
infamous reproach upon the hesitating Danes. For he
was of great bodily strength, and powerful in incanta-
tions. He also purposely asked the prize of the combat
and the king promised him the bracelets. Then said he:
'How can I trust the promise when thou keepest the
pledge in thine own hands, and dost not deposit the gift
in the charge of another? Let there be someone to whom

thou canst entrust the pledge, that thou mayst not be able to take the promise back. For the courage of the champion is kindled by the irrevocable certainty of the prize.'

Of course it was plain that he had said this in jest; sheer courage had armed him to repel the insult to his country. But Roricus thought he was tempted by avarice, and was loath to seem as if, contrary to royal fashion, he meant to take back the gift or revoke his promise; so, being stationed on his vessel, he resolved to shake off the bracelets, and with a mighty swing send them to the asker. But his attempt was baulked by the width of the gap between them; for the bracelets fell short of the intended spot, the impulse being too faint and slack, and were reft away by the waters. For this the nickname Slyngebond ['Hurler of the Arm-Band'] clung to Roricus.

[Despite the loss of the arm-rings, Ubbo went on with the duel, and won; thereupon the Slavs submitted to Roricus.]

5. *Hrólfs saga kraka* (c. 1400), chs. 10–12. See above, II E 8.

[Here Hrœrekr's name has been changed to Hrókr; he is the son of Signý and so nephew to Helgi and Hróarr, whose ring he covets. When he fails to get it for himself, he hurls it out to sea. Hróarr has him maimed as punishment, but he returns and slays Hróarr, only to be slain in turn by Helgi. The ring is eventually recovered from the sea-bed by Agnarr, a posthumous son of Hróarr.]

6. *Bjarkarímur* (c. 1400), VII, stanzas 5–34 (summary only).

[The two brothers, Ingjaldr and Hálfdan, quarrelled; Ingjaldr killed Hálfdan, took the kingdom, and begot two sons, Fróði and Hrœrekr Ring-Hurler. Meanwhile Hálfdan's sons Hróarr and Helgi were reared in hiding by old Vífill, till they were old enough to avenge their father by burning Ingjaldr in his hall, and win back the kingdom.

Hróarr and Helgi jointly owned the ring Svíagríss, which had once been Ingjaldr's; it was of superb workmanship and great value. Hróarr did not wish Hrœrekr ever to see the ring, but one day when they were on board ship together, Hrœrekr begged to see it, and Hróarr handed it to him. Hrœrekr flung it out to sea, saying no one should ever have joy of it. In their anger Helgi and Hróarr broke his bones and sent him home maimed, and he died soon after. But Ingjaldr had had another son, a bastard named Agnarr, who was a fierce berserk. He came to the place where Hrœrekr had thrown the ring into the waves, dived, and recovered it. Then Agnarr went to war against Hrólfr Kraki, but was killed in a duel by Bǫðvarr Bjarki—see above, I A 9(d).]

III. The Swedes

III A. ONGENÐĒOW—the phonetic O.N. equivalent would be Angantýr, but instead the name Egill appears.

1. *Wīdsīð* (seventh century) l. 31.

   Ongendþēow [ruled] the Swedes.

2. Ári Þorgilsson, *Íslendingabók* (*c.* 1130), Appendix III.

   [A genealogy of Swedish kings]

   ... Aun the Old; Egill Vendilkráka; Óttarr; Aðisl at Uppsala. ...

3. *Langfeðgatal* (twelfth century).

   ... Aun; Egill Tunni's-Foe; Óttarr Vendilkráka; Aðils at Uppsala ...

4. Snorri Sturluson, *Heimskringla* (*c.* 1223–35), *Ynglinga saga* ch. 26; quoting a stanza from *Ynglingatál* by Þjóðólfr of Hvin (*c.* 940).

   Egill was the name of the son of Aun the Old who was King of Sweden after his father. He was no warrior, but remained quietly in his own lands. Tunni was the name of a slave of his, who had been with Aun the Old and had been his treasurer; but when Aun was dead, Tunni took a great deal of money and buried it in the ground. Now when Egill was king, he put Tunni among the other slaves; but he took this very badly and ran away, and many slaves went with him, and they dug up the money he had hidden. He gave it to his men, and they took him as their chieftain. After that, many of the rabble flocked to him, and they lurked out in the forests and sometimes came down upon the inhabited regions and plundered men or killed them.

   King Egill heard of this and went to seek them with

his forces, but one night when he had taken quarters
for the night, Tunni came there with his forces and
attacked them unawares and killed many of the king's
host. But when King Egill learnt of the fighting he
turned to face them and set up his standard, but many
of his men fled from him. Tunni and his followers
attacked boldly, and King Egill saw no other choice
open to him but to flee. Tunni and his men pursued
the fugitives all the way to the woods, and after this
they turned back into the cultivated lands, and harried
and plundered without meeting any opposition. All the
wealth Tunni won in his raids he gave to his followers,
and in this way he grew popular and found many
followers. King Egill gathered an army and went to do
battle with Tunni. They fought, and Tunni won the
victory, but Egill fled and lost many of his men. King
Egill and Tunni fought eight battles, and Tunni was
victorious in all of them.

Then King Egill fled from the country and went out to
Zealand in Denmark, to Fróði the Valiant, and he
promised King Fróði tribute from the Swedes in ex-
change for help. Then Fróði gave him an army, and
champions of his own. King Egill then went back to
Sweden, but when Tunni heard of this he went with his
army to meet him. There was a great battle, and Tunni
fell there, and King Egill took possession of his own
realm. The Danes went back home. King Egill sent
King Fróði fine and valuable gifts every year, but never
paid tribute to the Danes, in spite of which the friend-
ship between him and Fróði held firm. King Egill ruled
his realm for three years after Tunni fell.

It so happened in Sweden that a bull which was meant
for the sacrifice was old and had been fed so richly that
he had grown vicious; when men tried to catch him he
ran off into a forest and went wild, and for a long while
he remained in the woods and did great damage to men.
Now King Egill was a great huntsman. It happened one
day that he had ridden out hunting with his men; he had
been chasing a beast for a long while and had pursued
it into the woods away from all his men. Then he caught
sight of this bull and rode up to it, meaning to kill it.
The bull turned to face him, and the king reached him

with a spear-thrust, but the spear tore its way out of the flesh. The bull stuck his horn into the horse's side, so that it fell to the ground at once, and so did the king. The king leapt to his feet and tried to draw his sword, but the bull stuck his horn deep down into the king's breast. Then the king's men came up, and killed the bull. The king lived on for a little while only, and he is buried in a mound at Uppsala. So says Þjóðólfr:

> The offspring, ever-praised, of Týr
> Fled abroad from Tunni's power.
> An ogre's-beast-of-burden stained
> In Egill's blood his bull's-head's-sword—
> A beast who long in eastern woods
> Had borne the burden of his brows—
> And this wild brute's sheathless sword
> Has pierced a Skilfing through the heart.

[The expression rendered 'bull's-head's-sword' might also be translated as 'boar's-snout's-sword'; this is preferred by some scholars, who believe that the poem alludes obliquely to the name of the warrior who, according to *Beowulf*, slew Ongentheow—Eofor, i.e. 'Boar'.]

III B. ŌHTHERE—O.N. Óttarr.

1. Snorri Sturluson, *Heimskringla* (c. 1223–35), *Ynglinga saga* ch. 27; quoting a stanza from *Ynglingatál* by Þjóðólfr of Hvin (c. 940).

Óttarr was the name of the son of Egill who took the realm and kingship after him. He was not on friendly terms with King Fróði [of Denmark], so then Fróði sent men to King Óttarr to claim the tribute which Egill had promised him. Óttarr answered that the Swedes had never paid tribute to the Danes, and that he too would act the same way. The messengers returned home. Fróði was a great warrior. It happened one summer that Fróði went with his army to Sweden, went raiding and plundering there, and killed many people and carried off others captive. He won a very great deal of booty. He also burned the inhabited districts far and wide and inflicted much destruction.

The following summer, King Fróði went off to plunder the Baltic coasts. King Óttarr heard that Fróði was not in his own country, so then he went aboard a warship and sailed out to Denmark, and plundered there, and met no opposition. He heard that a great host was gathered in Zealand, so then he turned westwards along the Baltic Straits, and then sailed south to Jutland and laid his course for Limfjord, and then plundered in the district of Vendel, where he burned and laid many places waste.

Vǫttr and Fasti were the names of Fróði's earls; Fróði had appointed them to guard the land of Denmark while he was out of the country. Now when these earls learnt that the Swedish king was harrying in Denmark, they gathered an army and hurried aboard ship and sailed south to Limfjord; their coming took King Óttarr quite unawares, and they began the battle at once. The Swedes faced them bravely. Many men fell on both sides, but however many might fall among the Danes, still more would come there from all the districts round, and also all the ships that were in the neighbourhood came to join them. The end of the battle was that King Óttarr fell there, and so did the greater part of his men. The Danes took his body and carried it to land, and laid it on top of a mound and let the wild beasts and birds of prey tear the corpse to pieces there. They made a wooden crow and sent it to Sweden, saying that that was all that their king Óttarr was worth now; after that they nicknamed Óttarr 'Vendel-Crow' [Vendilkráka]. So says Þjóðólfr:

> Óttarr fell beneath eagles' claws,
> Doughtily fell before Danish arms;
> The carrion bird, come from afar,
> In Vendel drove four talons in him.
> Vǫttr's and Fasti's deeds, I heard,
> Became a tale among the Swedes—
> How Fróði's earls who ruled the isles
> Had slain the lord who led in war.

BEOWULF AND ITS ANALOGUES

III C. ONELA—O.N. Áli—Lat. Alonis.

1. *Hyndluljóð* (date uncertain; included in *Flateyjarbók c.* 1375), stanza 18.

Áli was once the most famous of men.

[For Norse versions of the enmity between Onela and Eadgils see III E.]

III D. ĒANMUND—O.N. Eymundr—Lat. Hömothus.

1. *Hyndluljóð* (date uncertain; included in *Flateyjarbók c.* 1375), stanza 19.

He [i.e. Hálfdan of Denmark] allied himself with Eymundr the Noble.

2. For Hömothus, a Swedish chieftain slain by Hugletus of Denmark, see I B 4.

III E. ĒADGILS—O.N. Aðils—Lat. Adilsus.

1. For an allusion to Aðils in the *Bjarkamál*, see above, II G 3.

2. *Kálfsvísa* (date uncertain; included by Snorri Sturluson, *Edda* (*c.* 1220), *Skáldskaparmál* ch. 73.)

[A list of heroes and their horses.]

Áli was on Hrafn when they rode to the ice,
And eastwards another one under Aðils,
A grey one, stumbled, gashed by a spear.
. . . Aðils rode Sløngvir. . . .

3. *Leire Chronicle*—see above, II G 5.

4. *Skjǫldunga saga* (*c.* 1200) in an abstract by Arngrímur Jónsson (1596), ch. 12.

After this, hostility arose between this King Adilsus of Sweden and Alo, King of the Upplands in Norway, and both sides appointed to meet in battle; the place fixed on for the battle was Lake Wæner, which was frozen over. Realizing that he would be inferior in forces at this meeting, he begged his stepson Rolfo for help, promising in repayment that Rolfo could carry away as his reward whichever three most precious things he might prefer in the whole kingdom of Sweden; moreover, each of his twelve champions would be granted three pounds of pure gold, and each of the other warriors three marks of silver. Rolfo, though remaining at home himself, sent his twelve champions as reinforcements for Adilsus, and through their deeds he who would otherwise have been defeated obtained the victory. They demanded the reward that had been proposed for them and for their king, but Adilsus denied that he owed any reward to Rolfo, since he was absent; the Danish champions therefore spurned what was offered to them, as soon as they understood that their king was being cheated in this way, and when they returned home again they explained what had happened.

[For this saga's account of Rolfo's visit to Uppsala and the attempts of Adilsus to kill him, see above, II G 7.]

5. For Saxo's account of the dealings between Rolfo and Athislus, see above, II G 8.

6. Snorri Sturluson, *Edda* (*c.* 1220), *Skáldskaparmál* ch. 54.

There was a king who ruled at Uppsala whose name was Aðils; he was married to Yrsa, the mother of Hrólfr Kraki. He was at war with a king who ruled over Norway, whose name was Áli. They arranged to meet and do battle on the ice of the lake which is called Vænir. King Aðils sent a message to his stepson Hrólfr

217

Kraki that he should come with his forces to aid him, and promised rewards for all his host while they were on this campaign, and that King Hrólfr could have for himself any three treasures in Sweden that he chose. King Hrólfr could not go because of a war he was waging against the Germans, but he sent his twelve berserks to Aðils; one was Bǫðvarr Bjarki, then Hjalti the Noble-Hearted, Hvítserkr the Bold, Vǫttr, Veseti, the brothers Svipdagr and Beiguðr. In this battle fell King Áli and a great part of his men. King Aðils took from him, when he was dead, the helmet Hildisvín and his horse Hrafn.

Then Hrólfr's berserks asked to take their reward, three pounds of gold for each of them, and furthermore asked that they might take away for King Hrólfr the treasures they would choose on his behalf; these were the helmet Hildigǫltr and the corselet Finnsleif, on which no steel would bite, and the gold ring called Svíagríss, which Aðils' forefathers had owned. But the king refused all these treasures, nor would he pay the rewards. So the berserks went away, and were ill-pleased with their lot, and told King Hrólfr how things had turned out.

[For Snorri's account of Hrólfr's visit to Uppsala and the attempts of Aðils to kill him, see above, II G 10.]

7. Snorri Sturluson, *Heimskringla* (*c.* 1223–35), *Ynglinga saga* chs. 28–9; quoting a stanza from *Ynglingatál* by Þjóðólfr of Hvin (*c.* 940).

Aðils was the name of the son of King Óttarr, who took the kingdom after him. He was king for a long time, and was very rich; also he used to go on viking raids during some summers. King Aðils came with his host to Saxland, over which reigned a king called Geirþjófr, and his queen was named Álof the Mighty; nothing is said of any children of theirs. This king was not in his own country. King Aðils and his men ran up to the king's homestead and plundered it. Some of them drove a herd of cattle down to be carried off from the shore; there had been some slaves tending this herd, both men and women, and they took them all along with them. Among this company was a remarkably beautiful girl, who said her name was Yrsa. Then King Aðils went home with his booty. Yrsa was not among the slave-girls; it was soon found that she was wise, gifted with eloquence, and full of many accomplishments. Men thought very well of her, and the king most of all; so it came to this, that Aðils held his wedding feast with her. Then Yrsa was Queen of Sweden, and she was thought a woman of outstanding character.

At that time King Helgi, the son of Hálfdan, was reigning at Leire. He came to Sweden, with so great a host that King Aðils saw no other choice open to him but to flee. King Helgi went ashore there with his host and plundered, and took much booty; he captured Queen Yrsa and took her back with him to Leire and married her; their son was Hrólfr Kraki. But when Hrólfr was three years old, Queen Álof came to Denmark; she then told Yrsa that her husband King Helgi was also her father, and that Álof herself was her mother. So then Yrsa went back to Sweden to Aðils, and was queen there for as long as she lived. King Helgi fell on a raiding expedition. Hrólfr Kraki was eight years old at that time, and was accepted as king at Leire.

King Aðils had great disputes with a king who was called Áli the Upplander; he was from Norway. They fought a battle on the ice of Lake Vænir; King Áli fell there, and Aðils had the victory. There is a long account of this battle in the *Skjǫldunga saga*, and also of how Hrólfr Kraki came to Uppsala to see Aðils, and how Hrólfr then sowed gold over Fyrisvellir.

King Aðils was very fond of fine horses; he had the best horses of those times. His own horse was called Sløngvir, and there was another horse called Hrafn; this one he took from Áli when he lay dead, and from him he bred another horse, also called Hrafn. This last he sent to Halogaland to King Goðgestr; Goðgestr rode him and could not curb him, and so fell from his back and was killed. This happened at Ǫmð in Halogaland.

King Aðils was present at a sacrifice to the goddesses, and he rode his horse round the hall of the goddess. The horse stumbled beneath him and fell, and the king was thrown, and his head struck a stone so that the skull broke and his brains were smeared on the stone. That was the death of him. He died at Uppsala and was laid in a mound there; the Swedes call him a mighty king. So says Þjóðólfr:

> This too I heard: a being skilled
> In evil spells struck Aðils' life;
> Thus Freyr's offspring had to fall,
> Though valiant, from his charger's back.
> And mingled in the mud there lay
> The brains of a great hero's son;
> Thus Áli's foeman, ripe in years,
> Must meet his death at Uppsala.

8. For Aðils in *Hrólfs saga kraka*, see above, II F 12, II G 11.

[In this version there is no mention of the battle between Aðils and Áli; Aðils is responsible for Helgi's death because of their rivalry over Yrsa, and the feud between Aðils and Hrólfr is a consequence of this. Aðils is shown not merely as a miser but also as a wizard; the manner of his death is not told.]

9. *Bjarkarímur* (*c.* 1400), VIII, stanzas 17–18, 22–8.

Men came from King Aðals in the east [to the court of Hrólfr]. Laying letters on the board, they unfolded their errand to the king: Aðals meant to appoint a day of battle on the ice of Lake Vænir in the east; he was asking for help in his warfare against a king whom men named Áli, and he would offer gold red as blood in payment. The men said that this Áli ruled the Upplands, with so many men of note about him that I cannot tell of them—'And if the prince and his twelve warriors come, each shall have a pound in payment; the king himself shall have three choice treasures, if the champions slay Áli.'

The tale tells how Hrólfr's champions came to Vænir in the east; many a bow was bent to the bolt; there was creaking on the ridges of the waves. The warrior Aðals was glad when they came there in the east; they came with flashing spears, and hurled themselves into the fray. These heroes offered quarter to none; they worked well for their payment. Áli, young in the sport of weapons, fell there with all his host.

Hrafn was well known to be the finest horse, and him they took from Áli; Hildisvín was a famous helmet, and this Bjarki chose as payment. But the chieftain bade them hold no more idle talk about such bargains as these; he gave proof of his royal power—he snatched back the treasures from the champions. Boðvarr did not think well of this; he and Hjalti went away, saying that before winter was over they would come back to seek the gold. Then the heroes rode home and told the king of this, and he said that he would lay claim to it on their behalf.

IV. The Angles—O. E. Engle.

OFFA—Lat. Uffo.

1. *Wīdsīð* (seventh century) ll. 35–44.

Offa ruled over Angel, Alewīh ruled the Danes;
Alewīh was the bravest of all these men, yet he never
outdid Offa in deeds of valour. Offa, of all men, while
still a youth, won the greatest of kingdoms at one stroke;
no one of the same age as he ever did greater deeds of
valour in battle with his single sword. He fixed the
boundary against the Myrgingas at Fīfeldor, and ever
afterwards the Engle and the Swǣfe kept it as Offa's
stroke had established it.

2. *The Anglo-Saxon Chronicle* (MSS. Ā, B, C) for A.D. 755.

In this same year Offa succeeded to the kingdom [of
Mercia], and ruled for thirty-nine years; and his son
Ecgfrith ruled one hundred and forty-one days. That
Offa was the son of Thingfrith, the son of Eanwulf, the
son of Osmond, the son of Eawa, the son of Pybba, the
son of Creoda, the son of Cynewald, the son of Cnebba,
the son of Icel, the son of Eomer, the son of Angeltheow,
the son of Offa, the son of Wermund, the son of Wiht-
læg, the son of Woden.

3. Sven Aageson, *A Brief History of the Kings of Denmark*,
(*c.* 1187) chs. 2 and 3.

The son and heir [of Frothi the Bold], Wermundus,
succeeded to the kingdom; he was so outstanding for the
virtue of prudence that he got his nickname from it, and
for this reason was called 'the Prudent'. He begot a son
named Uffo, who suppressed his faculty of speech until
the thirtieth year of his life because of the burden of

disgrace which had fallen upon the Danes at that time, due to the fact that two Danes who had gone to Sweden to avenge their father's death slaughtered his slayer by attacking him both at once. For in those days it was reckoned a shameful and unseemly deed if two men slew one who was alone.

Now this under-king Wermundus held sway over his kingdom until his old age, and by then was so stricken in years that his eyes had grown blind with age. When the news of this infirmity reached the regions beyond the Elbe, the pride of the Teuton king began to swell and grow puffed up, so that he was no longer content with his own boundaries. So this emperor wreaked his fury upon the Danish people, seeing himself as having already conquered the Danish kingdom and won the Danish sceptre for his glory. Spearmen were therefore sent to carry the message of this puffed-up prince to the under-king of the Danes, that is, Wermundus; they set before him a choice of two courses, neither of which, however, was good to choose. Either he must give up his kingdom to the Holy Roman Empire, and pay tribute, or he must seek a champion who would dare to risk himself in single combat with the emperor's champion.

Hearing this, the king was filled with dismay; but, gathering a host from far and wide from his whole kingdom, he eagerly inquired of them what ought to be done. He declared himself to be perplexed as to who it was on whom fell the duty of settling the matter by battle, and also who would undertake the defence of the realm. Blindness darkened his own face, and the heir to the kingdom, having been turned speechless, lived in idleness, so that by common consent it was agreed that there was no salvation to be expected from him. From childhood Uffo had indulged the gluttony of his belly, studiously cultivating the pleasures of kitchen and cellar, according to the ways of Epicurus. Therefore he had called them together from far and wide from his whole kingdom to an Assembly, and had explained the ambition of the German king; the old man asked them, with repeated questions, what should be done about this choice, scarcely to be chosen.

While the minds of them all were full of dismay at

these dire straits, Uffo, the under-king, arose in the midst of the assembly. When the whole host caught sight of him, they could hardly have been more amazed, that a speechless man should express himself with the studied gestures of oratory; and since we know that every new thing deserves admiration, he drew the attention of them all on himself.

At length he began to speak thus: 'Let these provocations not move us, for it is an innate feature of the puffed-up Teutons that they glory in bombastic words and have learnt by experience how to dismay cowards and idiots with empty wind and threatenings. Nature has made me the one true heir to this kingdom, on whom, as you know, falls the duty of defending it; I therefore boldly offer myself for single combat at this crisis, seeing that either I alone will fall for the kingdom, or else I alone will win victory for my homeland. And so, in order that this threatening bombast may cease, let them take back this message to the Emperor, that the son and heir of the ruler does not fear to face the Emperor's most outstanding champion alone.'

So he spoke, uttering his words in a proud voice. When he had finished his speech, the old man inquired of his neighbours whose this speech had been; but when he understood from those standing near by that his own son, formerly as if dumb, had poured out these words, he ordered that he should be called before him for him to feel him. And when he had repeatedly felt his shoulders, biceps, buttocks, calves, shin-bones and other bodily members, 'I remember', said he, 'that I was like that in the flower of my youth.'

Why say more? The time and place for the fight were settled, and on receiving this reply the messengers set out again for their own land.

It therefore remained for suitable weapons to be found for the new warrior. Swords were brought, the finest that the king could discover in his realm, but Uffo, shaking them one by one in his right hand, shattered them into tiny pieces. 'Are these things the weapons with which I am to defend my life and the honour of the realm?' he cried.

When his father knew of this proof of his vigorous

strength, he said: 'There still remains one hope of safety for our kingdom and our life.' So he demanded to be led to a mound in which he had formerly hidden a very well-tried blade, and soon, guided by means of tokens marked on the rocks, he ordered that this most excellent sword should be dug up. Grasping it straightway in his right hand, he said: 'It is with this, my son, that I triumphed many a time, and always it was an unfailing protection for me.' So saying, he handed it to his son.

No more delay! See, the time fixed for this encounter swiftly draws near! When at length innumerable companies of warriors had gathered from every quarter, the site of battle was agreed upon, in the middle of the River Eidor, in order that the fighters should receive no assistance, being cut off from all aid from either side. So the Teutons seated themselves on the farther bank of the river, in Holstein, and the Danes took up their positions on the nearer side of the stream, while the king chose a seat in the middle of a bridge, since if his only son should fall he would throw himself into the eddies, and not linger on, deprived at once of child and kingdom, to take his grey hairs in sorrow to the grave.

Next, the champions sent from either side met in the middle of the stream. But when our noble warrior Uffo saw that two men were coming against him, like a lion he growled from his mighty chest, and with steadfast heart did not shrink from boldly opposing himself to two picked men; he wore at his belt the sword which his father had kept hidden, as we have mentioned above, and carried another, drawn, in his right hand. As soon as he had come face to face with them, he addressed them both, one by one; rarely does one read of such things happening, but this most elegant champion of ours roused his adversaries' spirits to the combat, saying: 'If ambition to win our kingdom spurs you on, so that you yearn to seize our riches and our lavish wealth, it is for you to outdo your vassal in hand-to-hand combat, so that you may extend the boundaries of your kingdom and win a name for valour under the gaze of your warriors.'

And in this fashion he addressed the champion: 'Now is the time to put your courage to a further test, if you will draw near for fighting hand-to-hand, and will not delay in making public to the Danes that glory which you showed to the Germans long ago. Now, therefore, you will be able to increase your reputation for vigour, and grow rich in most lavish gifts, if you outdo your lord and shelter him with your protecting shield. Let him strive, I beg, to teach the Danes that vigour in the various arts of war in which Teutons are expert, so that you will be able to go back to your own people exulting in triumph at the longed-for victory.'

When he had finished this exhortation, the champion smote at the other's helmet with all his strength, so that, so they say, his sword broke in two. The sound of its breaking rang out over the whole army, so that the host of Teutons raised a great clamour of exultation, while on the other hand the Danes, desperate and dismayed, uttered a great groan in their grief. And indeed when the king heard that his son's sword had split apart, he ordered them to place him upon the edge of the bridge.

But Uffo suddenly drew that which he had girded on, and straightway drew blood with that sword from the warrior's hip; with no delay he cut off his head as well. Such then is the sport of Fortune, which is as variable as the moon, mocking now at these, and now at those that follow them; those to whom her favours even now brought great exultation, she soon looks at with a step-mother's countenance and with a harsh glance. Learning of this, the old man, more confident, bade them place him in his former seat again. Nor did the victory remain in doubt much longer. For Uffo, pressing hard upon the Emperor's heir, drove him back to the river bank, and there, with little trouble, slew him with his sword.

In this manner, by being the victor alone over two others, he wiped out well enough by his magnificent and glorious courage the infamy which had fallen on the Danes in times long past. And when the Germans had gone back to their own people, disgraced, ashamed, and with their bombastic threats proved empty, Uffo reigned over his kingdom henceforth in peace and tranquillity.

4. Saxo Grammaticus, *Danish History* (*c.* 1200), §§ 106–17.

Wermundus, [Vigletus'] son, succeeded him. The long
and leisurely tranquillity of a most prosperous and quiet
time flowed by, and Wermundus in undisturbed security
maintained a prolonged and steady peace at home. He
had no children during the prime of his life, but in old
age, by a belated gift of fortune, he begot a son, Uffo,
though all the years which had glided by had raised him
up no offspring. This Uffo surpassed all of his age in
stature, but in his early youth was supposed to have so
dull and foolish a spirit as to be useless for all affairs
public or private. For from his first years he never used
to play or make merry, but was so void of all human
pleasure that he kept his lips sealed in a perennial silence,
and utterly restrained his austere visage from the business
of laughter. But though through the years of his youth
he was reputed for an utter fool, he afterwards left that
despised estate and became famous, turning out as great
a pattern of wisdom and hardihood as he had been a
picture of stagnation. His father, seeing him such a
simpleton, got him for a wife the daughter of Frowinus,
the governor of the men of Sleswik; thinking that by his
alliance with so famous a man Uffo would receive help
which would serve him well in administering the realm.
Frowinus had two sons, Keto and Wigo, who were
youths of most brilliant parts, and their excellence, not
less than that of Frowinus, Wermundus destined to the
future advantage of his son. . . .

[A Swedish king Athislus—not identical with
the Aðils of III E—made raids on Denmark and
killed Frowinus in single combat. Keto and Wigo,
though young, set out for Sweden in disguise, and
confronted Athislus, who boasted that he had
slain their father and could easily slay them, even
if they both attacked him at once, as, for their own
sakes, he advised them to do. Keto indignantly
refused, and attacked Athislus alone; however, the
Swedish king soon beat him to his knees, and
Wigo, seeing his brother's life in danger, broke the
rules of single combat by coming to his aid,

227

Together they killed Athislus, though realizing the deed was dishonourable. Wermundus honoured them for ridding him of a rival, but men of other nations blamed them for breaking the rules of duelling.]

When Wermundus was losing his sight by infirmity of age, the King of Saxony, thinking that Denmark lacked a leader, sent envoys ordering him to surrender to his charge the kingdom which he held beyond due term of life; lest, if he thirsted to hold sway too long, he should strip his country of laws and defence. For how could he be reckoned a king, whose spirit was darkened with age, and his eyes with a blindness not less black and awful? If he refused, but had yet a son who would dare accept the challenge and fight with his son, let him agree that the victor would possess the realm. But if he approved neither offer, let him learn that he must be dealt with by weapons and not by warnings, and in the end he must unwillingly surrender what he was too proud at first to yield uncompelled.

Wermundus, shaken by deep sighs, answered that it was too insolent to sting him with these taunts upon his years; for he had passed no timorous youth, nor shrunk from battle, that age should bring him to this extreme misery. It was equally unfitting to cast in his teeth the infirmity of his blindness, for it was common for a loss of this kind of accompany such a time of life as his, and it seemed a calamity fitter for sympathy than for taunts. It were juster to fix blame on the impatience of the King of Saxony, whom it would have beseemed to wait for the old man's death, and not demand his throne; for it was somewhat better to succeed to the dead than to rob the living. Yet, that he might not be thought to make over the honours of his ancient freedom, like a madman, to the possession of another, he would accept the challenge with his own hand. The envoys answered that they knew their king would shrink from the mockery of fighting a blind man, for such an absurd mode of combat was thought more shameful than honourable. It would surely be better to settle the affair by means of their offspring on either side.

The Danes were in consternation, and at a sudden loss for a reply; but Uffo, who happened to be there with the rest, craved his father's leave to answer, and suddenly the dumb as it were spake. When Wermundus asked who had thus begged leave to speak, and the attendants said it was Uffo, he declared that it was enough that the insolent foreigner should jeer at the pangs of his misery, without those of his own household vexing him with the same wanton effrontery. But the courtiers persistently averred that this man was Uffo, and the king said: 'He is free, whosoever he be, to say out what he thinks.' Then said Uffo, that it was idle for their king to covet a realm which could rely not only on the service of its ruler, but also on the arms and wisdom of most valiant nobles. Moreover, the king did not lack a son, nor the kingdom an heir; and they were to know that he had made up his mind to fight not only the son of the king, but also, at the same time, whatsoever man the prince should elect as his comrade out of the bravest of their nation.

The envoys laughed when they heard this, thinking it idle lip-courage. Instantly the ground for the battle was agreed on, and a fixed time appointed. But the bystanders were so amazed by the strangeness of Uffo's speaking and challenging, that one can scarce say if they were more astonished at his words or at his assurance.

But on the departure of the envoys Wermundus praised him who had made the answer, because he had proved his confidence in his own valour by challenging not one only, but two; and said he would sooner quit his kingdom for him, whoever he was, than for an insolent foe. But when one and all testified that he who with lofty self-confidence had spurned the arrogance of the envoys was his own son, he bade him come nearer to him, wishing to test with his hands what he could not with his eyes. Then he carefully felt his body, and found by the size of his limbs and by his features that he was his son; and then began to believe their assertions, and to ask him why he had taken pains to hide so sweet an eloquence with such careful dissembling, and had borne to live through so long a span of life without utterance

or any intercourse of talk, so as to let men think him
utterly incapable of speech, and a born mute. He replied
that he had been hitherto satisfied with the protection
of his father, that he had not needed the use of his voice
until he saw the wisdom of his own land hard pressed by
the glibness of a foreigner. The king also asked him why
he had chosen to challenge two rather than one. He said
that he had desired this mode of combat in order that the
death of King Athislus, which, having been caused by
two men, was a standing reproach to the Danes, might
be balanced by the exploit of one, and that a new en-
sample of valour might erase the ancient record of their
disgrace. Fresh honour, he said, would thus obliterate
the guilt of their old dishonour.

Wermundus said that his son had judged all things
rightly, and bade him first learn the use of arms, since he
had been little accustomed to them. When they were
offered to Uffo, he split the narrow links of the mail-
coats by the mighty girth of his chest, nor could any be
found large enough to hold him properly. For he was
too hugely built to be able to use the arms of any other
man. At last, when he was bursting even his father's
coat of mail by the violent compression of his body,
Wermundus ordered it to be cut away on the left side
and patched with a buckle, thinking it mattered little if
the side guarded by the shield were exposed to the sword.
He also told him to be most careful in fixing on a sword
which he could use safely. Several were offered him;
but Uffo, grasping the hilt, shattered them one after
another into flinders by shaking them, and not a single
blade was of so hard a temper but at the first blow he
broke it into many pieces.

But the king had a sword of extraordinary sharpness,
called 'Skrep', which at a single blow of the smiter
struck straight through and cleft any obstacle whatso-
ever; nor would aught be hard enough to check its edge
when driven home. The king, loth to leave this for the
benefit of posterity, and greatly grudging others the
use of it, had buried it deep in the earth, meaning, since
he had no hopes of his son's improvement, to debar
everyone else from using it. But when he was now asked
whether he had a sword worthy of the strength of Uffo,

he said he had one which, if he could recognize the lie of the land and find what he had consigned long ago to earth, he could offer him as worthy of his bodily strength. Then he bade them lead him into a field, and kept questioning his companions over all the ground. At last he recognized the tokens, found the spot where he had buried the sword, drew it out of its hole, and handed it to his son. Uffo saw it was frail with great age and rusted away; and, not daring to strike with it, asked if he must prove this one also like the rest, declaring that he must try its temper before the battle ought to be fought. Wermundus replied that if this sword were shattered by mere brandishing, there was nothing left which could serve for such strength as his. He must therefore forbear from the act, whose issue remained so doubtful.

So they repaired to the field of battle as agreed. It is fast encompassed by the waters of the River Eider, which roll between, and forbid any approach save by ship. Hither Uffo went unattended, while the Prince of Saxony was followed by a champion famous for his strength. Dense crowds on either side, eager to see, thronged each winding bank, and all bent their eyes upon this scene. Wermundus planted himself on the end of the bridge, determined to perish in the waters if defeat were the lot of his son; he would rather share the fall of his own flesh and blood than behold, with heart full of anguish, the destruction of his own country.

Both the warriors assaulted Uffo; but, distrusting his sword, he parried the blows of both with his shield, being determined to wait patiently and see which of the two he must beware of most heedfully, so that he might reach that one at least by a single stroke of his blade. Wermundus, thinking that his feebleness was at fault, that he took the blows so patiently, dragged himself, little by little, in his longing for death, forward to the western end of the bridge, meaning to fling himself down and perish, should all be over with his son. Fortune shielded the old father who loved so passionately, for Uffo told the prince to engage with him more briskly, and to do some deed of prowess worthy of his famous race, lest the low-born squire should seem braver than the prince. Then, in order to try the bravery of the champion, he bade him not skulk timorously at his master's heels, but requite by noble deeds of combat the trust placed in him by his prince, who had chosen him to be his single partner in the battle. The other complied, and when shame drove him to fight at close quarters, Uffo clove him through with the first stroke of his blade. The sound revived Wermundus, who said that he heard the sword of his son, and asked on what particular part he dealt the blow. Then the retainers answered that he had gone through no one limb, but through the man's whole frame, whereat he drew back from the precipice and came again on the bridge, longing now as passionately to live as he had just wished to die. Then Uffo, wishing to destroy his remaining foe after the fashion of the first, incited the prince with vehement words to offer some sacrifice by way of requital to the shade of the servant slain in his cause. Drawing him by these appeals, and warily noting the right spot to plant his blow, he turned the other edge of his sword to the front, fearing that the thin side of his blade was too frail for his strength, and smote with a piercing stroke through the prince's body. When Wermundus heard it, he said that the sound of his sword Skrep had reached his ear for the second time. Then, when the judges announced that his son had killed both enemies, he burst into tears from excess of joy. Thus gladness bedewed the cheeks which sorrow could not moisten. So while the Saxons, sad and shamefaced, bore their champions to burial with bitter shame, the Danes welcome Uffo and bounded for joy. Then no more was heard of the disgrace of the murder of Athislus, and there was an end of the taunts of the Saxons.

Thus the realm of Saxony was transferred to the Danes; Uffo, after his father, undertook its government; and he, who had not been thought equal to administering a single kingdom properly, was now appointed to manage both. Most men have called him Olavus, and he has won the name of 'the Gentle' for his forbearing spirit. His later deeds, lost in antiquity, have lacked formal record. But it may well be supposed that when their beginnings were so notable, their sequel was glorious.

I am so brief in considering his doing, because the lustre of the famous men of our nation has been lost to memory and praise by the lack of writings. But if by good luck our land had in old times been endowed with the Latin tongue, there would have been countless volumes to read of the exploits of the Danes.

Uffo was succeeded by his son Dan. . . .

5. *The Lives of the Two Offas* (*c.* 1200), by a monk of St Albans Abbey.

(*a*) Here begins the story of Offa I, who by his valour subjected the greater part of Angle to himself; Offa II was like to him.

Among the most illustrious kings of the West Angles, King Warmundus was honoured with particular praise by those who were in the habit not only of relating Anglian stories by word of mouth, but also of including them in their writings. He was the founder of a certain city which took its name from him, being called in English Warwick, that is, 'Warmund's Homestead'. He lived on into old age without any children, except for one son, whom he thought unfit to be his heir and successor, as he had suffered since childhood from a troublesome disability. It must indeed be granted that this only son, named Offa or Offanus, was tall in stature, sound in body, and a handsome-looking youth, yet he had remained blind from his birth till the age of seven, and till the age of thirty was dumb, uttering no human word. Not only the king, but also the nobles of the kingdom found this troublesome disability of his harder to bear than one can say. For great age had come upon his father, who did not know when he might die, nor did he know whom he could appoint as his heir and successor to the kingdom. One of the chief men in the kingdom, whose name was Riganus, together with an accomplice named Mitunnus (one ambitious man with another, a misleader with a traitor), seeing the king growing feeble and sinking into old age without hope of begetting a son, grew presumptuous and began to aspire to the heights of kingly rank, despising the other great men of the kingdom, and thinking himself alone more worthy than the rest. Therefore he plagued the king day after day, shamelessly pressing him as his heir. . . .

[When the king could not be persuaded to this, Riganus rebelled, proclaimed himself king, and gathered many supporters. King Wermundus summoned an Assembly.]

While they were debating publicly for several days, discussing this urgent crisis, the king's only son mingled with the speakers, listening with sharp ears to every man's speech, though he himself had hitherto been speechless and dumb. When he noted how his father was considered an old man, and how he himself was despised and blamed by everyone as being useless and inefficient in the business of kingship, he was so contrite and humbled in his heart as to burst into a flood of tears. His eyes were a channel for these waters, and his heart within him burned with most bitter grief. What he could not utter in words, God's inward prompting suggested to his heart, so that, groaning and inwardly repeating his tearful plaint, he prayed that he might receive comfort from the Holy Spirit, strength from the Father of Lights, and the grace of wisdom and salvation from the Only-Begotten Son of the Father. So, to be brief, He to whom everything lies naked and open, seeing the prayer of a contrite heart, opened the lips of the youth in clear and well articulated words.

Suddenly and unexpectedly he spoke thus of those puffed-up princes of the realm who had made a threatening tumult against his father and himself: 'Why, when my father and I are still alive, do you outrageously claim to lay hands on the government of the kingdom? And, excluding me, the born heir, why do you choose instead another man—ignoble, stained with crimes, and all too prone to burst out with proud threats and oath-breakings —so that we might, not unjustly, accuse you of wickedness? And what, I say, would strangers and foreigners do against us, when you, our own kinsmen and followers, want to expel us from our country, which our race has possessed till now by rightful hereditary succession?'

While this Offanus or Offa (for that was the name of

the youth), who now for the first time deserved to
receive a title of eternal fame and blessed memory, was
continuing his speech with fluent lips, eloquent rhetoric,
and a calm countenance, he drew to himself the eyes,
faces, and hearts of all who heard him, and they were
more astonished than one can say. And pursuing the
speech he had begun, he said, raising his eyes to Heaven:
'I call God to witness, and all the powers of the courts
of Heaven, that I will not suffer those who have kindled
such evil and dissension to remain safe and unpunished
—unless those who have begun to stumble return,
strengthened, to their former loyalty. But those who are
faithful and valiant I will treat with all honour and
favour.' . . .

[But Riganus and Mitunnus remain obstinately
rebellious, and both sides prepare for war.]

[The king's advisers] first counselled the king to have
his son adorned with a soldier's sword-belt, as he was
mature enough for this, both in years and character, so
that when he went to war he should strike fear and
horror into his foes. Submitting to the sane and whole-
some counsel of his men, the king girded his son with
a sword on an appointed day, with royal pomp and
solemnity. . . .

[The armies gather, among them two outstanding
young warriors named Otta and Milio, sons of one
of the rebel leaders. The armies encamp at an
appointed spot, on either side of a raging river;
nobody dares cross it, until Offa suddenly dashes
across, kills several of the enemy, and puts others to
flight. A long, bloody and indecisive battle ensues.]

By chance, the two sons of the powerful man who had
tried to usurp the kingdom came face to face with Offa.
The name of the elder was Brutus (or Hildebrand), and
of the younger, Sueno. They disrespectfully attacked
Offa with insults and foul words, and shamefully
attacked the youth with weapons as well as words,
before the eyes of the whole army. So Offa, deeply

affronted, glowing with fiery courage, and so inflamed with rage that he growled aloud, charged them boldly in his impetuous zeal. With one stroke of his sword he struck down one of them, Brutus, slashing off the crest of his helmet and piercing the skull to the brain, and casting him down, as the death rattle sounded, to lie under the horses' hooves. Then he rapidly pursued the other, who had taken to flight on seeing this, and humiliated him, prostrating him with a lethal wound.

[Offa puts the rest of the enemy to flight; Riganus is drowned in the river, and the men led by Mitunnus flee by night. Offa is welcomed home in triumph, and his father abdicates in his favour. Some years later, Offa marries the much-wronged daughter of the King of York, who had fled from home; she bears him two sons. Through the evil plots of her father, she and her children, when separated from Offa, are attacked and left for dead in a forest; a hermit heals them miraculously, and when Offa eventually finds them again he vows to build a monastery in thanksgiving, but forgets his vows.]

(*b*) The life of Offa II, King of Mercia.

[This Offa was a descendant of Offa I, several generations later; his reign was from 757 to 796.]

One day during his reign, at the time when the most victorious King Charlemagne was reigning in France, a certain girl who was a kinswoman of that monarch, who was lovely of face but shamefully wicked in mind, was legally condemned to a disgraceful death because of some exceedingly evil deed which she had committed; yet, out of respect for the king's honour, she was not condemned to die by fire or by the sword, but to be exposed to the winds and seas, with all their hazards, in a small boat lacking all gear, and equipped with very little food. After she had been long tossed to and fro by changeable storms, she was driven, as luck would have it, on to the shores of Britain, and as her boat came to land in the region subject to King Offa's power she was forthwith led into the king's presence. When she was

questioned as to who she was, she answered that she
was a kinswoman of King Charlemagne (as indeed her
native speech confirmed), and was called Drida; but
that she had been condemned to this peril through the
injustice of certain ignoble persons, whose offers of
marriage she had spurned, so as not to bring dishonour
on her race. With gushing tears she added: 'God, who
frees the innocent from the snares of the treacherous,
happily brought me as a captive beneath the wings of
your protection, O noblest of kings, so that my mis-
fortune might be changed into good fortune, and that all
future generations might say of me that I was more
blessed in my exile than in my native land.'

[Offa entrusts her to the care of his mother, who
feeds and comforts her; all admire her great beauty,
but she repays the queen mother's kindness by mis-
chief-making. Offa falls in love with her and marries
her, without consulting his parents, as he guesses they
would disapprove. From now on she is known as
Quendrida, 'id est regina Drida'. She now embarks
on a series of political crimes, plots and assassina-
tions, including attempts on the life of Offa himself.
After many years her wicked career is brought to
an end when she is murdered by robbers, who throw
her in a well, where she drowns. Offa founds the
monastery of St Albans in thanksgiving.]

6. *Annales Ryenses* (c. 1290).

Then Wermundus the Blind was king. . . . . In his
time, Keto and Wiggo, the sons of Earl Frowinus of
Sleswig, killed King Athislus of Sweden in vengeance
for their father. . . . Then reigned Uffo the Strong. He
had refused to speak from the age of seven until thirty,
right up to the day when he fought alone against the
son of the King of the Germans, and the best champion
of all Germany, at a place on the Eidor which is still
called Kunengikamp, and killed them both.

V. The Heathobards

(O.N.—cf. King Hǫðbrǫddr, II E 5 and II F 1, 2 and 8)

A. FRŌDA—O.N. Fróði/Frode—
Lat. Frotho/Frodo.

1. *Langfeðgatal* (twelfth century).

   [A genealogy of Danish kings.]

   . . . Frode the Bold; Ingialdr the foster-son of Star-kadr; his brother Halfdan. . . .

2. *Skjǫldunga saga* (c. 1200), in an abstract by Arngrímur Jóns-son (1596), ch. 9.

   As Alo had been born of a woman carried off in war, he was not considered fit for the succession [to the Danish throne], so Frodo succeeded, and Alo went off on Viking raids, from the success of which he got the nickname 'the Bold'. Frodo too began to grow glorious for many deeds, and to be called 'the Great' or 'the Famous'. He had his royal residence at Lethra [Leire] and at Ringsted; following his father's custom, he set up a court in which he maintained certain champions, powerful in their giant-like strength, and made Star-cardus their leader. He also had twelve earls subject to him.

   Meanwhile Alo, who as I have said was the brother of this Frodo on the father's side but not by the same mother, had won himself a kingdom in Sweden by his warlike prowess. . . . Then the Danish earls urged Frodo to lay a trap for his brother, for fear that this man, who was now so experienced in warfare, might turn his Swedish forces, his fleet, and his other warlike preparations against Frodo (as he was deprived of a share in his father's kingdom) and put an end to the safety of Denmark. Frodo listened to the evil counsels of his earls, and Starcardus was commissioned to perform this crime, since he indeed excelled the rest in courage and strength, and was the most willing to do Frodo's will. So he was induced to do this by the payment of 120 marks of refined silver, which the earls paid him as he set out. Starcardus yielded, though almost against his will; he left Ringsted, went to Sweden, and came with friendly greetings to Alo, by whom he was most honourably received and showered with rich gifts, since Alo suspected no evil. When he had already remained for quite a long while with the king, who treated him with the utmost favour and affection, it happened one day that the king, being about to wash in a hot bath, entrusted the protection of his life and limbs to Starcardus, whom he trusted more than the rest, even though he was a stranger. Then Starcardus, who had not forgotten his wicked vow (though up to now he had feared the very sharp glance of Alo's eyes, in which his power lay), seeing that the king's strength was considerably lessened by the bath, and that the force of his eyes and of his other senses was dulled, thrust a sword into his breast. Alo, at the point of death and grinning horribly with quivering nostrils, said: 'I see that my brother Frodo is the author of this deed!' And with a laugh he breathed forth his soul, while all others who were present dissolved into tears.

After he had committed this fratricide, King Frodo conquered King Jorundus of Sweden and ordered him to pay tribute, and did the same to a certain Swedish earl whose name was Sverting. At the same time Frodo carried off by force the Swedish king's daughter, and begot on her his son Halfdanus; she became his concubine. But later he married a different woman, and so had a son, Ingialldus, as his legitimate heir. . . .

[Starcardus, repentant, left Frodo's court and wandered abroad for many years. Ingialldus grew up and married Sverting's daughter, as a pledge of reconciliation.]

But the ties forged by this marriage could not save Frodo from paying the penalty he had deserved, by the power of the gods. By means of Starcardus he had killed his innocent brother; in his turn he was cut down by night, while carrying out the sacred rites of sacrifice, through a plot between King Jorundus of Sweden and his own kinsman-by-marriage, Earl Svertingus, whom no oath could bind. Starcardus was away in Sweden at the time; the Swedish king had enticed him with gifts, under the guise of friendship, to remain for a little while at his court, so that Svertingus should have a more convenient occasion for the killing he was to do.

[See also V B 4 below.]

3. Saxo Grammaticus, *Danish History* (*c.* 1200), VI §§ 182, 187–9.

Frotho . . . became from his very cradle and earliest childhood such a darling of all men, that he was not suffered even to step or stand upon the ground, but was continually cherished in people's laps and kissed. Thus he was not assigned to one upbringer only, but was in a manner everybody's fosterling. And after his father's death, while he was in his twelfth year, Swertingus and Hanevus, the kings of Saxony, disowned his sway and tried to rebel openly. He overcame them in battle, and imposed on the conquered peoples a poll-tax of a coin, which they were to pay as his slaves. . . .

[Arrival of Starcatherus at Frotho's court; description of his appearance; his past deeds.]

Meanwhile the Saxons began to attempt a revolt, and to consider particularly how they could destroy Frotho, who was unconquered in war, by some other way than an open conflict. Thinking it could be best done by a duel, they sent men to provoke the king to a challenge.

[But Starcatherus returns home unexpectedly, undertakes the duel on Frotho's behalf, and kills the

Saxon champion. The Danes then heavily increase
the taxes which the Saxons must pay.]

This Hanevus could not bear, and he meditated war
in his desire to remove the tribute. Steadfast love of his
country filled his heart every day with greater compas-
sion for the oppressed; and, longing to spend his life
for the freedom of his countrymen, he openly showed
a disposition to rebel. Frotho took his forces over the
Elbe, and killed him near the village of Hanover, so
called after Hanevus.

But Swertingus, though he was equally moved by the
distress of his countrymen, said nothing about the ills
of his land, and evolved a plan for freedom with a
spirit yet more dogged than Hanevus'. Men often doubt
whether this zeal was liker to vice or to virtue; but I
certainly censure it as criminal, because it was produced
by a treacherous desire to revolt. . . . The deed of Swer-
tingus was far from honourable . . . but the gains of
crime are inglorious, its fruits are brief and fading. . . .
For he had resolved to surprise the king under the
pretence of a banquet, and burn him to death; but the
king forestalled and slew him, though slain by him in
return. Hence the crime of one proved the destruction
of both; and thus, though the trick succeeded against
the foe, it did not bestow immunity on its author.

4. The enmity between Froda of the Heaðobards and the
Danes is also reflected in accounts of hatred between
Hálfdan and his brother Fróði—see above, II D.

V B. INGELD—O.N. Ingjaldr—
Lat. Hinieldus/Ingellus.

1. *Widsið* (seventh century), ll. 5–9.

Hrōðwulf and Hrōðgār . . . had humbled Ingeld's
battle-array, hewing down at Heorot the host of the
Heaðobards.

2. Letter of Alcuin to Bishop Hygebald of Lindisfarne (797).

... Let the Word of God be read when the clergy are
at their meal. It is seemly to hear a reader there, not a
harper; to hear the sermons of the Fathers of the Church,
not the lays of the heathen. For what has Hinieldus to
do with Christ? The house is narrow; it cannot contain
them both; the King of Heaven will have no part with
so-called kings who are heathen and damned, for the
One King reigns eternally in Heaven, while the other,
the heathen, is damned and groans in Hell. In your
houses the voices of readers should be heard, not a
rabble of men making merry in the streets.

3. *Langfeðgatal*, see V A 1 above.

4. *Skjǫldunga saga* (*c.* 1200), abstract by Arngrímur Jónsson
(1596), chs. 9–10.

Ingialldus the son of Frodo took as his wife the
daughter of that Earl Svertingus who was mentioned a
little while ago, in order, so it seemed to everyone, to
confirm friendship and reconciliation. ...

So when Frodo the Fourth had been slain, Svertingus
appeased Ingialldus, the son and heir of the slain man,
by ambassadors. But Halfdanus, brother of Ingialldus
by the same father, betook himself to Scania; he avenged
his father's fall by the slaughter of the twelve sons of
Svertingus, who had throttled Frodo with their own
hands. Then Ingialldus repudiated Svertingus' daughter
at the prompting of Starcardus, who had been utterly
hostile to his friendship with his father-in-law; he
then bestowed one third of the kingdom on his
half-brother Halfdanus, the avenger of their father's
fall. The repudiated wife bore to Ingialldus a son,
Agnarus.

[But later Ingialldus grudges his half-brother's
share of Denmark, and kills him. In due course
Ingialldus is killed in revenge by Halfdanus' two
young sons Roas and Helgo (i.e. Hróðgar and Hálga)
—see II D 2.]

5. Saxo Grammaticus, *Danish History* (*c*. 1200), VI §§ 189–90, 199–214.

Frotho was succeeded by his son Ingellus, whose soul was perverted from honour. He forsook the examples of his forefathers, and utterly enthralled himself to the lures of the most wanton profligacy. . . . For he was so prone to gluttony that he had no desire to avenge his father, or repel the aggressions of his foes. . . . Now the sons of Swertingus, fearing that they would have to pay to Ingellus the penalty of their father's crime, were fain to forestall his vengeance by a gift, and gave him their sister in marriage. . . .

When [Starcatherus] heard—for the rumour spread— that Ingellus, the son of Frotho (who had been treacherously slain), was perversely minded, and instead of punishing his father's murderers, bestowed upon them kindness and friendship, he was vexed to stinging wrath at so dreadful a crime. And, resenting that a youth of such great parts should have renounced his descent from his glorious father, he hung on his shoulders a mighty mass of charcoal, as if it were some costly burden, and made his way to Denmark. When asked by those he met why he was taking along so unusual a load, he said he would sharpen the dull wits of King Ingellus to a point by bits of charcoal. So he accomplished a swift and headlong journey, as though at a single breath, by a short and speedy track; and at last, becoming the guest of Ingellus, he went up, as his custom was, into the seat appointed for great men; for he had been used to occupy the highest post of distinction with the kings of the last generation. . . .

[In the absence of Ingellus, his wife, not realizing who this wild and filthy-looking warrior is, tries to turn him out of the highseat; in his rage Starcatherus shakes the walls of the hall and almost brings them to the ground. Ingellus returns, recognizes his foster father, and bids his wife wait on him.]

Then, learning too late the temper of the old man, she turned her harshness to gentleness, and respectfully

waited on him whom she had rebuffed and railed at
with bitter revilings. She wished to check his anger
with her attentiveness; and her fault was the less, inas-
much as she was so quick in ministering to him after
she had been chidden. But she paid dearly for it, for she
presently beheld stained with the blood of her brethren
the place where she had flouted and rebuffed the brave
old man from his seat. . . .

[There follows a feast, at which the sons of
Swertingus are present. Starcatherus refuses all
delicate foods and will only eat 'smoky and rancid
fare'; he flings an embroidered head-band which
the queen offers him back in her face; when a piper
appears to play to him he hurls a bone at his head—
'This man's hurt was ominous of the carnage that
was to follow at the feast.']

But when Starcatherus saw that the slayers of Frotho
were in high favour with the king, his stern glances
expressed the mighty wrath which he harboured, and
his face betrayed what he felt. . . . He said he had come
to Denmark to find the son of Frotho, not a man who
crammed his proud and gluttonous stomach with rich
elaborate feasts. . . . [Ingellus] bore the heaviest load of
infamy because, even when he first began to see service,
he forgot to avenge his father, to whose butchers, for-
saking the law of nature, he was kind and attentive.
Men whose deserts were most vile he welcomed with
loving affection; and not only did he let those go scot
free whom he should have punished most sharply, but
he even judged them fit persons to live with and enter-
tain at his table, whereas he should rather have put them
to death. Hereupon Starcatherus is said to have sung as
follows:

[The song is of seventy hexameters, including
complaints of the way he has been received, taunts
against gluttony, and contrasts between the austere
life at Frotho's court and the luxury at Ingellus'.
The parts most relevant to the theme of vengeance
are these:]

'Thou, Ingellus, buried in sin, why dost thou tarry

in the task of avenging thy father? Wilt thou think tranquilly of the slaughter of thy righteous sire? Why dost thou, sluggard, think only of feasting, and lean thy belly back in ease, more effeminate than harlots? Is the avenging of thy slaughtered father a little thing to thee?

'When last I left thee, Frotho, I learned by my prophetic soul that thou, mightiest of kings, wouldst surely perish by the sword of enemies; and while I travelled long in the land, a warning groan arose in my soul, which augured that thereafter I was never to see thee more. Woe is me that then I was far away, harrying the farthest peoples of the earth, when the traitorous guest aimed craftily at the throat of his king. Else would I either have shown myself the avenger of my lord, or have shared his fate and fallen where he fell, and would joyfully have followed the blessed king in one and the same death.' . . .

'Who would ever have borne to take money in ransom for the death of a lost parent, or asked a foe for a gift to atone for the murder of a father? What strong heir or well-starred son would have sat side by side with such as these, letting a shameful bargain utterly unnerve the warrior? Wherefore, when the honours of kings are sung, and bards relate the victories of captains, I hide my face for shame in my mantle, sick at heart. For nothing shines in thy trophies worthy to be recorded by the pen; no heir of Frotho is named in the roll of the honourable.' . . .

'Shame shall accompany thee far, and shall smite thy countenance with heavy disgrace, when the united assembly of the great kings is taking pastime. Since everlasting dishonour awaits thee, thou canst not come amidst the ranks of the famous; and in every clime thou shalt pass thy days in infamy. The fates have given Frotho an offspring born into the world when the gods were adverse, whose desires have been enthralled by crime and ignoble lust.' . . .

'Behold, a son of the tyrant Swertingus shall take the inheritance of Denmark after thee, he whose slothful

245

sister thou keepest in infamous union. Whilst thou delightest to honour thy bride, laden with gems and shining in gold apparel, we burn with an indignation that is linked with shame, lamenting thine infamies. When thou art stirred by furious lust, our mind is troubled, and recalls the fashion of ancient times, and bids us grieve sorely. For we rate otherwise than thou the crime of the foes whom thou now holdest in honour; wherefore the face of this age is a burden to me, remembering the ancient ways.

'I would crave no greater blessing, O Frotho, if I might see those guilty of thy murder punished for such a crime!'

Now he prevailed so well by this stirring counsel, that his reproach served like a flint to strike a blazing flame of valour in the soul that had been chill and slack. For the king had at first heard the song inattentively; but, stirred by the earnest admonition of his guardian, he conceived in his heart a tardy fire of revenge, and, forgetting the reveller, he changed into a foeman. At last he leapt up from where he lay, and poured the whole flood of his anger on those at table with him; insomuch that he unsheathed his sword upon the sons of Swertingus with bloody ruthlessness, and aimed with drawn sword at the throats of those whose gullets he had pampered with the pleasures of the table. These men he forthwith slew, and by so doing he drowned the holy rites of the table in blood. He sundered the feeble bond of their league, and he exchanged a shameful revel for enormous cruelty; the host became the foe, and that vilest slave of excess the blood-thirsty agent of revenge.

[Starcatherus sang again:]

'King Ingellus, farewell; thy heart, full of valour, has now shown a deed of daring. The spirit that reigns in thy body is revealed by its fair beginning, nor did there lack deep counsel in thy heart, though thou wert silent till this hour; for thou dost redress by thy bravery what delay had lost, and redeemest the sloth of thy spirit by mighty valour. Come now, let us rout the rest, and let none escape the peril which all alike deserve. Let the crime come home to the culprit, let the sin return and crush its contriver.

'Let the servants take up in a car the bodies of the slain, and let the attendant quickly bear out the carcasses. Justly shall they lack the last rites; they are unworthy to be covered with a mound; let no funeral procession or pyre suffer them the holy honour of a barrow; let them be scattered to rot in the fields, to be consumed by the beaks of birds; let them taint the country all about with their deadly corruption.

'Do thou too, king, if thou hast any wit, flee thy savage bride, lest the she-wolf bring forth a litter like herself, and a beast spring from thee that shall hurt its own father.'

VI. The Frisians and their Foes

A. FINN

1. *Wīdsīð* (seventh century), l. 27.

> Finn, son of Folcwald, [ruled] the Frisian race.

2. Nennius, *History of the Britons* (c. 800), § 31.

> Meanwhile there arrived three ships driven into exile
> from Germany, on board which were Hors and Hengest;
> these were brothers, the sons of Guictgils, the son of
> Guitta, the son of Guectha, the son of Woden, the son
> of Frealaf, the son of Fredulf, the son of Finn, the son of
> Folcwald, the son of Geta, who was, so they say, the son
> of God.

> [Cf. the Wessex genealogies, II B 1, 2, 3; Nennius
> has substituted Finn son of Folcwald for Finn son
> of Godwulf.]

B. FINN'S ADVERSARIES

1. *The Finnsburg Fragment* (eighth century?).

> '. . . gables burning.'
> Then Hnæf, the young warrior king, cried aloud:
> 'This is no dawn that breaks in the east, nor is there a
> dragon flying here, nor are this hall's gables burning!
> Nay, men bear weapons hither, the birds sing and the
> grey-coated wolf is howling, the spear rings out, the
> shield echoes to the shaft. Now the moon is shining,
> wandering through the clouds; now shall arise such
> deeds of woe as will satisfy the deadly spite of this race.
> So awake now, my fighting men, take up your shields,

248

set your minds upon valour, fight your way in the van, keep your courage high!'

Many a thane then rose up, his arms laden with gold, and girded on his sword. The lordly champions Sigeferth and Ēaha went to the doorway and drew their swords, and at the other door were Ordlāf and Gūðlāf, while Hengest himself followed in their tracks.

Meanwhile, Gūðere held Gārulf back, urging him not to betake himself in his armour to the door of the hall, and thus expose so noble a life in the first onslaught, now that a man hardy in combats meant to take it from him. But the bold-hearted warrior openly asked, above all the din, who it was who guarded that door.

'My name is Sigeferð,' said the other, 'I am prince of the Secgan, an exile known far and wide; many woes have I lived through, many hard battles. Whatever fate you seek of me, it is ordained for you here.'

Then the clamour of slaughter was heard in the hall— the hollow shield that guards men's bones now must break in brave men's hands, and the floor of the stronghold groaned—till Gārulf the son of Gūðlāf fell in this fray, first of all those who dwelt in that land, and around him fell many a fine man, a host of them, pale in death. The raven circled, dark and dusky. The gleam of swords flashed, as if all Finnsburg were ablaze. Never have I heard tell of sixty conquering heroes bearing themselves more nobly or more honourably in warriors' conflict than these, nor did youths ever give finer payment for their shining mead than Hnæf's young followers repaid him now.

They fought for five days, so well that not one among all those retainers fell, and still they held the doors. Then one warrior drew back and turned away wounded, saying that his corselet was broken, his warlike garb weakened, his helmet also pierced through. The guardian of the people [i.e. Finn?] asked him at once how those fighters bore their wounds, and whether any of those youths. . . .

2. *Wīdsīð* l. 29.

Hnæf [ruled] the Hocingas.

[cf. Hōc, father of Hildeburh and Hnæf, *Beowulf* l. 1076.]

3. *Widsið* l. 31.

Sæferð [ruled] the Sycgas.

[cf. Sigeferð of the Secgan, above.]

4. *Skjoldunga saga* (*c.* 1200) in an abstract by Arngrímur Jónsson (1596), ch. 4.

[A list of the six sons of Leifus, fourth king of Denmark, comprises the following names, of which three are reminiscent of names in the Finn Episode of Beowulf and in the Finnsburg fragment:]

Herleifus, Hunleifus, Aleifus, Oddleifus, Geirleifus, Gunnleifus.

VII. The Volsungs

SIGEMUND and FITELA—O.N. Sigmundr and Sinfjǫtli.

1. *Eiríksmál* (c. 955) ll. 16–19.

   [Óðinn bids dead heroes in Valhǫll welcome a newcomer.]

   > Sigmundr, Sinfjǫtli, spring to your feet,
   >   Go forth to meet the king!
   > Bid him come in, if Eiríkr it be;
   >   His coming we now await.

   [Cf. II A 1.]

2. *Hyndluljóð* (date uncertain; found in *Flateyjarbók c.* 1375) strophe 2.

   [Freyja praises Óðinn's generosity.]

   > To Hermóðr he gave a helm and corselet,
   > And to Sigmundr a sword for his own.

3. *The Death of Sinfjǫtli* (prose link-passage in the *Poetic Edda*, c. 1270).

   Sigmundr, son of Vǫlsungr, was king in the land of the Franks; the eldest of his sons was Sinfjǫtli, the second Helgi, the third Hamundr. Sigmundr's wife Borghildr had a brother. Now her stepson Sinfjǫtli and her brother both asked for the hand of the same woman, and because of this quarrel Sinfjǫtli killed him. And when he came home again, Borghildr told him to leave the country, but Sigmundr offered her money as compensation, and this she had to accept.

   Now at the funeral feast Borghildr carried the ale round. She took a powerful poison, a whole horn full, and carried it to Sinfjǫtli. But when he looked into the horn he realized that there was poison in it and said to Sigmundr: 'The drink is cloudy, father.' Sigmundr took the horn and drank it up. It is said that Sigmundr was so hardened that poison could do him no harm, neither outside nor in, and all his sons could bear poison externally on the skin.

Borghildr carried a second horn and bade him drink it, and everything happened as before. And again, for the third time, she carried the horn to him and heaped reproaches on him if he would not drink it up. Again he spoke to Sigmundr, in the same way as before. He said: 'Then let your moustache be the strainer, son!' Sinfjǫtli drank, and was dead at once.

Sigmundr carried him in his arms along distant paths, and came to a long, narrow fjord, and there there was a small boat with only one man in it. This man offered Sigmundr a passage across the fjord; but when Sigmundr had carried the corpse out to the boat, the skiff was fully laden. The old man said Sigmundr should walk inland along the fjord. The old man pushed the boat from the shore, and vanished straight away.

King Sigmundr did not remain long in Denmark in Borghildr's kingdom after he had married her. He then went south to the land of the Franks, to the kingdom he had there. Then he married Hjǫrdis, daughter of King Eylimi; their son was Sigurðr. King Sigmundr fell in battle against the sons of Hundingr.

[In Norse tradition the dragon fight is not ascribed to Sigmundr, but to his son Sigurðr, whose first exploit is the killing of the killing of the dragon Fáfnir. See below, XI.]

4. *Vǫlsunga saga* (*c.* 1200–70) chs. 2–8, 10–11.

[King Vǫlsungr of Hunaland] had ten sons and one daughter. The eldest son was called Sigmundr, and the daughter Signý; these two were twins, and were the handsomest and most outstanding in every way among King Vǫlsungr's children, even though all of them were mighty men. The memory of all this has been long kept alive, and there has been much praise of how the Vǫlsungs were men of heroic valour, and of how, as is told in ancient tales, they surpassed most men in knowledge and in feats of skill and in their eagerness to excel in every way.

It is said that King Volsungr had a splendid hall built, and it was so fashioned that a great fruit tree stood inside it, and the branches of this tree, with their fair blossoms, grew out through the roof-beams of the hall, while the trunk stood in the hall below; and they called the tree Barnstokk.

There was a king called Siggeirr who ruled Gautland; he was a powerful king, with many men under him. He went to visit King Volsungr and asked for Signý's hand. The king listened favourably to his speech, and so did his sons, but she herself was reluctant to agree; however, she asked her father to decide on her behalf, as he did in other matters which concerned her. Now the king thought it advisable to arrange her marriage, and so she was betrothed to King Siggeirr.

Now when the time came to hold the wedding feast and marriage, King Siggeirr was to go to King Volsungr's home for the feast. The king made the finest preparations he could for this feast, and when all was ready for the feast King Volsungr's guests and King Siggeirr's guests both arrived on the appointed day, and King Siggeirr had many notable men with him. It is said that large fires had been laid down the whole length of the hall, and that the great apple tree which has been already spoken of was standing there in the midst of the hall.

The next thing to be told is that as men were sitting by the fires towards evening, a man walked into the hall. This man's appearance was that of a stranger to them all. The attire the man had on was this: he had a hooded cloak of flecked cloth wrapped round him, and he was barefooted and had linen breeches bound round his legs. This man was holding a sword in his hand, and he walked up to Barnstokk; he had a hood pulled low over his head; he was very grey, aged, and one-eyed. He drew the sword and thrust it into the trunk, so that it plunged in up to the hilt. They all found that any greetings to this man froze on their lips.

He then began to speak, and said: 'He who draws

this sword out from the tree-trunk shall receive it from me as a gift, and he himself shall find it true that never in his life did he bear in his hand a better sword than this.'

Thereupon the old man went out of the hall, and none knew who he was or where he went. So now they stood up, for none of them would leave it to the others to take the sword, and whoever got it out first would think he had done best for himself. Then the men of highest rank went up first, and then the rest one after another, but no one who went up could get it out, for it would not shift at all when they took hold of it. Now there came Sigmundr, King Vǫlsungr's son, and took hold of the sword and drew it out of the trunk, and it was as if it lay loose to his hand. This weapon seemed so fine to them all that they none of them thought they had ever seen so fine a sword, and King Siggeirr offered to weigh him out three times its weight in gold.

Sigmundr said: 'You could have taken that sword just as well as I did from where it was set, if it had been right that you should bear it; but now that it has come to my hand first, you shall never get it, even if you offer all the gold you have in exchange.'

King Siggeirr grew angry at these words, and thought he had been given a scornful answer. But as he was by nature a very underhand man, he behaved now as if he did not mind the affair, though that very evening he thought of a way of paying him back for this, as later came about. . . .

[Three months later, Siggeirr invited Vǫlsungr and his ten sons to a feast and treacherously attacked them. Vǫlsungr was killed and his sons taken prisoner.]

Signý found out that her father was slain, and her brothers taken prisoner and condemned to death. So she called King Siggeirr to speak with her alone, and she said: 'I wish to ask you not to have my brothers slain so speedily; rather, have them set in the stocks, because I have come to the point when, as the saying is, "while the eye can see, the heart's content". The reason I ask nothing further for them is that I believe it would be of no use.'

Then Siggeirr answered: 'You are mad and out of
your mind to ask for more misfortunes for your brothers
than that they should be beheaded; yet I shall grant you
this, for the worse they suffer and the longer their death-
agony lasts, the better pleased I am.'

Now he ordered that things should be done as she
asked, and a large set of stocks was brought and fastened
round these brothers' legs at a certain spot in a forest,
and there they now sat all day long till night. And at
midnight a she-wolf, an old one, came towards them
out of the forest as they sat in the stocks. She was large,
and evil-looking too. What she did was that she bit one
of them to death, then ate him all up, and then she went
away. Later, in the morning, Signý sent the servant she
most trusted to her brothers to learn what had happened,
and when he came back he told her that one of them was
dead. She thought it hard to bear if they should all go
the same way, and she be unable to help them. The tale
is soon told: for nine nights on end this same she-wolf
came at midnight and bit them to death and ate them
one by one, until all were dead except Sigmundr, who
alone remained. And now, before the tenth night came,
Signý sent her trusty servant to her brother Sigmundr,
giving him a handful of honey and telling him that he
must smear it over Sigmundr's face and put some of it
in his mouth. So now he went to Sigmundr and did as
he had been told, and then went home.

Later that night the same wolf came, according to her
habit, meaning to bite him to death like his brothers.
But now she caught a whiff from him from where the
honey had been smeared on, and she licked his face all
over with her tongue, and then stretched her tongue
into his mouth. He mustered up his courage, and bit
into the wolf's tongue. At this she jerked violently and
pulled hard away from him, thrusting her paws against
the stocks so that they split right open, but he held on
so firmly that the she-wolf's tongue was torn out by the
roots, and this was the death of her. And some men do
say that this same she-wolf was King Siggeirr's mother,
and that she had taken on this shape by witchcraft and
evil arts.

So now Sigmundr had got loose and the stocks were

broken, and he took up his abode in the forest. Signý again sent men to know what had happened and whether Sigmundr was alive, and when they came there he told the whole affair, and how things had gone between him and the wolf. Then they went home and told Signý what had happened. She then went to find her brother, and they settled on a plan that he should make an underground chamber there in the forest; and so things went on for a while, with Signý hiding him there and sending him whatever he needed. But King Siggeirr believed that all the Vǫlsungs were dead.

King Siggeirr had two sons by his wife, and it is said that when the elder son was ten years old, Signý sent him to find Sigmundr, so that he would give him help if he wanted to try some way of avenging his father. Now the boy set off into the forest, and late in the evening he came to Sigmundr's underground chamber; Sigmundr made him more or less welcome, and told him that he was to make some bread for them both—'and I'll look for some firewood'. And he handed him a bag of meal, but he himself went off to look for the wood. And when he came back, the boy had done nothing about making the bread. Now Sigmundr asked whether the bread was ready.

He said: 'I didn't dare touch the bag of meal, because there was something alive lying in the meal.'

Sigmundr now felt sure that this boy had not got spirit enough for him to want to keep him with him; when he and his sister next met, Sigmundr said that even if this boy were by his side he would not think he was any nearer having a man with him.

'Then take him and kill him,' said Signý. 'There's no need now for him to live any longer.'

And so he did.

That year passed by, and a year later Signý sent her younger son to find Sigmundr, and there is no need to make a long story of it, for things turned out just the same, and at Signý's bidding he killed the boy.

The next thing to be told is that one day, when Signý was sitting in her own chamber, there came to her there a sorceress who was very skilled in evil arts.

Signý then spoke with her. 'It is my wish', said she, 'that you and I should exchange shapes.'

The other, the sorceress, said: 'It shall be done as you say.'

And now by her arts she brought it about that they exchanged appearances, and at Signý's bidding the sorceress took her place and went to King Siggeirr's bed that night, and he did not find out that it was not Signý beside him.

As for Signý, it is said that she went to her brother's underground chamber and asked him to give her shelter for the night—'for I've lost my way out in the forest, and I don't know where I'm going'. He said that she could stay there, for he did not wish to refuse lodging to her, a solitary woman, and he felt sure that she would not repay him for his good hospitality by giving him away. So now she took shelter with him, and they sat down to their food. He often happened to glance at her, and the woman seemed handsome and fair. And when they had eaten their fill, he told her that he wished her to pass the night in his bed; she made no resistance, and for three nights on end he had her lying beside him. After this, she went home and found the sorceress and said that they must change back into their own shapes, and the woman did this.

And when time had gone by, Signý gave birth to a boy-baby. This boy was called Sinfjǫtli, and when he grew up he was tall and strong and handsome to look at, and very much took after the Vǫlsung family; and he was not quite ten years old when she sent him to the underground chamber to Sigmundr. She had made a test on her other sons before she sent them to Sigmundr; this was that she stitched their kirtles to their arms through the skin and flesh. They had borne it badly, and had screamed at it. She now did the same to Sinfjǫtli; he did not flinch. Then she stripped the kirtle off him, so that the skin came away with the sleeves. She said he would find it painful.

'Such pain seems little enough to a Vǫlsung,' said he.

So now the boy came to Sigmundr. Sigmundr told him to knead dough from their meal, and said he would look for firewood for them; he handed him a bag. Then

he went off to get the wood, and when he came back
Sinfjǫtli had finished the baking. Sigmundr then asked
him if he had found anything in the meal.

'I have a certain suspicion', said he, 'that there was
something alive in that meal when I first started knead-
ing it; but whatever it was, I've kneaded it in with the
rest.'

Then Sigmundr laughed and said: 'I don't think
you'll have this bread for your food this evening, for
you have kneaded a huge poisonous snake into it!'

Sigmundr was so mighty a man that he could eat
poison without coming to any harm, whereas it was all
right for Sinfjǫtli to let poison touch his skin, but not
for him to eat or drink it.

The next thing to tell is how Sigmundr thought
Sinfjǫtli too young to seek vengeance with him, and
wanted to train him first by something that needed
courage. So now they ranged far and wide through the
forest that summer, and killed men for their wealth.
Sigmundr thought he very much took after the Vǫlsung
family, but still he believed that he was King Siggeirr's
son, and he believed that he had his father's evil nature
as well as the valour of the Vǫlsungs; and he reckoned
that he was not much attached to his kinsmen, as he
would often remind Sigmundr of his wrongs, and
strongly urge him to kill King Siggeirr.

Now it so happened one day that they went into the
forest again to win themselves wealth, and they came
upon a hut, and two men asleep in the hut wearing thick
gold rings. An evil spell had come on them, for there
were wolf-skins hanging above them in the hut; on one
day in every ten they could get out of these skins. They
were kings' sons. Sigmundr and Sinfjǫtli put these
skins on but could not get out of them again, for there
was still the same magic in them as before. They even
spoke in the speech of wolves, and both of them under-
stood this speech. They now set off into the woods, each
of them going off on his own; they made a compact
that they would risk their lives if there were seven men
against them, but not against greater odds, and that
whichever of them met with trouble would call aloud
in wolf-speech.

'Let's not depart from this plan,' said Sigmundr, 'for you are young and very reckless. Men will think it good sport to hunt you.'

Now each went off on his own. And after they had parted, Sigmundr came upon seven men and called out in wolf-speech, and Sinfjǫtli heard and came at once and killed them all. They parted again, and before Sinfjǫtli had gone very far into the forest he came upon eleven men and fought them, and it turned out that he killed them all. He was indeed badly wounded, and went to the foot of an oak and rested there.

Then Sigmundr came up to him and said: 'Why didn't you call out?'

Sinfjǫtli said: 'I didn't want to call on you for help. You accepted help in killing seven men, and I am just a child beside you, but I didn't call for help in killing eleven men.'

Sigmundr leapt at him so fiercely that he staggered and fell, and Sigmundr bit him in the throat. They could not get out of the wolf-skins that day. Now Sigmundr laid him on his back and carried him back to the hut, and wished the trolls might run off with those wolf-skins.

One day Sigmundr saw two weasels; one bit the other in the throat and then ran into the forest and brought a leaf and laid it on the wound, and the other weasel jumped up whole again. Sigmundr went out and saw a raven flying with a leaf, and it brought it to him. He passed it across Sinfjǫtli's wound, and he jumped up whole as if he had never been wounded. After this they went to the underground chamber and stayed there till they could get out of their wolf-skins; they took them and burnt them in a fire, bidding them never bring harm on anyone again. While under this evil spell they had done many daring deeds in King Siggeirr's realm.

By the time that Sinfjǫtli was full-grown, Sigmundr thought he had thoroughly tested him. Now it was not long before Sigmundr wanted to seek vengeance for his father, if this could be obtained. So one day they set out from the underground chamber and came to King Siggeirr's homestead late that evening, and went into an entrance hall which lay in front of the main hall;

there were casks of ale in it, and there they hid themselves. Now the queen knew where they were and wanted to come to them, and when they met they made a plan to try to avenge their father when night came.

Signý and the king had two children who were only young. They were playing on the floor with gold trinkets, rolling them along the floor of the hall and running after them; and one gold ring rolled out into the room where Sigmundr and his companion were, and the little boy ran after it to find the ring. Now he saw two men sitting there, tall and grim-looking, with helmets coming down over their faces, and bright coats of mail. He ran back into the hall to his father and told him what he had seen, so now the king suspected that there was treachery planned against him. Signý now heard what they were saying; she got up, took both children, and went out to the entrance hall to the others and said they ought to know that the children had given them away—'and I advise you to kill them'.

'I will not kill your children,' said Sigmundr, 'even if they have given me away.'

But Sinfjǫtli would not let his heart fail him, but drew his sword and killed both children and threw them into the main hall in front of King Siggeirr. The king now stood up and called on his followers to seize the men who had been hiding in the entrance hall all evening; some now ran out and tried to lay hands on them, but they defended themselves well and valiantly, so that for a long while whoever came nearest them thought himself worst off. But in the end they were overpowered by numbers and taken prisoner, and then laid in bonds and fettered, and they sat there all night.

Now the king privately thought over what was the slowest death he knew of to inflict on them. And when morning came, the king ordered a huge burial mound to be built of stones and turf; and when that mound had been made, he had a great slab of rock set up in the middle of the mound, in such a way that one edge of the slab was pointing upwards and the other down; it was so large that it stretched across from wall to wall, so that one could not get round it. Then he ordered Sigmundr and Sinfjǫtli to be taken and put inside the mound, one in one half and one in the other, for he thought it would be worse for them not to be together and yet to be able to hear each other. And while men were at work turfing the mound over, Signý came up with a bundle of straw in her arms and threw it into the mound to Sinfjǫtli, and told the slaves to keep this a secret from the king; they agreed, and then the mound was closed up.

When night came, Sinfjǫtli said to Sigmundr: 'I don't think we'll be short of food in here for some time; the queen has thrown a ham into the mound, and she wrapped it up in straw.'

He ran his hand over the ham again, and found that Sigmundr's sword was stuck through it; he recognized it by the hilt, for it was dark in the mound, and he told Sigmundr. They were both filled with joy. Now Sinfjǫtli thrust the tip of the blade over the slab of rock, and dragged it down hard; the sword bit into the rock. Sigmundr now took hold of the tip of the blade, and now they sawed through the slab between them, never pausing till the sawing was finished. As the poem says:

> By their strength they sawed
> The mighty slab—
> Sigmundr with sword,
> Sinfjǫtli too.

So now they were free together inside the mound, and they sawed through stones and iron too, and so got out of the mound. They now went back to the hall; by this time all the men were asleep. They brought wood to the hall and set fire to the wood, and those who were inside awoke to find smoke, and the hall blazing over their heads. The king asked who had started the fire.

'Here are the two of us,' said Sigmundr, 'myself and Sinfjǫtli, my sister's son. And now we mean you to know that not all the Vǫlsungs are dead.'

Then he bade his sister come out, and accept all the esteem and high honour he could offer her, for he wished in this way to make up to her for all her wrongs.

She answered: 'Now you shall know whether I remembered my grudge against King Siggeirr for the slaying of King Vǫlsungr! I had our children killed when I thought them too slow to avenge my father, and I went to you in the forest in the likeness of a witch-woman, and Sinfjǫtli is your son as well as mine. It is because he is King Vǫlsungr's grandson through both father and mother that he has such great valour. I have done all this so that King Siggeirr should meet his death; indeed, I have done so much in order that this vengeance should come about, that it is not fitting that I should live, on any terms. Gladly will I now die with King Siggeirr, unwillingly though I married him.'

Then she kissed her brother Sigmundr, and Sinfjǫtli too, walked into the flames, and bade them farewell; thereupon she met her death there, with King Siggeirr and all his court.

The two kinsmen gathered a host of men and ships, and Sigmundr set out for his ancestral lands, and drove out the king who had settled there after King Vǫlsungr. Sigmundr now became a powerful king, and was famous, wise and ambitious. He married a woman who was called Borghildr. . . .

Sinfjǫtli now set out raiding once again. He saw a beautiful woman, and grew very eager to possess her. The brother of Borghildr, Sigmundr's wife, was also asking for this woman in marriage; they fought out their quarrel in a battle, and Sinfjǫtli killed this other king. He now went plundering far and wide, took part in many battles and always won the victory; he became a most famous and outstanding man, and came home that autumn with many ships and much wealth.

He told his father the news, and Sigmundr told his queen. She ordered Sinfjǫtli to leave the kingdom, saying she never wanted to see him again. Sigmundr said he would not allow him to leave, and he offered to pay her compensation with gold and great wealth, though never before had he paid compensation for any man's death; he said there was no glory in keeping up a feud against a woman. So she could not carry this plan of hers any further.

She said: 'You shall have your way, sire, as is only right.'

Now, on the king's advice, she held a funeral feast

for her brother, and prepared this banquet with all the best cheer she could, and invited many men to it. Borghildr carried the drink round to the men. She came up to Sinfjǫtli with a great horn, and said: 'Now drink, stepson.'

He took it, and looked into the horn, and said: 'The drink is cloudy.'

Sigmundr said: 'Give it to me, then.' He drank it up.

The queen said: 'Why should other men drink your ale for you?'

She came a second time with a horn, saying: 'Drink now.' And she taunted him with many words.

He took the horn and said: 'The drink is tainted.'

Sigmundr said: 'Give it to me, then.'

She came a third time, and bade him drink it up, if he had the spirit of a Vǫlsung.

Sinfjǫtli took the horn and said: 'There is poison in the drink.'

Sigmundr said: 'Let your moustache be the strainer, son!' The king was very drunk, which was why he spoke thus.

Sinfjǫtli drank, and at once fell dead. Sigmundr rose to his feet, and his grief came near to being the death of him; he took up the body in his arms and went off into the forest, and so came at last to a fjord. There he saw a man in a small boat; this man asked if he would agree to be ferried across the fjord by him, and he said yes. The boat was so small that it could not take them both, and so the body was laid in it, and Sigmundr walked on along the fjord. And straightway the boat vanished from Sigmundr's sight, and the man too. After this Sigmundr returned home and drove his queen out of the country, and not long afterwards she died. King Sigmundr now ruled his kingdom as before, and he is thought to have been the greatest king and greatest champion in ancient times. . . .

[Sigmundr's last battle.]

King Sigmundr now sounded his horn, which his father had owned, and urged his men on. Sigmundr had by far the smaller host. Now there began a hard

263

battle, and though Sigmundr was old he fought hard, and was always foremost among his men. Neither shield nor mail-coat could hold against him, and all day he charged the host of his enemies, and none could foresee how matters would end between them. Many a spear and arrow flew through the air, but his guardian goddesses protected him so well that he was never wounded, and no man could reckon how many fell before him; both his arms were bloodied to the shoulders.

And when the battle had been going on for some time, there came into the fray a man in a black hooded cloak, with the hood pulled low over his face; he had one eye, and a spear in his hand. This man walked up to King Sigmundr and raised the spear to bar his way, and when King Sigmundr struck out strongly, his sword struck the spear and broke in two. After this the losses began to change, for King Sigmundr's luck had turned, and many of his host fell. The king would not look to his safety, but urged his host onwards, but now the saying proved true that 'none can hold out against numbers'. In this battle King Sigmundr fell in the forefront of his army.

5. A carved stone recently found in the Old Minster, Winchester, shows a bound man lying prostrate, while a wolf stands over him and thrusts its tongue in his mouth. It dates from the early eleventh or late tenth century, and may indicate that the story of Sigemund and the she-wolf was known in England. See the *Antiquaries Journal* XLVI ii (1966) 329–32 and Plate LXIIa.

VIII. The Goths

A. EORMENRĪC—O.N. Jǫrmunrek(k)r/ Erminrekr—Lat. Ermenrichus/Jarmericus/Hermanaricus.

1. Ammianus Marcellinus, *Rerum Gestarum Libri* (*c.* 385), ch. 31, 3.

So the Huns [*c.* 376] overran the lands of those of the Alani who are neighbours to the Greuthungi and who are customarily known as the Tanaïtes, killed and plundered many of them, and made the survivors ally themselves with them in a treaty of friendship; after forming alliance with these, they more boldly invaded, in a sudden onslaught, the broad and fertile districts of Ermenrichus, a very warlike king who was feared by neighbouring nations because of many and various mighty deeds. Daunted by the violence of this sudden storm, he tried for a long time to stand as far as possible firm and unshaken; but since rumour exaggerated the horror of impending events in spreading the news of them, he put an end to his fear of these great perils by a voluntary death.

2. Jordanes, *Getica* (*c.* 550), chs. 23–4.

When Geberich, King of the Goths, had departed this life, Hermanaricus, the noblest of the Amali, shortly afterwards succeeded to the kingdom; he subdued many very fierce tribes and made them obey his laws, so that some of our forefathers have compared him in merit to Alexander the Great. . . . And, that he might grow famous through enslaving so many, he would not rest until he had also slaughtered a great part of the tribe of the Heruli, whose ruler was Halaricus, and subjected the remainder to his rule. . . . After the fall of the Heruli, Hermanaricus waged war on the

265

Venethi, who at first tried to resist, for they were strong in numbers, though laughably ill-armed. But a host of unwarlike men can do nothing, especially when God permits their defeat, and there is also an armed host attacking them. Those of whom we said, at the outset of our survey and list of tribes, that they all came from a single stock, had by now developed three names, that is, Venethi, Antes and Sclaveni, and were all subject to the rule of Hermanaricus (though, for our sins, they are up in arms everywhere today). And in the same way, by his wisdom and valour, this same man subdued the whole nation that occupied the long coastal areas, and thus by his own efforts ruled over all the nations of Scythians and Germans.

But after no very long lapse of time, as Orosius tells, the race of Huns, who were more terrible than all the rest for their ferocity, mustered against the Goths. . . .

When the Goths saw this race whom nothing could hold back and who had forced their advance onwards through so many nations, they were filled with fear, and discussed with their king how to defeat such a foe; for, as we have already said, Hermanaricus, King of the Goths, had triumphed in combat over many tribes. But while he brooded over the coming of the Huns, the treacherous tribe of the Rosomoni, whom among others he held in servitude, seized the opportunity to betray him. So the king, full of rage, ordered that a woman of this tribe, named Sunilda, should, on account of her husband's traitorous flight, be bound between wild horses and torn to pieces as they galloped different ways. In vengeance for their sister's death, her brothers Sarus and Ammius drove a sword through Hermanaricus' side; maimed by this wound, he was reduced by weakness to the life of a cripple. Balamber, King of the Huns, got wind of his enemy's sickness and moved his battle array into the lands of the Ostrogoths. . . . Meanwhile Hermanaricus, unable to bear either the pain of the wound or the onslaught of the Huns, died, old and full of days, in the hundredth year of his life. His death gave the Huns the occasion to defeat the Goths who, as we have said, lived on the eastern seaboard and were named the Ostrogoths.

266

3. *Wīdsīð* (seventh century), ll. 5–9, 88–92, 109–11.

With the gracious lady Ealhild, he [i.e. Wīdsīð himself] came for the first time from Angel in the east to visit the home of Eormanríc, the Gothic king, that evil truce-breaker. . . . .

I [i.e. Wīdsīð] was with Eormanríc all that time; the King of the Goths treated me generously there; he, lord of those who dwelt in that fortress, gave me a ring which was valued at six hundred silver pieces, reckoned in shillings. . . .

From there I wandered through all the lands of the Goths; ever I sought out the noblest of companions— that was the household of Eormanríc.

[Among the names that follow, apparently as members of Eormanríc's court, are some which are Anglo-Saxon forms of names which are given in later Norse and German tales to kinsmen, counsellors or followers of this king; they are: Theodric, Becca, Sifeca, the Herelingas, Emerca, Fridla, Freotheríc, Rondhere, Wudga and Hāma; for the allusion to the last two, see below, VIII B 1.]

4. *Dēor* (eighth century), ll. 22–7.

We have heard tell of Eormanríc's wolvish thought; far and wide he ruled the folk of the Gothic kingdom— a grim king was he! Many a man sat, locked in sorrow, in expectation of grief, and wished again and again that that kingdom might be overthrown. That passed by; so may this.

5. *Hamðismál* (eighth or ninth century), stanzas 3, 10–11, 17–31.

[The poem opens with Guðrún, widow of Sigurðr the Vǫlsung, urging Hamðir and Sǫrli, her sons by a later marriage, to avenge their half-sister Svanhildr.]

'You two had a sister, her name was Svanhildr;
Jǫrmunrekkr trampled her down with his steeds,
With white steeds and black on the battle-road,
With grey steeds well tamed, the steeds of the Goths.'

[Guðrún laments her loneliness; her sons remind her how her wish for vengeance multiplied her past
267

tragedies; finally they accept the mission, though with forebodings:]

'For us too, O Guðrún, for us both you shall weep;
Doomed, we sit on our steeds, and far hence we shall
die.'
They rode from the courtyard with wrath in their
hearts;
Over wet mountains the youths made their way
Seeking vengeance for murder, on steeds of the Huns.

[The episode that follows is confused and obscure.
Hamðir and Sǫrli meet and kill their half-brother
Erpr, apparently because when they ask him how
he will help them, he replies 'as foot helps foot'.
Next, they come on a hanged man, apparently
Randvér, son of Jǫrmunrekkr and so stepson of
Svanhildr—see below, VIII A 9, 10, 11.]

The road ran onwards; a grim path they found,
And their sister's son on the gallows, sore hurt—
On the wind-cold wolf-tree west of the hall.
There birds' bait was swaying; there no man would stay.

There was din in the hall, and men merry with ale,
And no one to listen if horses might come,
Till the hero, bold-hearted, sounded his horn.

Then in went the earls, and they told Jǫrmunrekkr
That warriors in helmets were there to be seen—
'You should take counsel, for great men have come,
And you trampled their kinswoman down with your
steeds.'

Then Jǫrmunrekkr laughed, laid his hand on his beard,
Called for his beaker [?], grew fiercer with wine;
He shook his brown hair, at his white shield he gazed,
And bade the gold goblet be brought to his hand.

Jǫrmunrekkr said:

'I would count myself happy if I could but see
Hamðir and Sǫrli both here in my hall;
I'd bind the youths fast with the strings of my bows,
And Guðrún's fine sons on the gallows I'd hang.'

Then spoke Hróðrglǫð, standing near by—
Slender of fingers—spoke thus to the men:

'For this is the danger, that some will not heed,
That two men alone will cut down or bind fast
Ten hundred Goths in the stronghold so high.'

In the hall there was tumult and ale-cups were smashed;
Heroes lay in the blood that flowed from the Goths.

Thus then spoke Hamðir, the noble of heart:
'You wished for our coming, O King Jǫrmunrekkr,
That we sons of one mother might stand in your hall.
Look at your feet now, and look at your hands,
O Jǫrmunrekkr, flung in the heat of the fire!'

Then roared the king who was sprung from the gods,
Bold in his mail, as a bear roars aloud:
'Cast stones at these warriors whom no spear will bite,
Nor sword-blade nor iron, at Jónakr's sons.'

Thus then spoke Hamðir, the noble of heart:
'Brother, evil you found when you opened that bag;
Evil counsels have often come out of that bag.'

Sǫrli said:

　　'If you had wisdom, Hamðir, your heart would be great,
　　But a man who lacks sense is thought lacking in much.'

Hamðir said:

　　'His head would be off now if Erpr were alive,
　　Our brother, brave in battle, whom we slew on the road;
　　Most daring was he; me the goddesses drove,
　　So that I was the death of that valiant man.'

Sǫrli said:

　　'I think that we two should not act like wolves
　　　　That we should each other blame,
　　Like to the greedy grey steeds of the Norns
　　　　Reared in the waste lands wild.

'We have fought well; over slain Goths we stand,
Over sword-stricken men, like eagles on boughs.
We have won fame, though today or tomorrow we die;
No man lives till night, once the Norns' word goes
  forth.'

Sǫrli fell there, by the hall's gable-wall,
And Hamðir sank down at the back of the house.

6. Bragi Boddason the Old, *Ragnarsdrápa* (ninth century),
   stanzas 3–7; quoted by Snorri Sturluson, *Edda* (*c.* 1220),
   Skáldskaparmál ch. 51.

[The poem describes pictures illustrating heroic
tales and myths, painted upon a shield given to the
poet by Ragnarr.]

From a dream ill-omened
Did Jǫrmunrekkr awake,
Where warriors were blood-stained
In a whirling stream of swords.
There was fighting in the mead-hall
Of the head of Randvér's race,
When Erp's brothers, raven-swarthy,
Took vengeance for their wrongs.

From the bench the monarch's
Life-dew flowed to the floor;
Amid the gore there might be seen
His feet and hands hacked off.
He fell in the blood-mingled
Ale from goblets spilled—
Upon the shield 'tis painted—
And headlong he crashed down.

But there, to make a circle
About the prince's couch,
Stood his champions, wielders
Of shields in one piece made.
Swiftly then were Hamðir
And Sǫrli beaten down,
With one accord, by boulders,
The hard round stones of Earth.

The battle-rouser bade them
Crush Gjúki's grandsons down,
Since they had sought the life-blood
Of Svanhildr's wedded lord;
Blows and blades rang loudly;
All men paid them back—
The mighty sons of Jónakr—
With deep and gaping wounds.

I saw this fall of heroes
Upon the fair round shield;
This ship-moon and its stories,
'Twas Ragnarr gave it me.

7. *Quedlingburg Annals* and *Würzburg Chronicle* (both *c.* 1000).

[The texts of these two German chronicles are
virtually identical in these allusions to Ermenricus.]

At that time Ermenricus ruled over all the Goths—
a man more cunning than all others in his guile, and more
generous in his gifts. After the death of his only son
Fridericus, which was brought about by his own wish,
he hanged his nephews Embrica and Fritla on the
gallows. In the same way, at the instigation of his
nephew Adaccarus [i.e. Odoacer], he drove his nephew
Theodoricus from Verona and forced him into exile
at the court of Attila. . . .
Ermenricus, King of the Goths, was put to death in
a shameful manner, after his hands and feet had first
been cut off, by the brothers Hamidus, Sorilus and
Adaccerus, whose father he had killed.

8. Saxo Grammaticus, *Danish History* (*c.* 1200), VIII §§ 278–81.

[Saxo represents Jarmericus as a Dane; he begins
his account of him with a tale of how he was cap-
tured by Slavs in boyhood, but eventually escaped
and won the kingdoms of Denmark and Sweden for
himself, and subdued the Slavs.]

Jarmericus, being thus enriched with the spoils of
many nations, wished to provide a safe storehouse for
his booty, and built on a lofty hill a treasure-house of

marvellous handiwork. Gathering sods, he raised a mound, laying a mass of rocks for the foundation, and girt the lower part with a rampart, the centre with rooms, and the top with battlements. All round he posted a line of sentries without a break. Four huge gates gave access on four sides, and into this lordly mansion he heaped all his splendid riches.

Having thus settled his affairs at home, he again turned his ambition abroad. He began to voyage, and speedily fought a naval battle with four brothers whom he met on the high seas, Hellespontines by race, and veteran rovers. After this battle had lasted three days, he ceased fighting, having bargained for their sister and half the tribute which they had imposed on those they had conquered.

After this, Bicco, son of the King of the Livonians, escaped from the captivity in which he lay under those said brothers, and went to Jarmericus. But he did not forget his wrongs, Jarmericus having long before deprived him of his own brothers. He was kindly received by the king, in all whose secret counsels he soon came to have a notable voice; and, as soon as he found the king pliable to his advice in all things, he led him, when his counsel was asked, into the most abominable acts, and drove him to commit crimes and infamies. Thus he sought some device to injure the king by a feint of loyalty, and tried above all to steel him against his nearest of blood, attempting to accomplish the revenge of his brothers by guile, since he could not by force. So it came about that the king embraced filthy vices instead of virtues, and made himself generally hated by the cruel deeds which he committed at the instance of his treacherous adviser. Even the Slavs began to rise against him; and, as a means of quelling them, he captured their leaders, passed a rope through their shanks, and delivered them to be torn asunder by horses pulling different ways. So perished their chief men, punished for their stubbornness of spirit by having their bodies rent apart. This kept the Slavs duly obedient in unbroken and steady subjugation.

Meantime, the sons of Jarmericus' sister, who had all been born and bred in Germany, took up arms, on the strength of their grandsire's title, against their uncle, contending that they had as good a right to the throne as he. The king demolished their strongholds in Germany with engines, blockaded or took several towns, and returned home with a bloodless victory. The Hellespontines came to meet him, proffering their sister for the promised marriage. After this had been celebrated, at Bicco's prompting he again went to Germany, took his nephews in war, and incontinently hanged them. He also got together the chief men under pretence of a banquet and had them put to death in the same fashion.

Meanwhile, the king appointed Broderus, his son by another marriage, to have charge over his stepmother, a duty which he fulfilled with full vigilance and integrity. But Bicco accused this man to his father of incest, and, to conceal the falsehood of the charge, suborned witnesses against him. When the plea of accusation had been fully declared, Broderus could not bring any support for his defence, and his father bade his friends pass sentence upon the convicted man, thinking it less impious to commit the punishment proper for his son to the judgment of others. All thought that he deserved outlawry except Bicco, who did not shrink from giving a more terrible vote against his life, and declaring that the perpetrator of an infamous seduction ought to be punished with hanging. But lest any should think that this punishment was due to the cruelty of his father, Bicco judged that when he had been put in the noose, the servants should hold him up on a beam put beneath him, so that, when weariness should make them take their hands from the burden, they might be as good as guilty of the young man's death, and by their own fault exonerate the king from an unnatural murder. He also pretended that, unless the accused were punished, he would plot against his father's life. The adulteress Suanilda, he said, ought to suffer a shameful end, trampled under the hoofs of beasts.

The king yielded to Bicco; and, when his son was taken to be hanged, he made the bystanders hold him up by means of a plank, that he might not be choked. Thus his throat was but a little squeezed, the knot was harmless, and it was but a punishment in show. But the king had the queen tied very tight on the ground, and delivered her to be crushed under the hoofs of horses. The story goes that she was so beautiful that even the beasts shrank from mangling limbs so lovely with their filthy feet. The king, divining that this proclaimed the innocence of his wife, began to repent of his error, and hastened to release the slandered lady. But meantime Bicco rushed up, declaring that when she was on her back she held off the beasts by awful charms, and could only be crushed if she lay on her face, for he knew that her beauty saved her. When the body of the queen was placed in this manner, the herd of beasts was driven upon it, and trod it down deep with their multitude of feet. Such was the end of Suanilda.

Meantime the favourite dog of Broderus came to the king making a sort of moan, and seemed to bewail its master's punishment; and his hawk, when it was brought in, began to pluck out its breast-feathers with its beak. The king took its nakedness as an omen of his own bereavement, to frustrate which he quickly sent men to take his son down from the noose; for he divined by the featherless bird that he would be childless unless he took good heed.

Thus Broderus was freed from death, and Bicco, fearing he would pay the penalty of an informer, went and told the men of the Hellespont that Suanilda had been abominably slain by her husband. When they set sail to avenge their sister, he came back to Jarmericus, and told him that the Hellespontines were preparing war. The king thought it would be safer to fight with guile than in the field, and retreated to the stronghold which he had built. To stand the siege, he filled its inner parts with stores, and its battlements with men-at-arms. Targets and shields flashing with gold were hung round and adorned the topmost circle of the building.

Now it happened that the Hellespontines, before sharing their booty, accused a great band of their men of embezzling, and put them to death. Having now destroyed so large a part of their forces by internecine slaughter, they thought that their strength was not equal to storming the palace, and consulted a sorceress named

Guthruna. She brought it to pass that the defenders of
the king's side were suddenly blinded and turned their
arms against one another. When the Hellespontines saw
this, they brought up a siege-mantlet and seized the
approaches of the gates. Then they tore up the posts,
burst into the building, and hewed down the blinded
ranks of the enemy. In this uproar Othinus appeared,
and, making for the thick of the ranks of the fighters,
restored by his divine power to the Danes that vision
which they had lost by sleights; for he ever cherished
them with fatherly love. He instructed them to shower
stones to batter the Hellespontines, who used spells to
harden their bodies against weapons. Thus both com-
panies slew one another and perished. Jarmericus lost
both feet and both hands, and his trunk was rolled among
the dead. Broderus, little fit for it, followed him as king.

9. Snorri Sturluson, *Edda* (*c.* 1220) *Skáldskaparmál* ch. 50.

[Sigurðr the Vǫlsung and his wife Guðrún had a
daughter, Svanhildr. After Sigurðr's death Guðrún
remarried twice, the second time with a certain King
Jónakr.]

They had three sons, whose names were Sǫrli,
Hamðir, and Erpr; all three had hair as black as ravens,
like Gunnarr and Hǫgni and the other Niflungs. Sig-
urðr's daughter Svanhildr was brought up there, and
she was the fairest of all women.

King Jǫrmunrekkr the Mighty heard of this, and he
sent his son Randvér to ask on his behalf for her hand.
So when he came to King Jónakr's, Svanhildr was
entrusted to him, and he was to bring her to King
Jǫrmunrekkr. But then Earl Bikki said that it would be
far more fitting that Randvér should have Svanhildr,
since he was young and so was she, whereas Jǫrmun-
rekkr was old. This counsel pleased the young folk very
well. And the next thing was that Bikki told the king
about this, and then King Jǫrmunrekkr ordered that his
son should be seized and taken away to the gallows.
Then Randvér took his hawk and plucked its feathers,
and bade them send it to his father. He was then hanged.
But when King Jǫrmunrekkr saw the hawk, the thought

came to his mind that just as this hawk was stripped of its feathers and powerless to fly, in the same way his kingdom was now maimed, since he was old and had no son. And then once when King Jǫrmunrekkr was riding back from hunting in the forest with his courtiers, he set eyes on Svanhildr as she sat bleaching her hair. And they rode at her and trampled her to death under their horses' hoofs.

Now when Guðrún heard of this, she egged on her sons to avenge Svanhildr. As they were making ready for the journey she gave them mail-coats and helms so strong that no iron could bite on them; and she gave them this counsel, that when they reached King Jǫrmunrekkr they should come on him by night as he slept, and Sǫrli and Hamðir should cut off his hands and feet, and Erpr his head.

Now as they were on their way there, they asked Erpr what help they would get from him if they met King Jǫrmunrekkr. He answered that he would help them as the hand helps the foot. They said that it never happened at all that a foot got support from a hand. They were angry with their mother because she had driven them out by her bitter words, and they wished to do whatever would cause her most pain, and they killed Erpr, because she loved him best. Shortly afterwards, as Sǫrli was walking along, one foot slipped from under him, and he supported himself with his hand. Then he said: 'Now hand has helped foot. It would be better now if Erpr were alive.'

When they came on King Jǫrmunrekkr by night in the place where he was sleeping and hacked off his hands and his feet, he awoke and called out to his men and bade them awake. Then Hamðir said: 'The head would have been off by now, if Erpr were alive.' Then all the retainers arose and attacked them, but could not overwhelm them with weapons. Then Jǫrmunrekkr called out that they should bring stones, and this was done, and there they fell, Sǫrli and Hamðir. All the race and descendants of Gjúki were thus dead.

10. *Vǫlsunga saga* (*c.* 1200–70), chs. 40–42.

There was a king called Jǫrmunrekr, a mighty king in those days. His son was called Randvér. The king summoned his son to speak with him, and said: 'You must go and carry a message from me to King Jónakr, together with my counsellor, whose name is Bikki. Svanhildr, the daughter of Sigurðr Fafnir's Bane, is being brought up there, and I know she is the fairest maiden beneath the sun. It is her that I most wish to marry, and you must ask for her on my behalf.'

'It is most fitting that I should bear your message, sire,' said he.

So now they went on their way till they came to King Jónakr, saw Svanhildr, and thought her beauty was very great.

Randvér craved audience of the king, and said: 'King Jǫrmunrekr is offering to become your kinsman by marriage. He has heard tell of Svanhildr and wishes to choose her for his wife; and it is unlikely that she could be given to any man more mighty than he is.'

The king said that it was an honourable match, and that he was a famous man.

Guðrún said: 'Luck is a fickle thing, when you trust that it will not break.'

But because of the king's eagerness and everything that depended on it, the plan was accepted, and now Svanhildr went aboard ship with an honourable escort, and sat in the cabin at the side of the king's son.

Then Bikki said to Randvér: 'It would be fitting if you had so fair a wife, and not such an old man.'

That pleased his heart well, and he spoke gladly to her, and so did she to him. Then they came home to their own land and met the king.

Then Bikki said: 'It is right, sire, that you should know what has happened, though it is a hard thing to bear; it is a crafty betrayal, for your son has won Svanhildr's whole love, and she is his mistress. Do not leave such a man unhanged.'

He had already given him many evil counsels in the past, though this evil counsel of his cut the deepest. The king used to listen to his many wicked counsels. Now he said, for he could not master himself in his anger, that his son was to be taken and hanged on the gallows. And as he was being led to the gallows, he took a hawk and plucked all its feathers off, and said that it should be shown to his father.

When the king saw it, he said: 'One can see by this that he thinks I have been stripped of honour as the hawk is of its feathers,' and he ordered that he should be taken down from the gallows. But meanwhile Bikki had been at his tricks, and Randvér was dead.

Now Bikki said once more: 'There is no one to whom you should be more cruel than to Svanhildr. Let her die a shameful death.'

The king answered: 'That counsel we will follow.'

After this, she was bound to the gateway of the stronghold, and horses were set to gallop at her; but when she opened her eyes wide, the horses did not dare trample her. And when Bikki saw that, he said that a bag should be pulled down over her head; and this was done, and then she lost her life.

Now Guðrún heard of Svanhildr's death, and she said to her sons: 'Why do you sit so quiet and speak cheerfully, when Jǫrmunrekr has slain your sister and trampled her under horses' feet to dishonour her? You do not have the noble character of Gunnarr or Hǫgni—they would have avenged any woman of their kin.'

Hamðir answered: 'Little did you praise Gunnarr and Hǫgni when they slew Sigurðr, and you were red with his blood; and evil was the vengeance for your brothers, when you slew your sons. It might be better if we all slew King Jǫrmunrekr together; we cannot bear your taunting words, as we are thus egged on so bitterly.'

Guðrún went up to them, laughing, and gave them drink from great goblets; and after that she chose for them fine large corselets and other armour.

Then Hamðir said: 'Now here we must part for the last time; you will hear news of us, and then you will drink the funeral ale for us and for Svanhildr.'

After that they went on their way. . . .

Now as for Guðrún's sons, she had prepared their armour so that no iron could bite on it, and she had bidden them never to injure stones nor any other large objects, telling them that it would bring harm on them if they did not do as she said.

As they were going along the road they met their brother Erpr, and asked him what help he would give them.

He answered: 'Such help as hand gives to hand, or foot to foot.'

They thought that that was nothing, and they slew him. After this they sent on their way for a little while, until Hamðir tripped, put his hand to the ground, and said: 'Erpr must have spoken the truth. I would have fallen just now, if I hadn't supported myself with my hand.'

A little later Sǫrli tripped, but thrust a foot out and managed to steady himself, and said: 'I would have fallen just now, if I hadn't supported myself with my other foot.'

And now they said they had behaved badly towards their brother Erpr. Now they went on till they came to King Jǫrmunrekr's dwelling, and they went into his presence, and straightway made their attack on him. Hamðir hacked both his hands off, and Sǫrli both his feet.

Then Hamðir said: 'The head would be off now, if Erpr were alive—our brother, whom we slew on the road—and too late we see this!'

As it says in the poem:

> The head would be off now
> If Erpr were alive—
> Our brother, brave in battle,
> Whom we slew on the road.

In this way they had broken their mother's bidding, for they had injured stones. Now men attacked them, but they defended themselves well and valiantly, and caused harm to many a man. No iron could bite on them. Then there came in a man, grey-haired and old, with one eye; he said: 'You are fools, if you do not know how to do these men to death.'

The king answered: 'Give us your counsel, if you know how.'

He said: 'You should batter them down into Hel with stones.'

And so it was done, and stones came hurtling at them from all quarters, and that was how they lost their lives.

11. *þiðreks saga af Bern* (*c.* 1220–50) chs. 276–82.

Now King Erminrekr sat in his own kingdom. He was overlord of Rome and many other great realms, and all the kings and lords south of the mountains served him and did him homage, and in many other places too, and he was the mightiest among the kings in the part of the world called Europe, for the emperors themselves ruled Bulgaria and Greece. Erminrekr's kingdom reached all the way to the sea called the Adriatic.

It happened once that King Erminrekr sent his counsellor, whose name was Sifka, to the place called Sarkasteinn. He was to carry out all the king's business there, and pass judgments; and many knights went with him, and their journeying was most magnificent. So now Sifka went on his mission as King Erminrekr had bidden, but his wife, whose name was Odila, remained at home. She was the most beautiful woman men have ever seen.

And it so happened, as the king had intended, that Odila was lodging in a certain house alone, and before she realized it, King Erminrekr had come there secretly alone, and he told her that he wished to have her love, as he had often meant to do before. Now she certainly did not wish this, yet she did not dare have things otherwise than as the king wished, and so he did as he had intended and lay with her, though she had first struggled so that her clothes were torn in two, and she got rough handling in other ways too. So now he went away, and she went elsewhere.

Now Sifka came home, having accomplished his mission, and went into the courtyard and into his house, and found his wife Odila. But when she saw Sifka she rose and went to meet him, wailing and weeping bitterly.

Sifka said: 'Why are you weeping, wife? I would have thought that you would rejoice that I had come home, not weep.'

'It would be long to tell you why I am weeping,' she answered, 'but it is the fault of King Erminrekr and his wickedness. Once, when you had gone away, I was sitting in my little bower and sewing your silk shirt, when in came King Erminrekr—and never will you be able to repay him with evil enough for the dishonour which he did me before he left.' And she told him plainly everything that had happened.

Now Sifka answered: 'Be merry, wife, and act as if it had never happened. I shall so manage things that the king shall pay for this by dishonour of every kind, before I have finished.'

So now Sifka went before the king and bowed before him and greeted him, and was as cheerful as could be. And the king welcomed him warmly, and they now took counsel over everything together, as before.

One day King Erminrekr and Sifka and the counsellors were sitting in council, and Sifka said to the king: 'Sire,' said he, 'you are the greatest and strongest king in the world, and all kings and noblemen in the north do homage to you and serve your kingdom by great gifts of tribute, except that Ósantrix, the King of Vilkinaland, does not do you honour from his kingdom. This is a great grief to us, your dear friends, for he is no greater man than those who serve you honourably. It is my advice that you should send your son, the valiant Friðrekr, to bid him pay you tribute—courteously at first, but next by saying that you will come and make war on him. You must prepare his journey honourably, but do not send many men with him, for it is the custom for emissaries that they should not travel many men together.'

This pleased the king well, and he wished to have things thus. And now he summoned his son Friðrekr and told him how he must arrange his journey, and what his errand would be. So now Friðrekr made ready for the journey, and six knights with him, and so went on their way till they came to a stronghold called Vilkinaborg; an earl who was a vassal of King Ósantrix owned this stronghold.

Now Sifka had sent a man ahead, secretly but swiftly, and Sifka's messenger came to the earl with the message that when the earl learnt the king's son Friðrekr was on his way he was to send men out to kill him—and this earl was a kinsman of Sifka's. Now when Friðrekr arrived at the stronghold, the earl and his men came out against them and slew them all seven, and Friðrekr lost

281

his life there, as Sifka had plotted. Now when King Erminrekr heard of this, he thought that it must have been a plot of King Ósantrix, and that he must have plotted it because he was being asked for tribute.

On another occasion King Erminrekr and Sifka were in conversation and council together, and Sifka said: 'I suspect, sire, that you have received no tribute from England, and yet you ought to have tribute from there; and I know that if your seal-ring were to come there, the King of England would not dare refuse to pay you tribute. It would be my advice that you should send your son Reginbaldr, and many knights with him, and his journey will bring great fame to him, and to you too, O king! And it is my advice to you that you should make different arrangements for his journey from those of other men. You should have a ship made ready for him, as that is only half as costly but twice as splendid, and then his enemies cannot treacherously attack him, as they did his brother. And if, as I expect, he obtains the tribute, then it will be better to ferry the tribute by ship than carry it on horseback, and this way of travelling is far more easily managed than I can tell you.'

The king thought this plan well devised, and wished things to be done so, and he summoned his son Reginbaldr and told him what he intended; and Reginbaldr told his father to make all arrangements for his journey, and said he would do whatever he wished.

Now Reginbaldr went down to where the ships were lying in a river, and Sifka with him, and they found three ships there. And now Reginbaldr said he would have the best ship that was there. Sifka said that the king would not allow that, as he would want it himself if he should travel, and he pointed out to him the ship that was the worst of them, saying that it was quite good enough for so short a journey. But Reginbaldr would not go unless he had a good ship. Then Sifka answered that he would have to face his father's anger if he went back again to see him without having carried out his message. So Reginbaldr went on his way, and he had the worst ship; and when he had gone only a little way out to sea there came so great a storm that his whole ship broke in two, and he and all his men were lost.

One day King Erminrekr rode out hunting with his youngest son Samson, and with his counsellor Sifka, and Sifka was very gloomy, yet he rode beside the king all the time.

Then the king said: 'My good Sifka, why are you so gloomy?'

Sifka answered: 'Sire,' said he, 'I think it was a great dishonour that your son did me when he tried to force my daughter, the fairest of maidens, against her will. But it will never be avenged unless you avenge it in some way yourself, sire.'

Now the king grew angry with his son Samson; he was in the prime of youth, not yet full-grown, the youngest and most promising of the king's sons. King Erminrekr rode up to his son Samson in great wrath, and gripped him by the hair, so that he fell from his horse, and the king's horse trampled with all its hooves on the boy, and so the boy got his death. And now the king rode home; and the same evening the king heard that his son Reginbaldr was drowned, and now he had lost all his sons through Sifka's plotting, and he was now very gloomy.

Now it happened one day that Odila, Sifka's wife, went with all her maidens to her lady, King Erminrekr's queen, and they were all sitting there together drinking good wine and being merry, and Odila told the queen much about Egarð and Áki from Qmlungaland [Erminrekr's nephews]. Among other things, Odila said that if Egarð could, he would not spare the queen's honour, and she said she had brought her this message and bade her be on her guard. The queen was very angry, and thought Egarð's words had brought great shame upon her. Then King Erminrekr came in and sat and drank with them.

Now Odila said: 'The wind is from the west and south now, and the sun shines fair and warm, but sometimes there is a small, fine rain from the north and east. And what might be coming from that quarter, if not young Egarð and his brother Áki? Then there is no mercy for any wild beast or any bird of the forest, for wondrously great is the slaughter they deal out.'

The king was silent, and made no answer.

Then the queen answered: 'It is no wonder that birds and beasts get no mercy from them, since every time they come here there is no mercy for our serving-maids, if they can have their way.'

King Erminrekr was still silent, and he was paying close heed to what the women were saying. There had come in with the king a man whose name was Fritila, and who was the foster-father of Egarð and Áki.

And the queen spoke once more: 'Now certain words have proved true, that I myself must be on my guard against them, and that they intend dishonour to me if they can have their way.'

The king answered in great wrath: 'If you can get no mercy from them, my queen, then they shall get no mercy from me; and I swear that I will never sleep a second night where I have been one night, until I have found them, and then they shall be hanged so high that no man can ever hang higher.'

And Fritila said: 'So now Egarð and his brother Áki must pay for it because Viðga rode to meet King Þiðrekr of Bern! If he should reach home before his stepsons are hanged, many a helm would be cloven and many a head too, and many a mail-coat split and many a shield shattered, and many a man's son would never be seen again.'

And now the king answered: 'They will gain nothing by your high words, even though you are their foster-father; on the contrary, they shall now be hanged somewhat higher than I had first intended.'

And now Fritila said: 'So long as I and my son can stand up, I shall never see them hanging on the gallows.'

And now Fritila went to his horse and rode as hard as he could by night and day.

King Erminrekr ordered his trumpet to be blown, and summoned all his knights and rode to meet Egarð and his brother.

And when Fritila came to the Rhine one day, he and his men leapt from their horses and swam out into the river, taking their horses with them over the river. On the banks of the Rhine stood the stronghold of Trelinborg, and Egarð was in it. Now Egarð saw men swimming there, and he recognized them and said: 'It is my foster-father Fritila swimming there, and he will not wait for a boat, and so I know that there is some very great need for him to come.'

And now that Fritila had got across the river, Egarð and Áki went out to meet him and asked him why he travelled in such haste. But he answered: 'There is need enough. King Erminrekr is on his way with his host, and wants to slay you both. Save yourselves!'

Egarð answered: 'We will be reconciled if we meet; we ought not to be afraid of our father's brother.'

And now Fritila told them every proof of how things were, but they would not flee, but they sent for their men, raised the drawbridge over the moat, and meant to defend the stronghold. And now King Erminrekr and his men reached the stronghold, and before riding up to the stronghold he took his standard, and then rode as hard as he could to the moat and hurled the pole of the standard across the moat.

Now Egarð said: 'Sire, what charge do you bring against us? Why do you wish to storm our stronghold?'

Then the king said: 'Whatever charge I may bring against you, you shall both hang today on the highest tree I can find.'

Áki said: 'Before we lose our lives, you will have to pay dearly for them and lose many a valiant warrior.'

Now both sides flung spears at each other for a while. Then King Erminrekr had catapults set up, and had burning kindling placed in them, and had this slung into the stronghold, so that the castle and the whole place was on fire. Then Fritila spoke, bidding them die with honour, not burn in there, and now they came out, with sixty men. They now fought against King Erminrekr until four hundred of King Erminrekr's men had fallen. But now the brothers were taken prisoner and hanged, and now their lives had come to an end as Sifka had plotted. Now King Erminrekr went home.

VIII B. HĀMA—O.N. Heimir.

1. *Wīdsīð* (seventh century), ll. 124–30.

I visited . . . Wudga and Hāma; these were not the
worst of companions, even if I do name them last. Often
did a shrieking spear fly whistling from that troop to-
wards a hostile host; there as exiles Wudga and Hāma
ruled men and women by twisted gold.

2. *Þiðreks saga af Bern* (*c.* 1220–50) chs. 288, 429–36.

[In this saga Heimir is a rather fierce warrior, a
great lover of horses, owing loyalty to Þiðrekr
(i.e. Theodoric of Verona), and also to the latter's
uncle, King Erminrekr (i.e Eormanrīc). When the
two chieftains quarrel, Heimir sides with Þiðrekr.]

Now Heimir went in great anger to find King Ermin-
rekr, and said: 'You have done much evil against your
kinsmen, King Erminrekr. First you sent Friðrekr and
Reginbaldr to their deaths yourself, and slew young
Samson, and then you had your nephews Egarð and
Áki hanged, and now on top of all this you have driven
your kinsman Þiðrekr out of his own kingdom, and
also Þeðer, and your sister's son Úlfráðr, and the good
warrior Hildibrand and many another good knight—
some you have slain, and some driven away, and the
cause of all these evil deeds is Sifka the evil counsellor!'
Then Sifka answered: 'I told you long ago, sire, when
you brought Heimir here and made him so proud, that
he would defy you with his big words, as he is doing
now; it would be only right to send him back to the
forests where his father dwelt, and let him tend your
horses as his father did.'
Then Heimir said: 'God knows, if I had my good
sword Naglhring here, I would kill you like a dog.'
And he gave Sifka a blow with his fist on the cheek,
so that he fell to the floor at once at the king's feet, and
five teeth sprang from his mouth, and he lost his
senses.
And now King Erminrekr said: 'Up with you, all
my men, and seize him and hang him!'

When Heimir heard the king's words he rushed quickly to where his weapons lay and made himself ready as fast as he could. Then he ran to his horse Rispa and rode out through the castle gate, and sixty knights after him, all fully armed. And now Viðga [i.e. Wudga] reached the gate and ran to the middle of the gateway, and he had Mímung in his hand, and none of these knights dared ride out now; and so Heimir got away for the time being and rode out into the forest—and everywhere where farmsteads and property of King Erminrekr or of Sifka might be, there he would burn, and slay men, and he did not cease till he had burnt down five hundred farmsteads. And now he lay out in the woods; but Sifka never dared ride abroad with fewer than sixty men, and they were ever in fear of Heimir. . . .

Heimir Studason had been for a long time in the wild wastes of the forests, and often had ridden down to the cultivated lands to harm Sifka's domains, burning his farms and killing his men, and he went about thus by day and night. This went on for twenty years, all the time that King Þiðrekr was away from his kingdom.

But when Heimir learnt that Sifka had been slain, he realized how much evil he had done, and he now wished to repent of his sins. He rode to a monastery with all his weapons and with his horse Rispa. As he rode into the monastery yard, a monk asked who this man might be; he dismounted and bade them call the abbot to him. The monks told the abbot that a man in fine armour had come and wished to see him, and that they thought he must be a man of rank. So the abbot went to see the man, and asked him who he was.

He answered: 'My name is Loðvígr, and my family is in Qmlungaland. As for why I have come here, that you shall now hear.'

He took his shield from his neck, and next he took off his sword Naglhring and his helmet and mail-coat and his leggings of chain mail. He now laid all these weapons at the abbot's feet, and then prostrated himself, and said: 'My lord, these weapons and this horse, and myself, and my clothes, and the money which I have here (which is no less than ten pounds)—all these I wish to give for the service of God in this place, and to submit myself to your rule, and so make amends for my sins.'

Then all the monks said that God had surely put this in his mind, if he had been a warrior and a servant of the king. They could see by his weapons that he had been some man of noble rank, and the monks thought it a great matter that he should be bringing so much money to the place, and they said to the abbot: 'Raise this man where he lies prostrate; he will bring great glory to our monastery.'

But the abbot stood silent, and looked at the man, and marvelled, for it seemed to him that this man must be a man of high spirit who would not be obedient if he entered the monastery, and so for this reason he was afraid to take him in. All the monks begged him earnestly to take him in. The money pleased the abbot; so he took Loðvígr by the hand and led him into the chapel and choir, and led him to a seat and told him that he was to sit on that bench. And there in front of his seat he took off his velvet clothes and took black clothing like the other monks, and he was dedicated a monk that very day. The abbot now took all his wealth and armour and laid it among his own possessions, and Loðvígr now followed their rule. And if the brothers had known that this was Heimir Studason, then, though he might have never so much gold and silver, they would not have taken him in. He now served in this monastery for a while.

Now the giant Aspilian had many dwellings in this land of Lombardy; he was as big and strong and hard to deal with as ever. He had much increased his possessions by wrongful means, in gold and silver and fine treasures, and in homesteads and in land; and since they were small men beside him, they dared not keep what he wanted to have. There was a certain large rich homestead which the monks owned; the giant Aspilian claimed it for himself, and the abbot thought it monstrous that they should lose their farm. The abbot sent monks to meet the giant, and they asked what it meant that he should take their farm. The giant's answer was that he had taken a farm of his own, not theirs, and that he was better fitted to have it than they were. But the monks said this farm had been given to their foundation for the love of God.

The giant answered: 'I'll put an end to this argument with you. We'll put it to the test, which of us owns this farm. You must find a man who has the courage to fight me; if I am defeated, you shall have this farm and many others, but if I win, then God has shown that He wills me to have this farm.'

This was indeed the law of the country, that where two men were in dispute over something there should be a duel. The monks could answer nothing, as the giant had offered them legal terms, so they went home and told the abbot what answer the giant had given them. The abbot raised the matter before all the monks in the chapter, saying they would be forced to abandon their farmstead if they could not find a man who dared fight the giant. This did not please the monks, and they sent men far and wide to find whether anyone wished to win himself wealth and fight the giant, but none could be found.

One day they were debating this in the chapter, and grieving bitterly.

Then said Loðvígr: 'What are you debating, monks? What has Aspilian done to you?'

'Aspilian has taken our farm,' answered the abbot, 'and is offering us a duel if we lay claim to it. Now there is no one willing to fight the giant, though we promise in God's name that he who does so will be free of all sins which he has confessed.'

Then Loðvígr said: 'For the love of God I gave my wealth and weapons and my own self to this foundation, and now I will do this too, and fight with this giant. Where is my sword, and my armour?'

Then the abbot suspected that this must be some champion, and he said: 'Your sword you cannot have. It has been hacked in two, and a door-hinge made of it in the minster here; and the rest of your armour was sold in the market-place to bring wealth to our foundation.'

Then Loðvígr said: 'You monks are book-learned, but you have little learning in matters of chivalry. If you had known how good these weapons were, you would never have parted with them.'

And now he ran up to the abbot and gripped his cowl with both hands, and said: 'Truly, you were a fool if you could take no other iron for your church hinges but my good sword Naglhring! You shall pay for that!'

He shook the cowl, with the abbot's head in it, so hard that four teeth fell out. When the monks heard the name Naglhring, they realized that Heimir Studason had come there, and now the monks grew very much afraid, and they fetched the keys that belonged to a great chest in which all his weapons were. One took the sword Naglhring, another the mail-coat and the leggings of chain mail, a third the helm, a fourth the shield, a fifth his spear, and all these weapons had been so well kept that they were no worse now than when he laid them aside.

Now Heimir took up Naglhring, and saw how fair its edges and its gold flashed, and there came into his mind what trust he had placed in its edges, and now he was sometimes red as blood, and sometimes again pale, and he remained silent for a while. After that he asked where was his horse Rispa.

Then the abbot answered: 'Your horse used to drag stones to the church, and it is now many years ago that he died.'

Then the monks said: 'We will send men all over this realm to seek out the best horse that can be got. There are many good horses here in this place, so take whichever is the best.'

So now the monks sent for the finest horses and had them brought to the monastery, and called Heimir so that he should choose one. There were many of these horses that were well used to tournaments. Heimir went up to a horse and struck his hand against its flank, so that it fell down at once. And once again, he went up to the one that looked the finest there, and pressed his hand down on its back so that the spine broke in two; and he said that these horses were good for nothing, and he ordered them to bring him the best horse. Then the monks said one ought to fetch the old horse; the thin one should be taken and brought to him. Thereupon a horse was led forward; it was a large enough one, and very old by then. Heimir recognized this horse, for it was Rispa; he went up to the horse and gripped the forelock and tugged it with all his strength, but the horse stood quietly. Then he took hold of the tail and twisted it hard, but this horse did not flinch.

Now Heimir laughed, and said: 'So now you've come, my good horse Rispa, and however old you may be, and however thin, I know of none other in the world that I'd rather have than you!'

And now Heimir said to the monks: 'Take this horse, and give him some corn.'

So now Rispa was led to a stall, and he was given corn; he stayed seven weeks in the stall, and by then he was as fat and sleek as when he was young.

The Abbot sent word to the giant Aspilian that if he wanted to fight he should come to an island, and that a man who was willing to fight him would come there to meet him. And when the giant Aspilian heard this, he stood up quickly and armed himself, and for his mount he had a beast brought to him, one which men call an elephant.

Now the monks went with the abbot to accompany Heimir to the island, and took a boat and rowed out to the island. Heimir took his horse Rispa and made him ready with saddle and poitrel. He took his leggings and mail-coat, set his helm on his head, girded on his sword Naglhring, hung his shield round his neck, took his spear, and leapt on to his horse without touching the stirrup. Now the abbot spoke to Heimir, bidding him farewell and may God guard and help him—and all the monks said the same.

Heimir now rode across the island towards the giant; it was a fearful thing to fight him, but none the less Heimir rode fast towards the giant, praying God to guard him.

Then the giant shouted: 'Who is this man who is so small, and is riding towards me? What do you want? Are you thinking of fighting me? I would think it shameful to kill you—go home, and save your life!'

'Now you listen, you foul dog Aspilian,' answered Heimir, 'however large you may be and however much I may have short legs and a stumpy body, I shall be tall enough for you before we part—indeed, for all your

BEOWULF AND ITS ANALOGUES

mighty growth, you will have to look up to me. So listen, giant—I will not flee from you as things are now, even though I am alone.'

Now Heimir spurred his horse and rode at him, and drove his spear in under the giant's arm, but his armour proved so good that the stroke did not harm him. The giant flung his javelin at him, but Heimir bent down low over the saddlebow, and the javelin flew over him and buried itself in the ground so deep that it did not stick up at all, and nobody has ever found that javelin since.

Then Heimir leapt from the saddle and landed on his feet, grasped his sword by the hilt and swiftly drew it. The giant also leapt from his horse; he too drew a sword and brandished it and struck at Heimir, but Heimir dodged the blow, and the giant missed him and struck the ground. Heimir swung quickly round with his sword drawn and struck off the giant's right hand above his sword-hilt, and the hand and the sword fell to the earth. Heimir at once aimed another blow at his leg and slashed the leg open right to the bone, and the German folk say that he hacked off such a large piece of his leg that it was as much as a horse could drag. Now the giant saw that the victory would not be his, as he had lost his hand and received so great a wound that he would not a second time stand up to so great a blow. He drew himself up and meant to fall down on top of Heimir, knowing that it would be the death of him if he were underneath him. But Heimir was so quick-footed and bold that when he saw that the giant meant to fall on him he did not choose to run away but leapt towards the giant just as the giant was falling. The giant's legs were stretched along the ground, one leg to the left of Heimir and the other to the right; but Heimir stood safe and sound between the giant's legs, and then he struck blow after blow till each limb of his was off.

The monks who were guarding the ship heard so great a din that the land shook at it, and now they saw that the giant had fallen; they all raised a *Kyrie Eleison* and praised God for His miracle, and now came to the island to meet Heimir. He rode to meet them, and had no wound. Then he went on board ship with his horse, and they went to land, and so home to the cloister, and they

had come home before the hour of service. Now the
abbot came out to meet Heimir, and all the monks with
him, and they carried out the shrines and holy relics
and formed a noble procession, and thanked God for
the way he had saved them. Heimir dismounted at the
monastery gates, and the abbot took him by one hand
and the prior by the other, and so led him into church
to his seat. Now Heimir once again lived according to
the rule for a while, as before.

The news spread far and wide that the giant Aspilian
was slain, and that a monk had done it. Now when King
Þiðrekr of Bern heard this, he thought it very strange,
and wondered who the monk could be who had achieved
so great a deed. He remembered how all his champions
were dead, and he also turned over in his mind what
could have become of his dear friend Heimir, for he
had heard nothing of whether he was alive or dead. He
thought that there was no one as likely to have done this
deed as Heimir, if he was alive, but nobody was able to
tell him what had become of Heimir.

So now King Þiðrekr rode to this monastery with his
men, and arrived there one day towards evening; the
monastery was called Vadincusan. When he came to the
cloister he bade them call the abbot to him. The abbot
came out from the cloister and greeted King Þiðrekr
warmly and asked where he was going. The king said
he was going about on business of his own.

Then the king said to the abbot: 'Is there any monk
here in this monastery whose name is Heimir and who
would be the son of Studas?'

'I know the names of all the monks in this cloister,'
answered the abbot, 'and none of them is named Heimir.'

Then the king said: 'You must allow me to go into the
chapter-house and summon all the monks before me.'

At this moment there came out from the cloisters a
monk wearing his cowl and a wide-brimmed hat. He had
broad shoulders, and was short in stature; his beard was
broad and thick and as grey as a pigeon, and this monk
remained silent and spoke no word to King Þiðrekr.

King Þiðrekr turned to the man, and thought he
recognized him and that it must be his good comrade
Heimir, and he said: 'We have seen the snows of many

293

winters since we parted as good friends, my brother, and even so we find one another again. You are Heimir, my dear friend.'

Then the monk answered: 'I never knew the Heimir you mourn for, and I never saw him, and never have I been a man of yours in all my life.'

'Brother,' answered the king, 'remember now how our horses drank, out in Frisia, so that the waters of the lake diminished, big as it is.'

Then Heimir answered: 'I cannot remember that I watered any horses with you, for I never saw you before now, as far as I remember.'

Then said King Þiðrekr: 'Though you still refuse to know me again, you might well tell me of the day when you accompanied me as I was driven out of my kingdom, and then you went home to King Erminrekr and he drove you into outlawry. You will remember that well enough, though you declare you have never seen me.'

Then Heimir answered: 'I cannot remember what you are speaking of. I have heard King Þiðrekr of Bern and King Erminrekr of Rome named, but I know no more of any quarrels between them.'

'Brother,' said King Þiðrekr, 'many a snow has fallen since we two saw one another last. You must remember how as we were riding to a feast in Rome we found Earl Iron on the road before us with his great wound; and you remember his hawks, how they shrieked over his dead body, and his hounds, how they snarled, and his horse neighed, and how all his men had loved their lord, and not one of them would leave him.'

And Heimir now said: 'I do not remember that I was present when Earl Iron fell.'

Now King Þiðrekr answered: 'Brother, many a snow has fallen, but now you must remember how we came to Rome to King Erminrekr, and how our horses neighed, and how all the courtly ladies stood there and watched. In those days we had hair as bright as gold, beautifully curled; this same hair is now as grey as doves, both yours and mine. Your clothes are all of the same dye as mine. Remember now, my friend, these things of which I now remind you, and do not leave me standing here before you any longer.'

Then Heimir laughed and said: 'Good my lord King
þiðrekr, now I remember all the things of which you
have reminded me, and now I will go with you.'

Then Heimir threw off his cowl, and went back into
the cloister and took all his weapons and his horse, and
rode away with King þiðrekr, home to Rome. King
þiðrekr gave Heimir the warmest of welcomes, gave
him the highest place in his court above all his knights,
and bestowed great fiefs on him, and now he stayed there
for a while.

One day King þiðrekr and Heimir were talking to-
gether, speaking of the tributary lands, and Heimir
said: 'Sire, you are now the mightiest king in all the
world. You take tribute from all lands and every town
here in Lombardy, and far and wide elsewhere; many a
rich man pays this tribute, and many a poor one. Why,
sire, have you never claimed tribute from a place where
there must be gold and silver enough, since I know no
man takes tribute from it—neither you, sire, nor any
other—and that is the monastery where I was?'

'There must be great wealth there, as you say,' answered
King þiðrekr, 'and we have never had tribute from
there. But if we want to get it, you must be the first man
to ride there to claim the tribute.'

Heimir answered: 'I'll ride anywhere you wish, to
claim tribute.'

So a few days later Heimir was ready to ride off, and
went to the monastery; he rode alone, armed, to the
cloister. Now he came there, and the monks were aware
of his coming. They had been very angry that he should
have left the cloister without asking leave of the abbot,
though on the other hand they had thought it a great
gain that he should be gone, for they had all been afraid
of him. He was offered lodging there for the night, and
on the morning of the next day he went into the chapter-
house and summoned all the monks there.

Then Heimir spoke first to the abbot and then to all
the monks; he explained his errand, and said that þiðrekr
of Bern had sent him there on that errand because he
knew that there was so much gold and silver there, and
so much land owned, that not even the half of it was
spent on their foundation—'he wants to have tribute

from you, as from the other religious foundations. If you are willing to give him the tribute which is a king's due, I wish to hear it from you first'.

Then the abbot answered: 'We will keep the treasure here which belongs to God and Saint Mary, and no tribute shall be paid from here to any king, however great and free his crown may be.'

Then Heimir said: 'If you refuse to pay tribute to King Þiðrekr you will have to face his wrath, and it is a very strange thing that you should gather such immeasurable wealth and nobody should profit by it, but that you should be unwilling to pay tribute to the king.'

Then the abbot answered: 'You are certainly an evil man, Heimir. You ran away from the cloister to the king's court, but now you have come back and want to plunder the monastery. Now go home again to King Þiðrekr, as the fiend once already taught you to do, and live as a fiend, like King Þiðrekr.'

Now Heimir grew so angry that he drew his sword Naglhring and struck him on the neck with the first blow, so that it took off his head. And then he slew all the brethren and took the gold and silver there and everything which he knew the monks had hoarded, and he carried away all the wealth he could get hold of, loading it upon many horses, and then King Þiðrekr came to join him, and they set the place on fire and burned it all to cold ashes, but they carried all their wealth home and laid it in their treasury.

Now Þiðrekr heard tell of a giant who had hoarded much gold and silver, and they had never heard of more gold in any one place. This giant was now old, and he was the hugest and strongest of giants, so much so that no elephant could carry him; he himself was too heavy to move about, but lay always in the same place, and for this reason he had not become famous enough for men to know much about him. Heimir told King Þiðrekr about this giant, and said he meant to go and claim tribute from him on the king's behalf, and the king thought well of this. Heimir said that he did not suppose there was any man to be found in the land who had not paid tribute to the king, except this giant.

So now Heimir took his horse and his weapons and

rode off along the road that led to him, and in the end he
came to a high mountain where there was also a great
forest, and there he found a large cave. He leapt from
his horse and went into the cave. In front of him lay a
giant, the biggest he had ever seen, and this giant had
hair as grey as a dove, long hair, all hanging down over
his face.

Heimir went up to him and said: 'Stand up, giant, and
defend yourself. A man has come who means to fight
you.'

The giant awoke, and said: 'You are bold, my man,
but I won't stand up to kill you.'

Then Heimir said: 'If you won't stand up and defend
yourself, I will draw my sword from its sheath and kill
you.'

The giant leapt to his feet and shook his head and his
hair, and it stood straight up on end—it was fearful to
see! He snatched up his cudgel, which was both long
and thick. He brandished it and struck Heimir so might-
ily at the first blow that he flew through the air as far
and as fast as a bolt from a bow, and was dead before
he touched the ground. And that is the story of Heimir's
death. The news soon spread that so mighty a champion
had now lost his life.

VIII C. THE NECKLACE OF THE
BRŌSINGS—O.N. Brísinga men

1. *þrymskviða* (tenth century?; included in the *Poetic Edda c.*
   1270) stanzas 13, 19.

> Freyja grew wrathful and snorted with rage;
> At this the whole hall of the Aesir shook,
> And the mighty necklace of the Brísings broke.

[The gods disguise Þórr in Freyja's clothes.]

> A bridal veil they bound upon Þórr,
> And bound the great Brísing necklace on him.

2. Snorri Sturluson, *Edda* (*c.* 1220), *Skáldskaparmál* chs. 15, 23, commenting on and quoting a stanza from the poem *Húsdrápa* by Úlfr Uggason (late tenth century).

What names can be given to [the god] Heimdallr? He can be called 'son of nine mothers'. . . . He is also 'he who visited Vagi's Skerry and Singi's Rock'. On that occasion he fought Loki over the Brísings' necklace. . . . Úlfr Uggason has a long passage on this tale in his *Húsdrápa*, and it is said there that they had taken the form of seals. . . .

What names can be given to Loki? He can be called . . . 'Thief of the Brísings' Necklace' . . . 'Son of Fárbauti' . . . 'Quarrelsome Opponent of Heimdallr'. Thus Úlfr Uggason says here:

> The guardian of the bridge of gods,
> Far-famed, clashed in combat
> Against Fárbauti's cunning son
> Away at Singi's Rock.
> Stout-hearted, he, the offspring
> Of mothers eight and one,
> Was first—in poetry I speak—
> To gain that fair sea-gem.

3. Snorri Sturluson, *Edda* (*c.* 1220), *Gylfaginning* ch. 35.

Freyja owned the Brísings' necklace.

4. *Sǫrlaþáttr* (*c.* 1300–50), chs. 1, 2.

The region to the east of Vanakvísl in Asia was called Asíaland or Asíaheimr, and the people who lived there were called the Aesir, and they called their chief stronghold Ásgarðr. Óðinn was the name of the king who ruled it. There was an important place of sacrifice there, and Óðinn appointed Njǫrðr and Freyr as priests for the sacrifices. Njǫrðr's daughter was called Freyja; she accompanied Óðinn and was his mistress.

There were certain men in Asía, one of whom was called Áfrigg, another Dvalinn, the third Berlingr, and the fourth Grérr. Their home was not far from the king's hall; they were men of such skill that they could turn their hands to any kind of craft; people used to call men of the sort that they were, dwarfs. They lived

298

inside a rock. They used to mingle more with human beings in those days than they do now.

Óðinn loved Freyja dearly, and indeed she was the fairest of women in those days. She had a bower of her own, and it was beautiful and strong as well, so that people said that if the door was shut and locked no man could come into the bower without Freyja's consent.

It happened that one day Freyja went to that rock, and it was open; the dwarfs were busy forging a gold necklace, and it was by then very nearly finished. Freyja liked the look of the necklace very much, and the dwarfs too liked the look of Freyja. She said she wanted to buy the necklace from the dwarfs, offering gold and silver and other fine things in exchange. They said that they were not in need of money, but said they were each willing to sell his own share in the necklace, wanting nothing in exchange except that she should lie for one night with each of them. So, whether she found it easy to bring herself to this or not, this was the bargain she made with them. And when four nights had passed and the conditions had all been fulfilled, they handed the necklace to Freyja. She went home to her bower, and kept quiet, as if nothing had happened.

There was a man called Fárbauti; he was an old peasant and had an old wife whose name was Laufey, and she was thin and weak, and so she was nicknamed Nál ['Needle']. They had only one child, a son named Loki; he was not well-built, but he soon grew to be sharp-tongued, and quick-witted in his tricks. He was better than anyone else in cleverness of the sort that is called cunning; even in his youth he was very crafty, and so he was called Loki the Guileful. He went to Ásgarðr to Óðinn, and became his man. Óðinn always spoke up for him whatever he might do, and indeed he often entrusted difficult tasks to him, all of which he performed better than one might expect. Also he got to know almost everything that went on, and told Óðinn everything he knew.

Now it is said that Loki got to know that Freyja had obtained the necklace, and also what price she had paid for it, and he told this to Óðinn. Now when Óðinn found out about this, he said that Loki was to get the necklace and bring it to him. Loki said there was little chance of that, because nobody could get into the bower without Freyja's consent. Óðinn said he was to take himself off, and not come back till he had got the necklace; so then Loki went off howling. Most people were glad that things were going badly for Loki.

He went to Freyja's bower, and it was locked; he tried to get in, and could not manage it. The weather outside was very cold, and he quickly began to freeze. So next he turned himself into a fly, and then he fluttered all round the lock and along the door-frame, and nowhere could he find a hole big enough for him to get in by. Up he went, right up to the ridge of the gable, and yet the only hole he found was no bigger than you could stick a needle in—but through that hole he crawled in. And when he had got inside, he kept his eyes well open and looked carefully to see if anyone was awake, but he could see that everything was asleep in the bower. Then he went farther in, up to Freyja's bed, and noticed that she had the necklace round her neck, and that the clasp was underneath her. So then Loki turned himself into a flea. He settled on Freyja's chin and bit her, so that Freyja woke and turned over, and then went back to sleep. Then Loki took off his flea-shape, slipped the necklace off her, and then opened the bower and went away, and brought the necklace to Óðinn.

In the morning Freyja woke and saw that the door was open, but not broken, and that the fine necklace was gone. She felt pretty sure what the trick must have been, and as soon as she was dressed she went into the hall and appeared before King Óðinn, and said that it was a wicked deed which he had had done, to steal her fine treasure from her, and begged him to give her her treasure back. . . .

[Óðinn says he will give it back only if she undertakes to cause a feud between two kings and keep them fighting through all eternity.]

Freyja agreed to this, and took her necklace back.

IX. *The Fight Against Manlike Monsters*

1. *Anglo-Saxon Charters* etc. in which 'Grendel' occurs as a place-name element.

(*a*) Grant of land at Abbots Morton, Worcestershire, by Kenred of Mercia, (A.D. 708).

First from Grendel's Pit to Willow Mere, and from Willow Mere to the Red Swamp . . . from the pool along Piddle Brook as far as the marsh; and from the marsh back to Grendel's Pit.

(*b*) Grant of land at Creedy, Devonshire, by Æthelheard of Wessex (A.D. 739).

. . . from Dodda's ridge to Grendel's Pit; from Grendel's Pit to the ivy grove. . . .

(*c*) Grant of land at Ham in Wiltshire by Æthelstan (A.D. 931).

. . . from there north over the hill . . . to the fence of Beowa's Patch . . . then to the long meadow, and from there to Grendel's Mere. . . .

(*d*) A list of boundaries near Battersea (A.D. 957).

. . . from Goat Corner to Grendel's Mire; from Grendel's Mire to the rushy mere; from the rushy mere to Balham. . . .

(*e*) Grant of land at Swinford, Staffordshire, by Eardred (A.D. 958).

. . . along the ditch to Grendel's Mere. . . .

(*f*) Confirmation of land to Pershore Abbey by Edgar (A.D. 972).

. . . and thus from Grendel's Beck the boundary runs. . . .

(*g*) Account of inheritance of land near Edgware (A.D. 972).

. . . along the hedge to Grendel's gate, according to the king's boundary. . . .

2. *Grettis saga* (*c.* 1300–20), chs. 32–5, 64–5.

(*a*) [The farmstead of a man named Þórhallr is haunted, and he has difficulty in getting any shepherd to work for him; he is therefore advised to hire a certain Glámr, a Swede, 'big and strong, but not much to most people's liking'.]

One day Þórhallr missed two light bay horses, and went out himself to look for them—from which one may be sure that he was not a man of high standing. He climbed to the foot of Sleðás, and then went south along the mountain which is called Ármannsfell; there he saw a man coming down from the woods of Goðaskógr, carrying faggots on a horse. They soon met, and Þórhallr asked him his name, and he said he was called Glámr. This man was of tall stature, and his whole appearance was rather strange; his eyes were blue and bulging, and the colour of his hair was wolfish grey. Þórhallr raised his eyebrows somewhat when he saw this man, but he realized that it was the one who had been recommended to him.

'What kind of work are you most suited for?' said Þórhallr.

Glámr said he was well suited for tending sheep in winter.

'Will you come and tend my sheep?' said Þórhallr. 'Skapti recommended you to me.'

'You will find my stay works out best if I am my own master,' said Glámr, 'for I am easily annoyed if things don't please me.'

'That will do me no harm,' said Þórhallr, 'and I want you to come to me.'

'Maybe I will,' said Glámr. 'But are there any snags?'

'The place is supposed to be haunted,' said Þórhallr.

'I'm not frightened of these ghosts,' said Glámr; 'I think they make things less dull.'

'You'll need to be like that,' said Þórhallr. 'It's best not to be a man of little spirit there.'

After this they struck their bargain, and Glámr was to come in the first days of winter. Thereupon they parted, and Þórhallr found his horses in a place which he had just searched. Þórhallr rode home, and thanked Skapti for his kindness.

The summer passed by, and Þórhallr heard nothing more from his shepherd, and no one knew anything of him; but on the appointed date Glámr arrived at Þórhalls-staðir. The farmer gave him a good welcome, but every-one else took a dislike to him, most of all the mistress of the house. He took over the care of the sheep, and this gave him little trouble; he had a great strong voice, deep in pitch, and the sheep all flocked together as soon as he halloed at them. There was a church at Þórhalls-staðir. Glámr would not go near it; he had no faith, would not join in the singing, and was ill-tempered and full of spite; everybody loathed him.

So time went on, till it came to Christmas Eve. On that day Glámr got up early and shouted for his food.

The housewife answered: 'It is not the custom among Christian folk to take any food today, because tomorrow is the first day of Christmas,' said she, 'and so we are first bound to fast today.'

He answered: 'You have many superstitions, which are of no use that I can see. I don't know that men get on any better nowadays than when nobody did any-thing of the sort. I thought our ways were better when men were called heathen—and I want my food, and no tricks!'

The housewife said: 'I am sure something bad will happen to you today, if you do this wicked thing.'

Glámr told her to fetch the food at once, or else, he said, it would be the worse for her. She did not dare do otherwise than as he wished; and when he had fed he went out, and his breath was rather foul.

The weather had taken such a turn that it was dark wherever one looked, and snow came whirling down with a howling wind, and it grew far worse as the day wore on. At the beginning of the day men could hear the shepherd, but less often as the day wore on. Then the

303

snow began to pile in drifts, and by evening a storm
came on; men were coming for the service, and this went
on till nightfall, but Glámr did not come home. There
was some talk of whether one should not make a search
for him, but because there was this storm and it was
pitch dark, no such search was made. He did not come
home all that Christmas night; the men waited in this
way till after the service.

As soon as there was daylight enough the men went
searching, and found the sheep scattered far and wide
in the snowdrifts, battered by the storm, or running wild
up on the fells. Next they came upon a large area all
trampled over, high up in the valley; it looked to them
as if there had been some pretty violent wrestling there,
for rocks and earth had been torn up far and wide. They
examined the place carefully, and saw where Glámr was
lying, not far from them. He was dead, and as black as
Hel, and as big as an ox. They felt great disgust at him,
and they shuddered at the sight of him; nevertheless
they tried to carry him to the church, but they could not
manage to move him, except just to the edge of a ravine
a short way down from where they were.

So they went home leaving matters thus, and told
the farmer what had happened. He asked what it might
have been that was the death of Glámr. They said they
had followed some tracks as big as if the bottom of a
barrel had been slammed down, from the place where
the trampling was, and going up under the rocks high
in the valley; and great gouts of blood accompanied
them. From this men gathered that the evil creature
which had been there before must have killed Glámr,
but that Glámr must have dealt it some wound that had
taken full effect, for never again was there any sign of
that evil creature.

On the second day of Christmas there was another
attempt to carry Glámr to the church. Oxen were har-
nessed, but they could not manage to move him any-
where the ground was level, not downhill. So they went
away, leaving things thus. On the third day a priest
went with them, and they searched all day, but Glámr
was not to be found. The priest would not go again, and
the shepherd was found as soon as the priest was not

in the company. So then they gave up toiling to carry him to the church, and they buried him under a cairn just where he was.

Not long afterwards men noticed that Glámr was not lying quiet in his grave. This caused people great harm, for some fell in a faint if they saw him, and others went out of their minds. Just after Christmas some men thought they saw him at home there on the farm; they grew mightily afraid, and many men ran away. Next Glámr took to riding by night on the roofs of the buildings so as almost to break them. He walked almost night and day. People hardly dared go up the valley, even if they had some errand there, and men thought all this was doing great harm to the district.

In spring Þórhallr got himself some farmhands and started farming his lands. Then the walking began to grow less while the sun's course was at its highest, and so it went on till midsummer. That summer a ship came to Húnavatn, and on board was a man called Þorgautr. He was a foreigner by birth, a big and strong man, and he had the strength of two men; he was on his own and bound to no master, and he wanted to find some work, because he had no money. Þórhallr rode to the ship and met Þorgautr, and asked whether he would be willing to work for him. Þorgautr said that very well might be, and that he would make no difficulties.

'But you must be prepared for one thing, 'said Þórhallr, 'for it is no fit place for weaklings to be, because of the hauntings there have been there for some time; and I don't wish to lure you into a trap.'

Þorgautr answered: 'I won't think it's all up with me even if I do see some little ghosts. Things must be unpleasant indeed for others if I am afraid, and I will not refuse the place because of that.'

So now they were well pleased with their bargain, and Þorgautr was to tend the sheep in winter.

Now the summer passed by, and Þorgautr took charge of the sheep in the first week of winter; everybody liked him. Glámr was always coming to the farm and riding the roofs. Þorgautr thought this very amusing, and said: 'The thrall will have to come nearer if I'm to be frightened.'

305

Þórhallr told him not to say so much about it—'it will be best that you two should not pit your strength against one another'.

Þorgautr said: 'You really have had your courage shaken out of you! I won't drop down dead in the twilight because of this chatter.'

So things went on like that all winter till Christmas. On Christmas Eve the shepherd went out to the sheep.

Then the housewife said: 'I think what we need is for things not to go on again in the old way.'

He answered: 'Don't be afraid of that, mistress,' said he. 'There will have been something worth talking about if I don't come back.'

Then he went back again to his sheep. The weather was rather cold, with driving snow. Þorgautr was in the habit of coming home when it was getting towards dusk, but now he did not come home at that hour. The men who were coming for the service arrived, as was the custom; it seemed to them that things would very likely turn out the same way as before. The farmer wanted to send someone out to look for the shepherd, but these men made excuses and said they would not risk putting their lives in the hands of trolls by going out at night; and the farmer did not dare go himself, and so no search was made.

On Christmas Day, when the men had fed, they went out and searched for the shepherd. They first went to Glámr's cairn, as men reckoned that it must have been his doing that the shepherd had disappeared. And when they came near the cairn they saw that great things had happened there, and there they found the shepherd, and his neck was broken and every bone smashed in his body. Then they carried him to the church, and no man ever came to any harm through Þorgautr afterwards. But Glámr began to grow stronger once again. He made so much of himself now that all the people ran away from Þórhallsstaðir, save only the farmer and his wife.

Now there had been the same cowman there for a long time, and Þórhallr did not want to let him go, out of kindliness and care for him; he was getting to be very old, and thought it would be a hard thing to leave, and he also saw that everything the farmer owned would go

to rack and ruin if no one looked after it. Now some
time after midwinter it happened one morning that the
housewife went out to the byre to milk the cows at the
right time. It was then full daylight, because no one
would dare be out of doors earlier, except the cowman;
he used to go out as soon as dawn broke. She heard a
loud cracking in the byre, and hideous bellowing; she
ran back indoors screaming, and saying some sort of
horrible thing was going on in the byre. The farmer went
out and came to the cattle, and they were all goring one
another. He thought things looked bad there, and went
farther in, towards the hay-barn. He saw the cowman
lying there, with his head in one stall and his feet in the
other; he was lying on his back. The farmer went up to
him and ran his hands over him; he soon found out that
he was dead, and his backbone in two pieces—it had
been broken across the stone slab separating the stalls.
The farmer now thought it impossible to stay there,
and he left his farm with everything he could carry
away; but every living beast which was left behind
Glámr killed. Next he went through the whole valley
and laid waste every farmstead from Tunga upwards.
Þórhallr was then staying with friends for the rest of the
winter. No man could go up the valley with horse or
dog, for it would be killed at once. But when spring
came and the sun's course was at its highest, the walking
was somewhat lessened. Þórhallr now wished to go back
to his land; it was not easy for him to get farmhands, but
still he set up farming again at Þórhallsstaðir. Every-
thing went just the same way as before; as soon as
autumn came the hauntings began to increase. This time
the worst attacks were against the farmer's daughter,
and it turned out that she died of it. Much advice
was asked for, but nothing was done. Men thought
that things were coming to such a state that all
Vatnsdalr would be laid waste if no remedies could be
found. . . .

Grettir rode north to Vatnsdalr and came to visit
Tunga. Jǫkull Bárðarson, Grettir's uncle, lived there at
that time; he was a tall and strong man, and most over-
bearing; he was a seafarer, and a hard man to deal with,

but much respected. He gave Grettir a good welcome, and he stayed there three days.

There was so much talk about Glámr's walking that people spoke more of that than of anything else. Grettir questioned them closely about the events that had taken place, and Jǫkull said they were telling no more than had really happened—'and are you curious to go there, kinsman?'

Grettir said that was true.

Jǫkull told him not to do so—'for that would be pushing your luck too hard. Your kinsmen have a great deal at stake where you are concerned,' said he, 'and we think there is no one to equal you among the young men now. But as for Glámr, evil will come of evil, and it is far better to have to do with human beings than with such uncanny creatures.'

Grettir said he had in mind to go to Þórhallsstaðir and see how things were going there.

'I see now that it's no use hindering you,' said Jǫkull, 'but it's true what they say, that good qualities are one thing, but good luck is another.'

'When there's trouble in my neighbour's house, there's trouble knocking at my door,' said Grettir. 'Think how things may go for you yourself before this is over.'

Jǫkull answered: 'Maybe we can both see a little way into the future, but neither can do anything about it.'

After this they parted, and neither liked the other's prophecy.

Grettir rode to Þórhallsstaðir, and the farmer welcomed him warmly. He asked where Grettir meant to go on to, but he said he meant to stay the night there, if the farmer was willing that it should be so. Þórhallr said he would be thankful that he should be there—'but few people think there is anything to be gained by staying here for any length of time. You must have heard what reason we have to mourn here, and I would dearly wish that you should come to no trouble through me. And even if you yourself get away safe and sound, I know for sure that you will lose your horse, for no one who comes here can keep his beast safe.'

Grettir said there were horses enough, whatever might happen to this one.

Þórhallr was glad that Grettir wished to stay there, and welcomed him with open arms; Grettir's horse was securely locked up in an outhouse. They went to bed, and the night passed without Glámr coming to the house.

Then Þórhallr said: 'Things have changed for the better since your coming, for every night Glámr was in the habit of riding the roof of the house or breaking the doors open, as you can see by the marks.'

Grettir said: 'In that case, one of two things must happen—either he won't be able to hold himself in much longer, or he'll drop his habits for more than just one night. I'll stay here a second night and see how things go.'

Then they went to look at Grettir's horse, and it had come to no harm; the farmer thought that everything was pointing the same way. Now Grettir stayed there a second night, and the thrall did not come to the house. The farmer thought things were looking very hopeful, and he then went out to look at Grettir's horse. When the farmer came to the outhouse it was all broken open, and the horse had been dragged out and every bone of its body broken. Þórhallr told Grettir what had happened, and bade him save his own life—'for you'll be dead, for certain, if you wait for Glámr.'

Grettir said: 'I'll accept nothing less in exchange for my horse than a sight of this thrall.'

The farmer said that nothing good would come of seeing him—'for he is unlike any creature in human form. Yet I am glad of every hour you are willing to stay here.'

So the day passed; and when men were about to go to bed, Grettir refused to take his clothes off, and laid himself down in one of the open sleeping-stalls opposite the farmer's shuttered bed-closet. He had a shaggy cloak over him, and he held one end down firmly under his feet, and tucked the other over his head, and looked out through the neck-hole. There was a very strong post in front of this stall, and he braced his feet against it. The whole door-frame had been broken away from the outer doorway, and now a hurdle was tied across as a makeshift arrangement. The partition which had marked

309

the entrance to the sleeping-hall was all broken away, both above and below the cross-beam. All the bedding had been removed from its place; the room was hardly fit to live in. There was a light burning in the room all night.

And when a third of the night had gone by, Grettir heard a great din outside; then something climbed up on to the house and rode the roof above the sleeping-hall, drumming on it with its heels so that every timber creaked. This went on a long time. Then the thing came down from the house and walked up to the door; and when the hurdle opened Grettir saw the thrall stretching his head in—a head which seemed to him hideously large, and with the cut of the face remarkably big. Glámr came slowly forward, and once he was inside the door he stretched himself up to his full height; he towered up to the roof. He turned towards the sleeping-hall, and laid his arm along the cross-beam and craned his head forward into the hall. Not a sound came from the farmer, for he thought he had enough with what he heard going on outside. Grettir lay still and did not move at all.

Glámr saw some sort of heap lying in the stall, so now he made his way farther in along the hall and took a very firm grip on the cloak. Grettir braced his feet against the post, and did not yield at all. Glámr tugged it towards him a second time, far more strongly, and still the cloak did not move. The third time he took so strong a grip on it that he lifted Grettir up out of the stall, and now between them they ripped the cloak in two. Glámr looked at the torn bit he was holding on to, and wondered very much who could tug so strongly against him. And at this very moment Grettir ran in under his arms and gripped him round the waist and hugged his back as tightly as he could, thinking that this would make Glámr buckle at the knees; but the thrall went for Grettir's arms so hard that he quite gave way on account of his strength. Then Grettir retreated from one sleeping-stall to the next; posts were uprooted, and everything that came in their way was broken to pieces. Glámr wanted to get outside, but Grettir dug his feet in wherever he could, though even so Glámr managed to drag him out of the hall. Then they had a very hard tussle, for the thrall meant to get him right outside the farmhouse; yet, however hard it might be to have to deal with Glámr indoors, Grettir saw that it would be worse to grapple with him outside, and that was why he struggled with all his strength not to go out.

Then Glámr put on an added spurt of strength and, as they came to the entrance porch, he grabbed Grettir towards him. And when Grettir saw that he could not brace his feet to resist this, he did two things at once—he hurled himself as hard as he could against the thrall's chest, and braced both feet against a stone that stood, half sunk in the ground, by the doorway. The thrall was not prepared for this, as he had been tugging to drag Grettir towards him, and so he toppled over backwards and went flying head over heels through the doorway; his shoulders struck against the lintel and the whole roof broke in pieces, both timbers and frozen thatch. So he fell out of the house, head over heels and flat on his back, and Grettir came down on top of him. Out of doors the moonlight was very strong, with patches of open sky between thick clouds; from time to time these drove across the moon, and then cleared again. Now at the very moment that Glámr fell, a cloud swept clear of the moon, and Glámr turned his piercing eyes up towards it; and Grettir himself has said that this was the only sight he ever saw which was enough to make him flinch. What with all this put together, his weariness, and seeing Glámr's eyes staring up so fixedly, his strength ebbed away so that he could not draw his short-sword, but lay there between life and death.

And since there was far greater power for evil in Glámr than in most of the walking dead, he then began to speak thus: 'You have shown great eagerness to seek me out, Grettir,' said he, 'but it will hardly seem surprising if you win no great luck through me. Now this I can tell you: you have now attained only one half of the full-grown strength which would have been destined to be yours if you had not sought me out. I cannot now take away from you the strength you already have, but I can so ordain that you shall never become any stronger than you are now. Even so, you are strong enough, as many will know to their cost. Up to now you have become famous for your deeds, but from now on manslayings and

311

the penalties of the law shall fall upon you, and almost all your deeds shall turn to ill-luck for you, and the ruin of your good fortune. You shall be made an outlaw, and to live alone shall be your lot. And this I lay upon you, that these eyes of mine, such as they now are, shall be ever before your sight, and then you shall find it a heavy burden to be alone, and this shall lead to your death.'

As soon as the thrall had spoken these words, the weakness which had come over Grettir passed away; then he drew his short-sword and cut off Glámr's head and laid it between his thighs. Then the farmer came out; he had put his clothes on while Glámr was speaking, but he dared not come near before Glámr was dead. Þórhallr praised God for this, and thanked Grettir well because he had overcome this unclean spirit. Then they set to work and burned Glámr to cold ashes. After that, they carried his ashes away in a skin bag and buried them as far as possible from all grazing grounds or paths where men might pass. They went home after that, and by then it was almost daybreak. Grettir lay down, for he was very stiff.

(b)   [A farmstead called Sandhaugar has twice been raided at Yule by some supernatural being, and each time a man has disappeared, leaving only traces of blood. Grettir comes to offer his help to the mistress of the household, but as he is by now an outlaw he comes in disguise, calling himself Gestr.]

When he had eaten his fill, he told the servants to go to the far end of the hall. Then he took some boards and loose timbers and flung them down across the middle of the hall, and built a large barricade, so that none of the servants could get past it; none of them dared contradict him or grumble about anything. The entrance was in the side wall of the hall near the gable end, and near by was the cross-dais at the end of the room; Gestr lay down there, and did not take off his clothes. There was a light burning in the hall, opposite the door. So Gestr lay, until far into the night. . . .

As it drew near midnight he heard a great din outside. The next thing was that a great she-troll strode into the hall; she had a trough in one hand and in the other a knife, a rather big one. She looked round her as she came in, and saw where Gestr was lying, and rushed at him; but he jumped up to face her, and they attacked each other fiercely, and fought for a long time in the hall. She was the stronger, but he avoided her cleverly. They broke everything that came in their way, even the partition of the hall. She dragged him out through the doorway and into the entrance porch, and there he grappled grimly with her. She wanted to drag him out of the farmhouse, but before that could be done they had torn down all the framework of the outer door and carried it off on their shoulders. Then she went lumbering down to the river, and on towards the ravine. By then Gestr was very weary, but there were only two things to be done: either he must summon up his strength or else she would fling him down into the ravine.

They fought all night. He thought he had never grappled with so horrible a creature, as far as sheer strength was concerned. She held him so tightly clasped that he could make no use of either arm, except to keep a hold on her waist; but when they came to the river ravine he swung the hag right round. In this way he got his right arm free; then he quickly grasped the short-sword which he wore at his belt, drew it, and then struck at the hag's shoulder so that he cut her right arm off; and so he got free, but she hurtled down into the ravine, and so into the waterfall. Gestr was very stiff and weary by then, and he lay there for a long time among the rocks. Then he went home when daylight came, and lay down in bed; he was swollen and black and blue.

And when the mistress of the house came home from Mass, she thought her home had been pretty well turned upside-down; so then she went to Gestr and asked what had been going on, that everything should be broken and smashed to bits. He told her everything that had happened. She thought it a most noteworthy affair, and asked him who he was; then he told her the truth, and bade her fetch the priest, saying he wanted to meet him, and this was done.

And when Steinn the priest came to Sandhauger, he soon realized that it was Grettir Ásmundarson who had

313

come there, calling himself Gestr. The priest asked him what he thought had become of the men who had disappeared, and Grettir said he thought they must have disappeared into the ravine. The priest said he could not put any faith in his stories if he did not see some token to prove them. Grettir said that they would know the truth of the matter later. The priest went home.

Grettir lay in bed for many days. The mistress of the house looked after him well, and so Yuletide passed by. It is Grettir's own account that the she-troll hurtled down into the ravine when she got that wound; but the men of Bárðardalr say that the light of dawn turned her to stone while they were wrestling, so that her heart burst just as he cut her arm off, and that she is still standing there on the cliff, in the shape of a woman. The men of the valley hid Grettir there all winter.

One day after Yule, Grettir went to Eyjardalsár, and when he and the priest met, Grettir said: 'I can see, priest,' said he, 'that you don't put much faith in my stories. Now I want you to go to that river with me, and see how much likelihood you think there is in them.'

The priest did so. When they came to the waterfall they saw a cave high up under the overhanging cliff; the cliff-face was so sheer that there was no place to climb it, and it was almost sixty feet from the top to the pool below. They had a rope with them.

The priest said: 'It seems to me utterly impossible to reach that place, so you won't be able to get down.'

Grettir answered: 'Of course it's possible to reach it, but it is men who have some pluck in them who will come off best there. I will go and find out what there is in that waterfall, but you are to keep watch over the rope.'

The priest told him he could have his own way, and he drove a stake into the cliff, piled stones round it and sat down beside it. As for Grettir, he tied a stone in a loop at the end of the rope, and lowered it down to the pool.

'Now how do you mean to get down there yourself?' said the priest.

'I don't want to be tied up when I get to the waterfall,' said Grettir. 'I have a feeling it would be a bad thing.'

After this he prepared himself for the expedition; he had few clothes on, and wore a short-sword at his belt but had no other weapons. Then he leaped down from the cliff, down into the waterfall. The priest got a glimpse of the soles of his feet, but after that had no idea what had become of him.

Grettir dived down under the fall, which was very difficult because there was a great whirlpool there, and he had to dive right down to the bottom before he came up again behind the fall, where there was a jutting-out rock, and he got round to the far side of it and climbed up on to it. There was a large cave behind the fall, and the water poured down in front of it from the top of the cliff. Then he went into the cave, where a great fire of logs was burning; Grettir saw that a fearsome giant was sitting beside it, and he was terrible to look at. And when Grettir came towards him the giant jumped up and seized a pike and swung it at the man who had come in— for one could either swing or thrust with this weapon. There was a wooden shaft to it; men called a weapon made in this way a 'hafted short-sword'. Grettir struck back with his short-sword, and it struck the shaft and cut it in two. Then the giant tried to stretch his arm behind him for a sword that was hanging there in the cave. At this very moment Grettir struck him on the breast in such a way as to cut open almost all his rib-cage and belly, so that his guts came tumbling out and fell in the river and were swept away downstream.

And as the priest was sitting beside the rope, he saw some shreds sweeping down the current, all covered with blood. Then he was seized by panic, feeling certain that Grettir must be dead; instead of holding the rope he ran away and went home. By then evening had come, and the priest said it was certain that Grettir was dead, and he said that such a man was a great loss.

Now to speak of Grettir—he did not leave much pause between his blows until the giant died. Then Grettir went farther into the cave; he kindled a light and explored the cave. It is not said how much wealth he found in the cave, but men think that there was some; he stayed there till late in the night. He found the bones of two men there, and put them in a bag. Then he made his way out of the cave, and swam to the rope and shook it, thinking that the priest would be there; but when he realized that the priest had gone home he was forced to go hand over hand up the rope, and so he reached the top of the cliff. Then he went back to Eyjardalsár, and brought the bag in which the bones were to the church porch, together with a wooden rod inscribed with runes, on which these verses were extremely well carved:

> Into a dark gulf I went;
> The rolling rock-filled torrent
> Gaped its wet and icy mouth
> To swallow up this swordsman.
> The flowing current smote my breast
> In the ogress' dwelling;
> The whirlpool's hostile fury
> Beat about my shoulders.

And also these:

> The she-troll's ugly husband
> Left his cave to meet me;
> Long he fought against me,
> And hard, if truth be told.
> The hard-edged hafted short-sword
> I hewed from off its shaft;
> The giant's breast and belly
> I clove with my bright blade.

3. Orms þáttr Stórólfssonar (c. 1300), chs. 6–9.

[An Icelander and a Dane, Ormr and Ásbjǫrn, are visiting a district of northern Norway.]

There Ásbjǫrn learnt that two islands lay to the north of that district, both of them called Southey, and that the master of the outer island was a giant named Brúsi. He was a huge troll and a man-eater, and people thought he would never be defeated by human beings, however many they might be; his mother, however, was even worse to deal with—she was a coal-black she-cat, and as big as the sacred oxen, which are the biggest. The men of the district got no profit out of either of these islands because of these harmful creatures. Ásbjǫrn grew eager

316

to go to these islands, but Ormr persuaded him not
to go, saying there were few things worse than to have
to do with such fiends; and so nothing came of that
journey. . . .

Shortly after Ormr and Ásbjǫrn had parted, Ásbjǫrn
felt eager to go north to the Southey Islands. He went
aboard ship with three and twenty men, held his course
north past Mœr, and late in the day came to Outer
Southey, where they went ashore and pitched their
tents. They stayed there all night, and noticed nothing.

Early next morning Ásbjǫrn got up, dressed, took
his weapons and went up inland, but told his men to
wait for him. And when some little time had passed
since Ásbjǫrn had gone off, they became aware that a
horrible she-cat had come to the opening of the tent.
She was coal-black in colour and somewhat fearsome,
for there seemed to be fire burning in her nostrils and
mouth; nor were her eyes pleasant. They were very
startled at the sight, and grew full of terror. The she-cat
leapt in at them and seized them one after the other, and
it is said that some she swallowed and some she ripped
to death with her claws and teeth. Twenty men she
killed there within a brief while, but three got out, and
got away and boarded ship, and set sail at once from
that land.

But Ásbjǫrn went on his way till he came to Brúsi's
cave, and at once stepped inside it. Everything seemed
rather dark to his eyes, and indeed it was very shadowy
in the cave. He was aware of nothing before he was
snatched up into the air, and flung down so hard
that he thought it a marvel. He then became aware
that the giant Brúsi had come—and he looked rather
large.

Brúsi then said: 'You've certainly shown great eager-
ness to make your way here; now you'll get what you
came for, for you are going to lose your life here in such
torments that it will prevent any others coming to seek
me out in enmity.'

Then he stripped Ásbjǫrn's clothes off, for there was
such great difference in strength between them that the
giant could settle things between them unopposed.

Ásbjǫrn saw a great dividing wall across the cave, and a large opening in the middle of the wall; a large iron pillar also stood there, a little in front of the wall. . . .

After this Brúsi cut Ásbjǫrn's belly open and took hold of the end of his gut and tied it round the iron pillar, and led Ásbjǫrn round and round it; but Ásbjǫrn walked unfaltering, and thus in the end all his guts were wound out of him. . . .

It must be said that the three men who got away set to and rowed vigorously, and never halted till they came to the mainland; they told the news of what had happened in their journey, saying that they were of opinion that Ásbjǫrn must be dead, but they were unable to tell anything of how he had borne himself at his death. They joined the ship of some merchants, and so got a passage south to Denmark. This news now spread far and wide, and was thought to be tidings of importance.

At that time there came a change of chieftains in Norway. Earl Hákon was dead, and Óláfr Tryggvason had arrived in the land and was preaching the true faith to everyone.

Out in Iceland, Ormr Stórólfsson heard of the journey and death of Ásbjǫrn, as men thought it must have taken place. This seemed to him a very heavy loss, and he was unwilling to stay longer in Iceland, but got himself a passage at Reyðafjǫrðr and went abroad from there. They came to Norway by the northern route, and he spent the winter at Þrandheimr. By then Óláfr had ruled Norway for three years.

In spring Ormr made ready to sail to the Southey Islands. They were almost as many men on that ship as had been in Ásbjǫrn's company. They came to the smaller Southey late in the evening, and pitched tent on shore, and lay there that night. Men say that Ormr had been primesigned in Denmark, and had been baptized in Iceland. . . .

[That night a friendly giantess named Menglǫð, a half-sister of Brúsi, appears to Ormr in his
318

sleep and gives him magic gloves to help him move a
rock blocking the entrance of Brúsi's cave.]

Ormr then got up and woke his men; he sailed out to
the other island, went ashore, and bade his men wait on
board till the same hour of the next day, but to sail
away if he had not come back by then.

Now Ormr went on his way till he came to the cave.
He now saw that rock, so huge that it seemed impossible
for any man to move it away. Nevertheless he put on
the gloves, Menglǫð's gift, and after that he took hold
of the rock and moved it from the doorway; and Ormr
thought that that had proved the greatest test of his
strength.

Then he went into the cave, and placed an inlaid iron
blade in the doorway. But when he had come inside
he saw the she-cat come leaping at him with gaping jaws.
Ormr had a bow and a quiverful of arrows; he fitted an
arrow to the string and shot at the cat, three arrows;
but she caught them all between her jaws and bit them
in two. Then she threw herself on Ormr and drove her
claws into his breast so that Ormr's knees gave way
under him, and the claws went through his clothes so that
they pierced him to the bone. She then meant to bite
Ormr in the face; he found out then that nothing could
help him, and thereupon he vowed to God and to the
holy Apostle Peter to go on pilgrimage to Rome, if he
might overcome the she-cat and her son Brúsi. After
this, Ormr found that the cat's strength was dwindling.
He then gripped her by the throat with one hand and by
the backbone with the other, and broke the backbone
of her in two, and so left her dead.

Ormr then saw how there was a great dividing wall
across the cave. He went farther in, and up to it, and
when he came to it he saw a great pike sticking out and
through the wall; it was both thick and long. Ormr
then took a grip on the pike and pulled it outwards. Then
Brúsi tugged the pike back towards him, and it was held
so fast that it would not move at all. Brúsi was amazed
at this, and stuck his head out over the top of the dividing
wall; and when Ormr saw this he clutched Brúsi's beard
with both hands, but Brúsi jerked himself back to the

other side, and then they pulled hard against one another over the wall. Ormr had twisted the beard over his hand, and tugged so hard that he ripped off the whole area of Brúsi's beard, the chin, both jaws, and the fullness of the cheeks right up to the ears; and with this the flesh went too, right down to the bone. Brúsi puckered his eyebrows and scowled rather hideously. Ormr then leapt in over the dividing wall; they caught hold of one another and wrestled for a long while. By then the loss of blood was greatly wearying Brúsi, and he began to yield a little; Ormr then pressed forwards and drove Brúsi back against the wall and forced him backwards across it.

'Quite early on,' said Brúsi, 'as soon as I heard tell of you, I had a foreboding that I'd find trouble from you, and indeed it has come true now. Now, make quick work of it and cut off my head. Yet it's true that I cruelly tortured Ásbjǫrn the Magnificent when I wound all the guts out of him, but he did not give way at all till he died.'

'That was a wicked deed of yours', said Ormr, 'to torture him so cruelly—and he so valiant a man! You too must have something to remember that by.'

Then he drew a knife and carved the blood-eagle on his back, cutting all the ribs from the backbone and pulling the lungs out. Thus Brúsi lost his life, and with little valour.

After that, Ormr lit a fire and burned both Brúsi and the she-cat to ashes. And when he had finished this task he left the cave with two chests full of gold and silver; what was of most value he gave to Menglǫð, and the island too. He and she parted on most friendly terms. Ormr returned to his men by the appointed time, and thereupon they set sail for the mainland.

4. *þorsteins þáttr uxafóts* (*c.* 1300), chs. 10–11.

[þorsteinn and his friend Styrkarr have undertaken to hunt down a family of trolls in a Norwegian forest; they separate, and þorsteinn comes upon the house of the trolls.]

He went on farther into the hall till he came to a shuttered bed-closet, where a candle burned on a candlestick.

þorsteinn saw that there was a woman lying in the bed
(if one could call her a woman); she was both tall and
stout, and in every way like a troll. The cut of her face
was very large, and her complexion black or purplish;
she was lying wrapped in a silk shirt, and this looked
just as if it had been washed in human blood. For the
moment the ogress was sleeping, and snoring horribly
loud; a shield and sword were hanging above her.
þorsteinn climbed up on the edge of the bed and took
the sword down and drew it. He stripped the bed-
clothes off the ogress; he saw then that she was shaggy
all over, except for one spot under the left arm, which
he could see had only short hairs on it. He felt certain
that either it was here that iron could bite her, or else
nowhere at all. He laid the sword against that very spot
and threw himself hard against the hilt; the sword bit
so well that the point went right through to the feather
bed. The old hag then woke—not, indeed, because of
any good dream—and groped round with her hands and
jumped up. All in the same movement þorsteinn knocked
the light out and jumped up over the ogress and into the
bed. But she leaped out on to the floor, thinking that
her slayer must have tried to reach the doorway; but
when she reached it she was killed by the sword within
her, and died. Then þorsteinn went up to her and pulled
the blade out, and took it with him. . . .

[þorsteinn now spies on the rest of the troll
family, waits till they separate, and then kills one
of the daughters. He is then attacked by the father,
Járnskjǫldr.]

At that moment Járnskjǫldr came out; he had a drawn
sword in his hand, bright, and also so cutting that
þorsteinn thought he had never seen any like it. He
struck out at once at þorsteinn, who dodged aside from
the blow, but was wounded all the same in the thigh.
The sword was driven down into the ground right up
to the hilt; at this Járnskjǫldr bent forward, but þor-
steinn heaved up the sword 'Skjaldvǫr's Gift' powerfully
and quickly, and struck at Járnskjǫldr. That blow landed
on his shoulder and cut off his arm and foot; at this,

Járnskjǫldr fell down. Þorsteinn made only a brief pause between mighty blows, and cut off his head then and there.

After this Þorsteinn went back into the hall; but as he was going in, before he realized anything, he was snatched up and flung down. Þorsteinn discovered then that the old hag Skjaldvǫr had come back to life, and she was now far worse to deal with than before. She laid herself down on top of Þorsteinn, meaning to bite his windpipe in two.

Then it came into Þorsteinn's mind that He who made heaven and earth must be great indeed; he had also heard many remarkable tales about King Óláfr and the faith he was preaching. He now vowed, with a sincere heart and the whole of his mind, that he would accept that faith and serve Óláfr as long as he lived, if he could get away safe and sound and alive from all powers of magic. And just as she was meaning to sink her teeth in Þorsteinn's windpipe, and he had been binding himself by this vow, there came into the hall a ray of light, terrifyingly bright, and it shone straight into the hag's eyes. At the sight of this she turned so faint that all her strength and vigour were drawn out of her, and then she began to retch disgustingly. Then all her vomit gushed out of her down over Þorsteinn's face, so that he almost came by his death from the loathsomeness and stink of it. . . . They were both now lying between life and death, so that neither could stand upright.

[But Þorsteinn's companion finds him and helps him to break the hag's neck, and then they burn the corpses of all these trolls.]

5. *Samsons saga fagra* (*c.* 1300) chs. 3, 7-8.

There was a man named Gæli or Galinn who served the earl [of Brettland]; he was a miller, and always worked at this. His son's name was Kvintelin; he was a thief, and lurked away out in the forests. He knew many cunning tricks and had learnt many arts; he was a great master of harp-playing, and by this means he had lured many high-born ladies to come to him in the forest and had kept them with him there as long as he pleased, after

which he sent them home pregnant to their fathers or
husbands, and because of this he had an evil reputation
among all men. Nobody knew who his mother had
been, but many believed that Galinn must have begotten
him on the ogress who lived under the waterfall by the
mill. . . .

[The princess Valentina is lured away by Kvin-
telin, and no one knows what has become of her.
Samson the Fair sets out in search of her, and is
advised to ask help from Galinn the miller.]

Later, he came upon Galinn the miller; he was near
his mill, which stood beside a waterfall, and there was a
stream flowing very gently past the mill. But below the
waterfall there was a very deep pool with a great
whirling eddy.

The miller greeted him and asked him who he was.

Samson told him the truth, and—'I have come here',
said he, 'because I have been told that you know a great
deal about many things. I am seeking Valentina, the
daughter of King Garlant, whether she can be found
alive or dead. I want to have your help, that you should
join me in this search; in return, I will give you gold
and silver, and my friendship.'

Galinn answered: 'I think your friendship worth
having, but I think there's no hope of finding her; on
the contrary, I think some wild beast must have killed
her. But I am willing to bind myself to such a man as
you, if it can be of any use to you; and, if she is alive,
then I think there will be news of her.'

Then Samson took out a purse with sixty marks of
gold in it, and said to Galinn: 'I'll give you this money
for your friendship, and if we find the princess I will
make you a great man.'

Galinn answered: 'I think your money worth much,
and your friendship still more; and if I am in this search,
then she cannot be so well hidden in this world that we
will fail to find her.'

Samson was standing on the brink of the waterfall
while they were talking thus, and they clasped hands and
pledged friendship—and before Samson knew what was

happening, he was seized round both legs and jerked down into the fall. He found then that a she-troll had come, and he had no strength against her, but as soon as he could lay hands on her they grappled together, and sank to the bottom. And he realized that she was trying to tie him up with strong ropes, there on the bottom. He put up a great struggle, and managed to get hold of a knife which the princess Valentina had given him, and he set the point against her breast and slit open all her belly; and her guts gushed out, and the river looked just like blood. Samson was on the point of suffocating.

Now he got loose and dived down under the whirl-pool. He found that there must be a cave there, and he crawled up under the rock. He was now so exhausted that he had to lie there for a long time before he could move, but when he rose again he wrung his clothes out. Then he explored the cave, and thought he would never come to the end of it. Now he found an inner cave, where he saw a great deal of gear, and treasures of gold and silver. . . .

[Samson takes some of the treasures, and some clothes and jewels that had belonged to Valentina, but does not find her herself; he finds a way out from the inner end of the cave. Later Galinn tells Kvintelin that he thinks Samson must be dead; one manuscript adds the reason—'because the whole waterfall was stained with blood when they had been going at each other for a while in the fall'.]

6. Gull-þóris saga (c. 1300).

[The hero, þórir, hears tell of a group of dragons living in a cave behind a great waterfall and guard-ing a great heap of gold there. These dragons had once been human, a viking named Valr and his sons. On the advice of his dead uncle Agnarr, þórir sets out with several companions to win this gold.]

Úlfr tried to dissuade them from this journey, and offered them wealth if they would not go, and said that no one who had gone there had returned; also he said it would grieve him if the men whom his friend Sigmundr had sent him should be lost. But Þórir wanted to go in any case, and a little later he and his comrades set out on their journey, and went northwards past Finnmark till they came north to the foot of Blesaberg; that is the name of the mountain in which was Valr's cave, and it is in the north by the Arctic Sea. A great river comes rushing down from the mountain through a ravine, and flows out to sea. Then Þórir knew that they had come to the place to which he had been directed. They went up on to the mountain, and made the preparations which Agnarr had taught them; they grubbed up a huge tree and pushed its branches out over the edge of the mountain, heaping stones on its roots; then they took a rope and tied it to the branches. Then Þórir offered his companions the chance to go down, and each to have whatever wealth he got; but none of them would trust himself to get as far as the cave, even if that were the only danger, and they begged him to turn back.

Þórir said: 'There can be no question of that now; the likeliest thing is that I will take the risk myself, and have the wealth with the fewest possible other claims on it.'

They said they would not make any claims on the wealth, and said he would have done enough to deserve it, if he got it. They found that Þórir was a very different man from what he had been. Þórir took off his outer clothes so as to be lightly clad; he put on the kirtle which was Agnarr's gift, and took the gloves, belt, knife and slender cord which Agnarr had given him, and he also had the spear with a thong which his father had given him. He walked out along the tree; then he hurled his spear across the river, and it stuck fast in the woods on the other side of the river; after that he went down the rope, letting the cord guide him away from the cliff and under the waterfall. And when Ketilbjǫrn saw this, he said he would go with Þórir, and declared that the same fate would come to them both; so then he went down on the rope. Þórhallr Kinnarson also said he would go, and Þrándr the Tall said Sigmundr would

325

never hear say that he had not dared help those to whom he had promised his assistance.

By now Þórir had got into the cave, and he dragged those who came down towards him. There was a rocky promontory jutting out into the sea just in front of the waterfall, and Bjǫrn Beruson and Hyrningr went along there, and so came to the foot of the falls; they pitched a tent out at the point of the promontory, as one could not get nearer to the falls because of the vibrations, the falling water and the spray.

Þórir and his companions kindled a light in the cave and went on, until a wind blew towards them, and then the light went out. Then Þórir called upon Agnarr for help, and at once there came a great beam of light from the entrance of the cave, by the light of which they went forward for a while, until they heard the hissing of the dragons. But as soon as this beam of light reached the dragons they all fell asleep—and then indeed there was no lack of light, for it shone from the dragons and from the gold they were lying on. They saw where there were some swords, with their hafts sticking out by the dragons' sides; Þórir and his companions then quickly snatched up the swords, and then they leapt across the dragons and drove the swords in under their shoulders, and so to their hearts. Þórir managed to take the largest dragon's helmet away, but at the same moment the largest dragon caught hold of Þrándr the Tall and flew out of the cave with him, and so did the rest, one after the other, with fire pouring from their mouths, and poison too.

Now those who were outside saw a glow coming from the waterfall; they ran out of the tent just as the dragons were flying up out of the waterfall, and Bjǫrn saw that one dragon had a man in his mouth. They felt certain then that all those who had gone into the cave must be dead. The largest dragon was flying ahead, the one who had a man in his mouth; and as they flew over the promontory Bjǫrn ran up the mountain side and pierced the dragon with an inlaid spear. But as he received this wound much blood came gushing from the wound at Bjǫrn's face, and this was very quickly the death of him; and the blood and poison also touched Hyrningr's foot and set up such terrible pain in it that he could hardly stand.

As for Þórir and his friends, it must be said that they gathered great wealth in the cave, ample booty of gold and precious treasures for many men; it is said that they stayed three days in Valr's cave. There Þórir found the sword Hornhjalti ['Horn Hilt'] which Valr had borne. Afterwards Þórir hauled himself up first, and then dragged up the treasure, and then his friends.

7. *Þorsteins saga Víkingssonar* (c. 1400), ch. 23.

> [The hero has won the friendship of a dwarf named Sindri, who has given him a knife and promised to come to his aid if called. The hero then sets out with friends to slay a certain viking named Faxi, skilled in magic, 'as big as a troll, and no iron bites on him'. They fight on board ship; Faxi leaps overboard and swims to an island, with Þorsteinn after him; they fight again on the island, until Faxi once again plunges from a cliff into the sea.]

Then he headed out to sea, and Þorsteinn went after him; and when Faxi saw that, he turned back to meet Þorsteinn, and they grappled as they swam. Their tussles were strong and violent; each forced the other under water, but Þorsteinn now realized what a difference there was in their strength. It came to this, that Faxi forced Þorsteinn down to the bottom of the sea; he hindered him from swimming.

Then Þorsteinn felt sure that Faxi meant to bite his windpipe in two, and he said: 'Will I ever be in greater need of you than now, Sindri the Dwarf?' Thereupon Þorsteinn noticed something gripping Faxi by the shoulders so hard that the next thing was that he was down on the sea bottom, and Þorsteinn on top of him. He was by then very much wearied and worn out by the struggle. Then Þorsteinn took the knife that Sindri had given him; he drove it in under Faxi's lower ribs so that it sank in up to the haft, and then he slit the whole belly open, right down to the small guts. Yet he found that Faxi was not dead, for he then said: 'You have performed a great deed of valour in overcoming me, Þorsteinn, for I have taken part in ninety battles and been victorious in all of them save this. I have been victorious eighty times in single combat when I have undertaken to fight a duel, but I am ninety years old now.'

Þorsteinn thought that there was nothing to be gained by his chattering on any longer, if there was anything he could do about it; so then he tore out from his insides everything that was loose.

Now as for Angantýr and Beli [Þorsteinn's friends], they found themselves a ship and rowed out to sea, looking for Þorsteinn and Faxi, and for a long time could find neither of them. Then they came to a place where the sea was all mingled and red with blood, and then they felt sure that Faxi must be down on the sea bottom there, and must have killed Þorsteinn. And as time passed, they saw something loathsome floating on the sea; they went up to it, and saw huge ugly-looking bowels floating there. A little later, Þorsteinn came up to the surface, and by then he was so exhausted and overcome that he could not even float on the sea. Then they rowed up to him, and pulled him on board their ship.

8. *Gullbrá og Skeggi* (Icelandic folktale printed in Jón Árnason, *Íslenzkar þjóðsogur og Aefintýri*, 1862.)

[Gullbrá, a witch, realizes that she is dying.]

Then she called her servants to her, and instructed them to carry her to a certain ravine and lower her into it; she said she wished to lie somewhere where the sun could never be seen, and church bells never be heard. Now this ravine is so formed that there is a waterfall in a cleft of the rock facing north, and a cave in under it. The ravine is extremely deep, and also there is a whirlpool at the foot of the waterfall. Gullbrá went into this cave and lay down on her gold. After her death she walked again near the fall, and at once laid waste the farm Gullbrárhjalli; neither men nor livestock could remain among the rocks or on the mountain side and live. Ever since then, shepherds have thought the place haunted, but the walking ceased after a church was built at Hvammr. The place where Gullbrá had herself laid is called Gullbrá's Cleft and Gullbrá's Falls. . . .

It is said in the *Kristnisaga* and elsewhere that when þángbrandr the priest [a missionary sent to convert Iceland] was going round the West Fjords, he came to Hvammr; his words were badly received there, for the mistress of the house would not come out but stayed indoors conducting a heathen sacrifice, and meanwhile her son Skeggi made mock of þángbrandr and his companions.

It is said that this Skeggi had lived long at Hvammr and was a stout upholder of the heathen faith; he was himself skilled in magic and a strong heathen, like his mother. All the same, he did not have magic great enough to manage to stop Gullbrá's walking. She often killed his shepherds and beasts, when they came near Gullbrárhjalli. Skeggi was ill pleased at this, and all the more so because he had always set his heart on getting Gullbrá's chest of gold out of the waterfall; he said—as was true—that it would be better with him than with her, a dead ghost.

So he got himself ready one day when the weather was fine, and set out to go to Gullbrá's waterfall. It was a long way to the head of the valley, and it was beginning to grow dark when he came to the fall; there were two farm-hands with him, and they were to hold the rope. Skeggi lowered himself into the fall, and not much time had passed before the men at the top of the rope heard a great din, with crashings and shoutings; it sounded as if there was a hard tussle going on under the waterfall. They were very afraid, and it was touch and go whether they would run away; but at that moment Skeggi signalled to them to draw the rope up. They did so, but just as Gullbrá's chest had come up to the edge of the ravine they looked round, and it seemed to them as if the whole valley from Hvammr down was one blaze of fire, with flames reaching from one mountain side to the other. Then they were so frightened that they rushed away from the rope, and the chest crashed back down into the waterfall. As soon as they had come down from the rocks they could see nothing out of the common, but all the same they never stopped till they had reached home.

Skeggi got back much later, quite exhausted; he was black and blue and all bloody. Under his arm he was carrying a large cauldron full of gold; he had filled it from Gullbrá's chest, and had hauled himself up with it out of the ravine. The tussle between Gullbrá and Skeggi had been hard and long, and Skeggi had not been able to put an end to Gullbrá's walking, for indeed she had never been worse than she was after this. She killed Skeggi's shepherds one after another, and in the end it came to this, that no one could be found to tend the sheep, as they were all dead.

As for Skeggi, it must be said that he was never the same man again after he had gone into the waterfall, and this affected him so much, together with the killing of his shepherds, that he lay in bed a long while. But when it reached the point that no one could be found to tend the sheep, Skeggi got up from his bed one day and went out to the cattle. The day passed, and the night too, and Skeggi did not come home, but late on the second day he came home more dead than alive, for no one had dared go searching for him. He was carrying Gullbrá's chest on his back. He said that there would be no more trouble from her walking, but that he himself was likely to follow her; then he laid himself down, and never got up again. But before he died, he declared that the gold in the cauldron should be spent on church timbers, so that a church might be built at Hvammr.

He said that the first time that he went into the waterfall and grappled with Gullbrá, he had made a vow to Þórr, his friend, but he had failed him; but the second time, when he was in even greater straits, he had made a vow to spend the money on building a church at Hvammr if he escaped out of Gullbrá's claws. At this, a great light shone into her cat-like eyes, so that the first thing he knew was that she had turned into stone down there in the ravine—and her dead form can still be seen nowadays in Gullbrá's Falls. All the same, Skeggi would not accept the true faith or let himself be buried in the churchyard at Hvammr, but rather ordered that he should be laid in a mound to the north of his homefield. This was done, and Gullbrá's chest was laid beneath his head. There is a great stone there now, and it is called Skeggi's Stone.

9. *Folktale Analogue.*

[The folktale which shows closest analogy to the adventures of Beowulf is that classified by Antti Aarne as Type 301, *The Three Stolen Princesses.* Early folklorists also called it *The Bear's Son* or *Strong John,* but these names are now used for Aarne's Type 650A, which begins in a similar way to Type 301, Part I, but does not have the subsequent underworld adventures. About 600 examples of *The Three Stolen Princesses* have been recorded; some are printed by F. Panzer, *Studien zur germanischen Sagengeschichte: I. Beowulf,* 1910; more recent examples can be traced through the references in Antti Aarne and Stith Thompson, *The Types of the Folktale* (FFC 184, 1961), from which the following analysis of the tale is taken.]

THE THREE STOLEN PRINCESSES

I. *The Hero* is of supernatural origin and strength: son (*a*) of a bear who has stolen his mother; (*b*) of a dwarf or a robber from whom the boy rescues himself and his mother; (*c*) of a man and a she-bear or cow; or engendered (*e*) by the eating of fruit, (*f*) by the wind, or (*g*) from a burning piece of wood. (*h*) He grows supernaturally strong and is unruly.

II. *The Descent.* (*a*) With two extraordinary companions (*b*) he comes to a house in the woods or (*b¹*) a bridge; the monster who owns it punishes the companions but is defeated by the hero, (*c*) who is let down through a well into the lower world.—Alternative beginning of the tale: (*d*) The third prince, where his elder brothers have failed, (*e*) overcomes at night the monster who steals from the king's apple tree, and (*f*) follows him through a hole into the lower world.

III. *Stolen Maidens.* (*a*) Three princesses are stolen by a monster. (*b*) The hero goes to rescue them.

IV. *Rescue.* (*a*) In the lower world, with a sword which he finds there, he conquers several monsters and rescues three maidens. (*b*) The maidens are pulled up by the hero's companions and stolen.

V. *Betrayal of the Hero.* (*a*) He himself is left below by his treacherous companions, but he reaches the upper world through the help of (*b*) a spirit whose ear he bites to get magic power to fly, or (*c*) a bird (*d*) to whom he feeds his own flesh; or (*e*) he is pulled up.

VI. *Recognition.* (*a*) He is recognized by the princesses when he arrives on the wedding day. (*b*) He is in disguise and (*c*) sends his dogs to steal from the wedding feast; or he presents (*d*) rings, (*e*) clothing, or (*f*) other tokens, secures the punishment of the impostors, and marries one of the princesses.

[N.B. In some of the examples collected by Panzer, the episode corresponding to II (*e*) in the above analysis does not have a monster stealing from the king's apple tree, but a monster raiding the king's palace and fleeing, wounded, from the third prince's attack. Such a variation brings the plot particularly close to that of *Beowulf.*]

X. The Dragon Fight

1. *Fáfnismál* (date uncertain; included in the *Poetic Edda c.* 1270).

Then Reginn urged Sigurðr to slay Fáfnir. Sigurðr and Reginn went on to Gnitaheiðr, and there found the trail which Fáfnir made when he crawled down to the water. Sigurðr dug a deep pit across the path there, and went down into it. Now when Fáfnir came crawling from his gold he snorted out venom, which ran down over Sigurðr's head, but as Fáfnir crawled over the pit Sigurðr pierced him to the heart with his sword. Fáfnir shuddered, and lashed the ground with head and tail. Sigurðr leapt up out of the pit, and each of them gazed at the other. Fáfnir said:

'Youth, O youth, of whom were you born, O youth?
    And what man's son are you,
Who have reddened on Fáfnir your flashing blade?
    The sword now sticks in my heart.'

But Sigurðr concealed his name, for it was a belief of theirs in ancient times that a dying man's words would have great power, if he cursed his foe by name. So he said:

'"Noble Deer" is my name; I have walked my ways
    As a motherless boy;
No father have I, such as men's sons have;
    Ever I walk alone.'

F. said:
'If no father you have, such as men's sons have,
    By what wonder were you born?'

S. said:
'My lineage, I say, is unknown to you,
    And so am I myself;
Sigurðr my name is, Sigmundr my father,
    And I slew you by force of arms.'

333

F. said:

'Who urged you on, and why were you urged
  To seek to take my life?
A cruel father you had, O fiery-eyed youth!'

S. said:

'My own heart urged me, my own hands helped,
  And this keen sword of mine;
No man is bold when he comes to be old
  If in boyhood he is afraid.'

F. said:

'I know you were reared among loving friends,
  And men saw you fiercely fight;
Now a bondsman you are, a captive in war—
  A slave's heart always quails.'

S. said:

'You taunt me, Fáfnir, with being far
  From lands where my fathers lived;
No bondsman am I, though a captive of war—
  You have learnt that I live free.'

F. said:

'You reckon all these are but words of hate,
  Yet one thing I tell you true:
The ringing gold, the fiery-red wealth,
  And these rings, shall be your death.'

S. said:

'Every man must rule his wealth
  Till the last day of his life,
For a time will come when every man
  Must go from here to Hel.' . . .

[The hero and the dragon then exchange a series
of proverbs, wise sayings, etc.]

F. said:

'By the spell of terror I ruled men's sons
  While I lay upon my gems;
Alone, so I thought, I was stronger than all,
  Though never so many I met.'

334

S. said:

> 'The spell of terror keeps no one safe
>> Where wrathful men must fight;
> He that encounters many will find
>> No one man is always best.'

F. said:

> 'While I lay on my father's great legacy,
>> Poison I breathed forth.'

S. said:

> 'O flashing serpent, strongly you hissed
>> And showed your cruel heart;
> All the more hatred there is for him
>> Who rules by terror's spell.'

F. said:

> 'I counsel you, Sigurðr, to take my advice
>> And ride back home from here;
> The ringing gold, the fiery-red wealth,
>> And these rings, shall be your death.'

S. said:

> 'Your counsel you've spoken, but I will ride
>> To the gold where it lies on the heath;
> You'll lie here, Fáfnir, and struggle for breath
>> Till Hel takes you for her own.'

F. said:

> 'Reginn plotted my death, he will plot yours too,
>> And be slayer of us both;
> I see that Fáfnir must lose his life,
>> For your strength is the greater now.'

[Sigurðr's dragon fight is also described in Snorri's *Edda*, in the *Vǫlsunga saga*, and in *þiðreks saga*, and is alluded to in many passages of both Eddaic and Skaldic poetry.]

2. Saxo Grammaticus, *Danish History* (*c.* 1200) II §§ 38–9.

Hadingus [King of Denmark] was succeeded by Frotho, his son, whose fortunes were many and changeful.

When he had passed the years of a stripling he displayed the fullness of a warrior's prowess; and being loath that this should be spoilt by slothfulness, he sequestered his mind from delights, and perseveringly constrained it to arms. Warfare having drained his father's treasury, he lacked a stock of pay to maintain his troops, and cast about diligently for the supplies that he required; and while thus employed, a man of the country met him, and roused his hopes by the following strain:

'Not far off is an island rising in delicate slopes, hiding treasure in its hills and ware of its rich booty. Here a noble pile is kept by the occupant of the mount, who is a snake wreathed in coils, doubled in many a fold, with tail drawn out in winding whorls, shaking his manifold spirals and shedding venom. If thou wouldst conquer him, thou must use thy shield and stretch thereon bulls' hides, and cover thy body with the skins of kine, nor let thy limbs lie bare to the sharp poison; his slaver burns up what it bespatters. Though the three-forked tongue flicker and leap out of the gaping mouth, and with awful yawn menace ghastly wounds, remember to keep the dauntless temper of thy mind; nor let the point of the jagged tooth trouble thee, nor the starkness of the beast, nor the venom spat from the swift throat. Though the force of his scales spurn thy spears, yet know that there is a place under his lowest belly whither thou mayst plunge the blade; aim at this with thy sword, and thou shalt probe the snake to his centre. Thence go fearless up to the hill, drive the mattock, dig and ransack the holes; soon fill thy pouch with treasure and bring back to the shore thy craft laden.'

Frotho believed, and crossed alone to the island, loath to attack the beast with any stronger escort than that wherewith it was the custom for champions to attack. When it had drunk water and was repairing to its cave, its rough and sharp hide spurned the blow of Frotho's steel. Also the darts that he flung against it rebounded idly, foiling the effort of the thrower. But when the hard back yielded not a whit, he noted the belly heedfully, and its softness gave entrance to the steel. The beast tried to retaliate by biting, but only struck the sharp point of its mouth upon the shield. Then it shot out its

336

flickering tongue again and again, and gasped away life and venom together.

The money which the king found made him rich.

3. Saxo Grammaticus, *Danish History* VI §§ 180–1.

[On his return from a certain voyage, Fridlevus] was driven on to the shores of an unknown island. A certain man appeared to him in a vision, and instructed him to dig up a treasure that was buried in the ground, and also to attack the dragon that guarded it, covering himself in an ox-hide to escape the poison; teaching him also to meet the envenomed fangs with a hide stretched over his shield. Therefore, to test the vision, he attacked the snake as it rose out of the waves, and for a long time cast spears against its scaly side; in vain, for its hard and shelly body foiled the darts flung at it. But the snake, shaking its mass of coils, uprooted the trees which it passed by winding its tail about them. Moreover, by constantly dragging its body, it hollowed the ground down to the solid rock, and had made a sheer bank on either hand, just as in some places we see hills parted by an intervening valley. So Fridlevus, seeing that the upper part of the creature was proof against attack, assailed the lower side with his sword, and, piercing the groin, drew blood from the quivering beast. When it was dead, he unearthed the money from the underground chamber, and had it taken off in his ships.

4. *Ragnars saga loðbrókar* (*c.* 1300), chs. 2–3.

There was a powerful and noble earl in Gautaland whose name was Herruðr. He was married, and his daughter's name was Þóra; she was the loveliest of all women to look at, and the most courtly and accomplished in everything which it is better to have than to be without. She had a second name which she was known by, and this was 'Deer of the Stronghold', since she surpassed all other women for beauty, as the deer does all other beasts.

The earl loved his daughter dearly. He had a bower built for her not far from the king's hall, and there were wooden palings round the bower. The earl took as his custom that he would send his daughter something every day to amuse her, and he swore he would keep to this custom. The story goes that one day he had a little snake brought to her, a very pretty one, and this snake pleased her, and she put this snake in her ash-box and laid a piece of gold under him. He had not been long there before he began to grow big, and the gold under him also began to grow. It came to the point that there was no room for him inside the ash-box, and now he lay coiled round the outside of it. And later it came to the point that there was no room for him in the bower; and always the gold underneath him grew, just like the snake himself. So now he lay round the outside of the bower with his head and tail touching, and he became rather difficult to deal with, so that nobody dared come near the bower on account of this snake, except only the man who brought him his food—and he needed an ox for a meal. The earl thought this a very bad affair, and he swore an oath that he would give his daughter to the man, whoever he might be, who would be the death of this snake, and that the gold which was under him would be her dowry. This news became known far and wide through the country, yet nobody trusted himself to master this huge snake.

At that time Sigurðr Hringr ruled over Denmark; he was a powerful king, and had become famous through the battle which he fought against Haraldr Hilditǫnn at Brávellir, and in which Haraldr fell before him, as has come to be known all over the northern half of the world. Sigurðr had a son whose name was Ragnarr; he was of big build, handsome to look at and endowed with quick wits, generous to his men but fierce to his enemies. As soon as he was old enough, he got himself followers and a warship, and he became so great a warrior that his equal was hardly to be found. He heard tell of what Earl Herruðr had said, but he paid no heed and behaved as if he knew nothing of it. He had some clothes made for him which were of a very strange sort, and these were breeches and cape of shaggy fleece, and when they were ready he had them boiled in pitch; after this, he stored them away.

It happened one summer that he led his host to Gauta-land and beached one of his ships in a hidden creek, which was not far from where the earl ruled. And when Ragnarr had been there for one night he woke early one morning, rose, took these same protective clothes which have been spoken of, put them on, took a huge spear in his hand, and went off from the ship alone to a place where there was sand, and rolled himself in the sand. And before he went off, he took out the nail that held the head of his spear to its shaft.

So now he went off alone from his ship to the earl's stronghold, and arrived there so early in the morning that all the men were asleep. He turned his steps towards the bower. And when he had got inside the wooden palings where the snake was, he lunged at him with his spear and then jerked the spear back again. A second time he lunged, and this thrust pierced the snake's backbone; at this he struggled so hard that the spear came off its shaft, and his death-struggle made such a din that the whole bower shook. And now Ragnarr turned away. A spurt of blood caught him between the shoulders, but it did not harm him, for the clothes which he had had made protected him. . . .

[Ragnarr leaves without telling his name, but the spear-head remains in the dragon's body. To find his daughter's deliverer, Earl Herruðr summons an Assembly and declares that whoever can produce a shaft to fit the spear-head will be acknowledged as the dragon's slayer. Ragnarr does so, and marries Þóra.]

XI. *Funerary Customs: Literary Evidence*

1. Jordanes, *Getica* (*c.* 550), ch. 49.

[The funeral of Attila of the Huns.]

We must not omit to say a few words on a large subject, namely the way in which his departed spirit was honoured by his people. For the corpse was laid out in the middle of the camp between silk tents, and solemnly exhibited as a sight for all to wonder at. The finest horsemen in the whole Hunnish nation rode round and round the place where he was laid, as if in the circus games, while they proclaimed his deeds in a funeral dirge, in some such way as this: 'King Attila, outstanding among the Huns, born of Mundzuccus, lord of most valiant people, who held sole sway over the kingdoms of Scythia and Germany, by a power unheard of before; who struck terror into the captured citizens of Rome, yet, appeased by their prayers, accepted annual tribute rather than give over the rest of the city to plunder. After enjoying all this good fortune and success, he died—not of wounds dealt by a foe, nor through the treachery of his own men, but uninjured, without pain, happy, and in the midst of rejoicings. Who can think this end tragic, when none can judge it necessary to avenge him?'

After he had been mourned with such laments as these, they celebrated what they themselves call a *strava* by holding a great feast on his grave-mound; thus, linking opposite notions together, they carried out the funerary mourning with a mixture of gaiety, and then committed the corpse to the earth in the secrecy of night. They heaped his bier first with gold, then with silver, and thirdly with harsh steel, meaning by this that all these

340

things were fitting for a powerful king—steel, because he subdued nations; gold and silver, because he received both as public tribute. They added weapons acquired from enemies, and treasures rich with the gleam of many-coloured gems, and insignia of various kinds by which he might be honoured as befitted his princely glory. And, so that all human curiosity might be warded off from such great wealth, they slew those who had been assigned to the task, in ghastly payment for their toil, and thus instantaneous death came to those who buried him, beside him whom they had buried.

2. *The Travels of Ibn Fadlan.*

[Part of an eye-witness account of the customs of the *Rus*, Swedish merchants active in the region of the Volga, by an Arab, Ibn Fadlan, who visited their encampments *c.* 922.]

I had always been told that when a chieftain of theirs died many things took place, of which burning was the least; I was very interested to get information about this. One day I heard that one of their leading men had died. They laid him in a grave and closed it over him for ten days, till they had finished cutting and sewing clothes for him. This is how things are done: for one of the poorer men among them they take a small boat and lay him in it and burn him, but when it is a question of a rich man, they gather his wealth and divide it in three parts— one third for his family, one third for making clothes for him, and one third to make the liquor they drink on the day his slave-girl is killed and burnt with her master. They are indeed much addicted to liquor, for they drink day and night; often one has died with a beaker in his hand.

When a chieftain dies, his family say to his slave-girls and menservants: 'Which of you will die with him?' Then one of them says: 'I will.' When he has said this, he is forced to do it, and is not free to retract; even if he wanted to, it would not be allowed. It is mostly the slave-girls who do this. So when the man I am speaking of died, they said to his slave-girls: 'Which of you will die with him?', and one of them said: 'I will.' Two slave-girls were given the task of waiting on her and staying with her wherever she went, and often they would even wash her feet and hands. Then they began seeing to the man's things, cutting out his clothes and preparing everything that ought to be there, while the slave-girl drank and sang joyfully every day, and seemed to be looking forward to a coming happiness.

When the day came when he and his slave-girl were to be burnt, I went to the river where his ship lay. It had been dragged ashore, four props of birchwood and other wood had been set ready for it, and also something that looked like a great stack of wood had been laid all around. The ship was then dragged up on to this, and set in place on this woodpile. The men began walking to and fro, talking together in a language I could not understand; meanwhile, the dead man still lay in his grave, for they had not taken him out. Then they brought a bench, set it in the ship, and covered it with rugs and cushions of Byzantine silk; then an old woman whom they called the 'Angel of Death' came and spread these rugs out over the bench. She was in charge of sewing the clothes and arranging the corpse, and it is also she who kills the girl; I saw that she was an old, hag-like woman, thick-set and grim-looking.

When they came to his grave they cleared the earth off it, and also took the woodwork away. They stripped him of the clothes he had died in; I noticed that he had turned black, because of the cold in that land. They had laid liquor, fruit and a lute in the grave with him, and all these they now took out. Oddly enough, the corpse did not stink, and nothing about it had changed except the colour of the flesh. Then they dressed him in under-breeches, breeches, boots, coat, and a caftan of silk brocade with gold buttons on it; they set on his head a silk brocade hood with sable fur, and carried him into the tent that stood on the ship, and laid him on the rugs, and propped him up with cushions.

Then they brought liquor, fruit and sweet-smelling plants and laid them by him; they also brought bread, meat and leeks and threw them in front of him. Then they brought a dog, cut it in two, and threw it into the ship. Next, they brought all his weapons and laid them beside him. Then they took two horses and made them gallop about till they sweated, whereupon they cut them to pieces with swords and threw their flesh into the ship. In the same way they brought two cows, and these too they cut to pieces and threw into the ship. Then they brought a cock and a hen, killed them, and threw them in. Meanwhile, the slave-girl who had chosen to be killed was walking to and fro; she would go inside one or other of their tents, and the owner of the tent would make love with her, saying: 'Tell your master I did this simply for love of him.'

When it came to the Friday afternoon, they took the slave-girl to a thing like a door-frame which they had made. She sat herself on the palms of the hands of some men, and stretched up high enough to look over the door-frame, and said something in her own language; at this they set her down. Then they lifted her up again, and she did as she had done the first time. At this they set her down, and lifted her up for the third time, and she did as she had done the first two times. Then they handed her a hen, and she cut the head off and threw it; they took the hen and threw it into the ship. I then questioned the interpreter about what she had done. He replied: 'The first time they lifted her up, she said: "Look, I see my father and my mother!" The second time, she said; "Look, I see all my dead kinsmen sitting there!" The third time, she said: "Look, I see my master sitting in Paradise! Paradise is fair and green, and there are men and young lads with him. He is calling me, let me go to him!"'

Then they went off with her towards the ship. She took off two arm-rings she was wearing and gave them to the old woman called the Angel of Death, the one who was going to kill her; then she took off two ankle-rings she was wearing and gave them to two other women, daughters of the one known as the Angel of Death. Next, they led her up on board the ship, but did not let her go into the tent. Then came some men who had shields and sticks, and they handed her a beaker of liquor; she sang over it and drank it off. The interpreter told me: 'Now with this she is bidding farewell to all her friends.' Next, another beaker was handed to her; she took it,

343

and made her singing long drawn out, but the old woman hurried her to make her drink it off and go into the tent where her master was. I was watching her, and she looked quite dazed; she tried to go into the tent, but stuck her head between it and the ship's side. Then the old woman took hold of her head, and managed to get it inside the tent, and the old woman herself went inside with her.

The men then began to beat their shields with sticks, so that no sound of her shrieking should be heard, for fear other girls should become frightened and not want to seek death with their masters. Then six men went into the tent, and they all made love with her. After this they laid her down beside her dead master; two held her legs and two her hands, and the woman called the Angel of Death wound a cord with knotted ends round her neck, passing the ends out on either side and handing them to two men to pull. Then she stepped forward with a broad-bladed dagger and began to drive it in and pluck it out again between the girl's ribs, while the two men throttled her with the cord, and so she died.

After this, whoever was the closest kinsman of the dead man came forward. He took a wooden stick and set light to it, and then he walked backwards, with his back to the ship and his face to the people, holding the stick in one hand and with the other hand laid on his backside; he was naked. In this fashion the wood they had put just under the ship was set on fire, immediately after they had laid the slave-girl they had killed beside her master. Then the people came forward with wood and timber; each brought a stick with its tip on fire and threw it on to the wood lying under the ship, so that flames took hold, first on the wood, and then on the ship, and then on the tent, and the man and the woman and everything inside the ship. Thereupon a strong fierce wind sprang up, so that the flames grew stronger, and the ship blazed up even more.

A man of the Rus was standing beside me, and I heard him talking to the interpreter, who was near him. I asked the latter what the man had said to him, and he answered: 'He said: "You Arabs are stupid." I said: "Why so?" He answered: "Why, because you take the people you most love and honour and throw them into

344

the ground, and the earth and creeping creatures and growing things destroy them. We, on the other hand, burn them up in an instant, so that they go to Paradise in that very hour." Then he gave a roar of laughter, and when I asked him about that, he replied: "For love of him, his Lord has sent this wind to carry him away at the right time!"' And in fact, no great time passed before the ship and the timber and the slave-girl and her master had all turned into ashes, and so into dust.

After this, on the spot where the ship had first stood when they dragged it up out of the river, they built something that looked like a round mound. In the middle of it they set up a big post of birch-wood, on which they wrote this man's name, and the name of the King of the Rus; then they went on their way.

3. *Skjǫldunga saga* (c. 1200), in an abstract by Arngrímur Jónsson (1596), ch. 26.

[An aged Swedish king, Sigvardus Ringo (Sigurðr Hringr), wished to marry a certain Alfsola; her brothers preferred to poison her, and to face Sigvardus in battle.]

Thus after a fierce fight the brothers Alfus and Ingvo fell bravely, but Sigvardus was gravely wounded. And he, having been taken to the place of Alfsola's funeral, went on board a great ship laden with the bodies of the dead, he himself being the only living man aboard, and, placing himself and the dead Alfsola near the stern, he gave orders that the ship should be set on fire with pitch, bitumen and sulphur. When the sails had been raised and were filled with strong off-shore winds, he set the ship's course, and at the same moment laid violent hands upon himself. He preferred that he, who had achieved so many mighty deeds and possessed such great domains, should go with royal pomp to seek King Odin's realm (that is to say, the Underworld) according to the custom of his forefathers, rather than endure the weakness of helpless old age. He had spoken of this beforehand, with a cheerful heart, to his companions whom he left upon the shore; these men told how, before putting out to sea, he stabbed himself with his own hand. However, he had a sepulchre built on the shore, according to the custom of his time, and gave orders that it should be called Ringo's Mound; he himself, amid the tempests that drove his vessel onwards, sailed without delay across the waters of the Styx.

4. Saxo Grammaticus, *Danish History* (*c.* 1200), III § 74; V § 156; V § 264.

(*a*) The funeral of Gelder, King of Saxony.

Gelderus, the King of Saxony, who met his end in the same war, was set by Hotherus upon the corpses of his oarsmen, and then laid on a pyre built of vessels, and magnificently honoured in his funeral by Hotherus, who not only put his ashes in a noble barrow, treating them as the remains of a king, but also graced them with most reverent obsequies.

(*b*) The laws of Frotho III, King of Denmark.

So Frotho summoned the nations which he had conquered, and enacted that any father of a family who had fallen in that war should be buried with his horse and all his arms and decorations. And if any body-snatcher, in his abominable covetousness, made an attempt on him, he was to suffer for it, not only with his life, but with the loss of burial for his own body; he should have no barrow and no funeral. For he thought it just that he who despoiled another's corpse should be granted no burial, but should repeat in his own person the fate he had inflicted on another. He appointed that the body of a centurion or governor [local chieftain?] should receive funeral on a pyre built of his own ship. He ordered that the bodies of every ten pilots should be burnt together with a single ship, but that every earl or king that was killed should be put on his own ship and burnt with it.

(*c*) Funeral of King Harald Hilditǫnn of Denmark after the battle of Brávellir.

When Ringo heard that Haraldus was dead, he gave the signal for his men to break up their line and cease

346

fighting. Then under cover of truce he made treaty with the enemy, telling them that it was vain to prolong the fray without their captain. Next he told the Swedes to look everywhere among the confused piles of carcasses for the body of Haraldus, that the corpse of the king might not wrongfully lack its due rights. So the populace set eagerly to the task of turning over the bodies of the slain, and over this work half the day was spent. At last the body was found with the club, and he thought that propitiation should be made to the shade of Haraldus. So he harnessed the horse on which he rode to the chariot of the king, decked it honourably with a golden saddle, and hallowed it in his honour. Then he proclaimed his vows, and added his prayer that Haraldus would ride on this and outstrip those who shared his death in their journey to Tartarus; and that he would pray Pluto, the lord of Orcus, to grant a calm abode there for friend and foe. Then he raised a pyre, and bade the Danes fling on the gilded chariot of their king as fuel to the fire. And while the flames were burning the body cast upon them, he went round the mourning nobles and earnestly charged them that they should freely give arms, gold and every precious thing to feed the pyre in honour of so great a king, who had deserved so nobly of them all. He also ordered that the ashes of his body, when it was quite burnt, should be transferred to an urn, taken to Leire, and there, together with the horse and armour, receive a royal funeral. By paying these due rites of honour to his uncle's shade, he won the favour of the Danes, and turned the hate of his enemies into goodwill.

5. Snorri Sturluson, *Edda* (*c.* 1220), *Gylfaginning* ch. 49.

The gods took the body of Baldr and took it down to the sea. Baldr's ship was named Hringhorni, and it was the greatest of all ships. The gods wished to launch it and to build Baldr's pyre on it, but the ship would not move. So then a message was sent to Jǫtunheimr for the giantess named Hyrrokkin. And when she came, she was riding a wolf and had vipers as reins; she leapt from her steed, and Óðinn called four berserks to see to her steed, but they could not manage to hold it unless they stunned it. Then Hyrokkin went up to the prow, and

347

thrust it forward so violently at her first thrust that fire sprang from the rollers and the earth shook. Then Þórr grew angry, and grasped his hammer and threatened to crush her head, until all the gods promised her safety.

Then the body of Baldr was carried out on to the ship. And when his wife Nanna, the daughter of Nepr, saw this, her heart broke with grief and she died; she was carried to the pyre and laid in the flames. Þórr stood beside the pyre and hallowed it with Mjǫllnir. Now a certain dwarf whose name was Litr ran in front of his feet, and Þórr gave him a kick and sent him flying into the fire, and he burned to death.

People of many kinds came to this burning. . . . Óðinn laid the gold ring called Draupnir upon the pyre; it had such power that every night there dropped from it eight gold rings as heavy as itself. Baldr's horse was led to the pyre, in all its trappings.

6. Snorri Sturluson, *Heimskringla* (*c.* 1223–35), *Ynglinga saga* chs. 8, 10 and 23.

(*a*) Swedish funerary customs associated with the cult of Óðinn.

[Óðinn] decreed by law that all dead men should be burnt, and their goods laid beside them on the pyre, and the ashes thrown in the sea or buried in the ground. He declared that in this way every man would come to Valhǫll with as much wealth as he had with him on the pyre; he would also enjoy whatever he himself had buried in the earth. Men of high rank would have a mound raised to their memory, and all other fighting men who had been noted for valour would have a standing-stone; this custom remained long after Óðinn's time. . . .

It was a belief [of the Swedes] that the higher the smoke [of a funeral pyre] rose in the air, the higher would rise the man whose pyre it was; and the more goods that were destroyed with him, the richer he would be.

(*b*) Funeral of King Haki.

King Haki had received so great a wound that he knew his days would not be long. Then he ordered that a warship he owned should be fetched, and had it laden with dead men and weapons; then he ordered it to be launched, the rudder shipped and the sail raised, and that pine timber should be set alight and a pyre built on board ship. The wind was blowing from the land. Haki was at the point of death, or dead already, when he was laid on the pyre. Then the ship sailed blazing out to sea, and for a long while after this deed remained famous.

Archaeology and Beowulf

FEW of those arguing about the origin of the poem *Beowulf*
have taken into serious account the archaeological evidence.
It is bewildering to leave the sheltered world of libraries for
that of laboratories and excavation reports; moreover archae-
ologists have a wilful way of announcing changes in dating
in pontifical statements based on evidence from coins, pottery,
or soil analysis, demanding technical know-how of a kind
from which the literary man recoils. Yet it is likely to be
archaeology, rather than literary history, which will throw new
light on the poem's origins. A recently published anthology
of *Beowulf* criticism [1] illustrates this fact: here we have the
clamour of contradictory voices which Tolkien described in
his essay on 'The Monsters and the Critics', ending with only
one unanimous cry: 'It is worth studying.' If reluctant
students who feel no echo of this cry as yet in their own
bosoms will turn aside from grammatical intricacies and
literary theories to discover what archaeology can teach of
the life and ideals of the heroic society this poem presents,
they may return to the text with new understanding and
interest. The six centuries of Anglo-Saxon civilization is being
illumined now by each new season's work here and on the
Continent, extended by backroom study of craftsmanship,
art and symbolism, at a bewildering rate; it may be possible
from this wealth of evidence to find clues for the dating of
the poem, always bearing in mind the limitations of archae-
ology when used alone, clearly expressed by Rosemary Cramp
in a paper of 1957. [2] The progress made in Homeric studies by
this means may profitably be borne in mind.

In this brief survey I can only draw attention to the main
lines of approach which may throw light on the world of the
poem, but references to published work on the various topics

[1] *An Anthology of Beowulf Criticism*, ed. L. Nicholson, Notre Dame,
Indiana, 1963.
[2] 'Beowulf and Archaeology', *Med. Arch.* 1 (1957), 57–77.

will be found at the end. Let us begin with life in the king's hall, which forms so important a part of it. This is an idealized, cultured, in some ways sophisticated way of life, presented with enthusiasm and sometimes with nostalgia. The Danish king's hall is pictured as a place of just and noble rule, filled with mirth, music and feasting, arousing the hatred of the evil Grendel brooding in the darkness of the encircling fens. Within, it is splendid and adorned with gold, its light shining out over many lands (308, 311), a description recalling that of the halls of the gods in the *Edda* poems, and again that of the heathen temple at Uppsala, which according to an eleventh-century account had a gold chain across its roof. Lindqvist, however, suggested that the carved interlacing of the roof had been gilded to give this effect, while Rosemary Cramp notes references to buildings ornamented with precious metals in Anglo-Saxon times. Thus while Heorot is an idealized palace, it appears to have been based on knowledge of impressive timbered halls, like the larger buildings at Warendorf in West Germany, a village site of the seventh or eighth century, or nearer home, the royal palaces of Yeavering and Cheddar. A series of halls built at Yeavering (Illus. 1) formed part of the residence of Edwin of Northumbria, who ruled in the first half of the seventh century, and when full accounts of this excavation have been published it will add greatly to our knowledge of life in this period. There was a main hall of as much as 100 feet in length, surrounded by smaller buildings used as residential quarters, as in *Beowulf* (140, 1236, etc.). The ninth-century hall at Cheddar was 78 feet long, with a smaller building, probably of the same period, near by. The type of stave walling used at Yeavering could have been strengthened with iron clamps, as was that of Heorot (774). The effect of a large hall of heavy planks can be seen at Trelleborg in Denmark, a military camp of the eleventh century, where one can enter the reconstructed building, see the raised platforms on either side suitable for sleeping places (1239 ff.), and the fireplace under the smoke-hole in the centre, near where the king would sit (404) (Illus. 2). We now know that impressive halls of this kind were built as early as the seventh century in northern England, something very different from the primitive hut sites which were all we had to represent Anglo-Saxon dwellings a short while ago.

Terms such as *horngēap* (82), *hornreced* (704), and *bānfāg* (780), coupled with the name of *Heorot* ('hart') have led to suggestions that stags' heads or antlers were fixed on the gables; another possibility is that wooden animals were placed on the gable ends, as in later times. The horned stag on the standard from the Sutton Hoo ship-burial (Illus. 3) indicates the importance of this animal as a royal symbol in seventh-century East Anglia. The *stapol* on which the king stood to view Grendel's arm fixed to the roof (926) seems to have been a vantage point outside the building, and an interesting possibility is a platform like that near the hall at Yeavering, facing a kind of 'grandstand', which must have been used for open-air assemblies. The gleaming or coloured floor of the hall (725) might be suggested by Roman mosaics, or again a wooden floor, polished and cared for, might be so described; certainly the stone path leading to the hall (320) suggests a paved road surviving from the Roman period; but it may be noted that paved roads are known from the pre-Roman Iron Age in Denmark. Tapestries gleaming with gold were set up in Heorot for the banquet (994). Although no tapestries have survived from the early Anglo-Saxon period, fragments of gold brocading have been found in sixth-century graves and in the seventh-century Taplow barrow; these were from trimmings or ribbons on the clothes of the dead. It is therefore probable that gold was used for wall-hangings, while there may also have been oriental tapestries used in kings' palaces, like the Viminaeum gold tapestry from Hungary. Long strips of tapestry found in the late ninth-century ship-burial at Oseberg in Norway show how elaborate scenes from mythological and heroic tradition could be depicted on woven material.

There was ceremonial drinking in the hall, when the queen brought round the ornamented cup (620–4) to the king, to the honoured guest, and to the warriors in the hall in order of precedence. No drinking-horn is mentioned, for the words *ful*, *sincfæt* suggest a goblet or bowl, and many drinking vessels, including elaborate glass beakers, have been found in Anglo-Saxon graves of the sixth and seventh centuries. The two huge aurochs horns from Sutton Hoo, richly decorated with mounts of silver-gilt and each capable of holding about six quarts of liquid, must however have been intended for just such occasions, when men made solemn vows to support their king or to perform heroic deeds.

The playing of the harp is mentioned, and the completion of the hall was celebrated by the singing of a lay about creation, such as would fit into either a Christian or pre-Christian context, emphasizing the building of Heorot as a bright, enclosed sanctuary of order in the hostile wastes (90 ff.). The harp also accompanied the recitation of heroic poetry (1065), while its music represented the lost joys of a ruined hall (2458). The fragments of the little six-stringed harp from Sutton Hoo, placed in a bag of beaver-skin, have been reassembled to show the kind of instrument which might be passed from hand to hand in the hall, serving as a formal accompaniment to elegiac or heroic lay (like that of a guitar to a modern ballad). The inclusion of the harp in the grave indicates that it was among the ceremonial treasures of a seventh-century king, and there are remains of another harp from the Taplow barrow. In lines 2107 ff. it is implied that the instrument was played by the king himself.

The set of 'four gold-adorned treasures' (1027–9) offered to Beowulf as reward for his exploit are clearly of great significance, since they are described in detail and alluded to more than once. They consisted of helmet, coat of mail, sword and battle-standard, all objects included among the royal treasures of Sutton Hoo. Mr Bruce-Mitford was the first to point out how the description of the helmet in *Beowulf* is elucidated by the reconstruction of the magnificent Swedish helmet from the grave (Illus. 4). The ridge offering protection from a sword stroke, while the helmet was presumably padded below on the same principle as a motor-cyclist's crash-helmet, formed a kind of crest, inlaid with silver wire in curving patterns, exactly as described in lines 1030–4. Sheets of bronze overlaid with tin must have given it a shining whiteness which is in agreement with the description in line 1448.

The byrnie of ring-mail was not in a condition to be restored, but other examples of ring-mail from the Danish bog-finds of the Roman period and from Vendel in Sweden bear out the accuracy of the descriptions in the poem of the rings, 'hard and hand-locked', ringing as the wearer walked (322–3) and acting as a 'woven breast-net' against attack (551–3). It is now known how such ring-mail was made.

A sword adorned with gold could have resembled the type

of weapon found at Sutton Hoo, a splendid weapon with much gold on hilt, strap-ends and scabbard-mounts, and also resplendent with treasure in the form of brilliant cloisonné and millefiori work (Illus. 5). Gold-hilted swords are especially characteristic of the sixth and seventh centuries, and were probably made for kings to use on ceremonial occasions, while in the Viking Age silver, bronze or niello were more often utilized as forms of decoration.

The standard offered to Beowulf evidently had a boar on it, since it is called *eafor hēafod segn* (2152). The type of metal standard found at Sutton Hoo (Illus. 6), with a spike which could be stuck into the ground, and a figure of a stag dominating the heads of bulls farther down, would explain this phrase, if we imagine a boar replacing the stag. Such standards survive in the grave (2767 ff.), and it may be that this is an example of the *tufa* mentioned by Bede, carried before Edwin of Northumbria in the seventh century, of a different type from the vexillum or light embroidered banner used on the battlefield, to mark where the king stood or advanced with his men (1204, 2958). It has been pointed out that the O.E. term quoted by Bede (*tuuf*) is equivalent to the Old Norse *þúfa*, used of a cairn or burial-mound; it may thus be relevant to note that twice in the poem a standard marks the resting-place of a dead chieftain (47–8, 2767). Such an object could possess royal, ceremonial and religious significance.

We know that the boar was a religious emblem used by the royal house of Uppland in Sweden in the sixth century, linked with the cult of the Vanir, the deities of fertility. Bronze helmet-plates from the sixth century found in Sweden show warriors with boar crests (Illus. 7), while from seventh-century Anglo-Saxon England such a helmet has survived, recovered from the mound of Benty Grange in Derbyshire (Illus. 8). The boar is of gilded bronze, with gold spots and ruby eyes, and surmounts a metal framework orginally filled with plates of horn. Thus archaeological evidence corroborates descriptions of helmets in the poem, where the figure of the boar is said to shine above the cheekguards (303–4), even as it decorates the eyebrows of the Sutton Hoo helmet, and to protect the warriors who wear it (1453–4), while the boar cut by the sword in line 1286 implies a boar crest like the one on the Benty Grange helmet.

As additional gifts from Hrothgar, Beowulf received eight

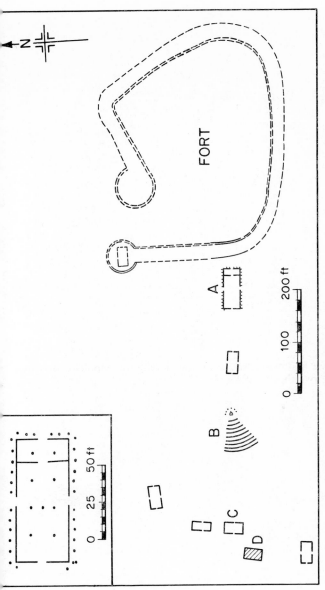

1. Yeavering, Northumberland: diagrammatic plan of buildings existing in the time of King Edwin (616–32); (after Hope-Taylor). A. Hall. B. Timber 'amphitheatre'. C. Possibly a pagan temple converted to Christian use. D. Building with a sunken floor. The inset shows the Timber Hall (A) to a larger scale.

2. Interior of reconstructed hall at Trelleborg, Zealand, Denmark, from the military camp built about

3. Bronze stag (slightly enlarged) from top of standard in ship-grave at Sutton Hoo (*by courtesy Trustees of the British Museum*).

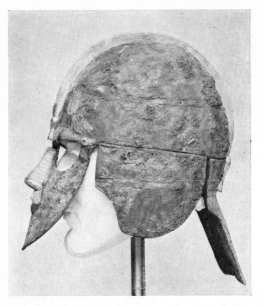

4. Reconstructed helmet from ship-grave at Sutton Hoo (*by courtesy Trustees of the British Museum*).

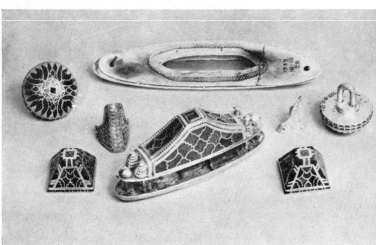

5. Gold and jewelled fittings from hilt and scabbard of sword from ship-grave at Sutton Hoo (*by courtesy Trustees of the British Museum*).

6. Metal standard when discovered in the earth during excavation of ship-grave at Sutton Hoo (*by courtesy Trustees of the British Museum*).

7. Warriors in boar helmets (actual size), on metal die for making helmet plates, found at Torslunda, Oland (*by courtesy Statens Historiska Museum, Stockholm*).

8. Bronze boar (9·5 cm. in length) on helmet from burial mound at Benty Grange farm, Derbyshire (*by courtesy Trustee of the British Museum and Sheffield Museum*).

9. Gold collar from Ålleborg, Västergotland, Sweden. (*Photo: I. Anderson, by courtesy Statens Historiska Museum, Stockholm.*)

10. Sword blade, showing marks of pattern-welding. In the Evans Collection at the Ashmolean Museum, Oxford, provenance unknown (*by courtesy Ashmolean Museum*).

11. Pommel of sword from cemetery at Gilton, Kent, showing runic inscription [2:1] (*by courtesy Liverpool Public Museums*).

12. Reconstruction of ship from Kvalsund, Möre, Norway, overall length 59 ft (*by courtesy Universitets Oldsaksamling, Oslo*).

horses, with gold-plated bridles, and one horse with special trappings and saddle, the royal war-horse on which the leader rode to battle, where he would dismount to fight on foot (1039–40). Beowulf later presented four matching horses to King Hygelac (2163–6), together with the four royal treasures, and three more horses to Queen Hygd, but presumably retained the war-horse for his own use. Although there is no evidence for the sacrifice of a king's horse at Sutton Hoo, the bones of a horse were found in Mound 4 in the same cemetery, and horses were buried beside warriors in many Anglo-Saxon and continental graves.

The queen presented Beowulf with two arm-rings and the 'greatest of neck-rings', described as *hrægl* and *brēostgewǣde*, something worn over the breast (1195, 1211). This he gave to the queen of the Geats (2172), but Hygelac himself is said to have worn it in his last battle against the Franks (1202 ff.) The unusual nature of this ornament is emphasized in the poem, and this, linked with the fact that a king chose to wear it in battle, may be explained by the series of superb golden collars, some of immense size, from treasure-hoards in Sweden (Illus. 9). These are formed of a series of tubes, ornamented with figures of men and animals in filigree work, and were made in Sweden in the fifth and sixth centuries A.D. There is reason to think that these collars were symbols of Odin, god of battle, whose cult flourished in Sweden at that time, and that they were worn by his distinguished royal worshippers. No such neck-ornaments have been found in England, but here we may have an allusion to some famous heirloom of this kind, resembling the great collars from Ålleborg or Möne in Västergotland.

The swords of the heroes are of great importance in the poem, some of them bearing names, like Hrunting and Nægling, famous in heroic tradition. The sword whose hilt Beowulf brought back from the lake is described in detail, and other swords are briefly mentioned. I have elsewhere [1] analysed all references to swords in *Beowulf*, and will here merely summarize my findings. The descriptions are general rather than specific, and the weapons are said to have richly ornamented hilts and patterned blades, while they are usually ancient heirlooms. No one particular weapon or style of sword is described, with the possible exception of the rune-inscribed

---

[1] *The Sword in Anglo-Saxon England*, Oxford, 1962.

hilt from the lake. On the other hand, there is a clear and knowledgeable tradition of swords with pattern-welded blades (Illus. 10). Considerable familiarity is shown with such patterns, which are compared to weaving and embroidery, twigs and branches, or serpents, while the blades are said to shine with a metallic gleam, and to have hard, steely edges. We know that such swords were being made from the second to the eighth centuries A.D. in Western Europe, and were being used by the Anglo-Saxons in the sixth and seventh centuries, since a number have been found in graves. By the ninth century, sword-makers were able to obtain ore of better quality, and to produce good swords without the use of this particular welding technique. The descriptions of blades in the poem are by no means vague and conventional ones, but appear to be based on close observation and some knowledge of forging technique, implying that such swords were well known and regarded as great treasures at the time when the poem was composed. There is one mention of a ringed hilt (2041), examples of which come from Kentish graves of the sixth century, while two examples of hilts with runic inscriptions, like the one from the lake, come from Kent (Illus. 11), and are of sixth- or early seventh-century date.

Other weapons are described in general terms. Spears are of ash with iron heads, and are left outside the hall together with the shields of linden wood (330). The evidence of Anglo-Saxon cemeteries is that spears were the weapons of the rank and file, while swords were carried by the leaders. The bow is occasionally referred to, but usually in the context of sport or hunting. Only in one passage (3117–19) is there a description of a storm of arrows, impelled by the bowstring, passing over the shield-wall. We know from the seventh-century Franks Casket that the bow could be a weapon in battle, but it did not become of military importance in England until later, as it appears to be in the battle of Maldon, according to the late tenth-century poem describing that event. The term *hornboga*, used once in the poem (2437), must be a technical one, for it indicates a composite bow, in which the 'belly' (the side nearest to the archer when shooting) is made of separate, incompressible material, usually horn, to render the weapon more powerful. This type of bow belonged properly to eastern Europe, and was a foreign import into the west. Clearly in *Beowulf* the essential weapons of the warrior are sword and spear; the axe, of importance among the Franks and in the Viking Age, is unmentioned.

Knowledge of ships is shown in the poem, and some of the terms used, like 'joined wood' (*bundenne*, 216), and 'foamy-necked' (*fāmigheals*, 218), indicate loving observation. The two features stressed are the curved prow, since such would appear to be the significance of the term *hring*, and the mast. Beowulf's ship had a sail, as is clear from the account of his departure from Denmark (1896 ff.). The Sutton Hoo ship had no mast, and the question of when masts were first fitted to sea-going vessels is a controversial one, since surviving ships are extremely difficult to date. However, the sail was in use by the seventh century, as may be inferred from a story quoted by Bede in his *Ecclesiastical History* (V, 1) and again from Adamnan's *Life of Columba*, (II, 15, 34), where tacking against the wind is described. These writers may refer to small boats, but the discovery of the Kvalsund ship at Sunnmøre, in Norway (Illus. 12), is relevant here. The structure of this vessel, with its external keel and efficient rudder, meant that a ship of this size could be built with a broad hull and could carry mast and sail, while its fine lines and the marked curve of its stem are especially noted, and Shetelig and Brøgger date the ship to about A.D. 600. A prow of this type might well have inspired descriptions such as *hringed stefna* and *hring naca* in *Beowulf*. Incidentally the hero's vessel, with its crew of fourteen, would be much smaller than that buried at Sutton Hoo, which had places for nineteen oars on either side.

The first ship mentioned is that used at the funeral of the Danish king Scyld, and the reference to its cargo of 'national treasures' brought from afar (36 ff.) has taken on new meaning now that we know of the royal ship-burial at Sutton Hoo, and a number of other ship-burials in East Anglia of seventh-century date. Ship-burial on an impressive scale began in Uppland, Sweden, in the same century, and the careful ritual by which the dead man was placed near the centre of the ship, with his possessions laid around him, is in agreement with the poem. The Vendel and Valsgärde chiefs, however, do not appear to have been given royal burials like that described in the poem. It is only in East Anglia that ceremonial objects like standard, sceptre, splendid purse and ceremonial sword, shield and helmet have been buried together in a ship at a time earlier than the Viking Age, to which the

357

rich Norwegian ship-burials belong. Moreover if, as seems likely, the Sutton Hoo ship was rowed along the Deben to the point where she was pulled up the hill to the grave prepared for her, then it is possible that the departure of a dead chief on his ship, rowed towards his last resting-place, was a practice witnessed up to the seventh century by the people of East Anglia. It is noteworthy that the opening section of the poem reads like a mythological commentary on the practice of ship-funeral: kings were burnt or buried in their ships because the first king of the Danes departed in a ship to the mysterious land from which he came. I have elsewhere [1] discussed the myth of the king from over the sea, and will here only comment that this section of the poem is hardly likely to have been composed at a time when Christians had repudiated the practice of ship-burial, and forgotten the mythological basis for it.

The same is true for what appear to be reasonably accurate accounts of cremation in *Beowulf*, although Lindqvist had difficulty in reconciling them with the cremation rites at Old Uppsala in the sixth century. The description of the pyre on which Hnaef and the other warriors were burned after death in battle is ruthless in its realism. The fire roars up to the sky while heads break up in the heat, old wounds reopen on the bodies, which are finally devoured by the greedy flames (1121 ff.): such a description is hardly likely to be based on vague traditions of a forgotten ritual. Mighty pyres were kindled at Uppsala in the sixth century at the funerals of the kings, with a good draught beneath the timber structure in order to produce the necessary heat, as Lindqvist has shown. The cremation of Beowulf himself is full of realistic detail (3110 ff.). Wood for the burning was collected by a concerted effort on the part of all owners of halls in the district. Helmets, shields and byrnies were hung on the pyre, and we know that it was customary to include the war equipment of the king in the burning, at Uppsala and elsewhere. The dead man was borne on a wagon, and unburnt treasures (the fact that in this special case these came from a dragon's hoard is not really relevant here) laid beside the ashes. If we leave Uppsala for Anglo-Saxon England, we find that cremation on a grand scale was still practised in certain areas by isolated families in the late sixth and even the seventh century. A cremation burial at

[1] *Gods and Myths of Northern Europe*, Penguin Books, 1964, pp. 104, 135.

Coombe, Kent, had a splendid sword of the late sixth century and other unburnt goods beside the cremated bones, and there are other examples of this combination of the two rites. Grave Mound 3 at Sutton Hoo held a cremation burial, also thought to be of late sixth-century date. A cremation burial on an impressive scale at Asthall Barrow, in Oxfordshire, was dated by Leeds to the seventh century. Here the burial mound was built over the pyre, and was surrounded by a drystone wall about 4 feet high; this is in accordance with the description of the mound erected over the ashes of the pyre in *Beowulf*, the building of which took ten days to complete, and the encircling of the ashes with a wall (3159–62). Nor is there any reason to reject the ritual of the twelve nobles riding round the burial mound, reciting a dirge in praise of the dead king, as being contrary to early Germanic tradition. One noteworthy difference between Swedish and Anglo-Saxon ship burials is that here animals were not sacrificed in large quantities at the funeral, as at Vendel and Valsgärde, where horses, sheep, cattle, pigs, dogs and birds were found in the graves. At Sutton Hoo there were a few traces of animal bones, but no signs of a holocaust on the Swedish scale, and the poem is in agreement with Anglo-Saxon tradition.

Thus in reviewing the evidence of archaeology it will be noted that there is a close link between objects and funeral practices as described in *Beowulf* and archaeological evidence from the sixth and seventh centuries A.D. The parallels are numerous and striking, whether we consider helmets and standards, pattern-welded sword blades and gold or rune-inscribed hilts, golden collars, well-built sailing ships, or cremation and ship funeral. Links with the royal ship-burial of Sutton Hoo are particularly detailed and impressive, and this is a seventh-century burial, previously thought to belong to the second half of the century, but now, on reconsideration of the coins found in the grave, definitely earlier than 650. Although timbered halls, sailing ships and patterned blades were also in use later than the seventh century, they were well established in Anglo-Saxon England at the time of Edwin of Northumbria and Redwald of East Anglia, while it may be noted that there are no allusions in the poem to objects or practices which must be dated later than the seventh century. Moreover the Sutton Hoo burial has shown how close were the links at this period between the East Anglian court and the Swedish kings at Uppsala, and this would account for the detailed knowledge of and interest in Scandinavian traditions shown in the poem. Particularly striking is the correspondence between the royal treasures given to Beowulf and those in the Sutton Hoo royal grave, some of Swedish and some of Anglo-Saxon craftsmanship. Whether this familiarity with seventh-century culture implies heathen lays utilized in a Christian poem, Christian editing of an early poem in later times, or consistent and skilful archaism on the part of a later poet, is a question beyond the scope of this chapter; such questions, as I pointed out at the beginning, cannot be settled on the evidence of archaeology alone. But the detailed accuracy displayed in *Beowulf*, in descriptions both of material objects and of funeral customs of the pre-Christian period, which the evidence of archaeology now forces us to recognize, must certainly be taken into account in theories about its origin.

ARCHAEOLOGY

GENERAL

C. L. Wrenn, 'Sutton Hoo and Beowulf', *Mélanges de Linguistique et de Philologie (Fernand Mossé in Memoriam*, Paris, 1959) pp. 495–501.

R. Cramp, 'Beowulf and Archaeology', *Medieval Archaeology* 1 (1957) pp. 57–77.

S. Pfeifstucker, *Spätantikes und germanisches Kunstgut in der frühangel-sächsischen Kunst* (Berlin, 1936).

S. Lindqvist, 'Sutton Hoo and Beowulf', *Antiquity* 20 (1946), 21 (1947).

THE HALL

W. Winkelman, 'Eine westfalische Siedlung des 8 Jahrhunderts bei Warendorf', *Germania* 32 (1954) pp. 189–213.

C. A. Ralegh Radford, 'The Saxon House', *Medieval Archaeology* 1 (1957) pp. 27–38.

P. Rahtz, 'The Saxon and Medieval Palaces at Cheddar, Somerset', *Medieval Archaeology* 6–7 (1962–3) pp. 52–66.

P. Nørlund, *Trelleborg*, Copenhagen, 1948.

P. Lauring and A. Hoff-Møller, 'Trelleborghusets rekonstruktion', *Aarbøger f. nordisk Oldkyndighed og Historie* (1952) p. 108 ff.

J. Larsen, 'Rekonstruktion af Trelleborg', ibid. (1957) p. 56 ff. (These last two have English summaries.)

Wooden animals: E. Sprockhoff, 'Das bronzene Zierband von Kronshagen bei Kiel', *Offa* 14 (1955) pp. 111–12.

stapol: T. Miller, 'The position of Grendel's arm in Heorot', *Anglia* 12 (1889) pp. 396–400.

Yeavering: Report of the excavations to be published by Brian Hope-Taylor. A short account appeared in the *Listener*, 25 Oct. 1956, 650.

H. M. Colvin, 'The King's Works before the Norman Conquest', *History of the King's Works* (London Stationery Office, 1963) pp. 1–5.

Temple at Uppsala: S. Lindqvist, *Uppsala Högar och Ottarshögen* (Stockholm, 1936).

Harp: H. M. Chadwick, *The Heroic Age* (Cambridge, 1912) pp. 83–7.

J. B. Beringer, 'Beowulf and the Harp at Sutton Hoo', *Toronto University Quarterly Journal* (Jan. 1958).

(Further work on reconstruction of the harp is in progress at the British Museum.)

Gold-worked Textiles: A paper on this subject by E. Crowfoot and S. C. Hawkes is to appear in *Medieval Archaeology* XI (1967).

A. Geyer and B. Thomas, 'The Viminacium Gold Tapestry', *Meddelanden f. Lunds Universitets Historiska Museum* (1964–65) pp. 223–36.

SUTTON HOO

The Sutton Hoo Ship-Burial: a Provisional Guide (British Museum).
R. L. S. Bruce-Mitford, 'The Sutton Hoo Ship Burial', *Proc. Suffolk Inst. Archaeology* 25 (1949) pp. 1–78.
C. Green, *Sutton Hoo* (London, 1963).

(These three all contain detailed discussion of the grave-goods.)

R. L. S. Bruce-Mitford, 'Saxon Rendlesham', *Proc. Suffolk Inst. Archaeology* 24 (1948) pp. 228–51. 'Sutton Hoo, A Rejoiner', *Antiquity* 26 (1952) pp. 76–82. Appendix to R. Hodgkin, *History of the Anglo-Saxons* (3rd ed. 1952) p. 11.

C. F. C. Hawkes, 'Sutton Hoo: Twenty-five years later', *Antiquity* 38 (1964) pp. 252–57.
The Smaller Mounds: R. L. S. Bruce-Mitford, 'Excavations at Sutton Hoo in 1938', *Proc. Suffolk Inst. Archaeology* 30 (1964) pp. 1–43.
Symbolism: K. Hauck, 'Herrschaftszeichen eines wodenistischen Königtum', *Jahrbuch für frankische Landesforschung* 14 (1954) pp. 1–66.
Dating by coins: J. P. C. Kent, 'Problems of Chronology in the Seventh Century Merovingian Coinage', *Cunobelin* (Year Book of British Association of Numismatic Societies, 1967) pp. 24–35.

HELMET

H. Maryon, 'The Sutton Hoo Helmet', *Antiquity* 21 (1947).
R. L. S. Bruce-Mitford, Appendix to Hodgkin, see above, pp. 707–8.

Benty Grange: R. L. S. Bruce-Mitford, *Annual Report Sheffield City Museum* (1956).

O. Doppelfeld, 'Das frankische Knabengrab unter dem Chor des Kölner Domes', *Kölner Domblatt* 20 (1961–2) pp. 118–26.

Boar Symbol: H. R. Ellis Davidson, *Gods and Myths of Northern Europe* (Penguin Bks. 1965) pp. 98–9. 'The significance of the Man in the Horned Helmet', *Antiquity* 39 (1965) pp. 23–7.

STANDARD

D. E. Martin Clark, 'Significant Objects at Sutton Hoo', in *Early Cultures of N. W. Europe* (Chadwick Memorial Volume, ed. Fox and Dickins, Cambridge, 1950) pp. 109–19.
W. Berges and A. Gauert, 'Die eiserne "Standarte" und das steinerne "Szepter" aus dem Grabe eines angelsächsischen Königs bei Sutton Hoo' in P. Schramm, *Herrschaftszeichen und Staatssymbolik* (Stuttgart, 1954) pp. 248–59.

SWORD

H. R. Ellis Davidson, *The Sword in Anglo-Saxon England* (Oxford, 1962) esp. p. 58 ff., 121–147, and S. Hawkes and R. I. Page, 'Swords and runes in E. E. England', *Antiq. Journ.* 47 (1967) p. 1 ff.

RING-MAIL

E. Martin Burgess, 'The Mail-maker's Technique', *Antiq. Journ.* 33 (1953) pp. 48–55.

NECK-RING

K. Hauck, 'Halstang und Ahrenstab als herrscherliche Würdezeichen' in P. Schramm (see above) pp. 145–92, 198 ff.
M. Stenburger, *Sweden* (London, 1962) pp. 134–5.

BOW AND ARROW

G. Rausing, *The Bow* (*Acta Archaeologica Lundensia*, 6), (Lund, 1967), esp. p. 64.

SHIP

C. Green, *Sutton Hoo* (London, 1963) 68–90.
A. Brøgger and H. Shetelig, *The Viking Ships* (Oslo/London, 1951–1953) pp. 52–8.

SHIP-BURIAL

R. L. S. Bruce-Mitford, 'The Snape Boat-grave', *Proc. Suffolk Inst. Archaeology* 26 (1952).
H. R. Ellis Davidson, *Pagan Scandinavia* (London, 1967) pp. 113–121.

363

HORSE BURIAL

Examples of this from Little Wilbraham (Neville, *Saxon Obsequies* (1852), grave 44); Marston St. Lawrence (*Archaeologia* 48, 328, grave 1); Saffron Walden (*Trans. Essex Archaeological Soc.* 2 N.S. (1884) p. 284.

From the continent: E. Salin, *La Civilisation Merovingienne* IV (Paris 1959) pp. 24–5.

CREMATION

A. Meaney, *A Gazetteer of Early Anglo-Saxon Burial Sites* (London, 1964) pp. 15–17.

C. Wells, 'A Study of Cremation', *Antiquity* 34 (1960) pp. 29–37.

Asthall Barrow: E. T. Leeds, 'Anglo-Saxon Cremation Burial of the Seventh Century in Asthall Barrow, Oxfordshire', *Antiq. Journ.* 4 (1923) pp. 113–26.

Coombe Burial: An account of this by H. R. Ellis Davidson and L. Webster is to appear in *Medieval Archaeology* 11 (1967).

INDEX OF SOURCES

INDEX OF SOURCES

367